DATE DUE

GAYLORD		PRINTED IN U.S.A.

THE INTERNATIONAL CATHOLIC LIBRARY

EDITED BY REV. J. WILHELM, D.D., PH.D.

VOL. VIII.

NIHIL OBSTAT

JOSEPH WILHELM, S.T.D.,

Censor deputatus.

IMPRIMI POTEST

✠ GULIELMUS,

Episcopus Arindelensis,

Vicarius Generalis.

Westmonasterii,

die 13 *Dec.*, 1906.

THE GREAT SCHISM OF THE WEST

BY

L. SALEMBIER

PROFESSOR AT THE CATHOLIC UNIVERSITY OF LILLE

AUTHORISED TRANSLATION BY

M. D.

LONDON
KEGAN PAUL, TRENCH, TRÜBNER & CO., LIMITED
DRYDEN HOUSE, GERRARD STREET, W.
1907

THE INTERNATIONAL CATHOLIC LIBRARY

Edited by Rev. J. Wilhelm, D.D., Ph.D.
Joint Author of the Manual of Catholic Theology

I. HISTORY OF THE BOOKS OF THE NEW TESTAMENT. By L'Abbé Jacquier. Vol. I. St Paul and His Epistles. Authorised translation from the 5th French Edition, by Rev. James Duggan. Price 7s. 6d.

II. HISTORY OF THE BOOKS OF THE NEW TESTAMENT. By L'Abbé Jacquier. Vol. II. The Synoptic Gospels. Authorised translation from the French, by Rev. James Duggan. [*In preparation.*

III. TEN LECTURES ON THE MARTYRS. By Paul Allard. With a Preface by Mgr. Pechenard, Rector of the Catholic University of Paris. Authorised translation by Luigi Cappadelta. Price 7s. 6d.

IV. THE CATHOLIC CHURCH. THE RENAISSANCE. PROTESTANTISM. By Alfred Baudrillart, Rector of the Catholic Institute of Paris. Translated by Mrs Philip Gibbs. Price 7s. 6d.

V. THE BLIND SISTERS OF ST PAUL. By Maurice de la Sizeranne. Authorised translation by L. M. Leggatt. With Frontispiece, 7s. 6d.

VI. SURSUM CORDA. Letters of the Countess de Saint-Martial, in religion Sister Blanche, Sister of Charity of St Vincent de Paul. With Memoir by her brother, Baron Leopold de Fischer. Authorised translation from the French. With two portraits. Demy 8vo, price 7s. 6d.

VII. MADAME LOUISE DE FRANCE. Authorised translation from the French by Meta and Mary Brown. With Illustrations. Demy 8vo, price 6s.

VIII. THE GREAT SCHISM OF THE WEST. By L. Salembier, Professor at the Catholic University of Lille. Translated by M. D.

IX. CHURCHES SEPARATED FROM ROME. By L. Duchesne. Authorised translation by A. H. Matthew.

X. THE FINDING OF THE CROSS. Historical Researches by Louis de Combes. Authorised translation by Luigi Cappadelta. Price 6s.

XI. THE TEMPORAL SOVEREIGNTY OF THE POPES. By Mgr. L. Duchesne.

KEGAN PAUL, TRENCH, TRÜBNER & CO., Ltd.
DRYDEN HOUSE, GERRARD STREET, W.

PREFACE TO THE FIRST EDITION

The period covered by our narrative is marked by one of the most distressing crises in history.

An unparalleled schism rends the Church in twain, weakens and lowers the papacy by dividing it, and lessens the respect which is its due. Simultaneously heresy breaks out afresh, and produces Wickliffe and John Huss, who in turn prepare the way for Luther. Sovereigns like the Dukes of Anjou twice invade the Italian peninsula, while, in the north, Robert of Bavaria, and in the south, Ladislas of Naples, take advantage of the decay of ecclesiastical power to get the upper hand of the Popes, so as to gratify their ambition or their avarice, to invade the Papal States, and even to desecrate the Eternal City herself. Finally, certain dogmatic errors, combined with the weakening of authority, give rise to a multitude of disciplinary and moral disorders, which the perplexities of the time prevent from being put down. All the past trials of the Church appear to revive, all her future crises exist in embryo in this unfortunate schism, which lasts nearly half a century (1378-1418).

It is not then surprising that this phase of history should have latterly attracted the special attention of authors, and have given rise to the deepest critical researches. To-day we are no longer satisfied with documents collected by certain annalists of the sixteenth and seventeenth centuries, who were less historians than romance-writers, led astray by prejudice, or too often blind with passion. The day will soon dawn when full knowledge will enable a just and final judgment to be pronounced on questions hitherto obscure.

In the course of our long and sometimes painful labours we have tried to observe the Ciceronian rule repeated twenty years ago by Leo XIII.: *Quis nescit primam esse historiae legem ne quid falsi dicere audeat? deinde ne quid veri non audeat?* [1] First, let the historian say nothing false: next, let him conceal nothing true.

Every conscience is bound by the first rule; but the sincerity of the historian is sometimes subjected to an almost intolerable strain by the second.

Is not the telling of certain special trials which touch our dear mother the Church almost like exposing family failings to the gaze of the public? Yet it must be done if conscience and historic truth are to be duly respected. If some Christians have been so ill-advised as to imagine religious truth would gain from the concealment of historic truth, if this is still a stumbling-block to some Catholics, let them bear in mind the words of the Gospel: "O men of little faith, wherefore do ye doubt?"

In the seventeenth century the learned Labbe, in his first volume of the *Councils*, remarks at the outset: "*Non tali auxilio nec defensoribus istis indiget Ecclesia.*" In a letter dated March 12, 1870, just before his death, Montalembert thus wrote to Baron de Hubner about

[1] *De Oratori*, ii. 15. *De studiis historicis*, a letter to Cardinals Pitra, de Luca, and Hergenröther, 1883.

his *Life of Sixtus V.*: "You have neither dissembled the shadows nor the stains so inseparably interwoven with the human element, which is so conspicuous and powerful in the Church, and therefore you throw into still greater relief the divine element, which always carries the day in the end, permeating our minds with its soft convincing light." Thus, too, Newman, in his *Historical Sketches*, ii. p. 231, speaks of "the endemic perennial fidget which possesses us about giving scandal: facts are omitted in great histories, or glosses are put on memorable acts, because they are thought not edifying; whereas of all scandals such omission, such glosses are the greatest."

The Sovereign Pontiff has just renewed this advice to the clergy of France; putting them in mind of this first principle of scrupulous scientific probity.

"God does not want our lies,"[1] he says. "The historian will be all the better able to manifest the Church's divine origin, so far transcending all that is purely terrestrial and natural, in proportion as he is faithful to keep back nothing of the trials which she has had to experience in the course of the ages through the frailty of her children, and sometimes even of her ministers. Studied in this fashion, the history of the Church in itself affords a splendid and conclusive proof of the truth and divinity of Christianity."[2]

The study of these great religious crises, which contrast so strongly with those of our own times, imbues the soul with indescribable consolation and strength. Our

[1] Job xiii. 7.

[2] Encyclical to the archbishops, bishops, and clergy of France, 1899.

trials of to-day are instinctively compared with the still more terrible trials of days gone by.

Pascal's profound saying is as applicable to the beginning of the fifteenth century as to the end of the nineteenth: "There is joy in the shock of the tempest, when you know your ship will weather the storm."

UNIVERSITÉ CATHOLIQUE DE LILLE,
Feast of our Lady of Mount Carmel,
July 16, 1900.

THE GREAT SCHISM OF THE WEST

CHAPTER I

THE CHURCH AND CHRISTENDOM AT THE END OF THE FOURTEENTH CENTURY

The Great Schism of the West brings the fourteenth century to a sad close, and dashes the beginning of the fifteenth with trouble and anxiety. It divides the political, as well as the ecclesiastical world, and breaks up Christian Europe into several hostile camps. It gave rise to problems which survived it, and some of them are still unsolved. Doubtless the religious disorders which then sprang up have disappeared; the doctrinal uncertainties which it perpetuated too long have been radically, if not universally, extinguished by the Vatican Council; but the historic question has made but little progress: On which side was the real Pope, the rightful successor of St Peter?

For forty years the Church was vainly trying to ascertain who was her true head, a Pontiff who could claim an undisputed recognition. What a fearful crisis was this for the Christendom of that era! How painful were these struggles, the consequences of which were felt right on into the middle of the nineteenth century, keeping alive in France the potential schism known as Gallicanism! Happily the trial is unique in the whole of the Church's history.

THE GREAT SCHISM OF THE WEST

It cannot be ignored: in a certain unhappy period of her history the Church had to see anti-popes rend her seamless robe in twain, and bring disunion into her divine kingdom on earth. The outcome of monarchical caprice or of popular revolution, these unscrupulous, rash, and transient intruders very quickly make their exit from the scene, in which they were only players, and their influence is as ephemeral as their titles were vain. The faithful quickly forgot, if they had ever known, the names of Ursinus, Romanus, and Novatian, and the sacrilegious pretensions of an intriguer like Gilbert of Ravenna, or weak-minded extravagances like those of Peter de Corbière.

It was not so with the fatal division which occurred in 1378. The dualism became immediately so plainly evident, was so strongly upheld by antagonistic interests, and so well sustained by opposing forces, that the conflict appeared incurable from the outset. Was it to go on for ever, despite the unity promised by Jesus Christ?

It was to be dreaded, especially when, later on, for a period of eight years, three Popes simultaneously assumed the tiara, and divided amongst themselves into three rival obediences a scandalised and perplexed Christendom.

"Things were going badly," wrote Froissart, "and had our faith not been strongly settled in mankind, and in the grace of the Holy Ghost, who enlightened the hearts of those who had gone or who had been led astray, and held them firmly united, it would have been ruined and thrown down."[1] Was the stream of tradition flowing from a divine source, after fourteen centuries to be split up into three branches, which would never reunite? An entirely different result was to follow, and an entirely

[1] Froissart (Kervyn de Lettenhove's Ed.), vol. xi. p. 251.

different conclusion would have to be inferred. "What was to them a curse in their days is for us the treasure-trove of history," says Le Maistre. "It proves that St Peter's throne is unshakeable, for what human institution could survive such a trial?"[1]

On this point our foes are as assertive as our friends. "A temporal kingdom would have come to grief," writes a sceptical historian, "but so extraordinary was the organisation of the spiritual kingdom, so indestructible was the papal idea, that this rift, though the deepest of all, only helped to demonstrate its indivisibility."[2]

The very excess of this evil was to afford a fresh and more striking and conclusive proof of the divine origin and necessary unity and perpetuity of the Church. The Catholic world, after forty years' suspense, awaited such a demonstration, and Providence was about to supply it.

§ 1. *The State of the Catholic World.*

What, then, was the state of Christian Europe on the outbreak of the Schism? This, the fundamental question, must be dealt with at the outset.

Catholicism had made nearly all the conquests it was to keep until the great Protestant revolt. In the West, the faith had spread along all the Atlantic coasts, from the frontiers of the Moorish kingdom of Granada to the farthest ends of Scotland, Ireland, and Iceland. It had even penetrated as near the North Pole as Greenland, as far as the icy regions discovered by the monks of Ireland. There flourished the mysterious Church of North America, soon to succumb to the blows of unknown

[1] De Maistre, *Du Pape*, lib. iv., end.

[2] Gregorovius, *Geschichte der Stadt Rom im Mittelalter*, Ed. 3, vol. vi. p. 620.

barbarians, a Church without a historian, like one of those martyrs interred in the catacombs, whose life and even name find no record in the annals of Christian antiquity, and who is known only by the palm and the phial of blood.[1]

In the North of Europe the three Scandinavian kingdoms, though Catholic for centuries, are powerless to maintain either peace at home or influence abroad. Towards the East, Livonia, Courland, and Finland have long abolished idols and adored the Cross. Prussia, with its Teutonic knights, is beginning to attain to a certain degree of religious prosperity, against the day when war without and fightings within shall accomplish its speedy downfall. Poland, under Ladislas and Casimir, is growing into a strong national organisation, and unites its straggling provinces under a single sceptre. Hungary, destined along with Poland to become the shield of Christendom, is preparing for the glorious days of Hunyadi; while on its borders Bohemia, turbulent and brutal, is preparing for a future of religious discord, and sees the birth of John Huss.

Farther down, the Eastern Empire is in the last agonies of senile decrepitude, more and more powerless to check the advance of Islam, the pressure of which grows tighter on all sides.

To the South of the Catholic world, Asiatic and

[1] The bishopric of Gardar, in Greenland, was founded *circa* twelfth century: it was then dependent on the archbishopric of Drontheim in Norway. Every year it paid Peter's pence in kind, as has been shown by recent research. In 1520, the last bishop of Gardar was consecrated, twenty-eight years after the discovery, or rather re-discovery, of America by Columbus. It is also at about this date that the diocese was wiped out. *Cf.* Elisée Reclus, *L'Amérique boréale*, p. 10 (Paris, 1890). Gams, *Series episcop.* (Ratisbon, 1873), p. 334. Eubel, *Hierarchia catholica medii aevi*, 1898, t. i. p. 270. Beauvais, *La Chrétienté du Greenland au moyen-âge*, *Revue des questions historiques*, 1902, p. 538.

African Christianity ekes out a precarious existence along the strip of land which borders the Mediterranean. Thence, looking as far afield as India, and the utmost limits of the known world, taking a survey of the great nations already seduced by Islam, or waiting to be gathered under the iron hand of Tamerlane, nothing is discerned but the shadow of death. Marco Polo's travels, and the apostolic journeys of Mont-Corvin in China, gave no solid or abiding results of conversion. They were rather extraordinary missionary excursions, than efforts to lay the foundations of abiding institutions. As for Africa, such, at any rate, as it appears in the maps of that era, it remains almost entirely closed to Christianity and civilisation ; it is fast asleep in all the errors and vices of Paganism and Islamism. For a long time to come it will be the great unknown and the land of mystery. But it would be unfair not to bear testimony to the efforts of Clement V., John XXII., and Clement VI., to keep alive the remains of Christianity in Abyssinia, and in all the barbarian states, and even in the extreme East. When the records of these great Popes have been fully published, the learned world will be able to estimate the loftiness of their political ideals, the resolution underlying their apostolical designs, the continuity of their undertakings in the propagation of the faith and of Christian influence. Here it need only be said that the final results did not correspond with the greatness of their conceptions, nor with the generosity of the sacrifices made.

Returning to the Christian world, we can discern the causes which paralyse it, and hinder it from conjuring the Mussulman danger, and from taking in hand the great work of internal reform. The first is at Byzantium, the second at Rome.

Christendom is ailing at its two centres, its two capitals, each the heir to an empire, but both apparently overwhelmed with the thought of bygone memories too great for their faintness of heart, both of them reduced to the shadow of a name. Constantinople is the victim of all the dissensions and rebellion of schism: Rome is abandoned to all the disorder and weakness of anarchy.

How is it possible to convey a true idea of the complex character of these Byzantines, who are wasting their powers in casuistical subtleties and ritual puerilities, while the Turks are encamped just across the Bosporus, and there are only temporary truces between Constantinople and Iconium? Doubtless the Latin crusaders shed upon Greece a last ray of military glory, while they defer the final catastrophe for a century, but they have grown tired of coming to the rescue of a country which repays them with contempt and treachery. The Western warriors who succeeded the Godfreys and the Baldwins, were such as Peter of Lusignan, Amédée of Savoy, Louis de Bourbon, Jean de Nevers, Jean de Boucicaut: they were full of fidelity and frankness, "they always wish to add to the good of Christendom and the honour of chivalry."[1] Moreover, they have a lofty disdain for the theologaster-emperors, the corrupt and corrupting ministers, the patriarchs who are both ambitious and servile, the monks who are sometimes vagabonds, sometimes sedentary recluses, but always fanatics, and for all this degraded people which makes and unmakes its rulers and has nothing left but the tombs of its departed, the shadows of its sages, and the relics of its saints.

On their side, the Byzantines, divided as to a thousand

[1] J. Delaville de Roulx, *La France en Orient au XIVe siècle*, p. 505.

different things, are only united in bringing against the Latins their scholastic arguments and insignificant liturgical variations, and in protesting above all against the primacy of the Roman Pontiff, which admits of no division. "Better the turban than the tiara!" This sacrilegious watchword will only make itself heard later on, but it was for centuries the root-idea of the Byzantine policy.

On several occasions imperial hypocrisy takes advantage of papal good faith, and deceives the Catholic West. Sometimes the Commeni and the Paleologi, assisted by a degenerate patriarchate, sketch out for the two Churches an ephemeral union founded on equivocation and almost immediately destroyed by treachery. The tyranny of the Greek sovereign imposes it for the needs or interests of the day, and for a like reason his servile subjects acquiesce in it, without conviction, and then reject it without regret. The Byzantine empire is already "the sick man." Death awaits it at an carly date.

While schismatical Constantinople suffers from being against the Pope, Rome, forsaken by her lawful ruler, suffers from being without him. For more than sixty years the Pontiffs had been obliged to leave their ancient capital, given over, as it was, to the revolutionary spirit, which seems to be endemic in this city, "widowed of a royal people," of whom she regards herself as the heir. Their prolonged stay at Avignon left Rome a prey to the factions which ravage, weaken, and disgrace her. The Romans of the fourteenth century appear to follow the fatal decline of the Greeks of the Lower Empire. Alternately they pay their insincere homage to emperors and tribunes, to despots and anarchists, until their final disenchantment, when they demand the return of the Popes with exclamations of repentance. At times they fling themselves at the feet of such Cæsars as Louis of Bavaria and Charles of Bohemia; at times they applaud such an enthusiastic tribune as the famous Rienzi, gifted with every talent that can dazzle the mob. One day there is the coronation of an emperor at St Peter's by the hands of an excommunicate; the next, the nobles recklessly destroy the palaces and walls and triumphal arches,[1] the venerable remains of a past of which they are ignorant, in order to build in the centre of each district a series of formidable citadels; or again, the crowd in a fit of delirium hurries to the capital with an excited demagogue, who goes mad with pride and finally succumbs to the revolutionary forces which had been his living.

During this era of madness and disorder the sovereign Pontiffs, in retirement on the peaceful banks of the Rhone, might learn to appreciate the truth of the observation addressed by St Bernard to his disciple, Eugenius III.: "What is more obvious than the arrogance and pride of the Romans? They are a people ignorant of peace, and accustomed to rebellion, recalcitrant and intractable, and, until now, only obedient when powerless to resist any more."[2]

Two years before the beginning of the schism, the author of the strange book entitled *Songe du Vergier*,[3] uttered similar complaints. "It is the iniquities of the Romans that led the Saviour to prefer France

[1] PETRARCH, *Var.* 48. *Cf.* BRESSOLANO, *Pétrarque et Rienzi*, 1899.

[2] ST BERNARD, *De Consideratione*, lib. iv. 2.

[3] *Somnium viridarii*, published by Goldast in his *Monarchia Sancti Romani Imperii*, t. i. p. 225. This pamphlet was written in 1376, two years

to Rome. The Roman is a spoiler, and, whom he cannot despoil, he hates. *Romanus rodit: quos rodere non valet, odit.*

"Nine times the Popes have been driven from the Eternal City; nine times our kings have restored them. France is the refuge of the Popes, Rome is their ruin. These hopeless pagans are the impenitent descendants of the murderers of St Peter and St Paul."

The mother and mistress cities of the Christian world both suffer from the same ailment: they have no Pope. But this malady, though incurable at Byzantium, is not beyond remedy at Rome. Nevertheless the city of the Popes will long be afflicted with it, and will make all Christendom suffer with her, till the end of that Great Schism, whereof we have now to recount the distant and proximate causes.

§ 2. *The Dogmatic Errors of the Fourteenth Century.*

Great historic events, however unexpectedly they may occur, have many and deep roots in the past. Their primary cause is almost always intellectual: and when the cause has to do with the Church, it is theological.

The most striking thing, in the troubled epoch under investigation, is the misunderstanding of pontifical authority, of its bases, its strength, and its privileges. It is the practical oblivion of the very constitution of spiritual sovereignty.

Doubtless the doctors of Paris and other centres could find the principles of what is to-day called "The Treatise of the Church" in the writings of the Fathers,

---

before the Great Schism, probably by Philip de Maizieres. *Cf. Revue des Sciences Ecclés.*, Serie vi. t. v. p. 45 (Amiens, 1887).

in the canons of the Councils, and in the papal decrees. But they had generally no idea of how to make a synthesis of this teaching, they had never reduced it to substantial unity, and they had no clear notion of logically co-ordinating the theses which compose it. They allowed themselves to be brought to a standstill by certain differences between the doctors, they were blinded by clouds which, in those troublous times, sometimes overcast fundamental truths; they too often considered indisputable points of dogma as if they were open questions.

St Thomas was providentially raised up to carry through the work of consolidation into a single whole, and to unite in one body of doctrine all the principles universally admitted by the old doctors. "On account of his great reverence for the Fathers," said his commentator Cajetan, "he has in a manner been the heir of their united learning." Unfortunately the monumental system of theology which he built up was never finished, and among the most celebrated successors of his school, none has inherited his synthetical mind, and none has set forth the teaching of the Church completely or systematically. And yet it would be fairly easy to restore the "Treatise of the Church" as a whole with the scattered fragments to be found in the work of the Angelic Doctor.[1]

The fourteenth century works that remain fairly often give us a report of the disputes of his school, of the eager scholastic discussions which took rise in the Rue de Fouarre in the professor's class, and were prosecuted in the cloister of the Mathurins, in Place Maubert, and in the whole of the Latin quarter of those days.

[1] This has been done by Dr Grabmann in his *Das Lehre des heiligen Thomas von Aquin von der Kirche als Gotteswerk*, Mainz, 1903.

One is astonished and startled to find on the lips of the intellectual combatants so many strange or suspicious theological propositions on every subject, especially about the authority of the Church. There is hardly an error, which has since then been condemned, that cannot be found among the singular questions raised by this decadent theology, among the risky theses of some newly budding doctor, or in the teaching of some lectures on the *Liber Sententiarum* by some B.A., more eager for novelty than truth. Often it is true that these propositions are put forth interrogatively, with restrictions suggested by fear of condemnation; but the venom works through these subtle openings and will soon infect Christian teaching as a whole.

First, John of Paris, a Dominican, attacks the temporal power of the Church; then Marsilius of Padua impugns the spiritual authority of the Pope, the primacy of St Peter and the power of the Keys. The part played by Marsilius with his accomplice John of Jandun, a Paris professor like himself, at the court of Louis of Bavaria, is well-known. After an interval of fifty years they played there the same part as was played by Peter Flotte and Peter Dubois at the court of Philippe le Bel. Their doctrines, which were both Cæsarian and revolutionary, have left more than one mark on the University schools.

But this theological evil grew specially virulent when William of Occam and some disputatious Franciscans took sides with William of Bavaria, at the time of his fatal struggle with John XXII. "Defend yourself with the sword," they said to the Emperor, "and we will come to your aid with the pen." Thus did traitors throw open to the foe the gates of the sanctuary which duty bade them defend.

The audacious theories of Occam found an echo in England, his native country. John Wicliffe, an Oxford theologian, raises a genuine revolt against throne and altar. On his death in 1384, the Great Schism had already broken out, and John Huss, the inheritor of his teaching, begins his studies at the University of Prague. There he will soon carry to extreme lengths his inferences against the Church and her head.

These doctrinal excesses give rise to a reaction, which is certainly less revolutionary, but not less erroneous. Already Augustinus Triumphus, the General of the Augustinians, had ascribed to the Pope an unlimited authority, and a direct dominion even over all things temporal. "The Sovereign Pontiff," said he, "himself does not know how far his supreme authority can extend."[1] Alvarez Pelagius, another old Paris student, follows the same errors, and teaches similar extravagances.[2]

It is easy to see how such contradictory doctrines must have perplexed University circles. According to the former, the Pope is Antichrist, and the curse of mankind; according to the others, he is a demigod, the master and supreme regulator of all things in heaven and on earth.

In this chaos of doctrinal monstrosities, where was one to find a true idea of the Church, her head, her magisterium, and her rights? On all these points the school is Babel itself. It has no doctrine, because it has too many doctrines.

This is why the events at Rome and Fondi, which we

[1] *Summa de potestate ecclesiae ad Joannem*, xxii. q. 1, a. 1.

[2] *De planctu ecclesiae*, lib. 1. *Cf.* Rocquain, *La Cour de Rome, et l'esprit de réforme avant Luther*, t. ii. p. 434 (Paris, 1897). The wise and learned Bellarmine refutes these two doctors. See *De Romano Pontifice*, lib. v. c. 1 and 5.

are about to narrate, the crisis of 1378, and the double pontifical election which resulted from it, were not the original cause of the Schism, but only the occasion for the free development, extension, and continuation of latent errors. The cardinal electors and the principal upholders of each of the two obediences were imbued with ideas taken from the great schools. On the other hand, the jurists by whom the princes were surrounded, the *milites legum* who inspired their counsels, had listened to the pernicious maxims of Peter Dubois and Marsilius of Padua. They were sure of a favourable hearing when with theories of autocracy they flattered the interests of kings, "greedy of sacerdotal power," to quote St Ambrose.

We shall see ecclesiastical authority, deeply undermined by Philippe le Bel and his legists, growing weaker and weaker throughout this period. A celebrated contemporary historian has called the attempt of Anagni a "generative fact."[1] And how rightly! The influence of the French king's unjust action, committed in 1303, will last throughout the fourteenth and following centuries: and from it dates the upsetting of institutions and ideas. From this era the principle of the divine right of Popes is in danger, and that of their social supremacy is done with.

The theological doctrine of the power of Pontiffs over kings and kingdoms seems to have been shaken by the perfidy of Philippe le Bel and by the sacrilegious violence of Colonna. "It is a vanishing principle, and was one of the greatest that had reigned over the mind

[1] Dom Tosti, *Storia del Concilio di Costanza*, t. i. p. 4. Victor Le Clerc, belonging to quite a different school, approves of the expression and the judgment of the Benedictine author: *Histoire littéraire de la France*, t. xxiv. p. 108. This is also the view of Comte and Littré, *Études sur les Barbares et le moyen-âge* (Paris, 1874), p. 372.

until then. Society too was hit by the same blow as had struck the Papacy. Henceforward, if we would rediscover the Middle Age, we must descend with Dante to visit the regions of the dead." [1]

§ 3. *The Question of Reform.*

Passing from dogma to discipline and morals, we discover a second cause of the Schism in the delays and obstacles which long-needed reforms had to cope with. Voices from cloister and altar, from the world and even from courts, demanded them with urgency: and the strongest of reasons underlay the complaints.

St Bernard very openly points out to Eugenius III. the abuses which call for correction in the very court of the Pope; [2] while St Elisabeth of Schoenau complains of the excessive wealth of the clergy, and predicts the disendowment of the Church as a judgment.[3] St Catherine of Siena expected to find the Roman court a paradise of virtue: she laments that she found there an odour of hell.[4]

From a less estimable quarter the pseudo-mystics draw their inspiration from the prophecies of the too notorious Joachim of Flori, and from a certain Cyrillus, General of the Carmelites. They fill the first years of the fourteenth century with their much-heeded denunciations of moral disorders.[4]

Poets join in this concert of recrimination and re-

[1] F. Rocquain, *Journal des Savants,* 1875, p. 199.

[2] St Bernard, *De consideratione,* lib. i. iii. and iv.

[3] *Cf.* W. Roth, *Die Visionen der hl. Elisabeth* (1884). Bolland, *Acta Sanctorum Junii,* t. iv. p. 499. Migne, *Patr. lat.,* t. cxcvii.

[4] Bolland, *Acta Sanctorum Aprilis,* t. iii. p. 891. *Cf.* Pastor, *Histoire des Papes,* ii. p. 135.

proach. Dante himself, *theologus Dantes,* scourges in vehement verse all the corruptions of the times. As a good Ghibelline, he cries out against the donation of Constantine, which he mistakenly supposes to be genuine, and which, according to him, is the origin of all the evils that afflict the Church; and sometimes he heaps insults on the heads of those whose feet he should embrace.[1]

Too much of a fine writer to avoid exaggeration, Petrarch calls Avignon the "Babylon of the Apocalypse," and blackens it with sweeping rhetorical phrases. He further exaggerates all the sorrowful blemishes which the Pontiffs are the first to acknowledge, while lamenting their helplessness in abolishing them.[2] The anonymous author of the *Songe du Vergier* is a well-informed pamphleteer, who echoes all the hatred of the lawyers against ecclesiastics, and all the attacks of free-thinkers on clerical morality.[3] Later on, St Antoninus will complain not without bitterness of foreign legates, and of the hostility they stir up around and against themselves.[4]

Each of these critics imparts to his complaints his own cast of enthusiasm, mind, or style. Eloquent invective, bitter reproach, doleful and supplicating sighs, prophetic warnings, ill-disguised or insatiable hatred, everything that can agitate the religious world is there: everything combines to urge the need of healthy amendment, moral awakening, and a total reform of both head and members so long demanded by the whole of Christendom.

[1] *Inferno,* xix. and xxvii.; *Purgat.,* vi.; *Paradiso,* xxii. and xxvii. *Cf.* Ozanam, *Dante et la philosophie catholique,* p. 369.

[2] Geiger, *Petrarca* (Leipzig, 1874), p. 198. *Lettres à Rienzi,* translated by Deuclay, 1886.

[3] *Somnium viridarii* (ed. Goldast, 1614), t. ii. p. 61 ff.

[4] *Chron.,* p. iii. c. i.

What is the principal cause of these undeniable abuses? It is to be traced, I think, to the continual wars that then laid waste the greater part of Europe, and which were more fatal to the Church than the wars of religion. Leaders, who were adventurers, ever in search of sword-play and plunder, were for more than a hundred years the terror and disgrace of Christendom. Robert Knolles, John Hawkwood, Arnaud de Cervole, Eustache d'Auberchicourt, Raymond de Turenne, Geoffroy de Boucicault are the leaders of international gangs destitute of faith or pity, without either flag or fatherland. Rival kings take them into their service; sometimes they get high protection from princes and nobles; and their violence is alike the terror of friend and foe.

Fire and pillage devastate episcopal and monastic buildings, and give rise to every sort of temporal disturbance and to every kind of moral decay.

Bishops cease to visit their dioceses; prelates forsake their residences ruined by the new barbarism. They fly to Paris or to the court of Avignon, and Gregory XI. is forced to fulminate against them to induce them to return to their duties.

Abbots send the Popes woeful complaints, and the pontifical replies betray the most perilous predicaments. The abbeys indeed have lost all their revenues, and some of them have been burnt down two or three times. Their lands, abandoned by the peasants, are uncultivated, the monastic possessions are alienated, churches no longer receive any assistance from the faithful, and chapters are reduced to pauperism. Through all these things combined, religious and ecclesiastical discipline is relaxed, and the moral ruin exceeds the material, and is still more deplorable. Everywhere the holiness of the religious life is under eclipse. It may be affirmed that for monastic conduct pauperism was as deleterious as riches became later on.

Most estimable bishops protest both by word and example, but in vain. Vain also are the orders, entreaties, and threats [1] issued by the general chapters of the religious orders. Disorganisation is perpetuated and intensified, and if reforms are effected, they are only local and limited.

There is no need to refer in detail to the abuses which then found their way into monasteries and churches through *annates*, *reservations*, and *expectations*.[2]

Suffice it to say here that these practices, which became so harmful later on, were at the outset simply the exercise of legitimate rights. The same is true of the *commendam*. In principle, a layman was temporarily entrusted with the management of the material interests of a monastery during an interregnum. But at the period we are speaking of, regular benefices were given in permanence to persons who were not only outside the order, but even out of the Church herself.

The Popes, specially those of Avignon, unhappily made use of and extended these irregular practices. Bishoprics, abbeys, parishes, priories, capitular appointments, all were seized and handed over to laymen, or to nephews who might be infamous, or to clergy who were too young, and held a plurality of benefices, quite illegally.[3] On their part rulers, with a munificence

[1] Martene and Durand, *Thesaurus*, t. iv. p. 1206 ff.

[2] D. V. Berlière, *Inventaire analytique des "Libri obligationum et resolutionum" des Archives Vaticanes*, 1904 (Paris, Champion), Preface, v.-xxv.; and also *Inventaire analytique des "Diversa Cameralia,"* 1906, *ibid.* Samaran and Mollet, *La Fiscalité pontificale en France au XIVe siècle*, 1904 (Paris, Pontemoing).

[3] St Bernard, *Tractatus ad Henr. archiep. Senonensem*, 7. *De moribus et officio episcoporum*, Migne, t. clxxxii. col. 826.

that cost them nothing, lavished the goods of the Church upon their creatures, plainly for the purpose of satiating them or acquiring an ascendancy over them.

The most venerated doctors, and general and particular councils, had often risen against these abuses, and proposed effectual remedies. But to drive these buyers and sellers from the temple demanded the strong arm and the avenging lash of a Gregory VII. or an Innocent III. When Popes Clement V. or Benedict XII. wished to do away with these fatal customs, they soon found to their cost, says Thomassin, that it is easier to make wounds than to heal them. However successful the cure may be, it always leaves a scar.[1]

At the time of the Great Schism all these open sores are rankling, and are not one of the least deplorable ills of the period. Each Pope, whether of Rome or of Avignon, specially of the latter, urgently demands taxes and more or less free subsidies, procurations, and plunder, not to speak of annates and charges. The meshes of the whole network of the ancient fiscal system are drawn tighter. To increase the number and kindle the zeal of his supporters, each pontiff bestows abbeys upon men more fitted to wear the helmet than the mitre, and on the thrones of the most venerated sees they place men who would be more at home in the seat of the money-changer than in that of the apostles. At Avignon, intrigue, favouritism, and nepotism have a free hand. Those who have compared this pontifical court to a Bourse or a commercial agency have doubtless exaggerated, but their assertions are not unfounded. Thenceforward, one can understand how interested

[1] *Ancienne et nouvelle discipline de l'Église,* 2e partie, lib. iii. ch. xx. *Cf.* Denifle, *Désolation des Églises de France,* v. ii. p. 603.

the protégés of the Pope were in the prolongation of a Schism which guaranteed the continuance of their simoniacal wealth.

History cannot dispute the existence of these deplorable practices and moral misfortunes. Let it be said once for all: the Church needs the truth only, and can countenance the use of no other weapons.

All these uncanonical disorders, all these practices of a too worldly spirit, impaired the respect of the faithful for their ecclesiastical superiors. This tendency to insubordination was shown even with reference to the rival Sovereign Pontiffs, when an astonished world saw them exchange anathemas, hurl lightly-regarded censures against those who were not on their side, and strive to increase their resources by methods which were unlawful. Listen to a historian whose authority is recognised everywhere by the learned: "The financial system adopted at Avignon," says Pastor, "contributed more than is generally supposed to destroy the prestige of the Papacy, and singularly facilitated the work of our foes."[1]

Is it then to be wondered at, if Wicliffe and John Huss contrived to assume the title of reformers; and if, in such favourable circumstances, they obtained such rapid and fatal success? For instead of aiming at reform within the Church and by the Church, as so many saints had done before them, they dreamt of effecting it in spite of and in opposition to the Church. They attacked the Pope and the cardinals, the bishops and the monks; and they wished to get rid of the very notion of authority and of the hierarchy. On the pretence of correcting abuses which were only too

[1] Pastor, *Histoire des Papes depuis la fin du moyen-âge*, t. i. p. 87.

real, they presumed to set up their personal fancies upon the ruins of the structure founded by Jesus Christ.

To this conception of reform through revolution, the Church opposed the idea of a reform inspired and directed by herself on the principles of the Gospel of which she is the interpreter, and according to the traditions of which she is the appointed channel. She resisted all these false teachers "who turned their rages into reasonings," to quote a word of Bossuet's.[1]

According to this great bishop, the two systems of reform were exactly represented by the two men whom he opposes to each other: "Luther," he says, "makes reformation depend on the destruction of the Papacy, whereas d'Ailly would have it to be a consequence of the perfect restoration of the authority established by Jesus Christ to maintain unity amongst His members, and to preserve the sense of obligation in the whole body."[2]

§ 4. *Fatal Influence of the Papal Residence at Avignon.*

The long sojourn of the Pontiffs in the country of Avignon, as has been shown already, was another originating cause of the Schism, because it gravely affected the belief that Rome was the indispensable centre of Catholicism, and because it put a multitude of hindrances in the way of attempts to begin a religious reformation.

No doubt, in the time of Clement V. and John XXII., there were very specious reasons for quitting an Italy torn with faction and its revolutionary metropolis.

[1] *Histoire des Variations*, i. 25. [2] *Ibid.*, i. 4.

What could the Supreme Pontiff do when Louis of Bavaria was proclaiming the deposition of the true Pope, and putting in his place the hypocritical and dissolute monk known as Pierre de Corbière, who was dragging in his train every fragment of schism and Ghibellinism in the peninsula? With what a saddened gaze must the head of the Church have regarded the abuse of power and the cupidity of the nobles, and how could he have met the declamation of a tribune of the people transformed into their king?

And yet one may ask whether the residence of the Pope in his capital might not have prevented all this: whether an open and generous struggle with the Empire, the nobility, and the people would not have been better than peace purchased by desertion? The energetic predecessors of the Popes of Avignon had better comprehended their pontifical obligations and their rôle as temporal sovereigns. When the Papacy sought refuge on the banks of the Rhone by voluntary exile, what did it gain in the way of outward respect either from kings or Christendom? And was it not forced to incur the invasion of luxury and of the worldly spirit within? Did it not deserve some still graver reproaches than fell even from the lips of the saints? In quitting Rome, their cradle, in separating themselves from the sacred sepulchre of the Prince of the Apostles, in ceasing to reign over the land which had been hallowed with the blood of the martyrs, the Popes seemed to hold cheap the support they derived from memories so august.

In their voluntary exile to the banks of the Rhone, the Pontiffs came under the power of the French kings; and the papal palace was far too much overshadowed by the menacing protection of the high towers of

Villeneuve, a French possession. In other countries they were regarded as the grand-almoners or mere chaplains of the court at Paris: they naturally became involved in the policy of the king, and had to take sides in the interminable quarrels between France and her neighbours, specially between her and England.

On the other hand, the Emperor did not forgive the Popes their residence at Avignon, which made it impossible for him to exercise his ancient rôle of outside bishop. Other sovereigns followed his example, and became jealous of even the spiritual authority of a Pontiff who appeared to be under the thumb of a rival monarch. The obedience of all of them had in it too many defiant reservations, and their respect was too often grievously withheld. "The universal father," they seemed to say, "should not appear to be the subject of one of his children," and when the Schism breaks out, England and the Empire will not follow the party of Avignon.

It was useless for the successors of St Peter to say: "We are still the Pontiffs of the Eternal City, only just now we prefer the banks of the Rhone to those of the Tiber." All the faithful of Italy and of other places replied: "But the Roman Pontiff ought not to live away from Rome, and cannot allow the inhabitants of his capital to be plunged everlastingly into political, moral, and physical catastrophes, brought about by the protracted absence of their legitimate ruler." In the eyes of many these seventy years of exile, which were termed the "Babylonian captivity," were bound to have a disastrous effect on the unity of the Church. Two capitals would prepare the way for two pontifical chairs, two colleges of cardinals, and two obediences, that is to say, for the Schism.

If the Catholic world had a presentiment of what was coming, the Popes themselves were not without their anticipations and fears. Sometimes they wished to break away from the charms and peace of Avignon to save Rome from disorders and numberless calamities. One day the blessed Urban V. plans this act of reparation. Escorted in triumph by all the galleys of Italy, he lands at Genoa, and sets out for Rome through pacified cities and respectful populations. The Eternal City has not seen her Pontiff since the days of Boniface VIII., that is to say, for sixty-three years. She receives Urban with enthusiasm and affection,[1] but he knows neither how to reign or die in his true capital. He refused to listen to the poetical plaint of Petrarch, then the most ringing voice in Italy; nor will he give any heed to the Franciscan Peter of Aragon, who predicts a fatal schism if he returns to France. St Bridget of Sweden has no better success when she forebodes for him a speedy death. And yet her prophecy is fulfilled to the letter. Urban only sees the sky of Provence to bid it a last farewell: he dies on arriving at the palace of the Doms, and Gregory XI. ascends the pontifical throne (1370).

Then occurs an event unique in Church history. In her bosom, as formerly among the tribes of Israel, arises a new kind of prophecy. Amid the troubles of these turbulent times comes forth a young girl, an angel of peace, and a missionary of reconciliation. Sprung from an obscure family, Catherine of Siena feels herself called by God to save the Church, and to restore the Vicar of Jesus Christ to his capital. She goes to find the new Pope on his throne, and does not allow herself to be

[1] Baluze, *Vitae Paparum Avenion*, t. ii. p. 768. Mirot, *La politique pontificale et le retour du Saint-Siège à Rome en* 1376 (1898).

alarmed by the brilliancy of his pompous court. With outspokenness and good judgment she demands reform and his return to Rome. She speaks eloquently on behalf of the city chosen by Christ, regenerated by St Peter, and watered with the blood of the martyrs. She succeeds, though not without miraculous help, in getting a hearing, and, as in Old Testament times, the prophet leads the priest. "Perhaps there was never in a human heart such faithfulness to the Church and to the Papacy."[1]

Does not a historic parallel here occur to everyone? Some fifty years later, another young girl, born in the marches of Lorraine, was listening to supernatural voices, which bade her take the Dauphin Charles to Reims. Joan of Arc sets out, appears before the prince, and speaks boldly and frankly in the presence of an effeminate and dispirited court. She gets listened to, and brings the future king of France to the city where kings are anointed and crowned.

When Catherine got Gregory to return to Rome, as when Joan led Charles to Reims, in each case everything seemed gained for a long time to come. God had shown His all-powerful hand. Italy in 1378 applauded as France was to applaud in 1427. All hearts seemed to have regained the right to hope afresh. And yet they were on the eve of an unexampled crisis, a fatal division, a long period of religious troubles and public calamities.

[1] Hase, *Katerina von Siena* (Leipzig, 1861), p. 197. *Cf.* Mignatz, *Caterina da Siena e la parte ch' ebbi nelle avenimenti d' Italia nel sec. XIV.* (Florence, 1894). L'Epinois, *Le gouvernement des Papes*, p. 346. Cerasoli, *Archivio Storico*, 1899.

CHAPTER II

THE ELECTION OF URBAN VI. AT ROME

It is not only in the fourteenth century that the historic problem of the origin of the Great Schism has divided and stirred men's minds. To-day this question is not cleared up for everyone. Though five centuries have gone by, Urban VI. and Clement VII. still have uncompromising upholders.

In 1378, who was the lawful successor of St Peter? Was it Bartholomew Prignano, Archbishop of Bari, or Robert of Geneva, formerly Bishop of Cambrai? The elect of April 8, or of September 20? The Pope of Rome, or he of Fondi, and afterwards of Avignon? Such was and such is still the starting-point of the discussion. The fact of the election is the central occurrence on which everything else depends. But each side tells the story in its own way, according to its convictions or emotions.

Whether one reads the explanation sent to the Christian princes by the Roman Pope,[1] or the *Declaratio* written by the dissentient cardinals;[2] whether one studies all the *Casus* of the period, in print or manuscript,[3] or

[1] Raynald, a. 1378, pp. 73-96.

[2] Du Boulay, *Historia Univ. Parisiensis,* t. iv. p. 468. Baluze, *Vitae Paparum Avenion.*, t. i. col. 1235. *Cf.* Christophe, *Histoire de la Papauté au XIVe siècle,* t. iii. p. 354.

[3] Gayet, *Le Grand Schisme d'Occident d'après les documents contemporains* —for the *Declaratio,* see next chapter, p. 57. The *Casus* are writings

whether one examines the documents preserved at the Vatican, and emanating from the rival Pontiffs,[1] one cannot but conclude that the critical point is always the account of the accession of Urban VI.

Was the moral freedom of the electors at the Council sufficiently assured? Must their choice of Bartholomew be considered legitimate and valid? Or, on the contrary, should the cardinals be considered to have so far yielded under pressure as to invalidate their acts, and, consequently, to nullify the election? This is the problem historians have had to handle, particularly since the fourteenth century.

Raynald, and the majority of writers outside France, defend Urban VI. They believe that his election was, if not unexceptionable, at any rate adequate, and moreover, that all invalidity was put out of the question later on.

Baluze and a certain number of French historians rather take sides with Clement, and are inclined to consider that the first election was invalid. This is the conclusion that follows from the testimony they bring forward, and which comes for the most part from French cardinals. Certain champions of Robert of Geneva and King Charles, especially in the seventeenth century, are rightly suspected of allowing themselves to be led away by political prejudices which have nothing to do with the discussion, through a sort of back-handed and mistaken patriotism.[2]

---

compiled by Urban, the cardinals, lawyers, and other writers, speaking in the name of each of the pretenders.

[1] *The Vatican Archives*, Ref. 291-309 for Avignon, 310-314 for Rome.

[2] The historiographer Mézeray is indignant with his fellow-countrymen who take sides with the Roman Pontiff, "without thinking that they are Frenchmen, and that they make out our kings to be schismatics and fomenters of schism." *Hist. de France* (Ed. 1685), t. ii. p. 479. MAIMBOURG, *Hist. du Grand Schisme*, lib. i.

In our days writers have treated the question afresh, but now relying upon documents which were unknown to the historians of the seventeenth century.

Hefele, Hergenröther, Pastor, Heinrich, Chenon, de Beaucourt, Denifle, have pronounced plainly in favour of the Roman Pontiff; Gayet, who has commented on many documents, rather leans towards Avignon; Noël Valois leaves the case in suspense and considers the rival Popes doubtful, and believes that the solution of this great problem is beyond the judgment of history.[1] All dwell upon the events which preceded, accompanied, or followed the election of April 8, 1378.

On this question of fact, history alone can speak; theology has nothing to do with it, and canon law can only pronounce later on, when the revalidation of the election of Urban VI. is in question, or when certain means have to be resorted to for bringing the Schism to an end. Until now the Church has not decided the matter by way of authority, and probably she never will. Some popes have shown their leanings, but none has imposed a fixed and formal decision on an important and still debated question. Nevertheless during the eighteenth century the learned Benedict XIV. had already remarked: "To-day the darkness is being dissipated and the legitimacy of Urban and his successors is growing plain."[2] Councils have formulated no judgment on the matter. Annalists and theologians of earlier centuries, who only had a limited quantity of

[1] Valois, *La France et le Grand Schisme d'Occident* (Paris, 1896), t. i. p. 8, and t. iv. p. 503. We shall often make use of information contained in this book, which cannot be too highly esteemed. M. Valois has utilised a large number of documents with great critical acumen. See also Lindner, *Histor. Zeitschrift*, t. xxviii. pp. 102-127.

[2] *De servorum Dei beatificatione*, lib. i. c. ix. No. 10.

official documents to survey, have reached different conclusions.

In the latter part of the nineteenth century, the erudite labours of historians and the discovery of numerous documents have shed enough light on the actual facts to enable one to form a reasoned conviction, which almost amounts to a certainty.

§ 1. *The General State of Mind.*

Gregory XI. had died on March 27, 1378. Following the example of his namesake, Gregory X., the deceased pope had taken every precaution to make the election of a successor easy, prompt, and indisputable. It was the first time since the departure of the Popes for Avignon, that is to say, the first time for sixty-three years, that a conclave was to be held in the Eternal City, and it was therefore more necessary than ever to surround the future choice of the cardinals with every guarantee of validity. Therefore Gregory desired the commander of the castle of Saint Angelo, Peter Gandelin,[1] not to give up the keys to anyone without an express order from six cardinals living at Avignon.

Everyone remembers Bossuet's saying in recounting the last moments of Alexander the Great: "He died full of mournful fancies about the confusion which would follow his demise." Such apparently were the apprehensions which haunted the last hours of the dying Pontiff.

[1] BALUZE, t. ii. col. 813, names this governor Pierre Rostainz, but a document recently published by Gayet calls him Gandelin de St Crispin (t. i. *Pièces justif.*, pp. 161 and 168). Pierre Rostainz was his uncle, of French stock, but an Italian by adoption (*Ibid.*, p. 156).

THE ELECTION OF URBAN VI. AT ROME

The decease of the Pope aroused various sentiments in Rome, but the dominant one was uneasiness as to the immediate future. Would the still unknown individual, on whose election the conclave was to decide, leave the Eternal City as Urban V. had done, or would he make up his mind to stay there like Gregory XI.? Was France to maintain her preponderance in directing the affairs of the Church, or would her influence pass to Italy? Was Rome again, and perhaps for ever, to be deprived of her Pontiffs, and would they return to Avignon? Was she to remain as a headless trunk, by the abandoned banks of the Tiber, a prey to anarchy and division, unprotected against the ambition of an Emperor like Louis of Bavaria or the agitation of a tribune like Cola di Rienzi? Such were the anxieties that filled every mind at Rome among the well-informed, whether priests, nobles, or *capitanei*.

The people, on their side, were animated with less lofty but more practical ideas. The Transtiberines were astir: they waylaid the cardinal-electors in the streets and called out to them: "For seventy years France has been gorged with Roman gold, it is our turn now to feast on French money."[1]

Was the Duke of Aragon going to be a true prophet when he foretold Gregory XI. the future that lay before the Papacy in the Eternal City? "If you go to live over there, said he, "the Romans are strange fellows and traitors and will take the upper hand of all the cardinals, and force them to make a Pope who suits their convenience."[2]

There might be some reason to fear it, for all the Roman citizens, rich or poor, were agreed in upholding

[1] Baluze, t. i. col. 1073. *Opera Gersonii* (Ed. Ellies-Dupin), t. i. p. 11.
[2] Froissart (Ed. Kervyn de Lettenhove), t. ix. p. 47.

a pretension, which is to-day regarded as extravagant, though for them it was a sort of undisputed dogma, that is to say, the right of the people of Rome to take part in the election of the Pope.

The turbulent and haughty nobility of Rome long believed that it had the right to make its influence felt, and to impose its preferences on the conclave. Ecclesiastical and civil history is full of frays between the Orsini of the castle of St Angelo and their eternal enemies the Colonnas of the Capitol. Rome had seen the Pierleoni of the Island in the Tiber dispute the tiara with the fierce Gaetani, who had fixed their eagle's nest in the fortified and monumental tomb of Cecilia Metella. Not merely a quarrel between two families, but the claims of a whole nation were now in question. The imperial capitulars and the privileges of Otho had confirmed the Romans in their century-long error. From another side, the national and democratic spirit of Arnold of Brescia and Cola di Rienzi had set in motion all sorts of claims opposed to pontifical authority. It is right to add that some blame attaches to the theologians of the times, who in this regard made too many advances to the degenerate Romans, and yielded in too many things to the pride of the quondam imperial people.[1]

Full of their own importance, the Roman people were ready to make their pretensions predominate within the conclave itself. The sad condition in which the exodus of the Popes to Avignon had left the town and patrimony of St Peter for seventy years, and the fear of a fresh and early departure, seemed to justify

[1] Pierre d'Ailly, "*De Ecclesiae, Concilii generalis, Romani Pontificis et Cardinalium auctoritate*," in the *Opp. Gersonii* (Ed. Ellies-Dupin), t. ii. col. 230 and 236. He terms the so-called right, *Jus naturale et divinum large sumptum.*

their complaints to a certain extent, and only encouraged them too freely to fill all ears with their overweening claims. On this point the bannerets and nobles were in perfect accord with the opinions and desires of the Roman plebs. "We want a Roman or at least an Italian Pope," was the cry heard everywhere in all the public places of the city. From another side six thousand Sabine mountaineers had descended upon Rome.[1] They camped in the streets and squares, and deafened the town with their fifes and drums. They ate and drank to excess, and meant ere long, according to custom, to plunder the residence of the future Pope-elect, and even of the cardinal-electors. The nobles and armed gentry could and should have prevented and suppressed popular risings, but they had been requested to leave the town forthwith. Thus there was a clear field for all fomenters of disturbance, who always find unwitting accomplices to act as their tools.

In the heart of Rome, with all its turmoil, what was to become of the Sacred College, called upon in such circumstances to discharge the gravest duties? It was not supposed to have been over troubled by such a state of things, which local passion, southern heat, and the rough manners of the contadini sufficiently explain. Most of the members took no precautionary measures to secure their personal safety. Later on

[1] St Vincent Ferrier, *De moderno Ecclesiae Scismati,* MS. Latin. Bibl. Nation., No. 1470, 2a pars, 3a obj. f. cclxiii. "*Homines rustici et ribaldi cellarium fregerunt palacii pro vino potando.*" This treatise was composed by the Saint in 1380 and sent to the King of Aragon, Peter IV., named the Ceremonious. M. Noël Valois wonders that so important a document has never yet found its way into print (t. i. p. 221). The Rev. Father Fages, author of a history of St Vincent, intends to publish the MS., but he has already been anticipated at Rome by Sorbelli (Purtet, 1900).

they declared that they trusted the true Romans, and never believed that their liberty was in serious danger.[1]

Furthermore, had they had any real fear, there were at hand two efficacious methods of securing protection. A few leagues from Rome were the formidable Bretons of John de Malestroit. These five hundred lances had long been the dread of all Italy. The mere news that they were coming would have been enough to inspire the plebs of the Transtiberines and the peasant mountaineers with salutary terror.

In the next place, the castle of St Angelo, commanded by the brave and trusty Pierre Gandelin, was ready to throw its doors open to the Sacred College, and to take them under the protection of its strong walls.

If these expedients crossed the timid minds of a few cardinals, they nevertheless did not think fit to resort to them. In short, there was no hindrance to prevent them from fulfilling their duty. They had put their confidence in the bannerets of the different quarters of Rome, and begged them to elect a captain, and the latter had chosen four constables. All swore according to law and ancient custom to uphold freedom of election. The three prelates appointed to guard the conclave took the same oath. The heads of the militia took energetic measures to keep order, and serious warnings were given to those who might disturb either the public peace or the personal security of the cardinals.[2]

Mounted men rode through the streets of the town to make these orders known. The executioner took his place in the Piazza of St Peter, and displayed his

[1] Gayet, t. ii., *Pièces justif.*, pp. 78 and 151. Baluze had before him many similar pieces of evidence, but has omitted to mention them.

[2] Gayet, t. i. p. 100, and several MSS. quoted by M. Noël Valois, t. i. p. 11. Knopfler, *Die Wahl Urbans* in the *Theolog. praktische Quartalschrift* of Passau, 1891.

primitive implements before everyone's eyes: a living and abiding threat calculated to inspire all the fomenters of disorder with due respect.

§ 2. *The Opening of the Conclave.*

Such were the circumstances of the meeting of the conclave on April 7, nine days after the death of Gregory XI. As he came out of Vespers, each cardinal entered into the Vatican, passing through the crowd massed in the Piazza of St Peter and on the steps of the church. As each *porporato* arrived, twenty thousand persons shouted: *Romano lo volemo, o, almeno, italiano.*[1]

The noisier among them added, as the foreign cardinals passed, "If you don't give us a Roman or at least an Italian Pope you will be torn in pieces."

Were all the cardinals ready to yield to the demands of this imperious mob? Whom did they wish to choose? Into what parties were the sixteen members present divided at this critical moment?

The Italians were in a minority. They were Francis Tibaldeschi, Cardinal of St Peter's, aged and infirm; Peter Corsini, Cardinal of Florence; Simon of Borsano, Cardinal of Milan, and James [2] Orsini.

The foreigners were more numerous and were divided into two sections. The Frenchmen included Hugh de Montalais, Cardinal of Brittany; Robert of Geneva, formerly Bishop of Thérouanne and Cambrai, afterwards Clement VII.; Peter Flandrin, Cardinal of St Eustache;

[1] *Dum Domini Cardinales vellent intrare Conclave pro Summo Pontifice eligendo, fere totus populus romanus armatus et congregatus in platea Sancti Petri vociferando et comminando: Romano lo volemo, o, al manco italiano.* St Vincent Ferrier, *op. cit.*, f. cclxi.

[2] Not *John* as he is called by Th. de Niem, a contemporary, and by his biographer, G. Erler, *Dietrich von Nieheim*, p. 324.

and Bertrand Lagier, Cardinal of Glandève. To them belonged also Peter de Luna, a Cardinal of Aragon, subsequently Benedict XIII.

The cardinals of the Limousin made a separate section. The three Avignon Popes, Clement VI., Innocent VI., and Gregory XI., were natives of that province. They had created numerous cardinals, chosen among their relations or fellow-countrymen. They were Guy de Malesset, Cardinal of Poitiers; John de Cros, Cardinal of Limoges; Gerald of Puy, Cardinal of Marmoutiers, William d'Aigrefeuille, and Peter de Vergne. At Rome, public opinion also credited them with Peter de Sortenac, Cardinal of Viviers; and William Noëllet, Cardinal of St Angelo.

In short, the conclave numbered four Italian, five French, and seven cardinals from the Limousin. Each party had its candidate, and hoped to carry him to victory by making alliances, compromises, and promises. In any case, the Italians and French seemed disposed to exclude the Limousin party, who for years had looked upon the Holy See as their own fief.

All the documents appear to agree that before the conclave there were negotiations between the smaller sections as to how to keep the Limousin party in check. The Italians and French combined were to agree upon a prelate taken from outside the Sacred College, and certain depositions claim that the name of Bartholomew Prignano, Archbishop of Bari, was then already mentioned.[1]

At this time it is curious to remark the attitude of Robert of Geneva, who, as Clement VII., was to become Bartholomew's rival. The Archbishop of Bari's candidature had no warmer partisan. "This time we will

[1] Gayet, t. ii. p. 10. Fleury, *Hist. Eccles.*, lib. xcvii. ch. 48.

have an Italian," he kept saying. "I will never vote for these Limousin traitors." And he added: "By these Holy Gospels, the Archbishop of Bari shall be our Pope."[1] He had spoken to Bartholomew in this sense, for this was the candidate of his choice. Peter de Luna himself, afterwards Benedict XIII., entered the conclave with the same idea, and proclaimed aloud that he meant to vote for Prignano.[2] It is also said that some of the Limousins, much agitated by the coalition against them, and feeling that they could not resist it, were not far from voting for Bartholomew.[3] Peter de Luna owns this, and his testimony is of primary importance.

Hence it seems certain that, from the very beginning of the conclave, from nine to ten of the sixteen cardinals intended to vote for the Archbishop of Bari. Antecedently he had much more than an absolute majority and almost obtained two-thirds of the votes. The differences between the electors paved the way for his success. From several of them he had received formal assurances of support, and everything leads one to suppose that he already counted on wearing the tiara.

There is then no need to assume that the election of the Archbishop of Bari was due to external pressure.

[1] Baluze, t. i. col. 1001.

[2] Gayet, t. ii. pp. 148-150. "The Romans," adds M. Gayet, "did not fabricate the election of Bartholomew Prignano: it was, I believe, in the nature of things. All they did was to compromise and injure the case of their candidate. The cardinals could not agree upon one of their own number: they had to look for a candidate outside of the Sacred College, and outside the Sacred College there was no one except the Archbishop of Bari" (t. ii. p. 286). As this avowal comes from a supporter of Robert of Geneva, it is all the more noteworthy.

[3] Valois, t. i. p. 28. Jahr, *Die Wahl Urbans VI.*, p. 46. Gayet, t. i. p. 152. Baluze, t. i. col. 1001 and 1077.

Moreover, the shouts that re-echo in the Piazza of St Peter do not call for Bartholomew by name, but for a Roman or at least an Italian.[1]

§ 3. *The Election of Prignano.*

The electors, received at the gates of the Vatican by the Senator, one by one ascend a staircase leading to the first floor, where the cells which they are to occupy have been got ready. Several staircases had been walled up to hinder the crowd from finding its way into the rooms of the conclave. Nevertheless a few men took advantage of the transition of the cardinals and members of the conclave to gain an entrance to the palace, and to continue to give loud expression to the wishes of the people of Rome.

The heads of districts (*caporioni*) then came forward and tried to exact from the united prelates a formal promise to elect an Italian. Cardinal d'Aigrefeuille, prior of the cardinal-priests, worthily replied to these illegal and disrespectful summonses: "I have not the right," he said, "to pledge the votes of my colleagues, nor can they command mine. Therefore retire. Fresh entreaties will only vitiate the election and succeed in making it null and void." Cardinal Orsini made them understand the impropriety of their proceedings still more keenly. The *caporioni*, after an hour's useless entreaties, withdrew in dissatisfaction. The people, who were expecting more definite pledges, showed themselves much disappointed. All night they took their stand in the Piazza of St Peter, breaking into and plundering the palace cellars,

[1] Gayet, t. i. p. 239. *Cf.* Valois, t. i. p. 37.

drinking stolen wine, and incessantly shouted—" A Roman or at least an Italian ! "[1]

On April 8, in the early morning, while the cardinals were hearing Mass, the alarm bell rang out in the town, and soon the bells of St Peter's mingled with its clanging their reverberating and ominous pealing. It seems as if a rising is on the point of breaking out in Rome, and that with the multitude of demonstrators the tumult is hourly increasing. The electors gathered in the chapel are perturbed : the Bishop of Marseilles, William de la Voulte, the guardian of the conclave, is the most alarmed of them all. He comes and cries out : " Make haste, my lords. The people want a Roman or Italian Pope ; if you make any opposition, you run the risk of being cut in pieces without mercy."[2]

The young Cardinal Orsini leaves the chapel and tries to check and calm the crowd, but with small success. All the cardinals return to the chapel full of agitation and perplexity. What are they to do ? Whom are they to choose ? Half an hour is spent in deliberation without result. At last two of the electors go and promise the mob that their wishes will soon be gratified. Here let it be noted once more that the Romans so far have suggested no one's name.

[1] "Vinolentia non violentia." "Such scenes are the result of noisy hilarity and impatience. They are the effect of the copious libations of the crowd." Thus writes a Protestant, Leo, *Histoire d'Italie*, t. ii. p. 315 (Ed. Dochez, Paris, 1844). *Cf.* Gayet, t. i. p. 244. *Pièces justif.*, pp. 77 and 154. Baluze, t. i. pp. 450, 485, 1211 ff. Valois, t. i. p. 39.

[2] St Vincent Ferrier, *loc. cit.* This writer adds : "Considerabant Domini Cardinales antiquam et consuetam experientiam malitiae Romanorum. Jam ab antiquo expertus est universus mundus quomodo Romani fuerunt semper assueti ad mala, faciles ad irascendum, subiti ad seditionem et audaces ad percutiendum et occidendum." F. 281. It must be remembered that the Saint is pleading for Clement VII., and that he was long on the side of the Popes of Avignon. *Cf.* Gayet, *Pièces justif.*, t. i. pp. 11, 17, 19, 36, etc. *Texte*, pp. 269, 275, etc.

Peter de Luna, with more determination and less timidity, gets the Cardinal of Limoges to vote for the Archbishop of Bari. This cardinal rises in his turn: "My Lords," he says, "since God has not given us to be of one mind as to the choice of one of the members of the Sacred College, I think we should elect someone from outside. I do not see anyone as worthy as the Archbishop of Bari. He is a saintly man, and known to us all, a man of ripe age and fitting attainments. I propose him freely and spontaneously."[1] Aigrefeuille, apparently anxious to have done with the question, exclaims: "I vote for Prignano as Roman Pontiff." Almost all express themselves in a similar way. A few seem to hesitate, but end in accepting Bartholomew. Orsini alone professes to think himself under too much constraint and that the election will be null.

On the other hand, Peter de Luna and many others protest that they choose the Archbishop of Bari with the express intention of making a true Pope.[2] It is nine o'clock. The election is over, but the cardinals propose to keep it secret until they receive an assurance of the consent of the elect. The Bishop of Marseilles has the Archbishop invited to come to the palace with several prelates, so that the people may not be in doubt as to the choice of the Sacred College.

Outside the mob continues to sway to and fro, and deafening cries re-echo round the palace, "Romano lo volemo!"

[1] Gayet, t. i. p. 313. *Cf.* Baluze, t. i. col. 1104 and 1463.

[2] "*Cum et animo et intentione ut sit verus Papa.*" Thus spoke the Cardinals of Limoges, St Peter, d'Aigrefeuille, Viviers, Milan, Luna, and perhaps of Poitiers. The Cardinals of Vergne, Glandève, and Marmoutiers, afterwards questioned as to what was then their intention, affirmed that they could not remember, so as not to have to make a reply. *Cf.* Gayet, t. i. p. 323. Valois, t. i. p. 45. These details, the importance of which is clear, are not denied by the opponents of Urban.

The cardinals begin to fear that the name of Prignano, who is not a Roman, will not be well received: nevertheless, as a comparative calm apparently falls upon the Piazza, they quietly take a meal. Then they return to the chapel, and one of the electors asks his colleagues: "Now that the excitement is over, let us take advantage of the opportunity to re-elect the Archbishop of Bari. Are we still of the same opinion?" "Yes, yes!" reply the majority of the cardinals: thirteen out of sixteen. Three of them had not yet come back to the chapel.

Assuming that the earlier election was invalid, Bartholomew is now elected lawfully and almost unanimously.[1]

While this was going on, Cardinal Orsini appears at a window where the conclave was met. "You have a Pope," he exclaims to the mob; but he does not utter the name of the elect. Different and contradictory rumours are current in the various knots of people. "It is Tebaldeschi, it is the old Cardinal of St Peter's," say some. "It's the camerlingo, John de Bar," cry out others. The latter, a native of Limousin, was detested by the Romans. The agitation grows and becomes threatening. Fresh clamour arises; doors are broken down, stones are hurled through the windows, and threats of death are uttered. The populace forces its way into the palace, wounds some of the members of the conclave, and begins to plunder. The prelates fail to restrain the mob let loose; misunderstanding continues and grows.

Then begins a scene strange and unparalleled in the

[1] *Cf.* Valois, t. i. p. 50. The three who were absent were the Cardinals of Brittany, Marmoutiers, and Vergne. The presence of the Cardinal of Glandève is not certain. *Cf.* Gayet, t. i. p. 359.

history of conclaves. A cleric imagines that the name of Bartholomew is not acceptable to the people, and the idea of presenting the old Cardinal of St Peter's as the elect of the conclave occurs to him.

Tebaldeschi protests : his colleagues in alarm beseech him to lend himself to the stratagem in order to save their lives. They seize the old man, who is almost impotent, and place him on the Papal throne, and crown him with a white mitre and cast around his shoulders a red cape, singing the *Te Deum* in the midst of the tumult. In vain the Cardinal cries out : " I am not the Pope at all. It is the Archbishop of Bari." He is lifted by force on to the altar, until at last the name of Prignano is heard and understood by the crowd.[1]

While this was going on, Bartholomew had arrived at the Vatican and heard the news of his election. A few Romans, disappointed of their ambitious hopes, tried to induce him to refuse the tiara ; but he managed to escape their entreaties, and succeeded in reaching the secret room. The cardinals, irked by the mystification which had just been gone through, vanish one after the other and get back to their houses. Six of them take refuge in the castle of St Angelo, after having run some risk. Four leave Rome for the shelter of neighbouring fastnesses.

√ Hence, in spite of shouts and threats, an election had taken place, and then a re-election. The great disorder and violence that broke out only came afterwards. No one dreamt of telling the Archbishop of Bari that his selection was the outcome of fear, and that this alone tainted it with irregularity.

Moreover, can it be said that the fears felt by the electors were strong enough to hinder them from per-

[1] *Ibid.* *Cf.* Muratori, *Rerum ital. scriptores*, t. iii. 2ª pars., p. 664.

forming a human and moral action, that is to say, an action possessing all the necessary attributes to ensure its being responsible in conscience? Urban's election had taken place in the midst of fears, but it had not been their outcome. Bartholomew then had a right to look upon himself as legitimately chosen, and the conduct of the cardinals during the following days could only confirm him in this conviction.

In mere virtue of their office, the cardinals were the principal factors in the Pope's election. Did they wish, and could they make a valid choice in the circumstances that have been related? If they were so far terrorised as to think that the election they have made was not valid, they will certainly hasten to declare it null and void immediately after peace has been restored; they will interchange opinions and proceed to a fresh election. If, on the other hand, they thought their choice was valid, they will act in harmony with this conviction and pay their homage to the newly-elect. Hence it is their action that will enlighten us as to the opinions that they entertain, now that all reasons for fear have disappeared. Let us note the steps they take.

The Archbishop of Bari awaits the homage of the cardinals, and he is not disappointed. The Cardinal of Florence is the first to meet him, and he is followed by the Cardinal of Milan. Both of these are Italians. Gerald of Puy, Cardinal of Marmoutiers, is from Limousin, and yet he gets his colleagues, who have taken refuge in the castle of St Angelo, to present themselves at the Vatican. The Frenchman Lagier, Cardinal of Glandève, and Peter de Luna of Aragon arrive in turn to pay their compliments to the new Pontiff. If the latter expresses some doubt as to the validity of the election, the cardinals present hasten to reassure him. The six prelates shut up in the castle make more difficulties, agitated as they are by the camerlingo, Peter de Cros. The remembrance of the commotion they had experienced and the insults they had received the day before seems to remain smarting within their breasts. But had they any velleity to contest the election of Prignano? They said so later on, but Cardinal d'Aigrefeuille contradicted them.

The honours with which they surround the new Pontiff testify to the impression they had at the time. Nor is this all: we see them at once sending their power of attorney, so that the enthronement of the Pontiff may proceed with validity in their absence. Yet that very evening they think better of it. Is it to express doubts as to the voting? On the contrary, it is to confirm it. They have decided to go to the Vatican in person, and to proceed, with their other colleagues, to the ceremony of enthronement. Hence they solemnly recognise Bartholomew as their elect. The Cardinal of Florence says in the name of them all: "My Lord, we have elected you." The latter accepts their election. He is dressed in the white cassock and pontifical decorations, and the *Te Deum* is chanted. The electors cast themselves at his feet and "do him worship." Meanwhile Peter of Vergne, a Limousin cardinal, opens a window, and, speaking so that all may hear, utters the customary form of words: "I have a great joy to tell you: you have a Pope, and he has taken the name of Urban VI."

The clergy and then the Romans enter the room in turn and prostrate themselves at the feet of the new Pontiff.

§ 4. *The Coronation of Urban.*

There is no hesitation and no manifestation of doubt. No delay is requested to examine into the question of validity, to see whether a new election will be required. The Pope, the cardinals, the clergy, and people, all are apparently at one. Later on, when the members of the Sacred College change their minds and proceed to a fresh election, Christendom will say to them: "My lords, if there has been any mistake, it is you who have deceived us. When we unanimously recognised Urban, we only followed your example. Why do you claim now to give us another Pope in the place of him whom you declared legitimately elected?"

Yet a few months later these same cardinals will want to make such a reversal: they will come to tell a catholic world, justly wondering at their right-about-face, "If we momentarily chose Bartholomew, it is because he was more involved than anyone else in the tumults of those days, and therefore could more easily comprehend the need of an immediate resignation of office."[1]

The Limousin cardinals, and particularly John de Cros, Cardinal of Limoges, there and then show themselves most anxious to obtain spiritual and temporal favours from the new Pope. They seem to be troubled

[1] Valois, t. i. p. 61. It is astonishing to see this strange reasoning repeated by St Vincent Ferrier: "*Domini Cardinales . . . nominarunt dictum Bartholomeum in papam, quem reputabant hominem intelligentem et devotum et in factis curiae satis expertum, quatenus ipsemet per suam scientiam et experientiam cognoscens nullitatem notorissimam illiusmodi electionis eam propter timorem Dei retractus nullathenus acceptaret, vel solum ad tempus eam acceptasse simularet ad liberandos Dominos Cardinales.*" *De moderno Ecclesiae scismate*, f. cclxiv. 6ª objectio. M. Gayet thinks the election of Bartholomew was the greatest mark of confidence that the cardinals could give him (t. i. p. 334).

by no scruple as to whether Urban has the authority to grant such privileges. They, and Cardinal Peter de Luna in particular, though soon after they will elect Clement, do not shrink from acknowledging these incriminating circumstances. Soon all the other members of the Sacred College, who had taken refuge in the neighbourhood, return to Rome. Robert of Geneva is among them, nor is he behindhand in offering his homage to Urban VI. Ceremonies follow one another throughout the month of April. The Pope gives his solemn benediction, known as *urbi et orbi*, distributes palms on Palm-Sunday, and utters an excommunication against the enemies of the Church.

Finally, on Easter Day, April 18, he is enthroned according to custom at St John Lateran; and then, at St Peter's, the cardinals solemnly proceed to the ceremony of the coronation.

It is Cardinal Orsini, the only one who would not vote for Prignano, who is charged with placing the tiara on the head of the new Pontiff. He has rallied completely.

Thus the whole of the Sacred College acclaims Urban, flatters his fancies, espouses his quarrels, and continues throughout the months of May and June to beg numerous favours at his hands.[1] Later on, the Clementine supporter, William de la Voulte, Bishop of Marseilles, will be obliged to admit that, for many months, he could not doubt but that the elect of April 8 had been recognised by them as the legitimate Pope.[2]

And, as a matter of fact, the Sacred College, in a collective letter, officially notified the accession of Urban to the six cardinals who had remained in Avignon

[1] Gayet, t. ii. p. 130.

[2] Valois, t. i. p. 63. *Cf.* Hefele, *History of the Councils*, t. x. p. 35.

(April 19),[1] and then to the Emperor (May 8), as well as to the rest of the catholic sovereigns. On April 14, Robert of Geneva, the future Clement VII., had written himself to Charles V.,[2] and then several times to the Elector Palatine, and finally to his relation Louis de Maele, Count of Flanders.[3]

On his side, Peter de Luna, subsequently Benedict XIII., had addressed to several Spanish bishops letters relating and approving in all particulars the election of April. Every day he used at Mass the prayer *pro Papa* for Urban.[4] "We have elected a real Pope," he wrote on April 8; "the Romans may tear me limb from limb before they get me to go back on to-day's election."

It is plain that the two future Popes of Avignon are most forward and emphatic in their defence of the legality of the acts of the conclave, and in making known Urban's election to the Christian world. There is no protest, no exchange of ideas as to the strange situation created for the Church, no fear for the future. All behave as if Urban's election could give rise to no serious dispute.

When later on the electors are confronted with the

[1] Raynald gives the full text of this document, a. 1378, No. 19. *Cf.* d'Achery, *Spicilegium*, t. i. p. 763. Du Boulay, *Historia Univ. Paris*, t. iv. p. 497.

[2] Pastor, *Geschichte der Päpste*, 2nd Ed., t. i. p. 686. Gayet, pp. 107, 141.

[3] Raynald, a. 1368, No. 17. Robert, Elector Palatine, in 1379, wrote to his cousin Charles V., that he had seen more than eighteen letters from the cardinals, of which some were in autograph. They had been written either from Rome, or outside Rome; some were from Robert of Geneva. All asserted that Urban had been elected by the guidance of the Holy Spirit, and that legal forms had been observed. Baluze, *Vitae Pap. Avenion.*, t. ii. col. 888.

[4] Gayet, t. ii. p. 140. *Pièces justif.*, pp. 148-151. Valois, t. i. p. 73. *Cf.* Baluze, t. i. col. 1482.

letters they had written immediately after the event, their replies will be weak and confused.[1] Their most subtle advocates will feel embarrassed, and fail to justify them fully.

On their side, as soon as they got the announcement of Urban's election, the six cardinals who had stayed at Avignon wrote to beg him to receive their homage and respect (June 24).[2] They have the armorial bearings of the new Pope put up in the town, and two of them order Gandelin to open the gates of the castle of St Angelo to the Pontiff.

Not until later will any doubts occur. The expression

[1] Proof enough is to be found in a speech at the Council of Cambrai in 1383 by Guy de Malesset, Cardinal of Poitiers, then Clement's legate, making an attempt to reconcile the Flemish to the authority of Avignon. I have published the text according to the Paris MSS. in the *Revue des sciences eccl.* (série ix. t. iii. p. 262), Bibl. Nat., 15561, f. 108, and Rome MS., Bibl. Vat., *Armarium* liv. vol. xiv. f. 93. Baluze has copied a few sentences from it, t. i. 1106. The cardinal attempts to reply to this objection: *Illas* (litteras) *non legi, sed supponatur quod ita contineatur . . . In facto, sic fuit veritas quod dictus Bartholomaeus litteras illas petiit a nobis omnibus, fuit sibi responsum quod nunquam de more Sacrum Collegium notificat per litteras electionem Summi Pontificis principibus vel aliis, et sic se habet veritas, et quaeratur audacter ab omnibus principibus christianitatis, si unquam alias ante illam intrusionem litteras de hoc a Sacro Collegio receperunt et recipient. Ipse tamen, hoc non obstante, cum instantia habere voluit. Ad quem finem? bene potest cogitare. Vidit enim quod, propter notoriam violentiam in electione factam, mundus non obedivisset ei, sicut nec debet. Ad attrahendum mundum in obedientiam sui litteras habere voluit, et multa alia dolosa ad finem istum operatus est, quae essent nimis longum enarrare."* These letters, he adds, prove nothing, because they were written in the very town where the cardinals were intimidated, because they cannot render valid an election which was simply null in law, and finally because they were contradicted and nullified by other acts of an authentic character which took place later on at Anagni or at Fondi, the same persons being the agents.

[2] These are Ange Grimoard, Cardinal of Albano; G. Aycelin de Montaigu, formerly Bishop of Thérouanne; John de Blanzac, Cardinal of Nîmes; William of Chanac, Cardinal of Mende; Peter de Monteruc, Cardinal of Pampeluna; and Hugh de Saint-Martial. Eubel, *Hierarchia*, p. 22.

sede vacante will only be made use of in official acts after September 12, that is to say, five months after the Vatican election.[1]

The cardinals on the banks of the Rhone are therefore in agreement with those on the Tiber as to acknowledging Urban VI. Out of the twenty-three members of the Sacred College, there is not a single exception. Furthermore, if there was some disturbance at the time of balloting, would it not be easy to find at certain dates of the Church's history conclaves still more agitated than that of 1378 ? Is there any need to recall the tumultuous elections of Popes Silverius, Vigilius, Felix IV., John XII., and many others ? But no one has ever doubted or doubts the validity of these elections.

The narrative just related rests on new documents, which mostly proceed from the future supporters of Clement VII. These records are, moreover, more numerous than those that proceed from the friends of Urban. When the Clementines are at one with the Urbanists as to certain questions of fact, or when the former put forth statements which are favourable to the cause of the Roman Pope, we may accept their opinion without fear of being mistaken.

Hence, as all acknowledge, there was perfect accord during the first few months of Urban's pontificate : the great excitement of the days of the month of April was apparently forgotten. The Pontiff who had been elected at Rome was accepted unhesitatingly not only by the Sacred College, but by all Catholic Christendom. But if the election of April is indisputable, the September election is unlawful. Urban and his successors are then the true Roman Popes, they belong to the true

[1] Conrad Eubel, *Das Itinerar der Päpste zur Zeit des grossen Schismas, Histor. Jahrbücher*, xvi.

line, which can be traced back to Peter, and which continues to Pius X. Those who, like M. Chenon[1] and M. de l'Epinois, call the future Pope Clement VII. an anti-pope, take their stand upon some of the surest of historical documents, and their opinion will certainly prevail in the future.

[1] *Histoire Générale,* published by Lavisse and Rambaud, t. iii. p. 319. I should, however, prefer the term *false Pope.* The election of the Popes of Avignon had not the odious character of the anti-canonical elections of anti-popes, who in preceding centuries unlawfully ascended the chair of St Peter. Later on it will be shown that the term Schism is also badly chosen from the theological point of view. There was no disobedience to the true Shepherd, which is Schism if one speak exactly, but it was possible to be mistaken as to who then lawfully held the power of the Keys. See further on, ch. ix. p. 187.

CHAPTER III

THE ELECTION OF CLEMENT VII. AT FONDI

§ 1. *Causes.*

A FEW weeks after the election of Urban, several cardinals, and particularly those of Glandève and Vergne, had taken counsel secretly with their colleagues who had remained at Avignon. They had also put the sovereigns of Europe on their guard against the official accounts which had already been sent. They had taken care to warn Charles V. above all, either by confidential letters or by official messages. Already an indescribable confused rumour of revolt and treason began to spread, and no news from Rome came to establish the truth in its exactitude.

On the contrary, the Pope's ambassadors had nothing more urgent to do than to betray their sender. Moreover, they had been sent off too late, just when the unfavourable rumours about Urban began to be disseminated. Further, the conduct of one of them seems to reveal an extraordinarily treacherous character. Peter de Murles, sent to King Charles, doubtless discharged his outward and public mission with correctness. But, being suborned by certain of the cardinals and by the camerlingo, this unscrupulous diplomatist disavowed in a whisper everything which he was commissioned to affirm aloud; he scattered doubt and awakened every kind of suspicion as to the lawfulness of the Pontiff who had sent him. He became the echo of every evil report, and related with much exaggeration all the violence shown by the Romans towards the Sacred College before and during the election.[1]

A second embassy, made up of James of Ceva, and Raymond of Capua, the confessor of St Catherine of Siena, whom William de la Voulte, Bishop of Valence, was to join, never reached the court of Charles V. Later on, William and Ceva took the other side.[2]

In Castile and in Portugal, the ambassador John de Roquefeuille played the same equivocal part. It was the fate of Urban always to be betrayed by those whom he selected to defend his case, and whom he had advanced to the highest dignities.[3]

Thanks to these disloyal manœuvres, a certain hesitation began to be shown beyond the Alps, at Paris, as at Avignon, among civil as well as among ecclesiastical authorities. People wanted to know, in their anxiety and curiosity, what was going to take place in Rome and Italy.

Soon events would reply.

First of all, as has been seen, the cardinal electors had never considered Urban's election illegal, and therefore to be set aside and replaced as soon as possible. They had got every personal advantage out of the situation that they could possibly obtain. Their scruples were but slowly aroused: their desire for a change, and their hope of getting together a fresh

[1] Valois, t. i. p. 92. Christine de Pisan, *Livre des fais et bonnes mœurs du sage roi Charles V.*, iii. 52.

[2] *Cf.* Denifle, *Chartularium*, t. iii. No. 1615. The ten letters published by the learned Dominican were recently discovered in the State archives at Siena, whither they were no doubt taken by Raymond of Siena himself. *Cf.* Valois, t. i. p. 124.

[3] Valois, t. i. p. 198; t. ii. p. 285.

conclave, appeared only by degrees: their interests and their hatred easily concurred for the overthrow of Prignano.

What were the causes of this sudden revulsion? They come out several times in the depositions of the Clementine cardinals. As soon as he was elected, Urban's character seemed to change. Until then he had been looked upon as a foe to vice, simony, and pomp, as a lover of corporal mortifications, exemplary conduct, and rigid integrity, and as an enlightened patron of literature and art. He had been a bishop for fifteen years, and he had not only been chosen for his Italian descent, but for his tried prudence, his knowledge of law, and his long practical experience. A vice-chancellor under Gregory XI. at Avignon and at Rome, he had shown himself equal to the discharge of the most delicate duties. "He would have been the worthiest man in the world to be Pope, if he had never been one," say the historians, copying a well-known saying of Tacitus.[1] Bartholomew Prignano had been irreproachable: Urban was far from being so, if we are to believe contemporary documents.

Too certain it is that the new Pontiff was no sooner raised to the chair of St Peter than he showed himself inflexible in his wishes, precipitate and fanciful in his plans of reform, more harsh than prudent, and more passionate than wise. We may well believe a judge whose impartiality is unquestionable, and so let us listen to St Catherine of Siena, speaking to the Pope, whose election she had welcomed. "Holy Father," she wrote, "you should be glad to find someone who helps you to see and avoid such things as might lead

[1] "*Capax imperii nisi imperasset*" (*Histor.*, lib. 49). *Cf.* Th. de Niem, *De scismate*, lib. i. c. 1.

to your discredit and the loss of souls: for the love of Jesus crucified, mitigate a little the sudden outbursts to which your disposition gives rise; by all saintly virtues, check your natural temper."[1]

Unhappily, Urban does not seem often to have put these wise counsels into practice.

Why is it that the high character of his learning, the worthiness of his moral conduct, and the indisputable greatness of his gifts did not protect him from such a want of tact and moderation? May it have been that the strong impression made by the dramatic events which had marked the beginning of his reign caused his mind to lose its balance at certain crises in his life?

Immediately after his coronation, the Pope uses roughly the foreign prelates who had come to the Vatican to offer him their homage. And does he not even treat them as perjurers, because they have temporarily abandoned their dioceses to make a brief stay in Rome?

A fortnight later he is preaching in full consistory and begins with the gracious words, "I am the good Shepherd." But the whole of his sermon is in constant contradiction with the text: it is couched in the most virulent terms, wherewith he attacks the life and conduct of the cardinals and prelates. A favourite of the late Pope comes to him to give back a certain sum he owed the treasury, and the newly-elect greets him with the reproach flung by St Peter at Simon the Magician: "Accursed, thy money perish with thee!"[2] Always angry, threatening, and harsh, he imperiously requires the princes of the Church to reform their household and style of entertainment, to repair at their own expense

[1] Niem, *De scismate,* lib. i. 4. Pastor, t. i. p. 137.

[2] St Antonin, *Summa histor.*, lib. iii. tit. 22.

the sanctuaries, the titles of which they bear, and to give up the gifts and pensions which sovereigns had been good enough to grant them. He addresses them with the bitterest invectives in public. Orsini, the prelate who had crowned him, is treated as a madman; and Robert of Geneva, the future Clement VII., has to hear himself characterised as a ribald person. The princes and nobles are sometimes reprimanded with a sharpness bordering on insult. No doubt all the plans of reform he was contemplating were such as might be expected from a Pontiff who had been chosen for his many fine qualities; but apparently the methods of Urban VI. were neither always prompted by prudence nor practised with nicety of form.[1]

At Rome an opposition came into being, and then it grew. Soon it had a headquarters, a leader, and troops. The castle of St Angelo had never opened its gates to Urban, in spite of the definite orders of the Avignon cardinals. At the very time of the election, Peter de Cros, the brother of the Cardinal of Limoges, had retreated thither with the pontifical treasure, and waged furtive but obstinate war against the new Pontiff. This fortress soon became a hostile centre where the lukewarm or discontented cardinals forgathered, where every suspicion found expression, all grievances were exaggerated, and where all revolts were hatched. The dissentients soon discovered a leader in the French cardinal John de la Grange, Bishop of Amiens. This prelate was not at Rome when Gregory's death and the election of Urban took place. Nevertheless he lavished every mark of outward respect on the new Pope; but he seems soon to have had doubts. No doubt the cause

[1] *Cf.* Pastor, t. i. p. 140. Hefele, *History of the Councils*, vol. x. p. 40.

is to be found in the violence of Urban's proceedings; for ever fuming and moping,[1] he had more than one altercation with John de la Grange, whom he loaded with bitter reproaches.

And this had serious consequences. The cardinal was a favourite of Charles V. More than once the King had had recourse to his indisputable talents as a diplomatist and financier, and he had loaded him with honours and riches. On the other hand, like all the French prelates, John de la Grange wished to see a return to Avignon, while Urban was of an entirely contrary opinion. Lastly, it was known at Rome, and the Pope made no secret of the fact, that he meant to create a considerable number of Italian cardinals as a counterpoise to the influence of the French.

All these circumstances combined to mark out John de la Grange as the leader of the opposition. Jointly with Robert of Geneva, he encouraged the commander of the castle of St Angelo to resist, and conferred with the captains of mercenaries. Soon the conspiracy was organised, and desertion of the Pope was as unanimous as adherence to him had been.

From the month of May, the town began to be hot, and the cardinals used this as a pretext for leaving and withdrawing to Anagni for reasons of health. Nevertheless they did not cease testifying all respect to Urban, and also continued to urge him to grant them new favours.

Perhaps they felt themselves obliged to dissimulate their plans of rebellion until they thought themselves strong enough in the support upon which they relied.

From the castle of St Angelo the camerlingo Peter de Cros called to their aid the famous captain of mercen-

[1] Froissart, t. xvi. p. 143.

aries, Bernardon de la Salle, Duguescelin's old companion. Almost immediately two hundred lancers of Gascony and Navarre, after putting to flight the Roman troops at Salaro bridge on their way, took the dissentient cardinals under their protection.

These preparations for reunion had at last aroused the attention of Urban,[1] and helped for the moment to bring him to more moderate views and to a clearer idea of the true situation. In the month of June he begged three members of the Sacred College, who had stayed at Rome (Borsano, Corsini, and Orsini), to betake themselves to Anagni to discharge a delicate mission to their colleagues: they were gently to upbraid these malcontents for their want of confidence, and to assure them that the new Pope would be as propitious to them as any of his predecessors. This step was taken, and in return the cardinals at Anagni gave the Pontiff an assurance of their loyalty. But this did not prevent their holding a meeting that very evening to affirm the invalidity of the April election, and to concert measures for the deposition of Urban. They even got the three deputies to stay in the town of Anagni, and to make common cause with them, but without at first succeeding in shaking their fidelity.

The three Italian cardinals wished to continue the negotiations; they tried their hand at diplomacy in order to prevent untoward occurrences, and to restore harmony between the Sacred College and the Pope. It is strange to make the statement, but the two principal means extolled later on, during nearly twenty years, for putting an end to the Schism, were put forward from the very beginning by his deputies in the

[1] Sheuffgen, *Beiträge zu der Geschichte des grossen Schismas*, p. 11. Bliemetz, in *Studien und Mittheilungen*, 1903, 2nd and 3rd quarters.

name of the Pontiff. The first of these means was the meeting of a *General Council*[1] in a safe town, say Venice, Pisa, or even Naples: it is the method that was to be crowned with success forty years later at Constance. The second was a sort of compromise that would have entrusted the election of a Pope to the care of six special delegates: it is a way which was to be vainly insisted upon many times during the years to come.

Neither the one nor the other of these expedients gained votes for the time being. The dissentient cardinals put aside the proposal to re-elect Bartholomew which would have put an end to all legal objections. They refused to consider the opinions on points of law and fact put forth in August 1378 by John of Lignano at Bologna, Balde at Perugia, and Colluccio Salutato at Florence: yet they were the three most clear-sighted lawyers of their time.[2]

From this time onwards the rebellion breaks out openly. The cardinals at Anagni first send Urban an insulting letter, calling him, amidst other abuse, the "old Bishop of Bari," and venture to wish him more reasonable ideas. They energetically dispute the legality of his election, and tell him that they had only enthroned him under the pressure of fear;[3] they

[1] Raynald, a. 1378, No. 43. Valois, t. i. p. 80. Gayet, t. ii., *Pièces justif.*, p. 188. Baluze, t. i. col. 1107. Scheuffgen, p. 7.

[2] Raynald, Nos. 31 and 36.

[3] St Vincent Ferrier (*De moderno scismate*, MS. Bibl. Nation. 1170, f. 265, 7o) also tried to excuse the cardinals on the ground of their fear of Urban, *homo furiosus*, as he was called by the Cardinal of Brittany. It is not until they are at Anagni, under the protection of the mercenaries, "*postquam fuerunt stipati armatis stipendiariis*," that they dare to declare that Bartholomew is an apostate and an intruder. Their pusillanimity seems to have lasted long. In April it had prevented their election of a true Pope. It clings to them for several months, and compels them to act against their conscience: first, they are afraid of the

denounce him as an apostate under anathema, and summon him to abdicate.[1] On August 2 they follow up this unedifying document with their famous *Declaratio*, a statement destined to become public. Therein they set forth an inaccurate and most impassioned narrative of the circumstances of the election of April 8, affirming afresh that they had only elected Prignano to please the people and from fear of death.[2] They thus constitute themselves accusers, witnesses, and judges in a cause against a Pope formally appointed and recognised by themselves. It is a declaration of war, and thenceforward events hurry on.

On August the 9th the thirteen cardinals issue to be read in public an encyclical addressed to all the faithful, in which they repeat their account of all that had taken place in April, and anathematise Urban as a usurper. They declare that they have put themselves under the special protection of Gaetani, Count of Fondi, whom the Pope had mortally insulted.

On August 21 they write to the University of Paris *de invasore Urbano*.

A few days afterwards, August 29, they leave Anagni for Fondi, nearer the States of the famous Jane of Naples. The sympathies of the latter had been at first on the side of the Roman Pope, but she had afterwards changed her mind, because Urban had, so she said, seriously offended her husband, Otho of Brunswick.

---

people, and then of the Pope! "Were the cardinal electors wrong to hold their peace so long?" asks the Saint. "Ought they to have preferred death to such dissimulation?" "I do not take the liberty of passing judgment upon them," he replies.

[1] Du Boulay, t. iv. p. 476.

[2] *Ibid.*, p. 468 ff. Baluze, t. ii. col. 821. Hefele, *History of the Councils*, vol. x. p. 4. Christophe, *Histoire de la Papauté au XIVe siècle*, t. iii. p. 354.

On September 7 the old Cardinal Tebaldeschi dies. He was a witness, and to some extent a victim, of the election of April 8. Up till the end he affirmed that he was convinced of the lawfulness of the choice of Urban.[1]

About September 15 the three Italian cardinals, tired of keeping up useless negotiations, rejoined their colleagues at Fondi. Possibly each of them may have been induced to this disloyalty by the hope of being elected Pope, for it appears that this fallacious promise had been held out to each of the three in turn :[2] and thus ambition prepared the way for treachery. Perhaps, too, they were persuaded by the news that Urban was on the point of creating twenty-nine new cardinals to fill the vacancies made in the Sacred College by the departure of the thirteen Frenchmen.[3]

The intervention of the King of France came to accelerate a solution which had thenceforward been anticipated. Worked upon by malicious confidential disclosures, Charles had more and more suspicions as to the legitimacy of Urban. The reports sent him by the dissentients only confirmed him in his unfavourable attitude towards the elect of Rome. On September 18 a letter from the King of France reached Fondi. The exact text is not extant, but its general tenor is known. It encouraged the dissentients to persevere in their plans, and to elect a Pope who would be acceptable to France, and that they might reckon on help in men and money.[4]

[1] Raynald, a. 1378, No. 41.

[2] Niem, *De scismate*, lib. i. 9. Baluze, t. i. col. 1050 and 1139.

[3] Baluze, col. 1239. Urban carried out his plan on September 18. *Cf.* Denifle, *Chartul.*, t. iii. p. 555 ff.

[4] Valois, t. i. p. 99 ff. About the same date, the King wrote to Jane

Doubtless this letter removed the cardinals' last scruples. On September 20 the thirteen prelates met in Gaetani's palace at Fondi, went into conclave, and unanimously, excepting one vote, elected Robert of Geneva. The three Italian cardinals, feeling that they had been trifled with, did not vote, but they regarded the election at Fondi as canonical. The new Pontiff immediately took the name of Clement VII. and was crowned on All Saints' Day.

§ 2. *Clement is Recognised by Several Nations.*

Robert was related to the principal families of Europe, and on his mother's side he was little cousin of the King of France. His brother was Count of Geneva and his mother the Countess of Boulogne. Appointed Bishop of Thérouanne while still young, he had occupied the see for seven years, then that of Cambrai for three years, and without giving his people any cause for serious complaint. At that time his age was thirty-six. He was of imposing stature, with a ringing voice, of an agreeable appearance, and of a light and taking wit. A man of high descent, he liked and protected the nobles, soldiers, and artists. But there was one blot on his life that nothing could efface. The year before, he had directed against the town of Cesena, which had rebelled against the Pope, some troops of foreign mercenaries, and he was said to have covered every sort of excess they had committed with the mantle of his authority. These cruelties had excited the horror of all Italy. They had come to look upon Robert rather as a leader of *condottieri* than as the living representative

---

of Naples to recommend the dissentient cardinals. This letter was discovered by M. Valois at the Cambrai library, MS. 940, No. 92.

of the good Shepherd. St Antoninus then compared him to Herod or to Nero.

It was not his conscience that put obstacles in his way. Thus he felt no scruple, as the sequel will show, in granting the King of France the nomination of the most important benefices in the kingdom,[1] and in disposing of the Papal States so as to suit his policy. For instance he did not hesitate to give over a large part of the sacred patrimony to the clever Duke of Anjou to enable him to create his fantastic and ephemeral kingdom of Adria.[2] It is even for this object that the elect of Fondi sacrificed his desire to take up his residence at Avignon immediately. He remained in Italy till the year following in order to foment and increase its discord,[3] and to try to establish in it his too precarious authority.

Thus, then, is the Schism completed. The cardinals of Fondi have rent the robe of Christ with their own hands. Were their reasons for so acting sufficient? I think not. And who can believe that they were? Were the fears which may have overhung the election of Urban certain to have impaired the freedom of the electors? Then, what can be said of the re-election which held good for so many months? Moreover, their conduct is too often marked with passion, and considerations of personal interest have too large a share in them. If only they could have foreseen how divided Christendom would be, how many consciences would be scandalised and souls tortured with doubt in all parts of the Catholic universe; if only they could

[1] Bull of Jan. 6, 1380, addressed to Charles V.

[2] Durrieu, *Le royaume d'Adria*, *Revue de Questions histor.*, 1880, t. xxviii. p. 45.

[3] Valois, t. i. p. 167. Froissart, t. xvi. p. 67. *Chronic. Karoli VI.*, lib. xi. c. 9.

have taken count of the progress of heresy in England and of its propagation in Bohemia; or had it been permitted them to hear the mockery and insults of the enemies of our faith![1] Or if, again, they could only have been forewarned that this sacrilegious division would last forty years, lowering the supreme pontificate in the eyes of the faithful and princes, adjourning indefinitely all plans of reform, and giving rise to every kind of religious and secular evil! Then doubtless they would have shrunk from the fatal consequences of actions as thoughtless as they were unjust. For the third time, had they thought it necessary they would have elected Urban, or they would have shown more patience in enduring the consequences of their first choice, of which they alone were the authors.

The inspired seer, Catherine of Siena, made bitter reproaches against the three Italian cardinals who had deserted Urban. These recriminations are only too well justified, and fall *a fortiori* on the French prelates who had instigated the rebellion. "You have turned to flight, like cowardly knights," she wrote them. "It is you who have taught me not to believe you. . . . Whoever is not for the truth is against the truth. Whoever at Fondi was not for Christ on earth, for Pope Urban,

[1] Here are the lines of an anonymous rhymester, whose quatrains were discovered at Rouen by M. Valois, t. i. p. 383.

Les sacrements faudront si le scisme demeure,	The sacraments will fail if the schism stays,
Juifs s'esjoiront, Sarrasins sans demeure	Jews will rejoice, Sarrasins without delay
Assaudront crestiens. Cis est nés de malheure	Will attack Christians. Born of woe
Qui contre le Conseil pour le scisme labeure.	Is he who is against the Council and for the Schism.

Cf. Opp. Gerson., ii. col. 115. Martène, *Thesaurus*, ii. col. 1159. H. de Langenstein, *Invectiva*, v. 243. *Epistola Pacis*, ii. 30. *Chronic. Karoli VI.*, lib. ii. c. 2. Froissart, t. xi. p. 251.

was against him. I tell you, you have done ill, you and the anti-pope, and I repeat that it is a member of the devil who has been elected. Had Clement been a member of Christ, he would rather have died than have consented to so great an evil, because like us he knows the truth, and cannot plead ignorance as an excuse."[1]

From the very day of the election, the cardinals took care to inform the Catholic world that they had elected Clement VII.

While the faithful, astounded and scandalised, were asking what could be the motive of such a sudden change of mind, Urban took measures to defend his outraged rights. On November 29, 1378, after due inquiry and with full knowledge, the Roman Pope hurled a bull of excommunication against Clement, and smote along with him all the principal fomenters of the Schism, "these workers of iniquity and perdition."[2] No one was to entertain them, and whoever took part in an expedition against them would gain the same spiritual benefits as a crusader in the Holy Land.

It was an immediate call to arms. Furthermore, the subjects of all princes who took the new Pope under their protection were released from their oath of loyalty, whether their masters were kings or bishops. It was an appeal to spiritual weapons.

Clement on his part did not remain inactive. He sent distinguished legates to the Catholic sovereigns and princes, and particularly to Charles V.

The King of France, as we have seen, was already gained to the cardinals' side. His political interests

[1] *Letter* 31ª, see Raynald, a. 1378, Nos. 55 and 59. *Ibid.*, a. 1379, Nos. 21 and 13. Du Boulay, t. iv. p. 518. Chavin de Malan, *Histoire de Ste Catherine de Sienne*, t. ii. p. 462.

[2] Raynald, a. 1378, No. 103.

inclined him towards Avignon and drew him away from Rome: he therefore had no difficulty in yielding to the arguments of Clement VII. and his party. But how were the University, the bishops, and the whole country to be dragged into the schismatical camp? The University had at the very outset sung the *Te Deum* on Urban's election. It had sent ambassadors to Rome to present him with the roll (*rotulus*), *i.e.* the list of those whom it nominated to benefices. Up till the month of July the Roman Pope was almost universally acknowledged in France. But, from this date and onwards, the cardinals had sent emissaries to the King, the Universities, and members of Parliament. On the way through Avignon these messengers had found five cardinals out of six gained over to the side of the revolt. These united their letters to those of their colleagues in Italy. All invited Charles to grant his protection to the Sacred College. "These good friends the cardinals belonged to the King and to his household," naïvely observed the *Great Chronicles of France*.[1]

The King then summoned a great meeting of the clergy, at which Clement's delegates spoke against the election of Urban. This little national council gave no formal decision, but advised Charles to take up an attitude of prudent watchfulness. "The matter is very high, perilous, and doubtful," said the members of this gathering.[2] The King paid respect to this counsel, and adjourned any further public declaration.

A few weeks later, a fresh exchange of correspondence between Paris and Anagni took place. Charles, more and more worked upon, let himself be persuaded by

[1] T. vi. p. 441 (Ed. P. Paris). *Cf.* Benoist, *La politique du roi Charles V.*, p. 218. Denifle, *Chartul.*, t. iii. p. 558.

[2] Benoist, p. 219. Du Boulay, t. iv. pp. 524 and 576.

degrees and declared in favour of the cardinals, even before the election of Robert of Geneva. The latter felt that he had to thank him for this later on. The emphatic expressions used by the elect of Fondi showed a warmth of gratitude which was not slow to manifest itself in subsequent actions.

A second meeting was held at Bois-de-Vincennes after Clement VII.'s election had been made known in France (November 16). The King was advised to declare openly in favour of his relation, who would doubtless establish himself at Avignon. This decision was clearly in accord with the inmost ideas of Charles, for he hastened to have the news of the second election published in all the churches with the usual ceremony.

Despite the declaration of the royal will, the University had some difficulty in changing its mind. The rector asked for delay before coming to a decision; England and Picardy said they would remain neutral.

Meanwhile the skilful John de Cros was sent by Clement to Paris to represent him and defend his interests. He had received authority from the latter to proceed against any Urbanists he might meet with in France and to strengthen the confidence of the Clementines.[1]

On April 6, 1379, the cardinal was received at Notre-Dame. A few days later he spoke warmly and with boldness before the King and the princes and prelates, and gave such an account of the election of Urban as might allay the scruples of his auditors. On May 7 he repeated his story at the castle of Bois-de-Vincennes before a new and selected audience. Doubtless he forgot to say that he had been the first to give his vote for Bartholomew, and that he had formerly expressed

[1] Valois, t. i. p. 130. Denifle, t. iii. No. 1621.

his intention of electing him definitely on rightful grounds. However this may be, two other cardinals who had recently reached Paris, Guy de Malesset and William d'Aigrefeuille, warmly supported what he had said, and the whole assembly expressed itself as convinced. It exhorted the sovereign to recognise the elect of Fondi, to offer him obedience and support.

Naturally the people followed their pastors. Even the University agreed to change its opinions and to submit, but the scholars of England and Picardy stood out. A rather celebrated doctor of theology, Simon Frèron, was bidden to inform Charles of the *Alma Mater's* decision to submit. He did it with such a lack of professional dignity as to have incurred the charge of platitude [1] from a historian; but those who were interested pretended to regard this adhesion as being as spontaneous as it was unanimous. The French people hastened to send Clement a list of its petitions, and wished to reap the fruits of its submission without delay. Peter d'Ailly, at that time a simple bachelor of theology, was commissioned to take it to the new Pope (before May 24).

Such, then, seems to have been the rôle of Charles V. in these delicate circumstances. As the advice he received perhaps corresponded with his secret wishes, and certainly with his political interests, he was drawn into the way of schism without his conscience being disturbed. The really culpable in such a conjuncture were rather the cardinals of Fondi, and next the Pope whom they had created. At the bar of history they have taken upon themselves a terrible responsibility, the gravest matter being perhaps their deception of the King, and their having induced him to become

[1] VALOIS, t. i. p. 139. *Cf.* DENIFLE, t. iii. No. 1624 ff.

the unwitting fomenter of the Schism, thus giving permanence to most lamentable division.

No doubt this important matter was not discussed in France under all judicial forms; no doubt pressure was put upon the University, then so influential; but we must not accuse Charles V. of bad faith and unfairness. Even on his death-bed he declared that he was determined to hold fast to the authority of Clement, because of what the cardinals had revealed. It is, then, upon the latter alone that the stern condemnation of impartial history must fall.

Let this much be granted: had not France upheld Clement, the rebellious party would have had little appearance of solidity. Thanks to Charles V., the kingdom of Naples decides for the Pope who had been elected on its borders. Scotland takes sides with France through their common hatred to England, which had declared for Urban. Castile, neutral at first, declares for Clement for like reasons.[1] Portugal is also won over through the renown of the house of France for orthodoxy. The Duke of Savoy takes sides with Clement because of his being a relation. Lastly, Aragon and Navarre later on adhered to the new Pope, owing to secret intrigues, and the consummate skill and indefatigable zeal of his legate Peter de Luna.[2] The incentives to these coalitions are not to be sought in the evidence of fact and proof. Furthermore, they were never made with unanimity, but were rather brought about by alliances and political passion.

[1] *Cf.* Valois, t. i. p. 210 *et passim.* Delalonde, *Étude historique et critique sur le Grand Schisme*, p. 93.

[2] Valois, p. 212 ff.

§ 3. *The Boundaries of the Two Obediences.*

It is now plain that the revolt had caught fire like a train of gunpowder throughout almost the whole of Western Europe. What, then, remained to Urban? The greater part of Christendom was faithful to him. First, the Empire, whose ruler, Charles IV., had declared in his favour from the beginning, and was always resolutely opposed to the Schism. He had his son Wenceslas recognised by the Empire as King of the Romans, and knew how to defend the pontifical election in the diet with success, as soon as it was disputed. In addition to the truth of fact which made the Roman Pontiff legitimate, diplomatic reasons likewise determined his conduct. Since the Popes had been at Avignon, the Emperor had lost almost all his influence in the Church. Since Urban wished to reign in Rome, it was good policy to defend him against the French cardinals.

Unfortunately for the Roman Pontiff, the Emperor died the very day of the election at Fondi, September 20, 1378. His son Wenceslas could not help following in his steps, but he did not equal his father, either in intellectual culture, or political skill, nor, above all, in moral dignity. Nevertheless, when the envoys of the King of France wished to drag him into the Schism, he gave them a pretty rough reception at Frankfort. At the meal which was offered them, they were served at a table by themselves, as if they were schismatics. This was in February 1379. In fine, despite a few partial defections,[1] the Empire remained true to the Roman Pope.

[1] Thus Duke Leopold III. of Austria sold his allegiance to Clement for 120,000 golden florins. Metz, Toul, and Verdun were from the outset

Perhaps this check to French policy must be attributed to the presence of ambassadors from England.[1] Here, again, the interest of the king across the Channel was in accord with the clearly Urbanist opinions of his clergy and faithful people. During the preceding half century the English had had to complain more than once of the secret ill-will of the Popes of Avignon. The Schism of Charles V., the hereditary enemy, indirectly confirmed the orthodoxy of Richard II. and his people. For its part, the Parliament showed a refractory intolerance of the supporters of Clement.

The Cardinal of Poitiers, Guy de Malesset, could never make his way into England in order to expound and defend the case of the elect of Fondi there. In the continental provinces which were under the authority or influence of England, the struggle between the two jurisdictions begins and continues long with varying fortunes. In the South-West, Urban carries the day; in Brittany, Clement holds sway, not undisputed. But on the other side, faithful Ireland declares for the most part in favour of Rome.[2]

In Flanders, the situation was more complicated. The country had long been attached to France by geographical position and political bonds, and by its prince, Louis de Maele, father-in-law of the Duke of Burgundy, the brother of Charles V. But the Flemish people, naturally and traditionally independent, had every interest, from a commercial point of view, in

enfeoffed to the Pope of Avignon. Albert of Bavaria, Wenceslas of Luxembourg, Adolphus of Cleves, Robert of Bar, and John of Lorraine also declared for Clement.

[1] Valois, i. p. 241 ff., develops the ideas contained in this and the following sentences.

[2] *Cf. Revue des quest. historiques*, July 1903, p. 302, and January 1905, p. 274.

looking towards England. When, in consequence of the war, English wool no longer reached Damme, Sluys, Ghent, Bruges, and Ypres, the powerful and stirring citizens of Flanders complained to the Count, and sometimes armed the warlike militia of the towns and country against him. This same year, 1378, the people of Ghent, supported by the English, had just broken out in a revolt that lasted seven years.

Moreover, the Flemish had excellent reasons for believing in the legitimacy of Urban and for remaining obstinately attached to him. For who had informed Louis de Maele of the Roman election and its canonicity ?[1] It was the very person who, six months later on, was to become the opponent of the Pontiff whom he had declared to be legitimate, it was Robert of Geneva. The Pope of Fondi had an awkward task in trying to struggle against a belief which was founded on his own word.

A few months later, Cardinal Pileo di Prata wrote from Venice to Louis de Maele and confirmed the first election of the Sacred College.[2] The letters in an opposite sense from Pampeluna could not make him change his mind. Lastly, the clergy of Flanders had got the Count to gather about him every possible source of enlightenment and to consult the learned University of Bologna. Their reply was favourable to Urban.

It is, then, with full knowledge that Louis de Maele separated from France and resisted all the solicitations of the party of Clement. He made it boldly known in a public document : " We are ready to refer the matter to a general council," he said. " In no wise would

[1] Meyer, *Annales rerum Flandricarum*, p. 169. Raynald, a. 1378, Nos. 17 and 62.

[2] Du Boulay, t. iv. p. 14. D'Achery, *Spicilegium*, t. iii. p. 743.

we become separated from the unity of the Church, but we will never desert the authority of Urban VI., who was elected in the first place, and whom we have held until now to be the true Pope." [1]

If the prince, the clergy, and the people declared for the Roman Pontiff, on the other hand the four bishops of this country turned towards Clement. John T. Serclaes of Cambrai, and Peter d'Orgemont of Thérouanne, were each of them successors of Robert of Geneva. The Bishop of Arras, Peter Mazuyer, like the two former, depended on the metropolitan of Reims in things spiritual: in temporal matters he was a subject of Marguerite, dowager Countess of Flanders, and devoted to Clement. As for Tournai, the town belonged to France since the time of Philip-Augustus: it was French in language and feeling, and its chapter had just elected Peter d'Auxy of Burgundy as bishop.[2]

So, then, this was the situation in Flanders; on one side the faithful, the prince, and the common clergy; and, on the other, the dignitaries of the Church. The counsels, the speeches, and the orders of the King of France, of his envoys, from the outset had no success there whatever.[3] Their accounts were regarded as suspect beforehand.

The Flemish, who belonged to the diocese of Cambrai, warned their bishop that they were minded to remain provisionally under the jurisdiction of Urban. Nor did those who were in the diocese of Tournai accept the Pope of Avignon with any greater readiness. The latter had recourse to John van West, Dean of Tournai,

[1] *Cf.* Baluze, t. i. col. 492 and 551.

[2] Valois, t. i. pp. 253 and 255.

[3] Mgr. Hautcœur, *Histoire de Saint-Pierre de Lille*, t. ii. p. 88. *Cf. Gallia Christiana*, t. iii. p. 229.

to whom Urban sent his bulls about 1380,[1] and who established himself at Ghent. Apart from the castellanies of Dunkirk, Bourbourg, and Cassel, which were dependencies of the Duchess of Bar, all Flanders obeyed the Roman Pope. After hesitating somewhat, Hainault remained neutral; and the Duke of Brabant behaved to Clement with cool politeness.

Italy is the centre of the great struggle. It too was at first divided between the two obediences, but became the principal bulwark of the Roman Pontiff. From the beginning of the revolt, the adherence of Queen Jane and her husband Otho of Brunswick procured for Clement the submission of the kingdom of Naples in the South, and of the Marquisate of Monteferrato in the North. Furthermore, the Gascon and Breton mercenaries, entirely at the beck of the elect of Fondi, held a part of the country through terrorism. But public opinion was hostile to the French, and to the Pope whom they called the "executioner of Cesena." Florence and Milan rallied to the Pope of Rome. In several encounters the foreigners were beaten, and the castle of St Angelo was retaken by the Romans (April 27, 1379). At this news the Pontiff of Fondi fled and took refuge in Naples. But three days later the town rose with shouts of "Long live Pope Urban! Death to Clement!" In fear of these disturbances and

[1] He died in 1384, and was succeeded by Willem de Coudenberghe, who died in England; then by William della Vigna, a Benedictine, Bishop of Ancona. At Malines, they recognised John Ysewyns, whom Rome appointed as spiritual and temporal administrator of the diocese of Cambrai in 1400. *Cf.* Neefs, "Notes sur la situation de la Belgique pendant le Grand Schisme," *Revue catholique de Louvain*, September 15, 1876. Baeten, *Verzameling van Naamrolen Betrekkelijk de Kerkeljke Geschiednis van het Aartsbisdom van Mechelen*, t. i. p. 5. Miraeus, *Opp. dipl. et hist.*, ii. p. 1030. *Cf. Revue des sciences ecclésiast.*, February 1902.

threats, and moreover with little confidence in such help as the Duke of Anjou might bring, Clement left rebellious Italy and embarked for Marseilles. After some tiresome vicissitudes he came to Provence, and only found complete safety under the sheltering walls of the pontifical palace. He reached Avignon on June 20, 1379.[1] There he found a peaceful capital, a magnificent palace, a court of cardinals, and a thousand reminiscences of power and greatness. He once more repaired the chain of periods gone by and the temporarily interrupted succession of the Popes of Avignon.

So, then, the seats of the two Popes are, from this time forward, definitely settled, and the great outlines of their respective obediences clearly marked out. The whole of the West on the borders of the Atlantic belongs to Clement, except England and most of her possessions in France. On the other hand, Germany in greater part, Flanders and Italy, with the exception of the kingdom of Naples, are under Urban. Starting from Edinburgh and drawing a boundary line between England and Scotland to the Irish Sea, then going on from Nieuwport to Liège, from Liège to Bâle, from Bâle to Constance, from Constance to the West of Genoa, and lastly passing between the kingdom of Naples, officially subject to Clement, and the Papal States, we shall obtain a fairly accurate geographical demarcation of the jurisdictions of Rome and Avignon.[2] As to

[1] Valois, t. i. pp. 158-178.

[2] Eubel and Haupt, *Das Itinerar der Päpste zur Zeit des grossen Schismas*, *Historische Jahrbücher*, xvi. p. 545. Noël Valois, pp. 292 and 305. Eubel, *Die provisiones praelatorum*, *Römische Quartalschrift*, Rome, 1894. The information furnished by Haupt is more extensive as to time, that given by M. Valois is more exact as to place. Moreover, it will always be difficult to establish fully the *series episcoporum* according to the archives either of Rome or of Avignon.

Greece, it will never either fall under Rome or Avignon, and apparently receives with some indifference nominations made by either of the Popes.

Only it is well to note that, even in the countries that are faithful to Clement, there is always a more or less numerous Urbanist party to be found; and it is the same with regard to Clement in the provinces which acknowledge Urban. Hence the frontier-boundaries and territorial divisions will always be rather uncertain. What is more, kingdoms, counties, and bishoprics will sometimes change jurisdictions because they have changed sovereigns or chiefs. Sometimes the same ecclesiastics, like the Bishops of Bâle and Constance, like William de la Voulte, Bishop of Valence and Die,[1] will offer their allegiance first to Urban, and then to Clement. At Dax, the opposite happens; the bishop, John Beaufaix, will go over to Clement. At Bayonne the chapter will be divided between the two jurisdictions; part of the diocese will support Urban, and the rest Clement. Gascony becomes a regular chess-board. At Coire, the head of the diocese will hold to Rome, while the chapter inclines to Avignon. Sometimes, as at Liège, the Clementine bishop will be overthrown by his people, and his successor receives the bulls of Urban. Some dioceses will have two pastors at once, and some monasteries two abbots; some religious orders, like the Carmelites, two generals; and a few orders of chivalry two grand masters.[2]

[1] ALBANÈS, *Gallia Christiana novissima* (Marseilles, 1899), p. 363. Four years later, William, who had been Bishop of Marseilles, and whom we saw guard of the conclave on April 8, was transferred to Albi, where he died in 1392.

[2] *Cf.* PASTOR, t. i. p. 154. DELAVILLE DE ROULX, *Un anti-grand-maître de l'Ordre de Saint-Jean de Jérusalem*, Bibl. de l'École des Chartes, t. xl. p. 523.

The Schism, which devastates the Church at large, will have its reverberations in little down to the smallest ecclesiastical circles; and anarchy in the government will engender a multitude of scandals and disorders, with a general diminution of hierarchical authority, as of the supernatural life.

In fine, Urban's obedience extends over larger numbers, and the motives that influenced its recognition were perhaps more disinterested and certainly more sound. The obedience of Clement looks the more dazzling, especially on account of the support given to the Pope of Avignon by the eldest daughter of kings and popes, the University of Paris, the mother and mistress of all the schools of Christendom. It is the University that takes care to give this assurance in a letter addressed to the King, not without a touch of self-satisfaction and vain-glory. "The obedience of Rome is the wider," they say, "*altera amplior*; but ours is the more intelligent and hale, *altera sanior*."[1] This affirmation is too interested to be free from suspicion: only the former part of it can be accepted.

[1] Froissart, t. xvi. p. 146. *Chronic. Karoli VI.*, lib. xvi. c. 3. t. ii. p. 160.

CHAPTER IV

THE DIVISION OF SOULS

§ 1. *Saints in both Jurisdictions.*

In spite of this ever to be regretted Schism, in spite of all the disorders which resulted from it, saints did not cease to appear, to shine in the Church, and to produce fruits of salvation, and even to exhibit those supernatural effects of divine action which are called miracles. They are to be found in either obedience. The sap of sanctity rises at all times and in all places; and the material and accidental irregularity of the mysterious channels used by the Holy Spirit does not prevent grace from producing in souls every kind of supernatural effect. God has never confined justification or sanctification to this or that section of the Church because of passing disorders for which the faithful are not in any way responsible. It would, then, be illogical to infer the lawfulness of one obedience and the unlawfulness of another, because such and such a saint supported one pope or another. On each side we find some of the beatified and even some wonder-workers. The saints who were present in Rome or lived near the theatre of events remained faithful to Urban; those who were born in countries where the rulers or bishops recognised the Pope of Avignon, adhered to Clement. All of them followed their natural guides.

There was, then, at Siena, one of the most remarkable saints the Church has ever honoured at her altars. Informed from the earliest age with the most remarkable graces, she was not satisfied with edifying her sisters in the cloister and ministering to the plague-stricken in her birthplace; she felt that she was called by God to give greater services to the see of St Peter.

We have remarked already that only a divine mission can explain the part she played in the affairs of the Church, the encouragements and subsequently the objurgations that she dared to address to the sovereign Pontiff, the reproaches wherewith she loaded the dissentient cardinals, the "evil pastors of the Church."[1] "What you want to have," she wrote to them, "is a French Pope."

Several times she takes upon herself to send her confessor, Raymond of Capua, on an embassy to Charles V., whom she wished to turn away from the Schism. In the very year in which she breathed out her great spirit to God (1380), Urban wished to send her as a delegate to Jane of Naples to rally the princess to the Roman obedience.[2] She was to have been accompanied by Saint Catherine of Sweden, her sister in saintliness and in faithfulness to the legitimate Pope. Nothing less than their combined influence could have converted this crafty queen, who was perverse and changeable. Unhappily for the Church and for the latter, the embassy was never sent; and the letters written by the famous Dominican saint to Jane remained unanswered and without result.

Catherine of Sweden, another light in the Church at the end of the fourteenth century, was at Rome at the

[1] Chavin de Malan, *Histoire de Sainte Catherine de Sienne*, t. ii. ch. xiii. *Cf.* Pastor, t. i. p. 143.

[2] Raynald, a. 1379, No. 21 ff. Bolland, *Acta Sanctorum Aprilis*, iii. p. 946.

time of Urban's election. She was obtaining from the pontifical court the beatification of her mother, Saint Bridgett. Herself an ocular witness of these great events, she always asserted with the utmost energy the legitimacy of Urban, and that from the beginning of the conclave the cardinals had intended to elect him.[1] Nevertheless she deplored the blundering severity of his behaviour. "The election was free," she stated solemnly before the judges; "the disturbance (*aliqualis rumor*) only broke out afterward. The cardinals had no doubt about it until the new Pope refused them favours and demanded reforms."[2] From another quarter, Ursula of Parma found her way to Avignon, and begged Clement VII. to resign an usurped pontificate.

Another of Urban's constant defenders was Peter of Aragon, of royal origin, who had entered the order of Friars Minor in his youth. He was reputed to be favoured with heavenly visions, enjoyed the gift of prophecy, and was venerated as a saint. Peter gave the bishops of Castile the best of advice. He took advantage of his royal kinship to reproach the King of Aragon bitterly for his desertion of the Roman Pontiff, and the King of France for his attachment to a Pope whom he characterised as an intruder. Unhappily, all his remarks remained without effect.[3]

In Urban's party, a conspicuous place was held by Gerard de Groote, whom Thomas à Kempis declared to be one of the lights of the Church. A fervidly eloquent preacher, he was the Vincent Ferrier of Holland

[1] RAYNALD, a. 1379, No. 20. *Cf.* BOLLAND, *Acta Sanctorum Martii*, iii. p. 515.

[2] "*Non erat blandus in eorum petitionibus et corrigere eos optabat.*" RAYNALD, *Ibid.*

[3] *Ibid.*, No. 5 ff.

and the North of Germany; as a reformer of the clergy, he is a forerunner of the mission of St Vincent de Paul;[1] as an educator of the young, he gives up his whole life to them like John Calazanzio; as the founder of an order, he is the father of the *Brothers of the Common Life*, a congregation which was very popular in our part of the world; he was the St John Baptist de la Salle of the fourteenth century.

This illustrious servant of God is attached to the most ardent of Urban's supporters, and he writes them an important, but hitherto unpublished letter,[2] on the question of the Schism. His influence and that of his disciples uphold and defend the Roman party in our northern provinces.

In the opposite camp we find persons as saintly as they were eminent who continue attached to the Pontiff of Avignon. There is no doubt that they were in good faith, but it is impossible to regard this as a presumption against the lawfulness of the Popes of Rome.

Certainly the most famous partisan of the Pontiffs of Avignon was St Vincent Ferrier. In every country to which his apostolic zeal carried him he left miracles on his track. Long he was attached to Benedict XIII., who was a Spaniard like himself and among his penitents.

[1] *Cf.* Bonet-Maury, *Gérard de Groote, un précurseur de la Réforme.* The writer, who is a Protestant, regards his hero as one of the Reformers before the Reformation. Petrarch, d'Ailly, Gerson, Clémangis, Nicolas of Cusa, and later on Savonarola were often forced into the ranks of these unconscious forefathers.

[2] Bibl. Vat. MS. Lat. No. 4927, f. 137. This letter is addressed to William de Salvarville, a doctor of theology, and canon of Paris and Rouen. *Cf.* Karl Grube, *Gerard Groot* (Köln, 1883). Pastor, t. i. p. 161. Valois, t. i. p. 367. A register bought at Lord Ashburnham's sale in 1899 by M. Léopold Delisle, f. 43, B. N. nouv. acq. Lat. No. 1793. *Cf. Journal des Savants*, 1899, p. 325.

In 1380, two years after the election of Fondi, he composed the remarkable treatise, which we have several times quoted, on the Schism. In it he asks three chief questions: (1) What belief in the true Pope is necessary to salvation in a time of schism? (2) Of the two claimants, who should be considered the true Pope? (3) How must this fact be preached to the Christian people? [1]

We shall make no detailed examination of the manifold divisions of this most important work. Suffice it to say that this ill-informed writer upholds out and out the second election of the Sacred College, then exalts the sovereign authority of the cardinals in such a case, and finally asserts that it is the duty of every Christian, and particularly of every prince, to defend Clement, even with the sword. This language, which appears to us violent, betrays Spanish warmth, and the extraordinary influence of Peter de Luna over his future persevering defender. Twice his extreme loyalty to the Avignon Pontiff brought the saint to the verge of the grave.

At last Vincent's eyes were opened, and he declared that the obstinacy of the Cardinal de Luna, become Benedict XIII., was an obstacle to the peace of the Church. On that occasion [2] the great and humble wonder-worker ascended the pulpit, blamed the Pontiff, and, with almost all Spain, renounced the obedience of Avignon. This was on January 12, 1416.

This news was greeted at the Council of Constance with unanimous acclamations and with a solemn *Te Deum*.

[1] MS. Bibl. Nat. Lat. No. 1470, f. 235.

[2] R. P. Fages, *Histoire de Saint Vincent Ferrier* (1893), t. i. App. O, p. xxx.; and t. ii. pp. 113 and 117.

Less well known, but not less winning, was the young Cardinal Peter of Luxembourg, the St Aloysius of the fourteenth century. As a University student, as hostage to the English at Calais, as a canon of Paris, as archdeacon of Chartres, and afterwards of Cambrai, wherever he went he left traces of an extraordinary sanctity, to which his extreme self-mortification bore witness, and which was enhanced by his simplicity and sweetness. Holding fast to the obedience of Avignon, he was nominated to be Bishop of Metz at the age of fifteen by Clement VII., and shortly afterwards he was invested with the insignia of the cardinalate and called to take his place in the pontifical court.

He stayed there with regret, for at Avignon he saw many things that offended him.[1] At the age of eighteen, already ripe for paradise, he piously departed without having ever expressed a doubt as to the legitimacy of the Pope in whom he had placed his confidence. Miracles took place at his soon glorious grave, and the common people regarded these prodigies as a striking proof in favour of Avignon.

Another wonder-worker was the devoted Colette, who was so full of the spirit of the seraphic Francis, and who, like Saint Theresa, became the reformer of a great religious order. She was born at Corbie, in the jurisdiction of Avignon, and had taken the veil at Genoa in 1406 from the hands of Benedict XIII. himself. At Poligny she had the honour of receiving a visit from Vincent Ferrier. Like the latter saint, she did not hesitate to abandon the Avignon Pontiff when she had palpable proofs of an obstinacy fatal

[1] Bolland, *Acta Sanctorum Julii*, t. i. pp. 428 and 483. Froissart, t. xiii. pp. 40 and 333. Raynald, a. 1387, c. ii. Du Boulay, t. iv. p. 561.

to the Church. Like Vincent, she sent the Council of Constance a letter of renunciation, which was read in public and made the august assembly rejoice.[1]

When these persons of eminent sanctity were seen to remain so long attached to the same obedience, their contemporaries were tempted to entertain a presumption in favour of the Pontiff recognised by such highly spiritual souls. But first it is to be noted that, among the upholders of Avignon, several retracted their opinion before dying. Further, this is how the most celebrated of them, St Vincent Ferrier, speaks of the matter. The saint had heard that supernatural effects had been obtained by the faithful attached to the authority of Bartholomew. "Some defenders of Urban," they said, "have enjoyed great spiritual favours. Therefore Urban is the true Pope. The Holy Spirit shows it by these signal graces."[2]

St Vincent endeavours to meet the objection, and these are the reasons he gives: "You must not," he says, "judge of Urban's legitimacy by prophecies, miracles, and visions, and this for three reasons. In the first place, the Christian people have been governed from the beginning by certain unchangeable laws against which extraordinary occurrences can avail nothing. 'If an angel of God,' said St Paul, 'teaches you any other doctrine than I have taught, let him be anathema.' As the Roman Church, that is to say, the College of Cardinals, has recognised Clement as the true Pope, no miracle or vision can make us believe

[1] Douillet, *Sainte Collette, sa vie, ses œuvres, son culte et son influence* (Paris, 1884). Corblet, *Hagiographie du diocèse d'Amiens* (Paris, 1868). Comte de Chamberet, *La parfaite Vie de Sainte Colette* (Paris, 1887).

[2] *De moderno Ecclesiae Scismate*, Bibl. Nat. No. 1470, p. 1, cap. v. The saint does not name Peter of Aragon, but probably he is in question. *Cf.* Valois, t. i. p. 222.

the contrary. And further, these extraordinary deeds are often neither infallible in what they announce nor certain in themselves; and sometimes the devil and not God is their author. Look at Pharaoh's magicians. Read Cassian, who will tell you how persons of importance were often misled by visions. Satan often changes into an angel of light. He will make use of this infernal power specially at the time of Antichrist; but this era of darkness is near at hand. So let us be on our guard."

This reasoning of St Vincent's may be set against those who rely precisely on the miracles of this wonder-worker to attempt to establish the legitimacy of the Pontiff of Avignon, whom he upheld. If these wonders had been wrought expressly to prove the solidity of the grounds upon which Clement's or Benedict's claims were based, we should have to yield to the argument. But this is not at all to the point. These extraordinary facts only show that, during this sad period of forty years, God did not deprive half of His Church of the most remarkable manifestations of His power at the hands of His chosen servants of both sexes.

The witness of the saints of this century is then neither unanimous nor decisive. Is that of the members of the two Sacred Colleges any more so? Here above all are to be found obstinate divisions and methods much to be regretted.

§ 2. *The Election of New Cardinals.*

Each Pope desires a full senate of cardinals, and thus to multiply his dependants. Urban, abandoned by all the Sacred College, makes another fully equipped by the promotion of twenty-nine princes of the Church.

No doubt there was never promotion on such a scale before. In obedience to a truly Catholic inspiration, he had chosen his cardinals from all nations. One alone refused, Peter de Barrière, Bishop of Autun. But soon the arbitrary, fantastic, and tyrannical proceedings of the Roman Pope lost him those who, until then, had shown themselves the most devoted to his person and cause. We have already had to speak of Pileo de Prata, Cardinal of Ravenna. At first he was strongly attached to Urban, and in his name discharged the most important missions in Flanders, Germany, at Liége, Wurzburg, and elsewhere.[1] But when he returned to Italy, and was dismayed to see the inconsistencies of the Pontiff's conduct, his cruelties, and the discredit into which he was falling more and more, he condemned and abandoned him. Several members of the Sacred College followed his example.

On the other side, Clement multiplied the number of his cardinals for the same reasons. From the month of December 1378, the Pontiff created at Fondi had introduced nine newly-elect into the Sacred College. The old ones behaved as the *missi dominici* of the Pope they had elected. Mention has already been made of the efforts of John de Cros, Cardinal of Limoges, of William d'Aigrefeuille, Cardinal of San Stefano, and of Guy de Malesset, Cardinal of Poitiers.

Themselves responsible for the creation of the Schism, they lavished their endeavours on behalf of Clement, and in doing this consisted both their interest and their justification. John de Cros signalled himself by his

[1] VALOIS, t. i. pp. 123, 258, 272. Later on he returned to the allegiance of Boniface, and won the cognomen of the cardinal *with three hats*. *Cf.* ZANETTO, *Il cardinale Pileo de Prata et la sua prima legatione in Germania*, 1378-82, Udine.

severity against the supporters of Urban, and by the numerous condemnations with which he visited them. D'Aigrefeuille, loaded with the bounty both of the Pontiff of Avignon and of the King of France, was entrusted by them with a mission to Germany. He found himself stopped at the frontier of the Empire by the definite orders of Wenceslas.[1] Malesset turned towards the North, and attempted to convert the Flemish, with what success will appear later on. We have already recorded the endeavours and triumph of the energetic Peter de Luna, Cardinal of Aragon, the future Benedict XIII., who strove with tongue and pen. Others less distinguished, less convinced, or less devoted, contented themselves with forming a court about the Pontiff of their choice at Avignon.

§ 3. *Doctors of Law and Divinity.*

In a less exalted station the doctors of law, *milites legum*, at this period had an influence which many excellent people considered excessive.[2] Several of them and of the most celebrated of them were consulted by kings and princes. Most of them decided for Urban, as has been seen. Suffice it to specify John of Legnano, Baldo of Perusia, Coluccio Salutato, Bartholomew of Saliceto. To all these names may be added that of John of Bournazel, a councillor of Charles V., who makes a summary of the contradictory allegations and gives no decision.[3]

[1] Valois, t. i. p. 284 ff.; t. ii. p. 277 ff. The cardinal only got back to Avignon from his mission on January 30, 1385. *Cf.* Baluze, *Vitae pap. Avien.*, i. col. 1011.

[2] Roger Bacon often complains of it. *Cf. Opera inedita*, Ed. Brewer, p. 84. Dante, *Parad.* ix. D'Ailly, *De materia concilii gen.*, pars. iii.

[3] Valois, t. i. p. 127. The treatises of Baldo and Legnano are in

Specially do ecclesiastics take part in this dispute, which, strictly speaking, is their own.

"Schism is a matter which appertains to the clergy," says a verse of those days.

Moreover, almost everywhere may be noted an outbreak of clerical pamphlets on one side or the other.

The earliest was perhaps that of Perfetto Malatesta, Rector of Sassoferrato in the marches of Ancona. In an imaginary dialogue between Rome and France, he puts the latter always in the wrong and lays the responsibility for the Schism upon this "ever deceitful and lying" nation (June 1379).[1] The saintly hermit Alphonsus, former Bishop of Jaen, also wrote a little treatise in Urban's favour.[2] About the same date, Henry of Hesse or of Langenstein published his *Epistola pacis* at Paris.[3] After a brief prologue, he puts on the scene in his eighty-eight chapters one of Urban's supporters and one of his opponents. The most important point is at the end of the book, where the Urbanist proposes the summoning of a General Council, and defends the suggestion against all sorts of objections brought against it by the upholder of Clement. Further the writer also puts forward the idea of gathering

---

Raynald (Ed. Bar-le-duc, xxvi.), p. 580. John Le Fèvre, Abbot of Saint Vaast of Arras, and king's councillor, replied to Legnano in 1379, and tried to refute him sentence by sentence. The MS. is at the Bibl. Nat. Lat. MSS. 1469 and 1472, and at the Bibl. Vat. 4153 and 5608. It is entitled *De planctu bonorum*.

[1] MS. Bibl. Nat. 1479, f. 141. *Cf.* Valois, t. i. p. 224.

[2] Raynald, a. 1379, No. 8.

[3] Valois, *Ibid.*, p. 324. *Cf.* Scheuffgen, *Beiträge zu der Geschichte des grossen Schismas*, 1889, p. 35. Kneer, *Die Entstehung der Konziliarien Theorie zur Geschichte des Schismas und der Kirchenpolitiken* (1893), p. 64. The work of Henry of Hesse is in MS. at Paris Bibl. Nat. 14,644, the St Victor texts at the Mayence Library, 241, at Vienna, 5097, and at the Burgundy Library at Brussels, 2243. *Cf.* Pertz, *Archiv.*, viii. 683.

together an arbitration committee, in which each of the two Popes, as well as the *neutrals*, shall be represented by two or three persons. This is his second method of restoring speedy peace to the Church.

At that time Conrad of Gelnhausen was still eminent at the University of Paris. He was a German like Henry of Hesse. He also advocated the proposal for a council in a short letter (*Epistola concordiae*), which soon became a full treatise, and which he dedicated to Charles V.[1] This book, compiled about the month of May 1380, appears to be the first treatise in which the "theory of a council" is set forth in a scientific and methodical manner. It shows that the assemblage of such a synod is useful, possible, and necessary. It refutes all objections, and particularly the one which alleges the impossibility of a General Council without the Pope's authority. Lastly, it begs the King of France to make every effort to summon such an assembly, which alone can put an end to all evils.

A little later on, in 1381, Henry of Hesse published yet another work entitled *Concilium pacis*, or, more accurately, to follow the metrical epilogue of the book, *Epistola concilii pacis*.[2] In the twenty paragraphs of his letter he shows the necessity and possibility of

[1] Valois, t. i. p. 325. *Cf.* Martène et Durand, *Thesaurus*, t. ii. col. 1200-26. Kneer, *Ibid.*, pp. 48-60. Scheuffgen, *Ibid.*, p. 58. Hubler, *Die Constanzer Reformation* (Leipzig, 1867), p. 364. This work of Conrad's is found in MS. in the secret archives at the Vatican. *Armar.* lix. t. xxi. f. 69, and at the Bibl. Nat. 14,643. *Cf. Journal des Savants*, 1899, p. 325, and the *Historische Vierteljahrschrift* (Kaiser), 1900.

[2] Von der Hardt, *Rerum Concil. Constant.*, t. ii. col. 361. *Opp. Gersonii*, t. ii. col. 809. Hartwig, *Leben und Schriften H. von Langenstein* (Marburg, 1857). L'Ecuy, *Essai sur la vie de J. Gerson*, p. 326. Denifle, *Die Universitäten des Mittelalters*, t. i. 1 (1885), p. 607. Roth, *Zur Bibliographie des Henricus Hembuche de Hassia* (1888), p. 97 ff. In 1899, at Lord Ashburnham's sale, the Bibl. Nat. purchased a new MS. of the *Concilium pacis*, f. 10 on the list. Valois, i. p. 356.

a General Council with energy and copiousness, but he does not limit its scope to the question of union. He insists on the need of reform in the Church, and depicts a sad picture of the religious and social evils of his time.[1] Between the treatise of Conrad of Gelnhausen and this last work there is such a likeness of thought and even of expression that the *Epistola concilii pacis* may be regarded as suggested by the *Epistola concordiae*, which had appeared a year previously. There is, however, this much difference, that Conrad ascribes to the bishops an authority which Henry would rather attribute to the general body of the faithful.[2]

Then appears upon the scene of politics and religion a young doctor who is to play the most important part until the end of these fatal divisions. His contemporaries called him Peter d'Ailly, " the eagle of France and the Hammer for Heretics." A modern critic could say of him with justice : " The development of the Schism, and particularly events at the Council of Constance, are unintelligible apart from the personal action of the Cardinal of Cambrai. The history of these forty years might be summed up under the heading—*Peter d'Ailly and his Period.*" [3]

Born at Compiègne in 1350, d'Ailly was sent to Paris from his early youth to begin his studies at the Navarre College. At this time, Realists and Nominalists were disputing in the Rue du Fouarre and on the Place Maubert with the same fury as the French and English on the battlefield of Poitiers or under the walls of Calais. At first victory seems to belong to the Nominalists, and

[1] Kneer, *Ibid.*, pp. 76-86.

[2] *Ibid.*, 106-26.

[3] Max Lenz, *Revue historique*, t. ix. (1879), p. 464. *Cf.* Paul Tschackert, *Peter von Ailli* (Gotha, 1879). L. Salembier, *Petrus de Alliaco* (Lille, 1886).

under their flag the young disciple enlists, following his masters. From this date onwards, Roger Bacon in science, and William of Occam in theology, will be and will remain his chosen masters. Made a doctor of divinity about the age of thirty-one, he immediately aspires to other contests than the pacific encounters of the schools. The question of the Schism provides him with a means of displaying at once his oratorical talents, his polemical wit, his theological learning, and his zeal for the highest interests of the Church.

From 1381, he throws himself into the fray, beginning with a pamphlet in keeping with the taste of the times, which he calls *A Letter from the Devil Leviathan.*[1] By a trick of writing, which was not without precedent[2] in those days, he puts into the mouth of Leviathan, the prince of this world, an encouraging speech addressed by this devil to all who wish to divide the Church and to make the Schism last. Taking up his part as Accuser, d'Ailly violently begins by attacking St Peter and St Paul, using scriptural phrases which he purposely takes in an opposite sense to the right one. Leviathan greatly rejoices in the divisions that have broken out in the Church and in the inefficacy of the means brought to remedy them. He is specially merry at the expense of the members of the University who

[1] Tschackert has published this text after MS. 11,804 of the Vienna Library (*Peter von Ailli*, App. V.). I have read this work in No. 531 of the Communal Library of Cambrai, and in No. 14,643, Bibl. Nat. f. 331.

[2] In 1351 was written a letter of Lucifer *ad malos principes ecclesiasticos* (*Histor. littér. de la France*, xxiv. p. 34). In 1408 appeared a letter of Satan to John Dominici, Archbishop of Ragusa. O. Hartwig quotes other examples in *Leben und Schriften H. von Langenstein*, ii. p. 9. *Cf.* Wattenbach, *Ueber erfundene Briefe in Handschriften, besonders Teufelbriefe*, in the Reports of the Berlin Academy of Sciences (1892). *Cf.* Pastor, *Histoire des Papes*, i. p. 187; iv. p. 136.

demand a General Council, and who propose thus to thwart all the devices of the devil.

"Here are the rats come out of their holes," he says; "and they dare to challenge us to fight. They are a ridiculous and base set of people, without birth or authority. And yet they laugh at my ministers, the prelates of the Church, and dare to look them in the face. These frogs have left their bogs, and their cries rise from the depths of the mud. A General Council! A General Council! they croak without ceasing. . . . They must be crushed, for this method is the only efficacious one. It would quickly secure the election of a single head and the peace of Christendom."[1]

In another paper, which is quite as curious, and which dates from the same era, Peter d'Ailly attacks false and bad pastors. He uses the same rhetorical device, and in the name of the Lord's prophet Ezekiel he makes the most cutting charges against them. He provides himself with the most terrible invectives of Holy Scripture and with the fiery objurgations of the Fathers to use against them. He ends with this prediction, which was only to be realised thirty-six years later: "I will save my flock, saith the Lord, and I will give it One Shepherd."[2]

It is also against these unworthy prelates that he raises his voice in his sermons of those days. He relies upon Joachim de Flore's prophecies of dubious authenticity and on the writings of St Hildegard to threaten them with signal punishments.[3]

In his panegyric on St Bernard, he addresses the clergy and prelates who are better acquainted with

[1] TSCHACKERT, *App.* v. pp. 17, 18.

[2] *Invectiva Ezechiel contra pseudopastores.* Cambrai Library MS. 531, p. 185. *Cf.* TSCHACKERT, App. iv.

[3] *Tractatus et Sermones ad finem,* Ed. Strasburg (1490).

the Code of Justinian than the law of Christ, who are called too young to minister to souls and even to episcopal charges, and who show themselves unworthy of them. D'Ailly exclaims: "If only another St Bernard could arise in our unhappy times to put an end to the Schism, soon would he restore us to peace and unity. May God send us a man who will stand as a wall against the rage for schism! O madness, whither dost thou fly? O error, till when shalt thou increase?"[1]

One of Peter d'Ailly's dearest friends[2] did not confine himself to these mystical reproaches and had no confidence in pacific methods. It is true that this combative theologian, before retiring to the Celestins of Paris, had long borne the sword against the infidels, and would have willingly drawn it against the schismatics. We are speaking of Philip de Maizières, former chancellor of the kingdom of Cyprus, a special friend of the Blessed Peter of Luxembourg, and, in the fourteenth century, the most ardent advocate of the Crusade. Unhappily *The Dream of a Fruit-garden* is ascribed to him,[3] an almost schismatical treatise, which had a most deplorable influence over men's minds, in this century and particularly in after times. If

[1] *Sermo de Beato Bernardo,* partly printed by Tschackert (*App.* vi.) after a MS. of Emmanuel College, Cambridge.

[2] To Philip de Maizières, d'Ailly dedicated his work entitled *Epistola ad novos Hebraeos.* I published it entire in 1889, in the *Revue des Sciences ecclésiastiques,* under the heading *Une page inédite de l'histoire de la Vulgate.* This letter is in MS. at Cambrai (No. 514), Reims (No. 466), and Brussels (Burgundy Library, 18,978). *Cf.* Tschackert, *App.* iii.

[3] *Cf.* Paulin Paris, *Mémoires de l'Acad. royale des Inscriptions et Belles-Lettres,* second series, vi. p. 336 (1841). See, too, the dissertations of MM. Le Foullon, Molinier, and A. Froment (1887), at the École des Chartes, and also the work of M. N. Jorga in the *Bibl. de l'École des Hautes Études* (1896). I defended the same opinion in the *Revue des Sciences ecclésiastiques* in 1887.

the Bollandists call him "a great servant of God" and the "most devout of Parisians," it is because he composed other works much worthier of praise.[1] Amongst them we may specially note *The Old Pilgrim's Dream.*[2]

In this rather discursive allegory, the old crusader shows himself the implacable enemy of Urban and the Romans. He exhorts Charles VI. to fall upon the Urbanists, as he has already done in Flanders, where he has just crushed Arteveld and the people of Ghent, who were partisans of the Pope of Rome. The King only showed himself too ready to follow this warlike advice, and to invade Italy "by force of arms in order to destroy all obstinate rebels."[3] Six years later on Philip returns to the charge, and supports the same military proposals, attacking afresh "the bad priests who would rule, but not according to God."[4]

The same warlike language creates some surprise when it proceeds from the prelatical pen of Robert Gervais, Bishop of Senez. He too is an adversary of the Roman Pontiff, whom he acknowledges that he does not know, but whom he nevertheless calumniates. He also is a declared enemy of the Italian canonists, whom he had not read at all, but whom he exerts himself to refute. He would have active measures taken, and force the recalcitrant Urbanists *manu militari*

[1] *Acta Sanctorum Julii,* i. p. 456 and 482.

[2] This work was finished about the end of 1389. (MS. at the Bibl. de l'Arsenal, 2682; at the Bibl. Nat. 9200 and 22,542; at the Vienna Library, 2251).

[3] *Cf.* JORGA, *op. cit.*, p. 466.

[4] *Lettre de Charles VI. à Richard II.* This letter is in MS. at the British Museum (Royal B. 4). *Cf.* FROISSART, xv. p. 376; xvi. p. 274. JARRY, *La "voie de fait" et l'alliance franco-milanaise,* Bibl. de l'École de Chartes, 1892, iii. p. 225.

to bow to the supreme power of the Pontiff of Avignon.[1]

It would carry us too far and be too tedious to quote extracts from all the printed or unpublished pamphlets that appeared at the end of the fourteenth century.[2]

The Schism was at this time the constant anxiety and the poignant grief of all the higher minds. Each writer has his panacea and sets forth his solution. Each, too, contributes his style, his type of mind, and his inborn or acquired prejudices.

§ 4. *Local Councils in each Obedience.*

And yet all these writers, however opposed to one another in opinion and in the means they would employ for making their view prevail, are in agreement on two points: the greatness of the evils under which the Church labours, and the increasingly recognised necessity for a single authority capable of inspiring confidence and respect in all.

[1] His work is entitled *Myrrha electa.* It is a perfume for dispersing "the stinking exhalations resulting from the putrefaction of the Schism." Bibl. Nat. MS. Lat., 1467. It was written about 1388. *Cf.* VALOIS, i. p. 375. *La via facti* was almost unanimously censured later on. *Cf.* JARRY, Bibl. de l'École des Chartes, iii. p. 10. DENIFLE, *Chartul,* iii. pp. 594, 598, 614.

[2] *Cf.* JOHN DE JENZENSTEIN, Archbishop of Prague, *Liber de consideratione scriptus ad Urbanum Papam VI.* (unpublished), Bibl. Nat. 1122, f. 434; *Compendio di dottr. eccles.*, of GIOVANNI DELLE CELLE (Bologna, 1861); *Concilium super schismate,* by NICHOLAS OF BITONTO (Bibl. Vat. 4192); *Dialogus de tollendo schismate,* by JOHN OF SPOLETO (MS. Bibl. Vat.); *Complainte de l'Église,* by JOHN PETIT, 1392. PETER DE LUNA, *cf.* GRILLE, vii. p. 515. PETER BOHIER, Bishop of Orvieto, *Tractatus compositus tempore hujus scismatis* (1379), Bibl. Nat. 14,643. JOHN DE MONTSON, *Tractatus informatorius de electione papae* (1389), Bibl. Nat. 1466. HONORÉ BONNET, *Somnium super materia scismatis* (1394), published by VALOIS in the *Annuaire de la Société de France,* t. xxvii. p. 193. GERARD GROOT, *De schismate* (DENIFLE, *Chartul.*, t. iii. p. 589).

Moreover, all the faithful and their pastors felt the need of assembling to find a remedy for the evils of the Church, and at times, in order to secure the triumph of their convictions as to the great question in dispute, "Which was the true Pope?"

As, for the time at any rate, they could not convoke the assembly of the General Council which most of them desired, they set themselves to work to summon local assemblies or great national councils of the clergy, almost everywhere.

In Castile, the Archbishop of Toledo had gathered all the bishops of the kingdom at Illescas in 1378. Any final decision was postponed, although the president had energetically defended Urban's cause.[1]

A second council was held at Burgos. Delegates were sent to Avignon, and then to Italy, to complete the inquiry and to enlighten the consciences of the prelates, who listened to sixty-three contradictory depositions (1380).[2] They gave a report on their mission at a third meeting at Medina del Campo. Finally, after a number of tergiversations and discussions, the result was proclaimed at Salamanca on May 19, 1381. Spain followed the example of France and swore allegiance to Clement. Did not King Henry of Trastamare and his son John owe their throne to the intervention of Charles V. and to the sword of Duguesclin?[3]

In Aragon, a local council was held at Barcelona, August 31, 1379, and perhaps at Calatayud in September. After an investigation made in 1386, this country too acknowledged the authority of Clement.[4] In Navarre, the clergy, the learned, and the lawyers met at Pam-

[1] Valois, i. p. 201. *Cf.* Raynald, a. 1379, No. 5.
[2] Valois, i. p. 209. [3] *Ibid.*, ii. p. 202. [4] *Ibid.*, p. 213.

peluna in 1390, and the result was also favourable to the Pope of Avignon.[1]

In the centre of Europe, these conciliar meetings end in quite a different way, for Urban triumphs everywhere.

At Prague, the University declares for Rome, and the Bohemian students quit the University of Paris in a body; the synods of the clergy, and specially the one held at Prague in 1381, confirm the people in their allegiance to Urban.

In Hungary, particular councils also maintain the cause of the Roman Pontiff. King Louis even decides to break with the French schismatics, and he has the extreme audacity of sending an embassy to Paris to announce his decision to his relation, the young King Charles VI. The Duke of Anjou undertakes to make the answer; by good words and presents he succeeds in calming the fiery Hungarians and in keeping peace between the two kingdoms.[2]

Poland incessantly furnishes fresh proofs of loyalty to the Roman Pope; and Austria rallies to his cause after Duke Leopold has found his death on the battlefield of Sempach (1386).[3]

In Germany, the diets of Nuremberg (1378-81) and Frankfort (1379) end in formal declarations on Urban's side. Like the Hungarians, the Germans send ambassadors to Paris to Charles VI., and all together they beg the King of France to unite with them in defending the Roman Pontiff, the true Pope.

We have already described the situation in Flanders, drawn in contrary directions by the Clementine bishops, and by the ordinary clergy who kept the Count and the

[1] Valois, p. 216. [2] *Ibid.*, ii. p. 274.

[3] *Ibid.*, p. 305; *Chronic. Karoli VI.*, i. pp. 72-80.

faithful in Urban's party. The indefatigable Cardinal Guy de Malesset had undertaken to win over this country to Clement's cause, and had arrived at Tournai in 1379. Louis de Maele would not allow him to enter his domains, and obliged him to go back to Cambrai. With the protection of the Clementine bishop, John T. Serclaes, Malesset persisted in wishing to force his entrance into Flemish territory.

Hear Froissart: "He wanted to go into Flanders to speak to the count and his country, but never went there, for the count had him told that nothing was to be done there for this cause, for he held that Urban was Pope, and would always hold him to be so, and would live and die in this state of mind."[1]

How were the obstinate Flemish to be converted to Clement's cause? The cardinal thought that a council would have some influence over these prejudiced minds, and he summoned them to meet at Cambrai in 1379. There he gave his own version of the disturbed election of Urban, and of the scenes at Fondi. This account cannot have differed widely from the tale he had told the King, clergy, and nobles at the meeting of Bois-de-Vincennes some time previously, nor from that which he related afterwards to the ambassadors of the King of Aragon.[2]

Next year we find him on the lookout at his usual post on the borders of Flanders. With more per-

[1] Froissart, xvi. pp. 147 and 520.

[2] In this important document, the cardinal complains much of his want of memory and repeats ten times: *Non recordor, non stat in memoria mea, nescio.* But he is obliged to acknowledge that he asked Urban for favours, and that he offered the latter presents, before the cardinals had left, at Anagni and Fondi. If the priests at the Synod of Cambrai objected these circumstances against him, they must have caused Guy de Malesset much embarrassment. *Cf.* Gayet, ii. *Pièces justif.*, p. 97 ff., *Bibl. de l'École des Chartes* (1896), p. 140.

severance than success, he is ever on the watch for the moment when he will be able to enter the country. On the first of October 1380 he held a new local council at Cambrai, and made a speech at it. We have the text[1] before us, and give a rapid analysis of its contents.

The first point brands certain abuses which hinder the recognition of the truth. They are due to Bartholomew's preachers and envoys, whose malice must be exposed. Guy then indirectly attacks the Count of Flanders. "Some," he says, "will not hear the upholders of both parties. This has many disadvantages. Truth is hidden, error is introduced, law is despised, God is offended, neighbours are scandalised, suspicion makes its way, division is increased, and civil friendship, which should reign amongst men, disappears. You bring the objection: but Clement's supporters are excommunicate, they are not in the true faith, but are schismatics to be avoided. I reply: That is no reason for refusing to listen to us. Do you act thus with regard to infidels? Do you avoid holding intercourse with them? What have you to fear from free discussion, if you are convinced of the lawfulness of Bartholomew?

"In this procedure there is a threefold error. You refuse to listen to those who alone know the facts, and you hearken to the Cardinal of Ravenna (Pileo de Prata) only, who was away from Rome, and happened to be in Flanders at the time of Urban's election.

"You are loath to admit the evidence of those who are above all suspicion, and you give credence to suspicious testimony, coming from persons on whom Bartholomew has lavished his favours.

[1] Bibl. Nat., MS. Lat. 15,561, f. 102.

"Lastly, you believe men whose witness is suspected and lying and often varying. On the other hand, Clement's cardinals have always repeated the same truth, to wit, that Urban's election was extorted from them by fear. Why, then, am I refused a reception in Flanders? Why insult him whom you will not hear? Why preserve an awkward silence in your relations with him?"

In his second point, the cardinal lays down three conclusions: 1st, Bartholomew's election was made under the influence of fear. The cardinals were put in this dilemma: either to die, or to satisfy the wishes of the rebellious Romans. 2nd, This election by the Sacred College gives Bartholomew no legal right. 3rd, Nothing that followed could legitimise the election.

Lastly, Guy de Malesset answers certain objections made with regard to the conduct of the cardinals after Urban's election, and sets himself, though without much success, to exculpate them. He concludes with a pathetic appeal for peace, for holding to the faith in its integrity, for the edification and extension of the body of the Church.

Such, stripped of its too dry construction, and of its numberless divisions, is the sermon preached by the Clementine cardinal, and hitherto but little known. It is not merely an isolated performance having only to do with Flanders: but it gives an accurate idea of the state of mind of the envoys of the Avignon Pope and of the opinions they set forth in the councils of the period. By way either of objection or answer it sums up the reasons of the two parties which then divided France and the entire Christian world.

It is clear that it is never a question of race-division, which would place on one side the Latin, and on the other the Germanic nations.[1] Nor is it exclusively a matter of French supremacy accepted on the one side and disputed or rejected on the other.[2] On the other hand, it would quite alter the nature of the conflict to put it down to a profane rivalry between the Sacred College and the Papacy.[3] The problem is of a still graver character, more perplexing and more profound: for it is the unity of the Church that is at stake. It is a question that everywhere disturbs the Christian conscience to its most secret intricacies. Neither the saints, nor doctors of law and divinity, nor particular councils could provide a solution acceptable to all, and everywhere the Schism continues its deplorable ravages.

[1] Höfler has maintained this singular view, *Anna von Luxembourg*, p. 119.

[2] *Cf.* Gottlob, *Karls VI. private und politische Beziehungen zu Frankreich*, p. 128. Valois, i. p. 302.

[3] Souchon's opinion. *Cf. Die Papstwahlen von Bonifaz VIII. bis Urban VI. und die Entstehung des Schismas* (Braunschweig), 1898.

CHAPTER V

THE DEATH OF URBAN VI.

§ 1. *The Death of the King of France*

CHARLES V. was forty-three when he found himself attacked by a disease from which he never recovered. It was sixteen years since he had ascended the throne of France, and he had undertaken the part of dressing the bleeding wounds of his country, wounds of honour and in finance, wounds of cruel defeat and foreign invasion, wounds of material ruin and material loss. Thanks to his long and skilful efforts, the kingdom was on the point of recovering its natural frontiers, and had regained almost all its provinces. It had resumed its secular rank in the midst of Christendom.

Froissart has well passed judgment on this "sturdily wise and clever prince, who made a fine show of these qualities as long as he lived. Staying at home in his own grounds, he regained all that his predecessor had lost in war, armed with helmet and sword."[1]

From the political point of view, this pacific king had succeeded almost everywhere in whatever he had taken in hand for the restoration of the country. But in his ecclesiastical relations he had been less fortunate. He felt it, and perhaps this check had much to do with hastening his end.

The scene of Charles V.'s last moments has been

[1] FROISSART, ix. p. 123.

admirably described by Philip de Maizières: it is one of the finest in our history. His last days are passed at the castle of Beauté, near Paris. His friends and councillors are gathered around him. "Thank you for having come at this last moment," says he. "All of you who are present know what the cardinals have done. You have read their reports. I have followed their advice, and believed that I was thus acting with the greatest safety. I believed then, and I still firmly believe, that Clement VII. is the true pastor of the faithful. No temporal or alien consideration influenced my choice. Further, I appeal to the General Council which should settle the question. May God not count it to me for blame, if I shall have done anything contrary to this future decision of the Church!"[1] (September 16, 1380.)

This ecclesiastical last will of Charles V. gives the summing up of his work, the true note of his intervention in the religious dispute. The King lays his conscience as bare to history as to the chiefs of his people. He believes that his judgment was not mistaken. And yet, may not the objurgations of Peter of Aragon and of Catherine of Siena have had some effect upon his mind? And may not, perhaps, the letters and offers of Urban, as well as the avowed tendencies of Clement, have suggested to him some tardy doubts? The monarch appeals to the decision of the supreme tribunal and accepts it in advance.

Thus do all the estimates made by foreign writers as to the rôle of Charles V., amidst these deplorable

[1] *Cf.* Hauréau, *Notices et extraits de qq. MSS. latins de la Bibl. Nat.*, i. p. 340. This account, first published by Hauréau, was the basis of what is to be found in *Christine de Pisan*, which is incomplete.

misunderstandings, fall to the ground. He did not allow himself to be guided purely by political considerations, by anxiety for French influence, and still less by a desire to subjugate the Papacy and to be, not only bishop-without, but Pope-within the Church. Charles had nothing of the fiery astuteness of Philip-le-Bel, nor had he the heroically saintly soul of Louis IX. His action was that of a Christian king, who lets himself be guided by conscientious motives, but who nevertheless rejoices to find that his political interests are in accord with what be believes to be the good of the Church. If the King was not in the good path, at least he was in good faith.

§ 2. *Events in Italy and Flanders.*

His son, who succeeded him as Charles VI., did not bring to the great dispute either the same breadth of view, or the same discretion in practice, or the same continuity.

The Duke of Anjou, regent of France, had special reasons for protecting Clement. His ambition, assisted by great political and military talents, sought a crown. As he could not aspire to that of France, he at one time wished to acquire that of Minorca. Now he claimed a throne in Italy, and reckoned on the Avignon Pope to help him in his hazardous design.

In 1379, Clement had already given him the title of a vassal-king of the Holy See. He had permitted him to carve himself a kingdom out of the Papal States, and because the provinces thus abandoned were along the Adriatic Sea, he gave this territory the name of the *Kingdom of Adria*.[1] Further, the French Pope entered into negotiations with Jane of Naples, who had no children, to adopt the Duke of Anjou as her son.

As a military expedition was bound to result from these proposals, Clement hoped that this would be a means of making the whole of the peninsula acknowledge his authority. This was the "path of action."

As a matter of fact, the campaign was undertaken at the beginning of 1382, but did not have the issue that the Pope of Avignon hoped for. He had, however, put the apostolic revenues at the service of the future King of Naples, and the latter had come down from the Alps at the head of one of the most brilliant French armies that had ever invaded the peninsula.

Like many other expeditions that have had Italy for their stage, this enterprise, so boldly begun, ended badly. Louis of Anjou met with an inglorious death, and his army melted in the sun, and the remainder was scattered, and the Avignon obedience gained no increase. A little afterwards, Clement deluded himself with the hope that the campaign against rebel Ghent, undertaken by Charles VI., would finally subdue the obstinate Flemish and bring them back to him. The King had hoisted the oriflamme because the Flemish were supporters of Urban and therefore schismatics. On his side, Philip van Artevelde returned the same compliment to the French, as being fomenters of the Schism.[2]

It was apparently a religious war. The striking

[1] Durrieu, *Le royaume d'Adria*, *Revue des questions historiques*, July 1, 1880. Jarry, *La "voie de fait" et l'alliance franco-milanaise*, Bibl. de l'École des Chartes (1892), p. 215.

[2] J. Meyer, *Annales rerum Flandricarum*, lib. xiii. p. 189.

victory of Roosebeke confirmed Clement in his confidence, specially when he saw the young King demand from the vanquished the recognition of the Avignon obedience. Further, next year, a descent of the English, who were Urban's supporters, on the territories of Flanders was a failure.[1]

Another event contributed to increase his hopes. Louis de Maele, Count of Flanders, had hardly been restored by the French army before he fell ill in January 1384, and died on the 30th of the month at the Abbey of St Bertin. He had been, it will be remembered, one of the most energetic defenders of Urban. The solemn funeral took place at Lille on March 1. He left an only daughter, Margaret of Flanders, who brought a rich inheritance to her husband, Philip the Hardy, Duke of Burgundy, and uncle of the King of France.

Philip had already taken possession of Lille, and the new count was by family ties attached to the Pope of Avignon. What was Flanders to do? The chapter of St Peter's was the first to submit, and on the very day of the funeral, four delegate canons placed their renunciation of Urban's obedience in the hands of the Bishop of Tournai, Peter d'Auxy, in the presence of the Archbishop of Reims and of the Bishop of Cambrai, John T' Serclaes.[2]

It was a great point to score, but the conquest of Flanders had yet to be won. Whatever may have been said to the contrary,[3] Philip the Hardy never consented to direct a violent persecution against the

[1] Walshingham, *Historia Anglicana*, ii. p. 88. Meyer, p. 194. G. Monteuis, *Le siège de Bourbourg*, 1895 (Lille, Taffin).

[2] Mgr. Hautcœur, *Histoire de l'église collégiale et du chapitre de Saint-Pierre de Lille*, ii. 97.

[3] Meyer, *loc. cit.* Kervyn de Lettenhove, *Hist. de Flandre*, iv.

Urbanists who were so numerous in his new states. He tried gentle means: the first method was the assemblage of a synod, which he presided over at Lille himself, on September 27, 1384, and the following days.[1] Deputies from the University of Paris were present and their names have been preserved. They were Guy Custelli, sent by the nation of Picardy; John Raulet de Roncourt, Canon of Meaux, sent by the French nation; and John d'Aramon, representing the faculty of Law. The last made the meeting a long speech, which has been recently recovered in the Barberini Library at Rome.[2]

We spare our readers the text of this technical argument, bristling with juridical quotations and re-

[1] No special compilation and not a single history had spoken till lately of this synod of Lille. I was put on its track by a passage of P. d'Ailly, which occurs in a MS. of Emmanuel College, Cambridge, and which Tschackert published fragmentarily in 1877. *Peter von Ailli*, App. vii. p. 24.

Peter d'Ailly had been delegated by the University of Paris to maintain an important suit against John Blanchard, Canon of Cambrai, Chaplain to the Pope, and Chancellor of the University. This cause had been taken before Clement VII. at Avignon in 1385, and the future Cardinal of Cambrai had opened his case. In the course of his argument he expressed himself thus: "Universitas Parisiensis declarationem seu adhaesionem suam sanctam et justam per diversas mundi partes publicavit, et, *quod in recenti memoria est, nunc etiam proprios deputatos solemnes ad sedationem scismatis in Flandriam delegavit.*"

I had further found in the *Histoire de l'Université de Paris* (Du Boulay, iv. p. 603), and later in Denifle (*Chartularium*, iii. pp. 332 and 591), the delegates' names, but I believed that the provincial council had not taken place, because no traces of it are to be found in the departmental archives of the North, which are otherwise so full. I confess I was mistaken (*Cf. Petrus de Alliaco*, p. 28).

[2] To M. Noël Valois I owe the knowledge of this MS., which is so valuable alike for the history of the Church and for our local annals. M. l'Abbé E. Bonduel was good enough to copy this interesting document for me, and I have published it in the *Revue des sciences ecclés.* (February 1902), and then in *Two Unknown Councils of Cambrai and Lille. Cf.* Valois, ii. p. 257.

ferences. This sermon, composed in the style of the period, would teach nothing to those who have read the account of the election as we have given it. Suffice it to say that John d'Aramon, with a great array of quotations, sets himself to prove that the cardinals chose Urban under the influence of fear, that the election was null, and that the subsequent acts of the electors could neither make valid nor add confirmation to an election which was invalid from the outset. We heard Guy de Malesset maintain the same proposition at Cambrai without success.[1]

As has been seen, the eloquence and the quotations of John d'Aramon apparently did not produce any immediate effect on the tenacious convictions of the out and out Flemish.

In the years that followed, a few Flemish towns recognised Clement, thanks to the personal influence of Philip and the touching exhortations of Margaret of Flanders; but this recognition was never quite sincere nor general.[2] Consciences were profoundly troubled in this land of living faith and powerful energy. The Urbanists of Bruges refused to hear mass said by Clementine priests. They made their Easter communion at Ghent so as not to communicate *in divinis* with schismatics.[2] Urban's partisans and Clement's had no more relations with each other than formerly the Jews had with the Samaritans, according to a later Flemish historian, James Meyer.[4]

[1] See last chapter, p. 96.

[2] Valois, ii. p. 268.

[3] Chronica Joannis Brandon, monachi Dunensis (1391), a work recently brought out (1870) by Kervyn de Lettenhove, p. 20. Bourgeois du Chastenet, *Nouvelle histoire du concile de Constance*, p. 140.

[4] *Annales rerum Flandricarum*, xiii. p. 210.

§ 2. *The Death of Urban VI. and the Accession of Boniface IX.*

In almost all parts of his jurisdiction the Pope of Rome could see these divisions and note partial defections. Urban, for some years before his death, had no more cruel enemy of his cause than himself. Strange and sad was the history of this Pope, so edifying before he was crowned with the tiara, but afterwards so extravagant to the point of cruelty through inconsistencies and mistakes.

Things came to such a pass that the cardinals contrived a plot, either to put him under ward, or else to give him into the hands of Charles de Duras, who had just issued as the successful competitor of Louis of Anjou for the throne of Naples.

Urban was informed of these designs and prosecuted the authors with cruelty. Thierry de Niem gives details of the punishments he inflicted upon them. They are such that we can scarcely believe his story, circumstantial as it is.[1] Either the chronicler makes use of exaggeration and calumny, or else Urban's reason was exceedingly shaken.

The Pope, besieged by the King of Naples at Nocera, succeeded in escaping, everywhere dragging along with him the pain without the glory of martyrdom, and took off the five cardinals as prisoners. At Genoa he got rid of them, and their manner of death, which has been hitherto almost unknown, has given rise to the most sinister conjectures.[2]

[1] *De scismate libri tres*, lib. i. 45 and 50.

[2] *Ibid.*, 60. *Cf.* Döllinger, *Lehrbuch der Kirchengeschichte*, ii. p. 282. Baluze, *Vitae Paparum Avenion*, i. p. 518. See also the Chronicles of John de Mussis, Minerbetti, and Gobelinus Persona, who relate the same

The other cardinals, terrified by this example, deserted him, and thought it their duty to make his conduct known. While his mercenaries were devastating the patrimony of St Peter and spreading terror there, Urban saw his authority set at nought in Tuscany and in the Romagnas. His party was everywhere falling to pieces, and Rome itself ceased to be faithful to him.

These manifold desertions and the mournful presage they might suggest to Urban finally shattered the old man's health, a martyr without any grandeur. On October 15, 1389, he died in the Vatican palace, which, eleven years before, had been the stage of the tumultuous scenes of his election.

From that time it was natural to hope that his discredited party would end with him, that all the cardinals would unite, and unanimously submit to Clement VII., thus restoring peace to the Church.

Had such not been their intention, might not the princes and nations have brought pressure to bear upon the fourteen cardinals of Urban who had met at Rome, to constrain them to rally to the authority of Clement? Alas! before the kings had time to get news of the almost sudden death of Urban, a successor had already been appointed in the person of the Cardinal of Naples, Peter Thomacelli (November 2, 1389). He took the name of Boniface IX., and all hope of seeing the end of the Schism disappeared, at

facts. I give no credence to the details, full of improbable cruelty, supplied by Andrew Gatarus in Muratori, *Rerum Italicarum Scriptores*, xvii. p. 480. Read the interesting documents in Sauerland (*Hist. Jahrbuch*, 1893, p. 820-832). They are supplied by certain cardinals nominated by Urban, but who became his enemies. The versatile Pileo de Prata is among them. Their aim is to stir up public opinion against the Pope.

least for the moment. The same deplorable blunders recommenced. Clement VII. excommunicated the newly-elect, and he, on his side, reiterated all the condemnations inflicted by Urban on the Pope of Avignon.

The latter had no reason to congratulate himself on the change of Pontiff at Rome, for Boniface was as popular as his predecessor had been the reverse. Kindliness and affability replaced severity and inconsistency on the Pontifical throne. In a few months the new Pontiff regained the ground lost by Urban in the affections of nations and kings.[1] Although the Romans began by revolting against him, he soon succeeded in repairing the castle of St Angelo and the Vatican, and restored the authority that had been momentarily compromised in the centre of the peninsula, and, in the jubilee of 1390, found a way of raising the moral prestige of the Roman Papacy at the same time as he increased its material resources.[2] The two obediences found themselves of equal power. The two competitors had less intention than ever of yielding, and the religious crisis was perpetuated in all the States of Christendom.

[1] Raynald, a. 1390, No. 15 ; a. i. 392, Nos. 1-6 ; a. 1393, No. 17 ; a. 1396, Nos. 1 and 4. *Boniface IX.'s letter to the King of France,* Bibl. de Cambrai, MS. 940, f. 57.

[2] John Guiraud, *L'État pontifical après le grand Schisme,* p. 11.

CHAPTER VI

ANARCHY IN DOCTRINE

§ 1. *The Forerunners.*

THE ever-increasing trouble at the heart of all the kingdoms of Christendom also produced disastrous results on people's minds. Whenever respect for spiritual authority decreases, intellectual and moral disorders creep in more easily and last longer, to the great detriment of souls.

At the end of the fourteenth century there is an increase and "redundancy in the number of hot, bitter, and quarrelsome heads," of which St Francis of Sales was to complain later on.

Nearly all the errors about the hierarchy, since condemned by the Church, were born or developed during this lamentable period. In many minds they upset the true idea of the Papacy and the Councils, and they often caused misunderstandings as to the necessarily subordinate position of the clergy and faithful laity with regard to authority.

To-day, thanks above all to the solemn decisions of the Vatican, everyone knows that the Pope is in the midst of the Church as an infallible doctor for teaching and as a sovereign monarch for government. It is he who, in virtue of his universal authority, summonses, presides over, and confirms general councils. Infallible when they are with the Pope, they cannot be so either without him or against him. The Pope is their only Head, and in a living organism like the Church, the head cannot be separated from the body which it animates and rules. On the other hand, the priests and simple laity are no part of the Church as a teaching body, nor can they be granted a share in its government. Their part is to be subject in mind and conduct to the hierarchical chiefs who have been divinely appointed. Whatever may have been the ideas of those who have looked upon the ecclesiastical body as a humanly constituted society, the Church is a pure and absolute monarchy, and cannot be regarded as an *aristocracy*, still less as a *democracy*.

Before dealing with a labyrinth of errors, it is important to recall these primary truths, which certain Christians of the middle age ignored, and which certain modern Catholics have failed to recognise.

As a matter of fact, the supremacy of the Papacy over Catholic royalties, and its social jurisdiction had been entirely denied by Philip le Bel at the beginning of the fourteenth century, and the brutalities of Anagni had only been the first and coarse manifestation of this revolt. At the period we have reached, the rebels go further: it is the internal jurisdiction of the sovereign Pontiff, it is his governmental authority, that they dispute; their attack is principally directed against his prerogative of infallible judge in matters of controversy. Moreover, erroneous opinions swarm, especially in the Universities. Side by side with professors who teach the whole truth, "the irrefragable word," the human but faithful echo of the divine utterances, there are others whose ignorance, temerity, and inconsistency are in the ascendant. It is a chaos of opinions, a very Babel. At Paris, the audacious Occam has more disciples than the learned brother Thomas or the pious brother Bonaventure have ever had. Theological hypotheses stray off to the utmost limits of absurdity, and even go beyond them at times.

To judge of the doctrinal disorder that then had sway over certain minds, it is enough to reproduce the questions that are asked in the schools about dogmas, which are the indisputable foundations of our faith. I will set forth a few, which will show the state of mind of those who had to guide the Christian society in the midst of the confusion caused by the election at Fondi.

"Is the Pope really necessary? Did our Lord build his Church on Christ or on Peter?[1] Or should, perhaps, the foundation be sought in Holy Scripture? If it was built on the Roman Pontiff, will it not be based on an unstable and perishable foundation?"

Such are the theological problems discussed by d'Ailly in one of his earliest writings, finished just when he was leaving the theological schools of Paris,[2] and the unexpected election of Clement VII. was beginning the Schism. "The jurisdiction of bishops and priests flows from Christ and not from the Pope: the Roman Pontiff is the head of the Church in the sense of being her principal minister: *ministerialiter exercens, administratione dispensans*"; and later on he adds,[3] "The subordination of the Church to the Pope is merely

[1] "Quis enim in Petri infirmitate Ecclesiae firmitatem stabiliat?" John Huss uses the same language in his treatise on the Church. HEFELE, *History of the Councils*, x. p. 357.

[2] *Recommendatio Sacrae Scripturae*, a treatise written in 1380. In the *Opp. Gersonii* (Ed. Ellies-Dupin), i. col. 604.

[3] *De Ecclesia, Conc. Gen. et Sum. Pontificis auctoritate, Ibid.*, ii. col. 928 and 951. ZABARELLA says on his side: "Potestas est in universitate, tanquam in fundamento, et in Papa tanquam *in principali ministro.*" *Cf.* SCHEUFFGEN, *Beiträge zu der Gesch. des grossen Schismas*, p. 114. *Cf.* the Bull, *Auctorem fidei*, pr. 3.

accidental."[1] "The Church universal alone is infallible;[2] every particular Church can err, the Church of Rome like the rest. The Sovereign Pontiff is not necessarily the Roman Pontiff, for the primacy formerly passed from the see of Antioch to that of Rome.[3] The Pope may err, and, as a matter of fact, has been mistaken more than once,[4] beginning with St Peter when he was rebuked by St Paul," d'Ailly continues.[5] The Pontiff may even become a heretic.[6]

In all cases where the faith is concerned, the Pope is subject to the General Council,[7] which can judge and condemn his teaching. It has even the right to pass judgment on his conduct and to depose him if he shows himself obstinate and is considered incorrigible.

[1] *De Ecclesia, Conc. Gen.*, col. 958.

[2] *Ibid.*, col. 953.

[3] *Ibid.*, i. col. 668, 690, 691.

[4] *Ibid.*, ii. col. 949, 959. "Papa est *deviabilis*," says Gerson, i. p. 8.

[5] See my *Petrus de Alliaco*, p. 249 (1886). This hypothesis of papal fallibility, of a purely hypothetical character, is found as an indiscreet conjecture put forward by certain ancient schoolmen. Gerson himself acknowledges that his teaching is new (*De pot. eccl.*, cons. xii. t. ii. p. 247). Still, a good number of doctors of this period admit its possibility at any rate. Here is the idea of Simon of Cramaud, patriarch of Alexandria, writing to the King of the Romans: "If the Pope scandalises the Church, he must be disobeyed: those who submit to him in such a case are guilty of mortal sin. To judge such a Pontiff, two or three judges suffice. He must be condemned irrevocably, like Lucifer of yore. . . . When the Pope falls into an already proscribed heresy, a new sentence is unnecessary, for he deserves less respect than any other Catholic." This text, which has been unpublished until latterly, dates from 1414. It has been published by Finke, *Acta Concilii Constanciensis*, (1896), i. p. 281.

[6] *Opp. Gerson.*, i. col. 689. *De materia, Conc. Gen.*, MS. in Bibl. Nat. Paris, fonds latin, No. 1571, p. 24. Gerson and Nicholas of Cusa are also of this opinion, with a good number of theologians of the period. Gerson adds that, on this hypothesis, the Pope could lawfully be put in chains, imprisoned, and even cast into the sea. *Opp. Gerson.*, ii. col. 221, *De auferibilitate Papae ab Ecclesia*.

[7] *Ibid.*, and *Opp. Gerson.*, ii. col. 951, 953, 959, 960. Hefele, x. 414.

This general synod, according to some theologians, is infallible. *It is only a pious belief*,[1] for, as a matter of fact, several ancient councils have erred as to the faith. The ecumenical synod, representing the universal Church, is above the Pope. D'Ailly sets himself to show this superiority by relying upon natural, divine, and canon law.[2] But in his defence it must be said that the dogma was much less explicit than it is to-day.

Such are the ideas that one of the most celebrated divines of the period ventures to set forth, and his influence was very considerable during all these events, and, according to Bossuet,[3] he often speaks for the whole Faculty of Paris. Such opinions remind one of those of the great and disastrous revolutionary known as Occam. Up till the fourteenth century, indeed, except among the schismatic Greeks, who rejected the primacy itself, one does not meet with this total denial of infallibility.

The Hussites, Protestants, and most audacious of Gallicans have hardly surpassed these Paris theologians in their most erroneous negations, when they dispute not only the limits, but even the origin of the rights of the Pope. Of this system I will only note an affirmation alleged and upheld at that time by more than one doctor, and since then adopted by the Gallican

[1] *Opp. Gerson.*, ii. col. 958. "According to some great doctors, a General Council can err *in facto, in jure, et quod magis est, in fide*," says the Cardinal of Cambrai, in the middle of the Council of Constance. Von der Hardt, *Rerum conc. œcumen. Constant.*, ii. col. 201. D'Ailly had scarcely finished his studies when he maintained this same opinion at Paris, *Utrum Petri Ecclesia rege gubernetur*. . . . *Opp. Gerson.*, i. col. 689. Like Bossuet, the Bishop of Cambria never wavered upon this point. But what is a pious opinion when contradicted by facts? *Cf.* Bouix, *De Papa*, i. p. 472.

[2] *Ibid.*, col. 956.

[3] *Defensio declarationis cleri Gallicani*, p. 11, lib. vi. c. 20.

Church as her own: *the General Council is superior to the Pope*,[1] whose place in the Church is simply a primacy of honour.

Does this mean that, in a time of ecclesiastical calm, the united bishops are superior to him who has to preside over them, and that the latter holds his powers from them, and, in a word, that the body is superior to the head? No, for the hypothesis would be absurd.

But the mischief of Gallicanism consists in taking advantage of exceptional periods of disorder and schism, and of the sometimes vexatious measures to which they lead, in order to divide that which should be united, in order to proclaim that the ecclesiastical aristocracy is above its natural sovereign, that it has the right to elect him, to deprive him of certain of his prerogatives, to pass judgment upon him, and even to depose him.

Doubtless the cardinals at Fondi had set a fatal example. Through their action, disunion reigned at this epoch in the Church. Doubtless the council, that is to say, the general assembly of the bishops, was perhaps the only way of finding a remedy for so many evils, but the exception must never be made into a rule, nor division be allowed as normal and natural. A temporary expedient, contrived to put an end to an accidental disorder, cannot become a perpetual law and less still a dogma of faith.[2]

[1] Th. de Niem, *De modis uniendi, Opp. Gerson.*, ii. col. 172 ff. This treatise was long ascribed to Gerson and placed among his works, but Lenz and Finke thought Thierry de Niem was the author. Others, with Schwab, Hartwig, and Sägmüller (*Hist. Jahrbuch*, 1895, p. 562), think on the other hand that this important work should be attributed to Andrew Escobar, a Spanish Benedictine, who died Bishop of Megara in 1428.

[2] "These (Gallican) doctrines will never be proclaimed except in troublous times for the Church," writes Bossuet to Le Tellier, at the time of the declaration of 1682. See chapter xv. of this work.

Yet this is what the imprudent theologians of Bâle and Constance will have the misfortune to bring about. What I want to show is that theories of the superiority of councils, now condemned, do not date from 1415 and the Council of Constance,[1] and still less from their codification drawn up in the four articles of 1682.

They were introduced into the Church by a certain group of theologians who were lovers of novelty, and they were invented and upheld from the end of the fourteenth century even in the University itself. Paris made Constance, or at any rate made it possible. At certain very troublous periods, at the Council of Bâle, as at the meeting of 1682, these false and fatal declarations, so inimical to the authority of the Roman Pontiff, come to light again.

This Gallican doctrine is an "opinion that the Pope endures and puts up with in spite of himself . . . held by only a few, contrary to general opinion and everywhere else a subject for ridicule, as it is even in France itself."

Such was the opinion of Peter de Marca, Archbishop of Paris, twenty years before the famous declaration of 1682.[2]

[1] Excellent theologians, like Ruard Tapper, Andrew Duval, Th. Raynaud, Bannez, Ballerini, etc. . . . profess the opposite opinion, and think that these doctrines were invented in their entirety at the time of the holding of the council. I think they can be shown to be mistaken. It would be easy to show, if it could be done without going outside of the matter in hand, that all the errors of these troublous times were first upheld in the bold discussions of the theological schools of Paris. *Cf.* HAURÉAU, *Notice sur le No.* 16,409 *of the Latin MSS. of the Bibl. Nationale*, Paris, 1895.

[2] A memorial requested from the Archbishop of Paris by the minister Le Tellier (1662). It was long in manuscript at Saint Sulpice, then at the Mazarin Library (2284) and at the Bibl. Nat. (17,614). M. Puyol gives long extracts from it in his book, *Edmond Richer*, ii. p. 435. *Cf.* BOUIX, *De Papa*, i. p. 566.

Nevertheless this schismatical view survived until the Vatican Council, in spite of the opposition of almost the whole Church, and in spite of the often repeated anathemas of Sovereign Pontiffs.

§ 2. *Democratic and Multitudinist Doctrines in the Church.*

The system we have just explained in accordance with d'Ailly is quite *aristocratic* ; in fact it sets up the predominance of bishops, of the ecclesiastical aristocracy, and also of doctors of theology and canon law, that is to say, a doctrinal or scientific aristocracy.[1]

The most celebrated disciple of the future Bishop of Cambrai, the chancellor, John Gerson, goes further, and maintains that parish priests have a definite voice in councils as well as bishops.[2]

The Council of Constance admits this doctrine. Simple priests, and even certain laymen, are allowed to sit there as judges. The conventicle of Bâle goes farther, and in its final schismatical throes, hardly admits anyone beyond ecclesiastics [3] of the second order, deliberating and disputing in utter anarchy.

[1] Von der Hardt, ii. col. 224. See chapter xv. of this work.

[2] Gerson, *De pot. ecclesiastica,* consid. xii. t. ii. col. 249. Item, *Sermo de privilegiis mendicantium, Opp. Gerson.*, ii. col. 436. A Protestant writer shows the relations existing between Gerson, Wicliffe, John Huss, and the reformers. *Cf.* Arminius Jepp, *Gerson, Wiclifus, Hussus* (Göttingen, 1857). Ém. de Bonnechose, *Les Réformateurs avant la Réforme, Jean Hus,* Introd., p. 71.

[3] At the 33rd session, which took grave decisions, there were only 20 prelates, whether bishops or abbots, and 400 other ecclesiastics. *Copistarum et paedagogorum grex,* says the Archbishop of Milan ; *colluvies copistarum,* exclaims Patricius ; *turba inconsulta et confusa, synagoga Satanae,* remarks Æneas Sylvius, the future Pius II., too long a supporter of the conventicle. These democratic notions influence first J. Almain, J. Courtecuisse, A. Tostat, and afterwards Saint-Cyran, Travers, Maultrot, and the schismatic authors of the *Constitution civile du clergé.*

Later on, the worst Gallicans take up these doctrines. Richer declares that simple priests are the necessary judges in all dogmatic difficulties, and that they have a deliberative and conclusive vote in virtue of their sacerdotal character.[1]

This might be called the *moderate democratic* system.

Others, with Gerson, go lower still, and end in that *absolute* or *radical democracy* known as *multitudinism*. According to them, spiritual authority resides entirely in the mystical body of the Church, which communicates it to the Pope and to the bishops. This system clearly corresponds with that of the democratic origin of authority in politics. The heads of the two societies of Church and State would only obtain their authority from the people as an intermediary.[2]

If this opinion is defensible in politics, it cannot be so in theology, for spiritual power comes from God through the mission of His Son and the apostles, and does not emanate from the people regarded either as origin or as channel.

Gerson also maintains that the right of correcting and even of deposing the Sovereign Pontiff belongs to the entire community, and not only to the General Council.[3] "Every one of the faithful can demand a hearing from the Council," he adds, "when the question in dispute has to do with public authority

[1] *Defensio libelli de eccl. et politica potestate,* lib. iv. c. iii. (1701). *Cf.* Puyol, *Edmond Richer,* i. p. 444.

The heretical and schismatical synod of Pistoja (1786) renewed this Gallican doctrine (the Bull, *Auctorem fidei,* pr. 9 and 10), and quite recently the Old Catholics also apparently adopted this presbyterian error. But it must not be confounded with the heresy of the Scotch Church, which does not recognise the episcopate.

[2] *Auctorem fidei,* pr. 2.

[3] *De auferibilitate Papae,* consid. xii. t. ii. p. 216.

in the Church, faith and morals." [1] Occam, with still greater temerity, asserted that even women should not be excluded from a General Council.[2]

It is well known how Protestantism, and especially Calvinism, took up these doctrines, and exaggerated them in introducing them into its religious system. "That is how the Reformation is preached," exclaims Bossuet, "that is how Christendom is torn to pieces and the way of Antichrist prepared." [3]

Clearly, all the errors about the reformation and hierarchical régime of the Church, about the power of councils, about the pontifical monarchy, and about the simple rights of priests, have their origin in theories which find their source, their encouragement, and their continuance in the Schism. The principal manifestations have been noted. It is hardly necessary to call attention to the opinions of the energumens who cry out: "After all, what does it matter about the number of the Popes? What does it matter whether there are two, three, ten, or a dozen? Every country should have its own Pope. Is it not the divine will that the Church should thus be divided for a time, or even for ever, perchance? In struggling against schism for unity, are people not perhaps struggling against God?" [4]

Here again seems to be a reflection of the most advanced of Occam's opinions, and another trace of the subversive influence of this evil genius in theology.

[1] *Cf. Sermones in Vigilia Domini Palmarum*, col. 205 (March 23, 1415). *Cf.* Schwab, *Johannes Gerson* (Würzburg, 1859), p. 507, note.

[2] *Dialogus*, lib. vi. c. 85. Apud Goldast, *Monarchia Sancti Romani Imperii*, ii. p. 392.

[3] Bossuet, *Histoire des Variations*, xv. No. 121.

[4] *Cf.* Pastor, *Histoire des Papes*, i. p. 192. The University puts forth these scandalous and heretical propositions in its last letter to Clement VII., July 17, 1394. *Cf.* Denifle, *Chartularium*, iii. p. 633.

§ 3. *Still more Extraordinary Opinions.*

Is it possible to be more rash and to wander still more imprudently away from the safe and beaten track? Does not a lower drop mean a fall into the midst of the wretched herd of heretics and free-thinkers, whose punishment we see and whose complaints are heard in Dante's eighth circle of the Inferno?

Several writers of the period seem to have had this irreverent hardihood; and, to be convinced of it, it suffices to add to the already gloomy picture a few more touches, equally true and still darker.[1]

There are certain theologians who consider as probable such propositions as these: "The Pope, the bishops, and all the clergy at once may fall into error. Only a few simple souls, a few poor lay-folk may preserve the deposit of revelation. Thus it was, say they, that, at the time of the Passion, the Blessed Virgin alone kept the faith."

But, on such a hypothesis, what becomes of the promised indefectibility of the Church? What becomes of its visibility and hence of its influence and authority? What is this supernatural society without an orthodox Pope, and without a faithful clergy? What is this

[1] D'Ailly himself relates all these hypotheses, which he finds to be plausible, in his treatise, *De Resumpta* (1380): *Utrum Petri Ecclesia rege gubernetur, lege reguletur, fide confirmetur, jure dominetur.*" *Opp. Gerson.*, i. col. 669, 689, 690. Occam, *Dialogus*, v. c. 1, 22, 28. *Cf.* Bouix, *De Papa*, i. p. 469. "Habemus Papam Christum, sufficit ut credamus in eum." A proposition repeated by Gerson, *De aufer.*, ii. col. 224: "Ecclesia non est aliud nisi conjunctio omnium existentium in charitate" (soul of the Church). P. Plaoul apud Denifle, iii. 552. This is the invisible Church of the Jansenists—"We have no Pope, except God and the Virgin our feminine Pope (papesse), and the Church is widowed." *Cf.* Teret, *La Faculté de théologie de Paris*, iii. p. 208. J. de Varennes, in *Opp. Gerson.*, ii. 841 ff. Andrew d'Escobar, *Gubernaculum Concil.*, etc.

temple devoid of doctrinal authority, and full of error and ruin? In these conditions, how could Christ guarantee the perpetuity of His Church?

These audacious innovators had discovered a reply to this question. "In this case," said they, "God would Himself ordain priests and bishops and supernaturally make this extraordinary ordination known to His Church. To deny the possibility of such an occurrence," they added, "was to dispute the omnipotence of God."

It must be acknowledged that this is to claim too extreme a liberty for the ridiculous. From such gratuitous and scandalous propositions to Protestantism there is but a single step, and that step will be taken. These simple souls, who believe that they alone have preserved the faith in its purity, have only to refuse to obey the decrees of a General Council, to appeal from them to another council, and to revolt openly. This is exactly what was done later on by the first reformers of 1517: it was the triumph of free-thinking. Still further, a fourteenth century theologian, who was long supposed to be Gerson himself, dares to assert that, on such an hypothesis, the council may be convoked by the emperor or other princes, by private individuals, by peasants, and even by some worthy female, *minima vetula*.[1]

What confusion of thought and what perturbation of mind is presupposed by the mere enunciation of these subversive theories. Are we wrong in saying, to begin with, that the *Treatise on the Church* did not

[1] A treatise, *De modis uniendi Ecclesiam in concilio*, composed either by Thierry de Niem, or by Andrew d'Escobar. *Cf.* Anglican Prayerbook, Article xxi.: "General Councils may not be gathered together without the commandment and will of Princes." Agreed upon by convocation holden at London, 1562.

exist, even in its most fundamental principles, for these decadent and wrong-headed theologians.[1]

What an extraordinary and scandalous production would result from summarising all the heteroclite opinions of the School of this period? A considerable number are compressed into the works of Wicliffe, whose heresy is the stepping-stone from the old Waldensian errors to the Protestant revolution.

At this time are to be seen many of those "extreme thinkers," spoken of by Bossuet, who are never weary of inquiring, and discoursing, and discussing, and whom St Gregory of Nazianz calls extravagant and insatiable."[2]

The innovators of those days are far from wishing, and even from perceiving, the logical consequences of their first steps. Anti-doctrinal blasphemy has always led, perhaps unconsciously, to all social disorders. The blows which strike the Roman See shake every throne, and, as has been said, a Luther in religion always begets a Luther in politics.

So, then, all these theological heresies soon reverberate in the social order, and Wicliffe will soon himself draw the conclusions that follow from his premises. Only read the incendiary propositions condemned by the Pope,[3] and then say if there is much between them and preaching anarchy.

As a matter of fact, in England, from the beginning of the Schism, the workman, Wat Tyler, and the Franciscan, John Ball, both Wicliffites, raised mobs by their fanatical preaching, and in 1381, twenty thousand rebels boldly encamped at the gates of

[1] Ch. i. p. 10.

[2] *Oraison funèbre de N. Cornet.*

[3] Hefele, *History of the Councils*, x. p. 504.

London.[1] Gregory XI., without condemning the heresiarch, justly remarks: "These propositions are not only erroneous as to faith, but their tendency is to destroy all political institutions."[2]

It is well known how, later on, John Huss introduced this permanent anarchy into Bohemia, when he set up a democratic and socialist republic. This unfortunate country long bore the sanguinary traces of the extraordinary disorders which accompanied his anti-patriotic and anti-religious effort.

On another side, the Beghards and the Waldenses were stirring up the whole of the east of Christendom and were preaching every kind of revolution.

§ 4. *The Prophecies of the Period.*

In this troubled epoch, predictions spread on all sides, announcing the coming of Antichrist preparatory to the approaching end of the world. It was not the first time that a similar phenomenon had occurred amidst the crowd, which is always eager for the marvellous. In every age, when an unusually grave calamity fell upon the faithful, they raised their eyes to heaven and waited in anxious dread the coming of the terrible and final adversary of Jesus Christ.

In the days of the first persecutions, they thought that Nero would rise from the dead and reappear in the world to set up the worship of idols and to fulfil

[1] *Cf.* Réville, *Le soulèvement des travailleurs d'Angleterre en* 1381 (Paris, Picard, 1898). Trevelyan, *England of the Age of Wycliffe*, in the *English Historical Review*. An English *Wyclif Society* is engaged in bringing out all the works of the heresiarch, who also composed a work on the Antichrist. It is his last production. *Cf. Revue historique*, xlv. (1891), p. 460 (1891), and lxxii. p. 460 (1899). J. Lingard, *History of England*, iv. ch. iii. (*cf.* French translation).

[2] Labbe, xi. p. 2041.

all that John had foretold of the Antichrist. In the third century, Tertullian, led astray by Montanist fancies, awaited the end of the world and set forth his fanatical hope with gloomy energy. He wrote at the time of the persecution of Septimus Severus and Caracalla, and would have people set themselves free from every earthly hindrance to meet martyrdom more readily. At the date when the fatal downfall of the empire was first foreseen, St Hilary saw the Antichrist at one time in Sabellius, at another in Arius, and then in the Emperor Constantius. About the year one thousand, Adso, the monk of Luxeuil, wrote his book *De Antichristo* to warn the wife of Louis d'Outremer against vain fears. At the date of the downfall of Constantinople two great men, Saint John of Capistrano and the learned Nicholas of Cusa, took up this disquieting question one after the other, until Luther and Cranmer came upon the scene to give out that the Antichrist was the Pope. Had one not been able to see with one's own eyes in France how, after the sad events of 1870, the same outpouring of predictions was invented by frenzy, accepted by the credulous, and propagated by the superstitious, one could not credit the possibility of the success met with by the most extravagant prophecies of the latter part of the fourteenth century.

In those unhappy times, seers arose on all sides, and their visions gained such an influence and diffusion as had been unknown before. A hermit called Telesphorus declaimed against the Church of Rome and the clergy, foresaw the Pontificate of an "Angelic pastor," and predicted the close of the Schism for the year 1393. "At that time," he said, "the imperial crown will pass to the King of France, who will become a universal monarch." Telesphorus is clearly on Clement's side, and therefore his book is refuted by Henry of Langenstein, a German, and a supporter of Urban.[1] On the other hand, in Flanders, Smet van Huysse prophesies in the name of Urban (1391). From another quarter, Gamaleon proclaimed the translation of the Holy See to Germany.

In some of the gravest sermons reliance was put upon these baseless predictions, and certain compilations of the day present a singular mixture of prophetic insanities, astrological forecasts, and doctrinal statements. In a discourse uttered during Advent in 1385, Peter d'Ailly gives the same importance to the pretended seer Cyril and the eccentric Joachim de Flore as to Saint John the Baptist and Saint John the Evangelist.

He gives credence to all the extravagances of these persons of sham spirituality, and does not shrink from saying that the Antichrist of the Apocalypse will reign within fifteen years. "There shall be signs in the sun, the moon, and the stars," he exclaims. "The *sun*, that is to say, the prelates; the light of their wisdom goes out: the *moon*, that is to say, the princes; the rays of their justice grow dim: the *stars* signify their numerous inferiors, for grace disappears from all." [2]

Others as well as D'Ailly made themselves an echo of these fantastic predictions, and like him announced

[1] *Contra quemdam eremitam de ultimis temporibus vaticinantem nomine Theolophorum*, published by Pez (*Thesaurus*, i. p. ii. c. 505). *Cf.* Valois, i. p. 373. Pastor, i. p. 165. Bibl. Nat. MSS. Lat. 3184, 14,643, 1617.

[2] *Sermo* iii., *De Adventu Domini.* D'Ailly was more happy in his forecast, when, relying on astrological calculations, he formally predicted in 1414 the revolution of 1789. *Cf.* my *Petrus de Alliaco* (1886), p. 187; *Revue des Sciences ecclésiastiques*, series viii. vol. viii. (Sept. 1898), p. 250.

the coming of Antichrist and the approaching end of the world. Clémangis, the disciple and friend of the Bishop of Cambrai, compiled a special treatise on this grave subject,[1] as also did Nicholas Oresme, Bishop of Lisieux.[2] Thierry de Niem asks if the Schism and its consequences are signs preceding the approaching arrival of Antichrist. "Yes, if one is to believe historians and prophets," he replies.[3] St Vincent Ferrier made it the ordinary subject of his sermons. Seven out of ten of them were about the Last Judgment which he believed to be near at hand.[4] On the other hand, mournful processions of twenty to thirty thousand persons overran all the centre and south of Italy. They were headed by great crucifixes from which ran blood and sweat. One of these pilgrims thought himself the prophet Elias and foretold that there would soon be an earthquake which would precede the end of the world.[5]

All these details agree so far as to show the profound perturbation of mind and the strange fancies by which people were haunted. Superstition oozed through all the gaps made in the faith.

On the other hand, public misfortunes awakened a true religious spirit, and everywhere aroused a fresh demand for prayer.

Charles VI. had just gone mad in the Forest of Mans,

[1] *De Antichristo, ortu ejus, vita, moribus et operibus* (Ed. Lydii, p. 367).

[2] *Cf.* MARTÈNE et DURAND, *Veter. Script. nova collectio*, ix. col. 1271.

[3] NIEM, lib. iii. xli. Thierry also composed a special treatise on the Antichrist to be found in SCHARDIUS, p. 834. *Cf.* BELLARMINE, *De Romano Pontifice III.*; BRUNET, *La France littéraire au XVe siècle* (1865).

[4] In a letter addressed to Benedict XIII., he wrote that Antichrist will come *cito, bene cito, valde breviter*. Bibl. Nat., Latin texts MS., 14669. This letter has been printed by R. P. FAGES, *Histoire de Saint Vincent Ferrier*, i., App., p. lxxvi.

[5] NIEM, lib. ii. 26. GREGOROVIUS, vi. p. 638.

and people saw in it a divine punishment.[1] From one end of France to the other they made processions and pilgrimages for the cure of their king. Notre Dame of Chartres, the basilica of Saint Denis, Saint Catherine du Val des Écoliers, the Sainte Chapelle of the Palace, and other miraculous churches received one after the other the homage and supplications of the French, who were brought in crowds by the misfortunes of the time to the most venerated sanctuaries. One day, in the midst of a crowd from the frontier-province of Lorraine, there arrived at Notre Dame du Puy, Isabel Romée, afterwards the mother of Joan of Arc. It was a first streak of dawn amidst the darkness of the night. At Avignon, the Pope himself composed a special mass for "peace," and promised indulgences to all those who would go to hear it.

Strange and cruel, indeed, was the situation of France. A mad king, a dissolute queen, and rival princes who put their own interests before those of the country. In a higher sphere, theological schools divided on important points, bishops uncertain of the legitimacy of their head, and, to crown the hierarchy, a doubtful Pope!

[1] "The common opinion of the realm of France was that the king would never be cured until the Church were in another state. . . . The king made this excuse: We believed the advice of those who have governed us until now, and if we have acted foolishly, theirs is the blame and not ours." Froissart, xvi. pp. 69 and 441.

CHAPTER VII

THE MEANS OF PACIFICATION

§ 1. *The Three Ways.*

ABOUT 1381, Peter d'Ailly had already pointed out the three most practical means of securing the suppression of religious discord: the way of compromise, the way of abdication, and the way of a General Council.[1] Other and not less celebrated writers were associated from the very beginning with the attempts of the future Bishop of Cambrai, and repeated his statements.[2]

The *compromise* consisted in entrusting the care of putting an end to the great dispute of twelve years' standing to arbitrators who should decide without appeal.

But where and how were they to be found? Were they to be cardinals? They would be both judges and suitors. They would be divided into separate camps by their sympathies and antecedents, perhaps by their interests.

Were other members of the clergy to be chosen? But they, too, would be divided for like reasons. Or should princes be selected? But is it their business to judge ecclesiastical matters? Or professors of law and eminent members of Universities? But, in addition to all the foregoing reasons that militate against such a choice, had not most of them, and the most

[1] *Epistola diaboli Leviathan apud Tschackert,* PETER VON AILLI, App. v. *Cf. Opp. Gers.* i. col. 157.

[2] *Cf.* DENIFLE, *Chartularium,* iii. pp. 596, 597, 667.

celebrated of them, already given their opinion on solemn occasions? Could a matter of an entirely spiritual character be treated by way of a compromise of this sort? Further, who would undertake to put the arbitrators in communication with one another? Finally, what sanction would the arbitration sentence possess? Would the decision of the arbitrators carry sufficient authority to force its acceptance? Who would be powerful enough to enforce it? [1]

As to the way of abdication, could it be thought of? The election of Boniface had given new strength to the Roman Papacy, which had in its favour, in addition to its primary right, all the votes that it had won since Urban's death.

Clement had been Pope for twelve years, and it was very improbable that he would now be willing to give up his dignified position. Further, how great were the practical difficulties? In whose hands could either of the Popes place his resignation? How, and by what college of cardinals, could his successor be appointed?

The summoning of a *General Council* [2] appeared to offer a more legitimate way, which was more effective and less difficult. If votes are counted, and even if they are weighed, it was the way which from the outset had received most sympathy.

From the beginning of the Schism, the powerful city of Florence, despite the urgency of the Duke of Anjou, appeals for a council to prove that she is wrong in remaining true to Urban.[3] The King of Castile, though canvassed by Charles V., desires to remain neutral, until a synod convoked by the cardinals has

[1] *Chronic. Karoli VI.*, lib. xv. c. 3 and 12. Denifle, iii. pp. 601 and 626.

[2] Denifle, iii. p. 611.

[3] Valois, i. p. 155.

been held.[1] The King of France as he was dying, also had rallied to this solution, demanding this gathering of the universal Church.[2]

Less known writers of the period advocate the same means. On this point German doctors and Urbanists, like Henry von Langenstein and Conrad von Gelnhausen,[3] were in accord with French authorities and Clementines, like Gerson. The latter recapitulates in one of his sermons the efforts made on behalf of a council by the University of Oxford, by Peter d'Ailly, and other famous professors.[4]

The knight Philip de Maizières joins his voice[5] with that of his brother-preacher, John de Montson.[6] With the Latin prose of the latter unites French poetry, then in its infancy. In 1381 a rhymester thus praises the meeting of the future council:—

> "Le général Conseil en sentence qu'il dit
> Ne mesprendra de rien : du tout à li m'affie.
> Donques qui du Conseil général se meffie
> Monstre qu'il ne sent pas bon droit pour sa partie."[7]

In 1385, the citizens of Ghent, too, in their quarrel with France, demand this sure method of putting an end to the Schism. No authority in the Church was greater

[1] Bibl. Nat., 14,643, f. 114. *Thesaurus novus anecdot.* ii. c. 1099-1120.

[2] Valois, i. p. 327. The citizens of Ghent display the same opinion in 1385.

[3] *Cf.* Aug. Kneer, *Die Entstehung der Konziliarientheorie zur Geschichte des Schismas.* Schwab, *Johannes Gerson*, p. 124.

[4] *Sermo coram Anglicis*, ii. col. 126.

[5] *The Old Pilgrim's Dream*, Bibl. Nat. MS. fr. 22542, f. 276.

[6] In his *Dialogus*, composed in 1391. Bibl. Nat. MS. Latin, 1466.

[7] Found at Rouen, by Valois, i. p. 385, in a MS. of Rouen Library, No. 1357.

> "The General Council in the sentence that it passes
> Will make no error : in all I will trust it.
> Who then distrusts the General Council
> Shows that he does not think that right is on his side."

than that of a General Synod at a period when the Pope was doubtful to a large number of people.

From 1380, however, the adversaries of a council expressed themselves thus by the mouth of St Vincent Ferrier. "Urban's case," he said, "was judged without appeal and with sovereign authority by the cardinals of Fondi. Why should the validity of Clement VII.'s election be called in question? What good is the decision of an Œcumenical Council? The wars that now devastate Europe deprive those who would take part in it of all security. Besides, the immense multitude of Italian prelates would infallibly crush the small minority of fathers from other nations." [1]

Others added: "No schism has ever yet been ended in this way. Who would summon this universal council? The two rival Popes? But they will never consent to do so. One of them? The other one's obedience would disregard him. The cardinals? Or the Emperor? They have not the right."

"Moreover, would sufficient numbers attend? If not, what would be the authority of a minority of prelates? Who would give it any authority? Who would preside over it? Who would accept its decisions? Is not a remedy so hard to apply worse than the disease?" [2]

I reproduce all these objections in detail, because they are re-echoed again and again throughout Christendom until the meeting of the Council of Constance.

[1] *De moderno Ecclesiæ scismate,* 2ª pars, c. iv. 2ª obj. Bibl. Nat. MS. Lat. 1470. Later on will appear (see chap. xv. of this work), the means used at Constance to neutralise the influence of the numerous prelates, *episcopelli italiani.*

[2] The University letter to the king, in 1394, refutes some of these objections. *Chronic. Karoli VI.,* lib. xv. c. iii. t. ii. p. 155. *Cf.* p. 231, a decision taken the same year by the *assembly* of Paris.

Even after the final decisions of the Council, these will still be the pretexts for disputing the value of the decrees of that assembly.

§ 2. *Useless Intervention of the University.*

The third means, which finally prevailed, was also the first to be put forward.

Immediately after the death of Charles V., the University discussed the proposal of a council, and the four Faculties agreed on recognising its utility. Peter d'Ailly was commissioned to sound the disposition of the court officially; but the princes of the blood, who were guardians of Charles VI., and above all the Duke of Anjou, caused the plan to fail.[1] From 1380 to 1394, that is to say for fourteen years, this was the great means advocated by France, and by the University of Paris and its disciples everywhere.

But from this date, men's minds are turned in a new direction, and the way of *cession* seems for a moment to gain upon the plan of holding a council.[2]

No doubt the *tres viae*, as the agents of the Faculties remarked, were still maintained and put forward together, but the absolute withdrawal of both candidates was what found the widest amount of support. No doubt also, when all the doctors of the University were called to the ballot in January 1394, and put their ten thousand voting-papers into the urn, each of the three procedures received a large number of votes, but the

[1] In 1412, D'Ailly wrote thus: "Taceo qualiter a principio schismatis materiam concilii generalis in concilio Franciæ *primus* ex parte Universitatis proponere diu instanter prosequi non *timui.*" *Apologia Concilii Pisani apud Tschackert*, Peter von Ailli, App. xii. p. 37.

[2] *Cf. Chronic. Karoli VI.*, c. iii. p. 142, and c. xii. p. 236. Denifle, iii. pp. 597 and 619.

way of *cession* the majority. It is curious to note that the professors had come to look upon the two Pontiffs as equally responsible for the Schism, and as intruders both, and that they wished to enforce not only the resignation of Boniface but of Clement also. It is the first desertion of the Avignon Pope, and a new way of regarding the solution.[1]

The same point of view is manifested by the University on another grave occasion. It wished to carry its complaint to the throne itself, and it appointed three of its best professors to explain to Charles what it deemed to be the best method. Peter d'Ailly, Gilles des Champs, Clémangis, and others therefore drew up a joint-letter, which has remained famous. The doctors supplied their ideas, and Clémangis threw them into Ciceronian form.[2] On June 30th, 1394, the members of the University were admitted to the king's room. William Barraut, prior of St Denis, gave voice to their complaints in the presence of a numerous assembly, and unfolded the ideas which had been developed in their written address.

[1] Henry von Langenstein composed the following verses in his *Carmen pro pace*, with regard to his belauded *cession*, though he had previously maintained the way of a *council* :—

"Qui prius hoc faceret Christo gratissimus esset,
Promptus ad hoc placitum sit quilibet ergo duorum
Sed quia *cedendo* jus unus non daret altri,
Ambo desinant electi . . ."

Cf. Denifle, iii. p. 598. The date of this document is June 8, 1393. Jarry, *La "voie de fait" et l'alliance franco-milanaise*, Bibl. de L'École des Chartes, 1892, p. 523.

[2] "Tulliana facundia singulariter pollens, eam coloribus rhetoricis exornandam suscepit." *Chronic. Karoli VI.*, lib. xv. c. ii. John de Montreuil calls him "vas eloquentiæ." The copy addressed to the king is lost, but the letter exists in MS. at the Bibl. Nat. MSS. Latin, No. 1463, f. 93, and 1463, f. 20, and at the Cambrai Library, MS. 940. The French translation, ordered by the king, is in the Vatican Library, 4791, f. 171.

The *cession* of both Pontiffs was recommended by them as the preferable method. Afterwards the cardinals of the two obediences should meet and elect a Pope who would be universally recognised. The letter threatened with most terrible judgments, and with the punishment of Dathan and Abiram, whichever of the two Popes should refuse to resign.[1] It is clear that the rival Pontiffs are once more put on the same footing. Was it the peremptory way in which they were judged, or the somewhat bitter threats of the deputation that displeased the king? One cannot say, but what is known is that Charles VI., urged by the astute Peter de Luna and the Duke de Berry, gave the University definite instructions not to busy itself any further with the Schism.

The steps taken by the authorities of Paris had made much noise, and their failure was still more talked about. The king's letter was made known everywhere, and gave rise to sharp answers from the party of Avignon.

One of them, a Dominican, attacks the address, which he calls "libellous, blasphemous, seditious. Theology, philosophy, rhetoric are all wanting in this document. It is the work of juniors without experience or practical sense. They ought to be arrested and punished."[2]

It is easy to imagine the vexation felt by the members of the University when they were rebuffed by the court and bitterly criticised by their opponents. It was not the first time their serious counsels had been treated with contempt, but they thought they had an infallible

[1] *Cf.* Denifle, iii. p. 617. Du Boulay, iv. p. 687. D'Achéry, *Spicil.*, i. 776. Raynald, a. 1394, No. 3.

[2] Denifle, iii. 634.

means of compelling the King to listen to them. They resolved to adjourn the courts, and to suspend all lectures and sermons, till their demands met with justice.[1]

It was the beginning of rebellion, not only against the Court, but further against their old protégé, the Pontiff of Fondi and Avignon. The authorities of Paris were as discontented with Clement as with the princes, and the grievances uttered by France were only too well justified. A few years previously the monk of St Denis had already drawn a sad picture of the fiscal doings of Clement. "By all these innovations," he wrote, "the will of the founders of churches is frustrated, the service of God is neglected, devotion among the faithful is diminishing, and the realm is denuded of money. Many ecclesiastics, wandering hither and thither, are loaded with poverty. The schools of the kingdom, formerly so flourishing, are abandoned, and the University of Paris, the tender mother of the liberal arts (*altrix dulciflua*), mourns the loss of her children who go abroad." [2]

Since this period, the buying and selling and the exactions of the Pope of Avignon had but increased. In the form of voluntary rates, tithes, annates, and various taxes, he had given permanent establishment to a system of forced loans. Nothing escaped this greedy finance, which watched everything and took advantage of everything. The Schism lay as heavy upon revenues as upon consciences.

Had only these extraordinary imposts some excuse in real and urgent necessities; but the Pontifical Court, more numerous than ever, abandoned nothing of its traditional luxury, and did not cut down its unjustifiable

[1] *Chronic. Karoli VI.*, lib. xv. c. 4. Denifle, *Désolation des églises*, pp. 603 and 731.

[2] *Chronic. Karoli VI.*, lib. ii. c. 2.

extravagances by a single halfpenny.[1] Moreover, the episcopate refused to pay these fresh dues. The king's Council took measures against the pontifical collectors and sub-collectors; and the University itself felt obliged to become the interpreter of a growing discontent.

§ 3. *Last Days and Death of Clement VII.*

Clement himself felt that his prestige was injured, and that his authority was diminishing among the clergy as well as amidst the people. He had above all to win back the good graces of *Alma Mater*.

For this purpose the Avignon Pontiff sent for Peter d'Ailly, Gilles des Champs, and some other influential members of the University. He needed, he said, to consult their advice. But they refused, not much attracted by an invitation as interested on the part of the Pope as it was compromising for themselves.[2]

Perhaps they were encouraged in this waiting attitude by Clement's legate at Paris, Cardinal Peter de Luna. The latter, at this time, highly approved of the way of *cession* in principle, though he would most energetically repudiate it later on.[3] Was he sincere at this date?

[1] Valois, ii. p. 388. *Cf.* N. de Clémangis, *De corrupto Ecclesiæ statu*, in Brown, *Fasciculus rerum exp. et fug.*, ii. p. 555. Protestants have often misused passages taken from this book, the declamatory and far-fetched tone of which is clear. Is this book, which takes the form of a pamphlet, the work of Clémangis only? Schubert raised the question in 1882: "Ist Nicholaus von Clemanges der Verfasser des Buches?" *De corrupto Ecclesiæ statu* (Leipzig). The work certainly belongs to this epoch.

[2] *Chronic. Karoli VI.*, lib. xv. c. 2.

[3] Thesaurus, *Nov. anecdot.*, ii. 1177. "When I heard that Peter de Luna had been elected Pope, I was extremely glad, because I had heard him preach and approve the way of *cession*, when he was legate in France." John Petit's declaration in 1406. *Cf.* Bourgeois du Chastenet, *Nouv. histoire du Concile de Constance*, Preuves, p. 206. Douet d'Arcq, *Choix de pièces inédites du temps de Charles VI.*, i. p. 144.

Was he a diplomatist with a succession of opinions? Was he merely serving his own end and nursing his future? God alone knows.

However this may be, the University then wrote the Pope of Avignon a letter that was energetic to the point of harshness: it was a final appeal to his conscience. The king, who had urged *Alma Mater* to take this step, himself sent Clement an address in which, a fortnight previously, the Paris doctors had reminded him of the three ways so long before put forward, and begged the Pontiff to bestir himself at last in order to end the Schism and restore peace.[1]

The bearer of this missive reached Avignon, and gave the letter to the Pope, who began to read it. He had scarcely perused half when he cried out in violent anger: "But this is a libellous indictment of the Holy See! This letter is full of poison, and does not deserve to be read."[2]

Rising abruptly, he asked the messenger who was awaiting his reply, "Do you understand Latin?" "Fairly well, Holy Father." Clement withdrew in great agitation, and the envoy did the same. The Pope understood: this letter was an ultimatum. His irritation was redoubled when he learnt that the Paris doctors had written at the same time to the cardinals, and that the whole Sacred College was prompted by this new spirit.[3] His cause then was lost, and his seat at Avignon was going to be lost to him for ever. This was true, but in another way than he supposed. At this critical and

[1] Denifle, iii. p. 631. *"Satis jam, satis hucusque cessatum est, satis tepuimus, satis quievimus, satis expectavimus. Exurgendum aliquando ad pacem est. . . ."*

[2] *Chronic. Karoli VI.*, lxv. c. 5.

[3] Du Boulay, iv. p. 700. D'Achéry, *Spicil.*, i. 785. Bibl. Nat. Paris, MSS. Lat. 1463, p. 98*b*, 14643, f. 24.

final moment Clement appeared to wish to repent, and to obey the counsels that reached him from all sides. He seemed resolved to resign, and disclosed his intention to several people. Then suddenly he was smitten with indisposition. He was ill several days, and then, thinking that he was better, he left his room to hear Mass. No sooner had he got back than he collapsed, smitten with a mortal affection. He hardly had time to invoke God, the Blessed Virgin, and the holy cardinal he had himself promoted, Peter of Luxembourg, but died almost immediately.[1] It was on September 16, 1394. The Pope's body was buried with great pomp in the Cathedral des Doms ; and then, seven years later, he was gathered to the venerated remains of the Blessed Peter of Luxembourg amidst the Celestins of Avignon.

It is rather difficult to arrive at an impartial estimate of Clement VII. His character was as complex as his life was agitated. Sprung from an illustrious race, gifted with every talent of wit and speech, an enlightened patron of literature and art, in less troubled times he might have been a Pope worthy of the tiara, a Colonna or a Borghese, a Martin V. or a Paul V.

As has been already said, Italy had never forgiven him the massacre at Cesena, which he had not prevented, nor yet his return to Avignon. France murmured, and submitted to his exactions and extravagance. Christendom will ever regret that he did not generously abandon the Pontifical throne which he had ascended through rebellion and intrigue, and in which he had been maintained by force of arms and an artfulness that was only too human. Clement VII. is incessantly thrown hither and thither by circumstance, by passion

[1] *Chronic. Karoli VI.*, lib. xv. c. 5.

and self-interest. One day he tries to gain the upper hand by policy, the next by force; one day by promising to assemble a Council (1387), the next by the *via facti*. For sixteen years he lives by expedients: promising benefices to a bishop, lavishing fine words on a king, encouraging this or that ambitious pretender, he tries to please or force himself upon the seven kingdoms that recognise him.

At one time he receives the King of France with the greatest magnificence in his palace at Avignon, and grants him the nomination to certain bishoprics, and to seven hundred and fifty benefices (November 1389). At another he prepares the young Duke of Orleans' invasion of Italy, unites his interests with the prince's, and aspires once more to force the Romans to accept him (1393). He does not repudiate the "use of brutal force," though it is unworthy of his cause and his sacred character. "He subjects the clergy to the civil magistrates and princes," says Clémangis, "and each of them is more of a pope than the Pope himself."[1] He always behaves as a clever but egotistical ruler, who lives rather for himself and his ambition than for his people and his duty. Tacitus might have written *Omnia serviliter pro dominatione*.

On December 13, 1294, just a century before, St Peter Celestin, for less grave reasons, had known how to leave the throne of St Peter and to make the "great renunciation," whereof Dante speaks.[2] "Would to God that this lofty example were followed!" exclaimed Peter d'Ailly, the biographer of the humble and valiant Pontiff. "In our own days, some have risen by

[1] "Ut principum benevolentiam facilius assequeretur, assecutam foveret, fotamque conservaret, conservatam amplificaret, plurima ultro dona et xenia illis dabat."

[2] *Inferno*, c. iii.

ambition to this climax of honour, and now for many years the Church continues rent asunder by a terrible and fatal Schism."[1]

Yet perhaps Clement was in good faith! Perhaps he ought to be pitied even more than blamed! There are times when the greatest difficulty is not to do one's duty, but to know it. King Charles VI. expressed long ago an idea that seems right, when he sent the Cardinals a laconic wish six days after Clement's death, a wish that was perhaps for him the best of funeral prayers: "May the Most High grant him pardon! *cui parcat Altissimus*."[2]

[1] *Vita Beatissimi Patris Domini Petri Cœlestini quinti*, apud BOLLAND., *Acta SS. Maii* iv. p. 428.

[2] *Chronic. Karoli VI.*, lib. xv. c. 6. In the list of Popes is another Clement VII., Julian di Medici, who donned the tiara in 1523, and died in 1534. Two centuries later, we find another Benedict XIII., Vincent Marie Orsini, who ascended St Peter's throne in 1724 and reigned till 1730. But this argument, taken alone, would not prove the illegality of the Popes of Avignon. Several names, borne by alleged anti-popes, were not taken afterwards by legitimate Popes (Leo VIII., Boniface VII., Benedict X.). *Cf.* GAYET, Preface, xvii.

CHAPTER VIII

BENEDICT XIII.—THE WITHDRAWAL OF OBEDIENCE

§ 1. *Election of Benedict XIII.*

On the death of Clement VII., there was a unique opportunity for the French cardinals to put an end to the Schism. They had only to abstain from electing a successor, and the peace of the Church was restored.

Unhappily, too many interests and passions were involved for the members of the Sacred College either to be able or to wish to take advantage of this favourable opportunity. Scarcely had the body of Clement been laid beside that of John XXII. in the Cathedral vaults (September 18, 1394), than the cardinals went into conclave.[1]

In these delicate circumstances, what will the King of France, the recognised protector of the Avignon Papacy, do? On the news of the Pontiff's death, Charles called together his privy council. They unanimously decided to beg the Sacred College to defer the election until the King of France had sent a special and important message to the Cardinals. A letter was despatched immediately to make this decision known.

On its side the University did not remain inactive. Its influence was increasing amidst these divisions. It

[1] The names of the twenty-one members of the Sacred College then at Avignon are in Baluze, i. col. 566, and also in the document published by Ehrle in 1889, *Archiv für Literatur und Kirchengeschichte*, v. p. 401, Fribourg. The article is called: *Aus den Acten des Afterconcils von Perpignan.*

sent Charles a deputation of professors, commissioned to present him four requests : " That the Cardinals should delay the opening of the conclave until the king had settled the method of procedure. The way of *cession* seems to us the best and easiest. An assembly composed of prelates, barons, and members of the University, and notables should meet to select the surest means of succeeding. That the King should write to the Pope of Rome and his principal partisans. That Charles should finally have prayers offered and solemn processions made to obtain the restoration of peace from God." [1]

The King acceded to all these demands, then in his turn he begged the professors to resume their lectures and teaching functions. They eagerly consented. On the same day, September 23, Charles resolved to send a deputation to Avignon, for the purpose of hindering a fresh election and trying to put an end to the Schism.

Unhappily, when the first message reached the Sacred College, all the members had already met in conclave.[2] Doubtless the prelates guessed the contents of the royal letter, for they resolved to open it only after the election had been accomplished. Nevertheless, as they were anxious to be conscientiously in order, and as they did not wish to have to face the reproaches of the King, they pledged themselves by solemn oath to work for the suppression of the Schism by helping the new Pope, and by putting no obstacle in the way of his good will. Each of them promised, if elected, to use the best means for the restoration of religious unity, even were it necessary for that end to renounce the papacy, should this be thought indispensable for the good of the Church.[3]

[1] *Chronic. Karoli VI.*, lib. xv. c. 7. *Cf.* Valois, iii. p. 7.
[2] *Ibid.*, c. 8. 26th September 1394. [3] Niem, lib. ii. 32.

Therefore the way of *cession* was adopted in principle by the whole Sacred College, and seemed to be on the point of triumphing.[1]

After a promise of such grave import, the twenty-one cardinals together invoked the light of the Holy Spirit, and then unanimously elected the former legate at Paris, Peter de Luna of Aragon, who took the name of Benedict XIII.

The vacancy of the see had only lasted twelve days.

Born of a noble family of Aragon, Peter de Luna had studied to good effect in France, and professed canon law in the University of Montpellier. Gregory XI. made him a cardinal, and took him as a companion when he returned to Rome. First of all convinced of the legitimacy of Urban VI., he was one of the last to rally to his rival; but his loyalty, though late, was absolute and effective. It is he who brought over the whole of the Spanish peninsula to the cause of Clement VII. A conqueror in Spain, he was a temporiser in Paris: but on both sides of the Pyrenees he showed himself a consummate diplomatist. In 1394 he was sixty-six years of age.

At the conclave of Avignon he was a supporter of *cession*. "He acted as a very Lamb of God, to a marvellous degree: and I should have gladly given him my vote, had I been able to vote for him," said Simon de Cramaud afterwards.[2] As, until then, he had seemed insinuating and eloquent, exemplary in life and pacific in character, he was chosen by all the members of the Sacred College. They were convinced that he would do

[1] Three cardinals, however, refused to swear, says the document in EHRLE, p. 402. BALUZE says there was only one, the Cardinal of Pampeluna, *op. cit.*, p. 571.

[2] Speech at the Council of Paris, 1406. *Cf.* BOURGEOIS DU CHASTENET, *Nouvelle histoire du Concile de Constance*, Preuves, p. 216.

even more than he said, and that under him, union would meet with no hindrance, at any rate on his part. Moreover, he had wished to refuse the honourable post that was offered him.[1] During the first five months of his reign he apparently justified the most optimistic expectations. One day he said, as he was taking off his cope, "I would resign the Papacy as readily as I put aside this vestment."[2] "I would rather be a friar than keep the Church in such a state of Schism," he added, and people were convinced that what he said was true.

§ 2. *The new Pope's State of Mind.*

Unhappily, in Benedict XIII., as in Urban VI., it was soon plain that there was a deplorable change in his conduct and character.[3] Was it the result of ambition which had been until then dissimulated and was now revealed? Was it that, after having become used to honours and the highest dignity in the world, he found the sacrifice of giving them up too hard? Who can say?

Nevertheless, Benedict's first inclinations had been excellent. Immediately after his election, he had hastened to write to the King. "I give you notice of my promotion," he said in substance, "and at the same time I assure you of my fixed and sincere desire of bringing the Schism to an end. I have made use of your

[1] *Diu renitens,* says Ehrle's document, p. 405. *Invito et diu renuenti inthronizatus,* p. 403.

[2] *Chronic. Karoli VI.,* lib. xv. c. 10. The religious of St Denis reports the same fact and attributes it to Clement VII., lib. iii. c. 14. *Cf.* Valois, ii. p. 401. Both may have made the same proposal.

[3] "Petrus ille de Luna, homo nunquam non lunaticus, turbavit omnia." Meyer, *Annales rerum Flandricarum,* a. 1406, p. 225.

good counsels, and of those of the princes, your uncles, that to you may belong all the glory of having rendered this great service to the Church. To arrive at my object, I shall employ all reasonable and possible means: but I beg you to despatch an important embassy to Avignon at once. I will accept without any tergiversation everything proposed by it. I would rather end my days in the desert or the cloister than contribute in any way to prolong a state of disorder so prejudicial to every one."[1]

A letter from Alma Mater reminded the new Pope, in pressing terms, of the desire he had always manifested on behalf of union:[2] "To-day," she said, "the moment is favourable and heaven seems to second your aspirations. Without delay carry out the peaceful designs which you have so long mentally decreed. If you hesitate, flatterers, courtiers, and persons of ambition will come to petition you in an opposite sense. You will insensibly get a taste for honours and act like your predecessor. Who knows how long you will possess the authority God has entrusted to you? The peace of the Church is in your hands, for your rival will no doubt have to imitate you. Should he refuse to do so, everyone will be convinced of your good right, and he will be overthrown like the most hardened of heretics. The safety and unity of the Church depend then upon you."[3]

The Pope at first received this touching request favourably, and gave a kind welcome to the list of promotions sent him by the University on behalf of its professors and disciples. Benedict desired them to depute him an extraordinary embassy, and Charles thought that he

[1] *Chronic. Karoli VI.*, lib. xv. c. 9.
[2] Denifle, *Chartul.*, iii. p. 602.
[3] *Chronic. Karoli VI.*, lib. xv. c. 19.

could not do better than send the Pope his almoner, Peter d'Ailly, to prepare the way. The doctor, young and famous, had been for five years chancellor of the University of Paris, and he had just been promoted to be treasurer of the Sainte-Chapelle.[1]

Through these important posts he belonged both to the University and to the Court, and he was about to represent them both to the new Pontiff of Avignon. Moreover, through his correspondence with the most important personages of the period,[2] by his diplomatic spirit, and by his sincere desire to put an end to the Schism, he was naturally marked out for this confidential mission (October 1904).

The discourses pronounced by Peter d'Ailly on this important occasion have been preserved, and I have read them in MS. in the Cambrai Library.[3] The skilful ambassador, in a style, the taste of which in these days would seem somewhat inflated, first paid the Pope some prophetic compliments which the future did little to justify. He hoped to see the end of the Schism, thanks to the good-will, the power, and the learning of Benedict. He gave an anticipatory greeting to the dawn of peace and of the reformation of the Church.

Then d'Ailly speaks in the name of Wenceslas, King

[1] Ehrle, p. 406. Tschackert, *Peter von Ailli*, p. 91. Valois, iii. p. 24.

[2] Letter from P. d'Ailly to the King, June 6, 1394 (Denifle, *Chartul.*, iii. pp. 620, 624). Letter from Clement VII. to P. d'Ailly (*Ibid.*, 483 and 485). Letter from B. Alaman to d'Ailly about his treatise *de scismate*, (*Ibid.*, p. 600). Letter from P. d'Ailly to Henry von Langenstein, and the latter's reply (*Ibid.*, p. 637).

[3] MS. of Cambrai Library, No. 531, f. 203 verso. Tschackert and Valois are mistaken in thinking that this discourse was uttered during the embassy of which d'Ailly had just been given charge in 1398 (*Peter von Ailli*, p. 353). But the orator says that the Schism has lasted sixteen years, so that this document must date from 1394. Before 1843, Pertz had already noted this MS. at Cambrai (*Archiv.*, viii. 431).

of the Romans; but in these speeches there is no mention of the way of *cession*. Was it that just then he judged it better to reserve this delicate subject for the private conversations he was to have with Benedict? Was it that he already read the secret thought of the Pope, and distrusted his sincerity? [1]

What was the adroit Pontiff's reply? It appears that it was simply to gain time, and that d'Ailly received no positive assurances. In fact, on his return to Paris, the ambassador, after having given the King an account of his secret mission, appeared in the midst of the great assembly of the clergy, held at the royal mansion of St Paul, February 1, 1395. Peter d'Ailly again highly extolled the way of *cession* as the most expeditious, the most simple, and the most advantageous.[2] The meeting approved, and next day eighty-seven prelates out of a hundred and nine declared for the same method. They expressed a similar opinion in the instructions given to the messengers the King meant to send to Avignon. "If the Pope will accept this means," they added, "it will be necessary to inform the princes who belong to the Roman Pontiff's obedience before letting the intruder Boniface know himself. If he

[1] In this MS. are traces of *concetti* that are frequent in rhetorical works of the period. D'Ailly says to the Pope: "Fiet pax ista vera utique et perfecta si sit *misericordia in affectu* quantum ad inchoationis ingressum, si sit *veritas in effectu* quantum ad mediationis progressum, si sit *justitia in profectu* quantum ad consummationis egressum." But it contains no mention of the way of *cession*. Yet it is certain that he spoke of it to Benedict, for the Duke of Burgundy makes allusion to such a communication in 1398, when a new withdrawal of obedience is at stake. But the Duke is mistaken when he asserts that this request was made in full consistory. *Cf. Choix de pièces inédites* par Douet-d'Arcq, i. p. 145.

[2] *Chronic. Karoli VI.*, lib. xv. c. 11. Hefele, *History of the Councils*, x. p. 87. Jarry, *Louis de France*, p. 131.

refuses, the sovereigns will have an excellent resource against him: withdrawal of obedience."[1]

Alas! it was against the obstinate Benedict, and not against Boniface, that the French clergy would soon have to enforce this rigorous measure. The solemn embassy which was to leave for Avignon was composed of the Dukes of Berry and Burgundy, the Duke of Orleans, the King's brother, as well as of a brilliant company of nobles and professors of the University. On May 21, the delegates reached Villeneuve-lez-Avignon, and next day they were received with apparent friendliness by the Pope. Benedict was already distrustful of such counsels as he might get from Paris. Also a few days later, when the embassy ventured to ask him again for the text of the oath the future Pope had taken before the conclave like the other cardinals, the Pontiff at first refused. But when urged energetically by the deputies, he finally consented to allow it to be copied.[2]

[1] *Chronic.*, lib. xv. c. 12. Valois, iii. p. 36.

[2] *Chronic. Karoli VI.*, lib. xvi. c. 2. In the whole of this narrative I shall follow the document discovered by Father Franz Ehrle, S.J., in the Calvet Museum at Avignon. This text, published in 1889 in the *Archiv für Literatur und Kirchengeschichte des Mittelalters*, is much more complete than that of Baluze (*Informatio seriosa*, *Vitae Pap. Avenion.*, ii. col. 1107).

Certain reserves, however, should be made, for this document is brought forward by one of Benedict's partisans, who sets himself to justify all the Avignon Pontiff's actions to his contemporaries and to posterity. Father Ehrle has collated his text, which is of a later date, with that of Baluze and with a Vatican MS. The Roman document, like that of Baluze, dates from 1399. The original edition has undergone erasures and modifications, which are very strongly substantiated in the second text published by Ehrle, and drawn up in 1408. Benedict's position was changed, and that was why these alterations were made.

The first part of the documents given by the learned Jesuit contains, after the introduction, the first period of Benedict's government until the Treaty of Château-Renard (1394-1403). The second contains an account of negotiations with Gregory XII. (1404-1408). The third relates the rupture of the negotiations, Benedict's flight, and the circumstances that

This obstinate and equivocal resistance can only be explained by supposing that Benedict had already no intention of keeping his promise. He was anxious that the official document he had signed should not be able to be used against him.

§ 3. *The Pontiff's Designs.*

What the Avignon Pope wanted, as he soon declared to the ambassadors, was a joint-conference between himself and Boniface and their respective colleges of cardinals in a safe place not far from France and under the King's protection. "This new way," it was claimed by Benedict, "is wiser and easier than cession."[1]

A few days later, Gilles des Champs[2] answered him in the name of the King's envoys. He urgently begged the Pope to adopt the means proposed by the court of Paris. "It is the King's express wish," added the Duke de Berry. "If that be so," answered the Pope, "let Charles give me his written notification of it." "There is no need of writing," said Gilles des Champs; "the whole of our proposals may be summed up in one word: *cession*." "I want the requisite time and leisure for reflection," replied Benedict at last. "More-

characterised the pseudo-council of Perpignan (1408-1409). The manuscript found by Ehrle modifies all the facts hitherto acknowledged in several points, and fills up some important gaps.

[1] *Chronic.*, c. 3. VALOIS, iii. p. 48.

[2] He was from Rouen diocese. First educated at the Collège d'Harcourt and a master of arts, he became a doctor of theology in 1383. Then he was rector of the College of Navarre in 1389. Made a cardinal with P. d'Ailly on June 6, 1411, he held the administration of the Church of Coutances, of which he had been appointed bishop, October 2, 1409. He died at Rouen in 1413.

over, I assure you that I am still most ready to secure the peace of the Church."

The cardinals, gathered at Villeneuve and consulted by the ambassadors, each gave their opinion on the point. They also rejected the Pope's evasions, and all were for the great word: *cession*. The only exception was the Cardinal of Pampeluna, who openly pronounced in favour of the "way of action," and called for the use of force. "The true way according to God and right," he said, "the way to restore peace and union to the Church, is to expel the intruder by armed force as far as possible." [1]

In spite of all this opposition, the Pope continued his tergiversation and hesitation. He had prepared a bull, and he handed a copy of it to the Dukes. "The way of *cession*," he said in it, "is not admissible in law as a means of putting an end to schisms. It has never been employed, but on the contrary always rejected as unsuitable. Any innovation in this direction would be prejudicial to the Church, and make a regrettable precedent." [2]

Then Benedict set forth his own plan, which was, as has been said, to have an interview with his rival and the cardinals of the other side, so that they might respectively explain their reasons. "If the interview leads to no result," he added, "let an arbitration tribunal be formed, and let it decide either unanimously or by a majority of two-thirds." The Avignon Pope was already beginning to give proofs of that unhappy obstinacy in which he was to continue till the day of his

[1] Ehrle, pp. 23-28. *Cf. The Embassy Minutes*, by Goutier Col, the King's secretary. *Veterum scriptorum amplissima collectio,* vii. pp. 466, 472, and 492. The cardinal was called Martin de Salva.

[2] *Chronic. Karoli VI.*, lib. xvi. c. 4 and 5.

death. He resisted all the entreaties of the Sacred College and the Embassy.

He was even accused of having the famous bridge between Avignon and Villeneuve burnt down, so that the dukes who lived there "might not have an opportunity of coming to him," says the irascible John Petit, who formed part of the legation.[1] He went so far as to refuse to receive the delegates of the University in public audience. The latter, it was said, asked for one at hours and places which did not suit the Pontiff. Was this a reason or an excuse?

As lavish of the property of the Church as he was sparing of his own, he offered the dukes to conquer and take possession of the countries that constituted the Pontifical patrimony in Italy, and which, moreover, were not under his dominion as yet. In this he only followed the somewhat dishonourable proceedings of his predecessor, who sixteen years before had given up the Kingdom of Adria to the Duke of Anjou.

The uncles of the King of France scornfully replied that they had no need of his assistance. While this was going on, the relations between the ambassadors and the cardinals became more and more friendly and frequent. In Avignon they often met in the Cordeliers' monastery, and they planned together what requests and replies they should send to the Pope. In all these cautious negotiations, the details of which would be tiresome, the Pontiff clearly sought only to gain time and tire out the royal envoys. A last interview took place in which they could get no concession from the inflexible Benedict, notwithstanding his most solemn pledges (July 8).[2]

[1] Speech at Paris University, 1408. *Cf.* Ehrle, p. 475.

[2] *Chronic. Karoli VI.*, lib. xv. c. 14. Jouvenel des Ursins, a. 1395. Michaud collection, p. 400. Valois, iii. p. 62.

Before leaving the papal palace, the dissatisfied dukes convoked the cardinals and several other persons whom they had chosen. All met on July 9, 1395. Four orators harangued the crowd in the name of the King and of the University, and endeavoured to justify their conduct and censure that of the Pontiff. As for the cardinals, they were almost all won over to the King's side; all their benefices were in France: their supplies were threatened and their zeal corresponded with their interests.

§ 4. *The Displeasure of the King of France and the other Rulers.*

From this period, the new Pope only seemed to use his ability, which was great, his knowledge, which was profound, and his tenacity, which was astounding, in finding out political expedients or legal subtleties to put off the day of his downfall. One of his historians puts him down as *homo contentiosus*.[1]

First, the obedience of Avignon began to doubt the Pope's promises and to distrust his good faith. Jouvenel des Ursins takes note of this state of mind. "Many suspected that it was all make-believe," he writes of Benedict, "that he said one thing and meant another."[2]

There was no backwardness in accusing him, when he was seen to be multiplying difficulties. The impetuous John Petit loudly denounced him later on at the Council of Paris: "The Pope of Avignon only follows his own wishes," said he in a vehement prosecuting speech.

[1] *Auctor Vitae Innoc. VII.* apud MURATORI, iii. 836. John Petit's speech in the Council in 1406. *Cf.* BOURGEOIS DU CHASTENET, *Nouvelle histoire du Concile de Constance*, Preuves, p. 107.

[2] *Histoire de Charles VI.*, p. 387.

"He has owned more than once that he would rather beg for bread than give in."[1]

Still less respectful was the Archbishop of Reims when he added a few days later: "Benedict comes from a good mule-country: when they take to a road, it is easier to skin them than to get them to turn back."[2]

When the ambassadors had returned to Paris after a hundred and twenty days' useless negotiations,[3] King Charles saw clearly that he could not count upon the Pontiff of Avignon for the restoration of peace to the Catholic world. He decided thenceforward to join with other Christian princes for the object "of bringing the ship of the Church safe to port," as the monk of St Denis observed.

At the close of 1395, on the advice of the University, he sent a deputation to the archbishops and German princes, but it soon returned without having accomplished anything. An embassy to England was courteously received by Richard II., who then desired the hand of the young Isabel of France. The King promised to work for union, but advised the deputies not to open up relations with the University of Oxford, which was heartily on the side of the Italian Pope.[4] In reality, England did nothing to help Avignon.

Next year, Charles VI. sent ambassadors again to all the neighbouring princes. The King of the Romans at that time was the drunken and debauched Wenceslas. As an old translator of Boccacio said of him: "he had no remembrance of the marvellous exploits of

[1] Bourgeois du Chastenet, *op. cit.*, Preuves, p. 117.

[2] *Ibid.*, pp. 147 and 226.

[3] Bibl. Nat. MS. f. 10,431, 594. They returned to Paris, August 24, 1395.

[4] *Chronic.*, c. 14.

his predecessors, and loved the glory of Bacchus of Thebes more than he added splendour to the Italian Mars."[1]

Such a prince could not be zealous for the cause of union. He refused to receive the delegates of the University, but nevertheless welcomed the envoys of the King with a certain amount of courtesy, and promised to deliberate over their proposals.[2]

The King of Hungary was more definite, and approved the way of *cession.* So did the archbishops of Trèves and Cologne, and the archdukes of Austria and Bavaria. In another direction, the sovereigns of the Spanish peninsula gave some encouragement to the designs of the King of France.[3]

Meanwhile, news came to France (December 25, 1396) of the sanguinary defeat of John the Fearless at Nicopolis and of the dearly purchased victory of the Sultan Bajazet. The stupor resulting from the unsuccess of this chivalrous enterprise and solicitude for the liberation of the French prisoners were a hindrance to the prosecution of the great matter of putting an end to the Schism. The ambassadors of France, England, and Castile only went to see the Pope towards the middle of June 1397. Benedict again refused to listen to pacific counsels, and put forward as an alternative his plan of compromise.[4] The French representatives, that

[1] *Histoire littéraire de la France,* xxiv. p. 141. According to P. Paris, French MSS., i. p. 254. Bliemetzrieder, *Studien und Mittheilungen* (1903).

[2] The ambassadors reported on their mission to the Parisian Synod, (Aug. 16-31, 1396). I say no more of this assembly for fear of complicating my narrative. Though there were forty-three prelates present, it produced no result.

[3] *Chronic. Karoli VI.,* lib. xvii. c. 1, 5, 11, 18. Du Boulay, iv. p. 773. Raynald, *Foedera* (Feb. 13 and Aug. 17).

[4] *Chronic. Karoli VI.,* lib. xvii. c. 33. *Cf.* Ehrle, p. 422.

is to say, Gilles des Champs, John Courtecuisse,[1] and the Chevalier de Calleville, were very dissatisfied when the way of *cession* was once more rejected. Calleville made a solemn announcement to the obstinate Benedict: "If by Candlemas," he said, "the Church is not ruled by a single Pastor, the King of France will take energetic and efficacious measures."[2]

The deputies then went to see Boniface at Rome. He, like his competitor of Avignon, intrenched himself behind pleas in bar, and only sought to gain time. "I will examine the matter at leisure with my brethren the cardinals," he said. "I will consult the princes within my jurisdiction, and then I will inform the sovereigns who have sent you of my decisions."

About the same time Wenceslas, urged more and more by the King of France, and impelled from another side by the University of Prague, resolved to quit the cause of the Roman Pope, to brave the dissatisfaction of a few nobles, and to agree to an interview with Charles VI. at Reims, to work together for the restoration of religious peace.[3]

The French sovereign, delighted with this decision, went to meet the King of the Romans, and conducted him in state to Reims, March 31, 1398. He gave him great presents, and offered him magnificent entertainments, which more than once put the sobriety of the German prince to the proof.

In a moment of presence of mind, Wenceslas promised the King of France to bestir himself with Pope Boniface

[1] "Breviscoxa." He was afterwards Bishop of Paris, then of Geneva. *Cf.* Launoy, *Navarr. Gymn. Historia*, p. 264.

[2] Hefele, *History of Councils*, x. p. 104. Martène et Durand, *Vet. Script. nova collectio*, vii. pp. 556 and 622. Christophe, *Histoire de la Papauté pendant le XIVe Siècle*, iii. p. 164.

[3] Cambrai Library, 940, f. 42 ff.

to beg him to abdicate. He had at hand a negotiator of special fitness: Peter d'Ailly had given up the see of Puy [1] to take possession of that of Cambrai. As Count of Cambresis, he had just taken an oath of fealty to the King of the Romans (April 3, 1398). Wenceslas begged him to betake himself to Avignon to get the way of *cession* accepted there.[2]

Peter d'Ailly took his departure immediately, taking with him Wenceslas' intimate private secretary, Nicholas of Jewicka. When he reached Benedict's court, he was received in public consistory, in the presence of the cardinals, prelates, and a large number of laymen. He spoke and made a speech full of gentleness, facility, and captivating wit. "The King of the Romans," he said, "agrees with the King of France in urging you to restore the peace of the Church, and to realise the holy aspirations you have so long manifested." [3] The Bishop of Cambrai plainly takes the liberty of reminding the Pontiff of the promises he had made at the time of his election.[4]

[1] He had been appointed to Puy in succession to Itier de Martreuil, April 2, 1395, but he never went there. His translation to Cambrai was made by a bull dated Nov. 15, 1396, and he took the oath of allegiance at Soissons, June 5, 1397.

[2] *Archiv. Vatic.*, Arm. lxiii. t. 85, p. 30.

[3] Cambrai Library, MS. 531, f. 205-208.

[4] There are three authentic proofs of this embassy. The first is in the speech of Peter Ravat, Bishop of Saint-Pons, at the Council of Paris, May 29, 1398, a month after the event. The second is in a memorial against the two Popes read before the 5th session of the Council of Pisa, April 24, 1409 (Hardouin, viii. col. 60; Mansi, xxvi. col. 1198). The third is in a similar document read at the 32nd session of the Council of Constance (Hardouin, viii. col. 772; Mansi, xxvii. col. 1083). Froissart's account (xvi. p. 116) is in every way erroneous. It puts d'Ailly's embassy in September, whilst it took place in April. He thinks the Bishop of Cambrai was sent by the King of France as well as by the King of the Romans, and adds that he was accompanied by the Marshal de Boucicaut, so that everything he affirms is mistaken. Lastly, like

The Pope replied to this pressing invitation now in the most definite way. "Never," said he, "have I consented to the method of *cession*, and never will I do so. I believe it would be a mortal sin to use this means."

These words largely upset those who were present. They saw that every hope of reaching a settlement in this direction was vanishing. Moreover, they all remembered an emphatic utterance of Benedict's, which he had addressed a year previously to the Chevalier Louis de Tignonville: "The King wants to force *cession* upon me: I shall do nothing of the kind. I would rather be flayed alive than cede."[1]

Did Peter d'Ailly and his companions go to Rome, as Froissart asserts, and he is followed in his statement by several historians? Did they hear the words which the inventive chronicler puts into the Pope's mouth: "My children," he makes the Pope say to the people, take comfort and assurance from my resolve to remain Pope, and whatever the kings of France and Germany and their counsellors may have said and done, I shall not submit to their will."[2]

The reality of this journey has been much and justly called in question. It is, however, certain that the

---

Livy, he puts into the mouth of a bishop, who was indeed a devoted partisan of Benedict's, a speech that was an insolent ultimatum. The chronicler of Valenciennes, who was on special terms with his neighbour, the Bishop of Cambrai, ought to have remembered that the latter did not abandon the cause of the Avignon Pope until much later, towards 1408.

Finally, it is to be noted that the cardinals, writers, or editors of the two latter documents took an active part in all these negotiations. Hence the official accounts are much more reliable than Froissart's sometimes fanciful stories.

[1] Bourgeois du Chastenet, *op. cit.*, Texte, p. 24; Preuves, p. 36.

[2] Froissart, xvi. pp. 86 and 117. *Cf.* Martène et Durand, vii., Preface, p. lii. Tschackert, *Peter von Ailli*, p. 103. Raynald, a. 1409, No. 50. Valois, iii. p. 135.

Bishop of Cambrai returned to Wenceslas, and that the latter sent to Paris to inform Charles of the negative reply he had received from Benedict.[1] Then the King thought that an energetic line should be adopted, and that the Church should be saved, as he maintained, without the Popes and in their despite.

§ 5. *The Withdrawal of Obedience.*

However, Charles did not wish to undertake this grave responsibility alone. He convoked all the clergy with the professors of the University at Paris. On May 22, 1398, eleven archbishops, sixty bishops, thirty abbots, a large number of inferior prelates, and representatives of the Universities of the realm met in one of the halls of the royal palace.

The masterful Patriarch of Alexandria,[2] Simon of Cramaud, spoke first and set forth the state of the case since the death of Clement VII., and the efforts made by the King of France to attain peace by the way of *cession*. "Since Benedict obstinately refuses," he said, "we must find out whether the Church of France is going to throw off all obedience so far as he is concerned, or whether a partial withdrawal of allegiance would suffice to make the Avignon Pope reflect." Six commissioners were appointed to defend Benedict, and six

[1] Lindner, *Geschichte des deutschen Reichs unter König Wenzel II.*, p. 394.

[2] He played a great part in all these events. Coming from Orleans, he was appointed Bishop of Agen in 1382, of Béziers in 1383, and of Poitiers in 1385, and Patriarch of Alexandria in 1391. He was called to the see of Reims in 1409, by Alexander V., and made cardinal in 1413. Died 1423. His tomb was found in Poitiers Cathedral. *Cf.* Abbé Auber, *Relation*, 1859.

to set forth the grievances that might be brought against him.[1]

On May 29, Peter Ravat, the envoy of the Pontiff of Avignon, made a Latin speech to sustain his case. He asserted that Benedict must be obeyed in all his orders, however wrong he might be in conduct, and even if he were suspected of heresy, until he were declared to be heretical by a lawful sentence. He attempted to show the probable evil results of withdrawal and tried to exonerate Benedict from the charge of extortion that had been brought against him. "Moreover," he added, "even if the Pope gave in, many persons would doubt whether such a cession were valid. . . . The kings of France have always been protectors of the Pontiffs; sometimes they have restored them to their see; I cannot believe that Charles VI. will be the first to persecute them." Two others spoke in the same sense. Then the president, the Chevalier de Tignonville, and Professor Gilles des Champs maintained the opposite thesis: they uttered a good number of Gallican propositions, cited many legal passages, and quoted certain very mistaken historical precedents.[2] After a few replies, the University of Paris, by the mouth of Professor Peter Plaoul, declared against the Pope, and demanded an entire withdrawal of obedience.[3] The Universities of Angers, Montpellier, and Orleans declared in the same sense.

On July 28, in the midst of a fresh assembly, the

[1] Bourgeois du Chastenet, Texte, p. 8; Preuves, p. 4.

[2] *Cf.* Ehrle, *Archiv. für Literatur*, vi. p. 274 ff.

[3] Du Boulay, iv. p. 835. As to Plaoul, *cf.* Froissart, xvi. pp. 69 and 278. This prelate was one of the clergy of Liège, and the monk of St Denis says of him: "*In sacra pagina excellentissimus professor.*" Later on he was interpreter to the Sorbonne at the Council of Pisa. He died Bishop of Senlis, on April 11, 1415.

Chancellor of France, Arnaud de Corbie, spoke in the name of the King, and declared that, out of three hundred prelates called upon to vote, two hundred and forty-seven were for the entire abandonment of obedience, until the Pontiff of Avignon had effectively adopted the way of *cession*.[1] The Duke of Bourbon pronounced in the same sense ; the Dukes of Burgundy, Berry, the Count of Alençon, the Duke of Lorraine, and others also acquiesced in this decision.[2]

M. Noël Valois maintains, contrary to generally accepted opinion, that the withdrawal of obedience was only voted by a rather narrow majority of the clergy, viz. about three-fifths of the meeting, and even that because of royal pressure. The Duke of Orleans and thirty prelates demanded that a fresh summons should be sent to Benedict. Others to the number of fifty pronounced in different ways. This eminent historian, who has discovered and counted the voting-papers, therefore accuses the Chancellor of having falsified the returns of the ballot, of having lent himself to a sharp piece of juggling, and of having led the Gallican Church into error.[3]

At this same important session the Chancellor, on the King's behalf, forbade anyone to speak directly or in-

[1] *Chronic. Karoli VI.*, lib. xix. c. 2, 6. Mansi, xxvi. p. 90. Du Boulay, iv. p. 848. Bourgeois du Chastenet, p. 51.

[2] These notes were published by Douet-d'Arcq, *Choix des pièces inédites*, i. pp. 142-149. French History Society (1863). *Cf.* Jarry, *Louis de France*, pp. 207, 439.

As to the divisions of opinion at this time, see a letter of one of Benedict's confidants, recently discovered by Father Ehrle in a Vatican MS. (*Archiv.*, vii. p. 102).

[3] *La France et le grand Schisme d'Occident*, iii. p. 173. An important document published by Father Ehrle (*Archiv.*, vii. p. 79) says : "Non fuerunt publicatae voces in substractione quando fuit facta, quia multi, ut dicitur, erant contradicentes."

directly against the decisions adopted. The Duke of Berry went further. "Whoever," he said, "is rash enough to venture upon such an attack will be deprived of his benefice, if he is a member of the clergy. If he be a layman, he shall be handed over to the secular arm for exemplary punishment."[1] Thus exaggerated threats were used to uphold an illegitimate decision, which the energy of Benedict would make futile.

A few days later, on August 8, Charles VI. declared the collations made by the Pope[2] null and void, and placed the confirmation of monastic appointments in the hands of the bishops.[3]

On August 22, an organic law ordained that, during the withdrawal of obedience, all records should date from the year of Benedict's election and no longer from the current year of his pontificate.[4] France hoped not to be alone, and to drag several other kingdoms of the West in her defection.

Thus the rupture between the Court on the one hand, and the Avignon Pontiff on the other, was a *fait accompli*. But what would the French cardinals do ?

On the first of September, two royal councillors, Robert Cordelier and Tristan du Bosc, arrived at Villeneuve, near Avignon, to notify the Pope of the Royal decrees. They had them published at once, and ordered all French subjects, whether clergy or lay-folk, to abandon the Avignon obedience. Most of the cardinals did not hesitate : they came to join the royal envoys at Villeneuve and gave their adhesion to the withdrawal of obedience. Nevertheless seven of them refused :

[1] *Chronic. Karoli VI.*, lib. xix. c. 2. Bourgeois du Chastenet, p. 52.
[2] Martène et Durand, *Thesaurus*, ii. p. 1153.
[3] *Chronic.*, c. 4. *Archives nat.*, J. 508, f. 291.
[4] Martène et Durand, *loc. cit.*

five took refuge in the palace of the Doms with the Pope, and two withdrew to their own homes.[1] All who had posts at the pontifical court imitated the example of the majority of the Sacred College, and the citizens of Avignon also gave up the side of Benedict, who began to fortify himself in the palace of the Doms. How was he to be forced to recognise the decisions of the Council?

In the South of France there was at this time an impecunious adventurer whose violent and warlike nature had already won him an unenviable reputation. Ready for every desperate enterprise, even the most disreputable, he was above all covetous of ecclesiastical property. It was natural that such a highwayman should eagerly seize an opportunity which was so favourable to making a fortune without running much risk.[2] Still he was a king's chamberlain, and bore a name that his eldest brother was to make famous. He was Geoffrey de Boucicault.[3]

[1] Ehrle, p. 424. *Chronic. Karoli VI.*, lib. xix. c. 8. *Cf.* P. Doizé, *Études religieuses*, 1903, p. 378.

[2] Valois, iii. p. 194.

[3] Froissart, xvi. p. 121. One can hardly understand how Froissart, Jouvenel des Ursins, and many other historians after them, made the mistake of identifying the great Boucicault with the common *condottiere*, his younger brother. Froissart, too, was a friend of Peter d'Ailly, and must have been informed by him about the siege of Avignon, and the embassy, of which, he says, the bishop was in charge.

At this time, John de Boucicault was at war, in the King's name, with the Count de Périgord, and had taken forcible possession of the castle in which his enemy had taken refuge (at the end of 1398, and beginning of 1399). Immediately afterwards he was sent to defend the Greeks against the onslaughts of Bajazet. So that he could not have been in command of the army that laid siege to, and then blockaded, the city of the Popes. The *Mémoires* of John de Boucicault, written by a contemporary, do not allude to the fact. It is scarcely to be understood how the cardinals took Geoffrey into their pay. It is he who imprisoned, and, in October 1398, disgracefully ransomed the cardinals of Pampeluna and St Adrian. Appointed governor of the Dauphiné in 1399, he was guilty of innumerable exactions, caused numerous complaints, and was excommunicated in

It was this mercenary blade who was summoned by the cardinals to their aid to treat the citizens of Avignon and the cardinals who were in revolt against the Pope with a high hand. Geoffrey came at once, and, at his call, from the mountains of Auvergne, Velay, and Vivarais, down swept all the adventurers who, ten years previously, under the command of Raymond, were all that was left of the *Great Bands* of hired braves who, to the number of three thousand, had formerly laid siege to Urban V. at Avignon. The investment of the papal city was about to begin.

Let us go back for a moment and inquire by what right the King and clergy had decided on the withdrawal of obedience. Many theologians and politicians of those days believed in the justice of this rigorous measure. The utility and the policy of the action were discussed rather than its lawfulness. If, at the Council of 1398, we listen to Benedict's accusers, Simon de Cramaud, Peter le Roy, and Peter Plaoul, all their arguments may be summed up thus: The Pope promised on his oath to agree to *cession*; but he is obstinate, and is suspected of heresy and schism. Hence it is not only lawful, but desirable and even necessary, to refuse to obey him. This withdrawal is the only way to secure union, for it is France that provides Benedict with all the indispens-

---

1404 by the Archbishop of Vienne (Chevalier, *Le Mystère des trois Doms*, p. 735). Later on, in 1424, Geoffrey was prosecuted by the King's command, for his crimes and misdeeds (*Histoire de Languedoc*, ix. p. 1077, Ed. 1885). In 1426 he begged and obtained from Martin V. complete pardon for the offences and depredations he had committed with his accomplices at Avignon and the county in 1398. This ruffian's repentance and resolution of amendment did not last long, for he began his outrages in the province at the beginning of 1428. He died in 1429.

Cf. Ehrle, *Archiv.*, v. p. 465. Chevalier, *Bulletin d'histoire eccl. de Valence* (1884-1885), p. 129. Delaville le Roulx, *La France en Orient*, i. p. 189.

able supplies. Taking them away from him is to deprive the Schism of its advocates, upholders, and advisers.

The King, continued these disrespectful prelates, has the right to resolve on withdrawal without troubling about the Pope's opposition. For, if all the faithful are bound to do their utmost to restore unity to the Church, still more so are all Christian princes. There is no need of a citation or a suit or a sentence, since Benedict's crime is notorious. Moreover, law provides many ways of obviating the disadvantages that might result from this revolt.[1] They could do without the Pontiff and apply to the primates for reserved cases, dispensations for marriages, nominations of bishops, etc.[2] Such, then, was the unfortunate position of the Church. She was abandoned by the King, and the conduct of Charles and his councillors was considered as just and lawful by the prelates themselves. Already, twenty years previously, Charles V. had supported the rebel cardinals when the election of a fresh Pope was in question. To-day, Charles' son allied himself with the Sacred College to overthrow the successor of the Pontiff whom his father had recognised and upheld. From the election at Fondi, the intruded Pope of Avignon had put himself under the patronage of the King of France. To-day the sovereign, who only ought to be an external bishop, became a Pope within. Secular authority took the sway over men's consciences and claimed to withdraw them from pontifical power.

Through a phenomenon that was happily almost unique in its history, our country was about to break

[1] Bourgeois du Chastenet, p. 15. Preuves, p. 17 ff. *Cf.* Ehrle, *Archiv.*, vii. p. 72.

[2] Ehrle, *Ibid.*, pp. 92 and 103.

off all relations with the supreme authority in religion of its own accord. It had never recognised the Pope of Rome, and was about to repudiate him of Avignon.

It would be necessary to trace down our annals to the worst days of the Revolution before France would see a similar crisis, and become at the same time witness and victim of so strange a situation. For five years the power of the Pope was non-existent so far as she was concerned.

It may be declared and affirmed that the King of France, or rather those who spoke in his name, evidently outran their authority. No doubt the Avignon Pope was doubtful in law, but in fact the Gallican Church had formally recognised him several times. In breaking with Benedict, France made a schism within the Schism, and sowed the germs of division, which were formulated at Constance in 1415, and at Paris in 1682. The assembly of 1398 inaugurated a sort of civil constitution of the clergy, and prepared the way for a kind of national Church in the narrowest and most schismatic sense of the word, a Church like that of Byzantium, Moscow, or London. It paved the way for the despotic proceedings that Napoleon would afterwards carry out with regard to Pius VII.

It went even farther than the Emperor dared to go. What can be said of this order issued by the Council of Paris in 1398? "As to those who scruple in conscience as to obeying the decree of withdrawal, it is laid down that they are bound to conform to the King's resolution, and to put their scruples on one side, and if they would not do so, the King would provide for it, and ought so to provide." Thus, everything that was taken from the Pope was benevolently granted to the King, Charles VI., the least intelligent prince who had ever ruled in France.

He it was who thus laid violent hands on people's consciences, and became the chief director of souls, and claimed to point out to the clergy themselves what they ought to believe about the gravest matters. Without the least scruple he was granted an infallibility that was laic, but unlimited. The monarch, or rather the high chancellor of France, thus was made for five years the arbiter of the Church, and her director in all her ways, and acted as if he were the real French Pope.[1]

[1] Du Boulay, iv. pp. 882, 883.

CHAPTER IX

THE CHURCH OF FRANCE DURING THE WITHDRAWAL OF OBEDIENCE

§ 1. *The Siege of Avignon.*

Avignon was not only the sumptuous abode of the French Popes, the city ringing with a thousand belfries; it was also a first-class fortress, of which the massive towers and battlemented walls, four yards thick, even to-day astonish the world. The ready pen and quick imagination of a child of Provence thus describes the city of the Popes: "Nations drank at the Rhone," says Mistral; "churches, chapels, and oratories were counted there by thousands. In continual motion the carillons of a hundred belfries resounded joyfully all through the town, and during the night the corners of the streets shone with illuminated madonnas.

"Astride of the rocky escarpment, the enormous castle that reaches the clouds flung into the sky the colossal mass of its seven hard stone towers, the mouldings of which looked like those of a habitation for giants. The colossal structure was reflected in the river that flowed below it, and its height commanded the vast surrounding plain. Striding over the swollen Rhone, like a road of triumphal arches, a stone bridge of unheard-of height and length linked together France and Provence, Villeneuve and Avignon. When the awful sounds of the mistral made themselves heard over the city, you would have said that God's breath was on its way to distribute the Pope's blessing amongst the nations." [1]

The pontifical palace is to-day one of the wonders of mediæval architecture and the glory of Avignon. "Both fortress and monastery, prison and palace, the provisional residence of the Popes is curiously like a faithful picture of the lot that befell the Papacy in France, and of its declension. It is at once a pontifical prison and a feudal castle of the period when the chiefs of Christendom took without blushing the rôle of vassal to the King of France, and the title of Count of Venaissin and Avignon." [2] If at any time this was a true picture, it was so when Geoffrey de Boucicault came to besiege and then to blockade Benedict XIII. in the palace built by Benedict XII. and strongly fortified by Clement VII.

In September 1398, Avignon, as has been said, was by no means inclined to make resistance.[3] The people of the town cried out loudly that they neither could nor would maintain a war against France. Benedict answered them: "Your city is strong and well-provisioned. Defend yourselves. Sooner or later I shall get relief from Aragon, my native country, or

[1] Mistral, *Nerto*, a Provençal tale.

[2] Pastor, *Histoire des Papes*, i. p. 98.

[3] It has been said that Froissart's otherwise picturesque story of Peter d'Ailly's embassy at Avignon, just before the siege began, to deliver an ultimatum in the name of the King of France, is untenable (xvi. p. 121). This account has been refuted by Ehrle (*Archiv.*, 1889, v. pp. 394-492). *Cf. History of the Councils*, Hefele, 2nd Ed. German by Alois Knoepfler, (Freibourg, 1890), vi. p. 855, n. 2. The *Chronic. Karoli VI.* does not speak of this embassy. No doubt Froissart confused it with the mission of the month of April, spoken of in the last chapter, p. 163. See an interesting letter of King Martin of Aragon in Döllinger, *Beiträge*, iii. 353.

from elsewhere. I will be responsible for the defence of my palace."[1]

Indeed, the energetic Pontiff was ready. He had long before had the formidable papal castle put into a state of defence. The halls in which Petrarch had sung resounded with the cries of sentries; cupboards, formerly filled with precious manuscripts, were stored with swords and bolts; and the Gothic windows with their broad bays, whence John XXII. and Urban V. delighted in watching the majestic banks of the Rhone, were changed into narrow loop-holes, whence Benedict's two hundred Aragon soldiers surveyed and disturbed the besiegers.

Thanks to the efforts of Boucicault and his adventurers, the county of Venaissin was in full revolt; the people of Avignon cared little about the defence of their Pontiff; either of their own accord or under pressure they openly took the side of the fugitive cardinals. They opened their gates to the enemies' troops, committed more than one act of violence, and joined in the attack on the fortified palace. The Cardinal of Neufchâtel, forgetful of his dignity and of the oaths that bound him to the Pope, went further than all the others, riding through the town on horseback and in armour, and exciting the people to rebellion. All the people vied with one another in crying out, "Long live the Sacred College." "Long live the city of Avignon."[2] A few days later the Cardinal was himself smitten with fatal sickness, and many thought his sudden death was a divine punishment. The mines had been carried below the towers, and bombards and crossbows were incessantly

[1] *Chronic. Karoli VI.*, lib. xix. c. 8; lib. xx. c. 5. Martène et Durand, *Vet. Script.*, vii., Preface, p. lxii. Baluze, ii. p. 1122.

[2] *Cf.* Ehrle, v. p. 427; vii. pp. 180, 234. Baluze, ii. p. 1123.

discharging great stones and bolts. Benedict, who energetically directed the defence, was wounded by the splinter of a stone in one of these attacks. Wherever he turned, there was no ruler inclined to give him consolation or afford him help.

Indeed, many princes and towns had followed the example of France, and forsaken their obedience to the Pontiff of Avignon.

Mary, Queen of Naples, had abandoned him;[1] Castile and Navarre henceforward refused to obey; in the North, Cambrai and Besançon, depending on the Empire, broke the bonds that tied them to Benedict. On the other hand, his confessor St Vincent Ferrier had not been willing to be shut up with him in the citadel the French were endeavouring to capture. He strongly disapproved this armed resistance. Everything seemed to be wanting to Benedict at the same time, and the fortress of Avignon, which he had so well provided with food and arms, was every day more closely pressed. A vast store of wood had been burnt by the Greek fire that was flung by the besiegers, helped by the revolters[2] of Avignon; the garrison was unable to cook its food, fresh provisions were wanting, wine and remedies were lacking, and illness began to spread amongst the besieged.

The obstinate Pontiff then seemed to be ready to negotiate. Three of the cardinals who had remained with him,[3] on October 24, had an interview with three who had left him, to come to an arrangement. They could not come to terms: the treacherous Geoffrey de Boucicault kept the three negotiator cardinals as hostages

[1] *Vet. Script. nova collectio,* vii. p. 600 ff.
[2] *Cf.* Ehrle, vii. pp. 68 and 200.
[3] *Ibid.,* vii. p. 70.

in his camp, and held them in captivity in his castle at Borbon, where he usually resided.[1] They were the Cardinals of Pampeluna, Buyl, and St Adrian.

On the 26th of the same month, a captain of Geoffrey's troops, named Richard, nearly took the castle by surprise. He had found that it was possible to get into the place by the kitchen drains. He had the audacity to slip in through this opening, and his men followed him one by one. A victory was about to spring out of these hollow recesses, when the soldiers of the Pope, warned, as by miracle, says the chronicle,[2] came up and seized these rash assailants. A little later they discovered the mines, and hindered the besiegers from blowing up the walls of the castle of the Doms.

On the other hand, an attempt made by some Catalonians, who were the Pope's friends, to raise the blockade of the town by using the Rhone water, had miserably failed. Geoffrey made no headway, but death was decimating Benedict's troops. Nearly a hundred people had been victims of the hostilities, and the besiegers were as tired as the besieged of the ravages and slowness of the siege. They agreed to cease hostilities on both sides and to conclude a temporary truce.

§ 2. *Paris Opinion becomes more Moderate.*

Meanwhile three cardinals, those of Preneste,[3] Thury, and Saluces, betook themselves to Paris to compass fresh rigorous measures against the besieged Pontiff. But public opinion had changed, and the ideas of the King and court had undergone a complete revolution.

[1] *Ibid.*, v. p. 429; vii. pp. 70 and 180.

[2] *Ibid.*, vii. p. 198.

[3] This was Guy de Malesset, who in 1383 had given up his title of Cardinal of Poitiers for that of Preneste.

There was no wish to carry things to extremes, and the partisans of violence daily became fewer.

The three members of the Sacred College were received more than coldly by the nobles and people, who so far forgot themselves as to insult them openly.[1]

The prelates, indeed, had not hesitated to pronounce Benedict guilty of heresy, injustice, perjury, and dissoluteness. They had accused him of bringing dishonour upon the office of Pope. Such conduct towards the Pontiff whom they had helped to elect, and the excessive care of the cardinals for their own interests, conduced to bring back public sympathy to the persecuted and wronged Pope.

On February 20, 1399, an assembly of the clergy was held at Paris.[2]

The King began by asking for subsidies to meet the expenses incurred by the business connected with the union of the Church. The prelates granted tithe payable by all holders of benefices and even from monasteries that were exempted; but at the same time they demanded that the clergy, and not the King's officers, should be entrusted with collecting it. The Dukes accepted the proposal, at the same time remarking that the sum thus obtained would not be sufficient. Moreover, and perhaps by way of compensation, the prelates of their own accord abolished all the debts they had to pay to the apostolic Chamber, as well as all expectancies, whether they came from Clement or from Benedict. The cardinals protested energetically, but without success.

[1] *Chronic. Karoli VI.*, lib. xix. c. 12; lib. xx. c. 2.

[2] The monk of St Denis' narrative only hints part of the truth. The true character of this meeting comes out in the letter of one of the clergy, apparently on the side of the dissentient cardinals. It was written from Paris, and addressed to the members of the Sacred College who had stayed in Avignon. EHRLE, p. 41.

The University showed itself particularly eager in making claims on behalf of its partisans. More than a thousand of them were on the lists of benefices presented to the Pope (*rotuli*). Every day they made clamorous and fresh demands in the midst of the assembly. Certain prelates, as full of shame as of sorrow, left the meeting before it ended.[1]

In fine, this assembly had only to do with material interests. The prestige and authority of the clergy gained nothing at it. Royal pretensions increased directly in proportion to episcopal surrenders. The ambition of princes and the cupidity of courtiers were unlimited.[2]

Besides this, religious opinion began to be uneasy as to the treatment that was meted out to him whom the majority of Frenchmen still regarded as the true Pope. Furthermore, the chivalrous side of the several months' defence regained for Benedict the affection that his obstinacy had previously caused him to forfeit. No doubt the Pope enclosed at Avignon had a precarious position, " but he was not easily aghast at trifles," says Froissart, " and he kept within the palace, which is the fairest and the strongest house in the world, and the easiest to defend."

On the other hand, the friends whom Benedict had kept were not discouraged. The ambassadors of King Martin of Aragon [3] to the King of France had passed by way of Avignon and had seen themselves the distress of

[1] Ehrle, *Ibid.*, p. 43.

[2] *Chronic. Karoli VI.*, lib. xx. c. 2. *Cf.* Lesqueux et Mollat, *Mesures fiscales exercées en Bretagne par les Papes d'Avignon, Annales de Bretagne*, 1903, Rennes.

[3] Ehrle, vii. p. 15 ff., gives many details about this prince's part from 1397. He continued the constant defender of Benedict. *Cf.* Zurita, *Annales de la corona de Aragon*, x. p. 491.

the Pope. When they reached Paris, they gave an account of it to the court of King Charles. The King made the Pontiff proposals of peace, which were taken to Avignon by ambassadors.

On April 4, 1399, they offered them to Benedict that he might confirm their arrangements. Benedict, driven by necessity, in fact accepted the following points on April 10 :—

"If his opponent Boniface renounced the tiara, or died, or was driven out, the Pontiff of Avignon would abdicate in turn, so as to allow of the election of an undisputed Pope. If a meeting was held for securing union, Benedict would be bound to attend it.[1] In return, Charles was pledged to take Benedict under his protection with a hundred of his supporters, and to have him treated in a manner worthy of his rank. But it was stipulated that the Pope should not leave the pontifical residence without permission." The preliminaries of agreement were drawn up in these terms : prisoners were exchanged, the cardinals of Pampeluna and St Adrian were given up after having paid a ransom of 18,000 francs to the greedy Geoffrey, and the siege was changed into a kind of blockade. Benedict was to be confided to the keeping of the Duke Louis of Orleans, the King's brother, who was very devoted to him and had taken a great part in these negotiations.[2]

For four and a half years the Pontiff would thus remain a captive, and the question of unity was not to advance by a single step. Partial assemblies, long and learned dissertations, dark intrigues, embassies of cardinals and courts, and prolix discussions only resulted

[1] Ehrle, v. p. 438. Martène et Durand, vii. col. 636 ff.

[2] Douet-d'Arcq, *Choix de pièces inédites*, i. p. 203. Jarry, *Louis de France, Duc d'Orléans*, p. 225.

in drawing much sympathy to the persecuted Pontiff, and in increasing the ever-growing number of adversaries of the withdrawal of obedience, the advantages of which were clear to nobody.[1]

A correspondence, in August 1399, sent to Avignon from Paris by an agent of Benedict's, throws a great deal of light on the situation of the Pope as well as on the state of mind of the French at this time. This document, recently discovered by Father Ehrle in the Vatican Archives,[2] fills the lacunæ in the rare official reports that remain of these facts. Composed of very different materials, it was probably destined to provide the substance of a memorial which the Pope meant to address to his faithful friend the Duke of Orleans. I give a brief analysis : " All that is done against Benedict takes place in the name of the King and of the dukes. Therefore the royal family, noble and ancient as it is, becomes responsible for it at the bar of history. For the love of God, in the name of godliness, humanity, and religion, be on your guard. If you succeed in saving the Pope from a cruel and disgraceful death, you will win immortal glory."

Benedict's confidant enumerates, from the beginning of the siege of Avignon, the sacrilegious murders that accompanied the invasion, the acts of depredation and violence, the threats addressed to the inhabitants in the King's name, and the insults hurled at the Pontiff himself. Then he relates at length all the circumstances of the investment of the place, and gives interesting details about the meeting of the clergy, which resolved on the withdrawal of obedience.

" If Benedict dies," he adds, " or if cession is forced upon him, the position of the Church will be as bad as it

[1] EHRLE, vii. p. 102. [2] *Ibid.*, p. 59.

was under Celestine V., Boniface VIII., or John XXII. Let the Duke of Orleans readily accept the undertaking of watching over the Pope. Above all, this work should not be given to the dissentient members of the Sacred College."

The unknown author of the document then makes a very unflattering portrait of the Cardinal of Amiens, and especially of Cardinal Thury, whom he paints as avaricious, jealous, intriguing, and as particularly anxious to occupy the pontifical throne. It is he who falsified the messages which the Pope had intended for the King, and sent false letters from Paris to Avignon in the name of the royal council. "Benedict is better than they," he adds, "he has not fallen into the nepotism of his predecessor. If he is imprisoned or put to death, let the kingdom of France beware![1] It should have repented of the ill-treatment accorded by Philip to Pope Boniface; and still greater chastisement would have been inflicted on us, had not the Pontiffs of Avignon protected our country. Even now the French king's people treat Benedict as if he were a Jew or a Saracen; they persecute him in every possible way in his besieged palace."

Finally the author enumerates the means to be used to lift the Church and the Pope out of this false and dangerous situation.

This humble anonymous writer appears to me to give very valuable information as to the Pontiff's state of mind, and also as to that of certain cardinals, of some princes, and of all the principal actors in the great drama, the slow vicissitudes of which were being unfolded both at Avignon and Paris.

[1] Ehrle, vii. pp. 83 and 84.

§ 3. *Negotiations at Avignon and Rome.*

The Duke of Orleans, to whom doubtless this memorial was sent, cherished an intention of acting in accordance with the wishes expressed by Benedict, but above all he held to the Pope giving in his submission. He wanted the Pontiff to be obliged to condescend to all the wishes of the dukes, his uncles, and of the royal council.

Even in captivity Benedict took the highest care of his pontifical dignity. In October 1399 he declined the proposals of the Duke of Orleans with courtesy but with resolution. He accepted him as correspondent and friend, and even up to a certain point as protector, but he would not admit the troublesome patronage of the French court.[1]

At the end of 1399, or at the beginning of 1400, Benedict gave the Duke this reply through his ambassadors: "If I submit to the King's desires," he said, "I am sure to draw upon myself the animadversions of the Kings of Castile and Aragon, who are my protectors. On the other hand, the cardinals will not allow this decision to be left in the hands of a layman, and will not hesitate to reproach me for it. Lastly, among the royal councillors I have some determined enemies who will certainly oppose all suggestions that can be made."[2]

In conclusion, he asked the Duke to come to Avignon himself, or at any rate to get him letters of safe-conduct signed by the King.

Louis d'Orleans showed that he was little pleased with

[1] Ehrle, vii. p. 123 ff. The unedited papers printed by Father Ehrle, of which we give a summary, acquaint us with a number of incidents in the captivity of Benedict which were hitherto unknown, and also with the whole set of negotiations between the Pope and France.

[2] Ehrle, vii. p. 127. *Cf.* Martène et Durand, vii. col. 661.

this reply, which was too vague for his liking, and also with the pride that neither persecutions nor misfortunes had been able to destroy. He asked the Pope afresh by his ambassador, Peter Beaublé, Bishop of Uzès, whether he agreed to submit to the conditions originally proposed, yes or no, and whether he would meet the expense that would be incurred by the sending of a bodyguard (March 1400).

In a carefully calculated reply, Benedict informed the Duke that he accepted the second request, but that he wanted time for ripe reflection as to the first. On receiving fresh entreaties from the envoy, he replied that in July he would inform the Duke of his decision by trustworthy intermediaries.

As a matter of fact, on July 31, the Pope sent to Paris three monks commissioned to set forth to Louis d'Orleans all the sorrow and shame of his position. With all the forms of respect demanded by the necessity of the moment, Benedict declined the royal proposal afresh, and refused to submit unconditionally. At last the King of France consented to send official letters of safe-conduct for the Pope and the hundred persons in his retinue, and ordered the Duke of Orleans to protect the Pontiff (October 18, 1400).[1] Without going into tedious details of the negotiations that then ensued, let us recall one or two salient facts. A council was proposed at Metz, but the project broke down;[2] another attempt to assemble the bishops of the party of Avignon met with no better success. The dissentient cardinals persisted in their distrustful and contemptuous attitude towards the papal prisoner: and they had little regard for the King's intentions, though they energetically repudiated the charge of trying to annoy

[1] Ehrle, vii. p. 137 ff. [2] *Ibid.*, pp. 55 and 160.

Benedict and his captive companions with disrespect. The Pontiff's situation became daily worse, long memorials were exchanged to no purpose, pacific proposals came to nothing; they merely marked time and beat the air. At the beginning of 1402, such were the difficulties amidst which the Avignon Papacy was discussed.

And what had become of the Pope of Rome on his side? Events in France have caused us to lose sight of what was going on at the same period in Italy. Had Boniface regained all the authority and prestige that had been lost by his rival? Had he agreed to accept the way of *cession*, which Wenceslas, in agreement with Charles, had tried to force upon him? How had his relations with the King of the Romans and the electors of the Empire turned out?

When Wenceslas, at the time of the interview at Reims, consented to request voluntary abdication from the two Popes, Boniface felt that his position was becoming perilous and precarious. To win back the good graces of the King of the Romans, he offered him the imperial crown (September 4, 1398).[1] Wenceslas, more and more brutalised by drunkenness and debauchery, made no reply to these advances. Apparently, from this time onwards, folly and error constantly increased their hold on the mind of this sorry monarch. The elector-princes of the Rhine there and then resolved to get rid of Wenceslas, and were not hopeless as to getting Boniface to approve of their conspiracy. The head of this redoubtable opposition was Robert of Bavaria, who openly aimed at obtaining the Empire.

It was in vain that the King of the Romans, at length growing uneasy, sought to assemble the diets, to

[1] Lindner, ii. p. 365.

arouse the nobles to draw the sword and his subjects to defend themselves. Even his relations abandoned him. His brother Sigismund, who was at war in Moravia, on his own account, scarcely thought of helping him. The electors went so far as to arraign Wenceslas at the bar of their tribunal, and to wish to sit in judgment on their own chief. It was not only in the Church, but in the Empire, that subversive and revolutionary ideas prevailed. The King of the Romans refused to submit to these orders, and the electors regarded themselves as thenceforward freed from their oath of fealty. They met not far from Coblentz, in a little chapel that exists still, and impeached Wenceslas. They reproached him with having injured the Empire, committed horrible cruelties, and with not having secured the peace of the Church, and condemned him as a "useless, stupid, and worthless holder of the Holy Roman Empire."[1]

On August 20, 1400, the Archbishop of Mayence solemnly read the sentence of deposition, and then next day the prince-electors met at Koenigstuhl and chose Count Robert of Bavaria to succeed him. He was crowned at Cologne on Jan. 6, 1401.

No doubt Robert was more able, worthy, and moral than Wenceslas; but the illegal and revolutionary character of his election was salient, and could not be excused by the stupid, coarse, and tyrannical doings of him whom he replaced.

Moreover, the Roman Pope at first refused to recognise the choice of the electors and to crown Robert. It was only at the close of 1403, after a number of tergiversations and negotiations, that Boniface pronounced in favour of the new King of the Romans, and confirmed the deposition of Wenceslas. For his part, Robert

[1] Janssen, *Frankfurt's Reichscorrespondenz*, i. p. 56.

promised to use all his forces for the advancement of the Catholic Church. Perhaps from conviction, in any case through gratitude and personal interest, he thought himself henceforward bound to recognise the Roman Pope as alone legitimate, and to defend him in all circumstances.

Thus religious peace was more and more set back, since the new Emperor brought Boniface forces at least as powerful as those offered by the King of France to his rival, in restoring him the obedience of which he had been deprived for five years.

§ 4. *What becomes of Authority in the Church?*

At the date now reached, in 1403, the Avignon Pope is in a state of semi-captivity and kept a prisoner, never out of sight of his palace, while his Roman rival has just concluded with the new King of the Romans a peace, the precarious and dubious character of which is concealed from nobody. It is the sharpest moment of the crisis of the great Schism.

Looking higher, the Christian may ask himself this sad question that closely touches the faith itself:

In such critical circumstances, in the midst of the Schism and of the withdrawal of obedience, what became of the supreme authority wherewith Jesus Christ had indued His Church. Is the captive of Avignon, or the helpless Roman Pontiff, the unique depositary of the authority granted by the Divine Founder? Is the half of the Church, which in reality does not cleave to the true Pontiff, at that time known to God alone, really a schismatic section, and therefore deprived of rights of jurisdictions, especially that of giving absolution, which belongs to the legitimate hierarchy only? Can it be that this half had reached the point of losing the very power of conferring the Sacrament of Order and the valid consecration of the sacraments?[1]

There is no need for piety and faith to take alarm. God has never taken away from a considerable portion of His Church, led astray by its bishops into errors of fact made in good faith, the power of the keys and of the benefits depending on its exercise. The Pope, whoever he may then be, is at least possessed of what canon law calls a coloured title, in these conditions of general and practically invincible error, perfectly adequate for the administration of the sacraments, and for keeping and conferring exterior jurisdiction.

The faithful are mistaken as to who is the head perhaps, but what does it matter? Their error is involuntary, and their good faith perfect. The sacraments they receive are efficacious, because administered by true priests: and the authority they acknowledge produces all its legal effects.

The instructions given by the national Synod, held at Paris in February 1395, exactly show this position: "In the great schisms of the past," they said, "it was clear and plain that one was intruded, however much he may have been upheld in fact by some nobles. But now, however false the intruder's party may be, it is nevertheless highly specious and based on different documents and arguments, and maintained by more of the well-known clergy than there are under the obedience of our holy father Benedict; and it is certain that the two elect, at the beginning of

[1] Exaggerated theses on this point have been sometimes maintained by theologians of Avignon. *Cf.* Ehrle, vii. p. 209.

the Schism, were elected by the whole College of Cardinals."[1]

These quite peculiar circumstances were well appreciated at the time by St Antoninus. He is specially competent in these events, for he was long connected with an eminent man, who was mixed up with all these difficult matters, the blessed Cardinal John Dominici: "No doubt it must be believed that there is only one Church, and one vicar of Jesus Christ," wrote the learned bishop. But in a schism, if it happens that several Popes are elected, it is not necessary to salvation to know that this or that one is the true Pontiff. It is generally enough to be ready to obey him who has been canonically elected. The faithful laity is not obliged to know canon law: it can and should leave it to the opinions of its superiors and prelates. The erring Christian is then excused by an ignorance that is almost invincible."[2]

Now let us listen to one of the best authorities among recent theologians: "After a Pope has been elected, and before his death, or resignation, if a new election takes place, it is schismatical and null. The newly-elect does not belong to the apostolic succession. This is what happened at the beginning of what is called, not quite rightly,[3] "*the Great Schism of the West*," which from a theological point of view was merely a schism in appearance. Had two elections occurred at the same or almost at the same time, one according to laws that had previously been made, and the other against them, the Pope elected according to law would be

[1] *Archives nationales*, 5518, f. 84, *verso*. *Cf.* Valois, iii. p. 35.

[2] *S. Antonini Summa Histor.*, pars iii. tit. xxii. c. 2. *Ibid.*, tit. xxiii. c. 8.

[3] *Cf.* Bouix, *De Papa*, i. p. 461.

apostolical, and not the other ; and, even if there were perplexities, doubts, disputes, and grievous ruptures connected with the matter, as at the time of the so-called *Western Schism*, it would not be less true, or less the fact, that apostolicity would belong objectively to the *true* Pope. What would it matter if this objectivity were not plain to all, and if its general recognition only were to occur long afterwards ? I know that treasures have been bequeathed to me, but I do not know whether they are to be found in the chest marked A or in the box B : am I therefore any the less possessed of these treasures ? "[1]

This opinion re-echoes that of the fifteenth century, uttered by the great Archbishop of Florence, who was publicly acclaimed as the " Antoninus of Counsel."

So, then, the well-spring of all saintliness, of all legislative and judicial authority, was not dried up in one half of the Church. The true Pope was present in her : he continued the mighty soul of this great body. This governmental authority did not pass to the bishops, nor to the multitude of priests and faithful laity, nor to the University of Paris, nor to French or foreign princes, sometimes too covetous of sacerdotal powers, as St Ambrose said.

The sanctifying force in the Church lost nothing of its efficacity. In this fatal period, dearth and war united with religious difficulties to disturb mankind.[2] Through all the western nations, the Black Plague pursued its devastating career, and seemed to corrupt all the sources of natural life. The world, dismayed and downcast at the combination of so many evils, seemed plunged in despair. The Church alone remained standing, and bearing in her holy hands the treasure of the sacraments

[1] Didiot, *Logique surnaturelle objective*, No. 823 (Lille, 1892).
[2] Denifle, *La désolation des Églises de France*, ii. pp. 57-63.

that nourish, fortify and uplift, with divine consolation and supernatural hope upon her lips. In this age of disaster, as in the happier times of St Francis and St Dominic, each of the two parts of the Church brought forth and gave increase to those ripe products of spiritual life called Saints, and through them she revived and healed and edified mankind.

If legislative and judicial power are considered, and without these there can be no rule, how precarious they were in the royal hands of those times! The revolutionary spirit had breathed over Christendom, and from the time of Philippe le Bel it had weakened all monarchies. In England it had produced Wicliffe, and in Bohemia was soon to give rise to John Huss. These subversive doctrines were soon to pass into actions. In England, Richard II. had just been dethroned by his cousin Henry of Lancaster, who was soon afterwards to have him assassinated. In Germany, Wenceslas had just been unlawfully deposed and replaced by Robert of Bavaria, and was soon to be cast into prison.

In Hungary, Ladislas and Sigismund disputed the throne of St Stephen; while in Castile, Henry of Trastamare killed his brother, Peter the Cruel, with his own hand.

In Navarre reigned Charles the Bad, whose name says enough. In Aragon ruled Peter the Ceremonious, who had the legate, who had been ordered to excommunicate him, hung up by the feet.

In Italy, debauch gave rise to cruelty, and immorality led on to murder. In January (1382), Jane of Naples, protectress of Clement VII., had her first husband strangled from the most shameful motives, and herself died in 1382, stifled by the orders of her nephew. In

1386 Charles de Duras fell assassinated at Naples by Queen Elisabeth of Hungary, who is put to death in turn by the ban of Croatia. In the north of the Peninsula, the Ghibeline Barnabô Visconti stained himself with a multitude of debaucheries and cruelties, until his nephew Galeas rid the country of him in 1385. Returning to France, the picture becomes filled with more detail, but gains nothing from the additions. Charles VII. only had lucid intervals of sanity, and Isabel of Bavaria casts away both her reputation and her realm. The throne is as shaken as the altar.

In reading the account of all these tragic revolutions, certain fine lines of Lucretius come to mind. He, too, relates the different ills engendered by ambition, and depicts the miserable existence of rulers, exposed to envy like mountain summits to the thunderbolts.

> Ergo regibus occisis subversa jacebat
> Pristina majestas soliorum et sceptra superba. . . .

"The kings are slain and the time-honoured majesty of the throne is stricken down: proud sceptres lie prone upon the earth, and the bloody crown laments its disgrace."[1]

In the Church, on the contrary, despite the troubles arising from the Schism, the power of the tiara and the keys remains undiminished in the midst of either obedience. One of the two is doubtless in error, but its wish is nevertheless to be faithful to the true successor of St Peter. The true and divinely appointed hierarchy continues its existence, and its authority circulates like sap in the two parallel branches, which spring from the same stock. Whoever is generally considered, through a mistake that could hardly be helped, by the

[1] *De rerum natura,* lib. v. 1134, 1135.

Christian people to be the true head of the body ecclesiastic, he gives his subordinates the same authority that would be granted by the undisputed Popes, such as Gregory VII. or Innocent III.[1] Valid orders and valid jurisdiction, then, were not wanting in the case of any representative of Jesus Christ in the two spheres of obedience. It was only later on that Peter de Luna, when left by the whole Church and legitimately excluded from the Papacy, remained without authority and was reduced to the sad and ridiculous position of a solitary and formal schismatic in the Church.

Thus the bond of moral and religious unity remained unbroken among all the members, notwithstanding the momentary division of the two obediences. There was always *una fides, unum baptisma, unum corpus*, in the sense of St Paul and Christ.

[1] Father Conrad Eubel, p. vi. of the Preface of his "*Les Ordres mendicants de l'obédience d'Avignon* (Paderborn, 1900), remarks that the acts of government and grace of all the Popes of all these obediences were respected alike by Martin V. and his first successors. Indeed, in the official writings of the new Pontiffs, the former Popes are never called Anti-popes, but thus designated: "*called Popes in their own obedience.*" Dr P. A. Kirsch, in the *Archiv. für kath. Kirchenrecht*, (1900, No. 2, p. 418), is clearly of this way of thinking. See also in the *Römische Quartalschrift* (1896), a remarkable article by Eubel, on the procedure followed during the Schism, when a bishop, appointed in one obedience, went over to the other.

CHAPTER X

THE RESTITUTION OF OBEDIENCE

§ 1. *Flight of the Pope of Avignon.*

THE University and the Court, France and foreign countries, grew more and more uneasy at the abnormal and intolerable situation of the Pope, who had but lately been recognised as legitimate by almost the whole of Western Europe. Until this troublous period it had been the historical rôle of the eldest daughter of the Church to deliver Popes from captivity when Lombard kings or German emperors had temporarily brought them into subjection. The world had not been at all accustomed to the sight of a French king and princes undertaking the responsibility of keeping the Vicar of Jesus Christ in bondage.[1]

If the people wondered, the clergy showed that it was dissatisfied with the heavy and novel charges that had been imposed upon it since the sovereign had usurped the place of head of the Church. On its side, the University had manifested its discontent more than once :[2] it was grieved to see its professors and members less favoured in the matter of preferment since the French bishops had taken the place of the Pope in the distribution of favours. This learned corporation had

[1] EHRLE, vii. p. 212. The Cardinal of Pampeluna's instructions to P. Ravat, Bishop of Saint-Pons.

[2] EHRLE, p. 43. DENIFLE, *Désolation des Églises de France*, ii. *passim.*

even resumed its grand method of uttering protests, and since 1400 it had suspended its lectures.[1] Some of its most honoured professors receded from the position they had assumed with regard to withdrawal of obedience: Gerson and Clémangis published letters and writings in which they definitely demanded a return to the obedience of Benedict.

The University of Toulouse was still more energetic. Its deputies spoke before the King at Paris with such vigour that the Duke de Berry, governor of Languedoc, had them all imprisoned.[2] The University of Paris replied to this violent attack, and later on, the national council thought it necessary to condemn the memorial of the doctors from Toulouse.[3] From another side, the Bishop of Saint-Pons, Peter Ravat, had spoken energetically and had dared to reproach the three cardinals, who had attacked Benedict, for their deplorable disloyalty: "If the Pope should die," he said to the King, "they could take no part in the election of his successor, for they are guilty of high treason."[4] Moreover, the other cardinals tended toward reconciliation with the imprisoned Pontiff. The court itself was divided. If the Dukes of Berry and of Burgundy were rooted in their hostile sentiments towards Benedict, the Duke of Orleans, the King's brother, continued to be the chivalrous defender of the Pontiff.[5] He understood France's terrible responsibility, should harm happen

[1] *Chronic. Karoli VI.*, lib. xx. 20. Du Boulay, iv. pp. 284 and 871. Hefele, *Histoire des Conciles*, x. p. 126.

[2] A number of manuscript documents referring to this period were purchased by M. Léopold Delisle in 1899, at Lord Ashburnham's sale. See the list in the *Journal des Savants*, June 1899.

[3] Bourgeois du Chastenet, p. 234. Vaissette, lib. xxxiii. t. ix.

[4] *Chronic. Karoli VI.*, lib. xxiii. 1. Schwab, *Johannes Gerson*, p. 153.

[5] Ehrle, vii. pp. 66 and 92. Jouvenel des Ursins (Éd. Godefroy), p. 135.

to the Pope during the too prolonged blockade. Violent disputes on this question sometimes arose between them, even at the most important meetings. In another direction, the court of Castile and Aragon had just succeeded in making the echo of their too well grounded complaints as to the long captivity of the Avignon Pontiff reach Paris. A reaction was in progress.

Benedict, encouraged by this sympathy, took advantage of an opportunity for escape that presented itself. A Norman knight who was entirely devoted to the Duke of Orleans, Captain Robert de Bracquemont, was entrusted with guarding the Pope. He enjoyed the privilege of free entry and exit of the palace at Avignon. The clever captive hailed him, told him of his plan, and secured the captain's assistance.

In the evening of March 11, 1403, Benedict put on borrowed attire, placed the Blessed Eucharist on his chest, and a letter bearing the royal seal of Charles VI. in his clothes, and boldly left the papal castle with three companions. Under the guidance of the daring captain, he successfully passed all the sentinels and reached a house in the town where several French knights waited for him and offered him their homage and their help. With them he came up with an escort of four hundred men, whom Braquemont was keeping in reserve. At sunrise he embarked on the Rhone, then ascended the Durance, and came to Château-Renard,[1] under the protection of the King of Sicily. When Avignon awoke, it heard of the flight of the captive, and the population allowed the rest of the Pope's servants to rejoin him. The cardinals themselves and several bishops went to

[1] *Chronic. Karoli VI.*, lib. xxiii. c. 16. *Cf.* Ehrle, p. 449. Du Boulay gives March 16 as the date of the Pope's flight. This is certainly an error.

offer to the Pontiff now at liberty the homage they had sometimes refused him when in prison: they were reeds swayed by every wind, said the Chronicler of St Denis.[1]

The very day of his arrival at Château-Renard, Benedict addressed the King of France, his council, and the University in three letters of the same tenor. He said to them in substance: "Our detention did not bring about the peaceful results that were expected of it. We have set ourselves free, and we give you notice thereof, as of a thing whereat you should greatly rejoice. We hope that divine grace will make our flight subserve to the glory of God, and to the prosperity of the Church, as well as to the honour of the royal house of France."[2]

Perhaps there is a touch of irony in the latter words, addressed to those who had made him a captive. It may seem to some that Pius VI., Pius VII., and Pius IX., when leaving Rome in circumstances that recall those just mentioned, afford a spectacle of a more dignified and lofty character.

Yet Benedict knew how to show magnanimity. He was reconciled with his cardinals (March 29, 1403), and took no vengeance on the people of Avignon, who had been so long in rebellion, but who returned to their obedience to the Pope with the same versatility as they had shown in deserting him.[3] The Pontiff repealed all the censures pronounced against them, and only obliged them to repair the ruins they had made in the castle where he had defended himself with such energy.

[1] *Chronic. Karoli VI.*, lib. xxii. c. 16. [2] *Ibid.*

[3] Martène et Durand, *Thesaurus*, ii. col. 1268. Ehrle, p. 449 ff. Valois, iii. p. 331.

§ 2. *The Question of Obedience.*

At Paris, Benedict's good fortune produced the same pacificatory results. The King and the dukes were not really sorry for this ending of a situation that was a greater perplexity to them than they cared to acknowledge. The Pope of Avignon sent two cardinals, who had not always been so favourable to him, to the court: that is to say, Guy de Malesset and Cardinal de Saluces. On being admitted to a royal audience, on May 25, the former spoke and attacked the withdrawal of obedience with both eloquence and vigour. "As long as it lasts," he said, "you can do nothing for union. Although this step was taken to move the culpable obstinacy of Benedict, yet it was resolved upon too lightly. I ask for a modification of it, if not for its abolition."

These words were important, and called for a fresh reconsideration of the religious policy of France: and they were destined to bring it about, though not without delay. The King replied that for this matter he had convened all the bishops of the realm, and that they themselves would make their reply. Guy de Malesset could not have spoken thus openly had he not been sure that public opinion was prepared for a revolution and political stroke of this sort.

Gerson indeed was glad of the deliverance of Benedict, and, in an eccentric comparison, he had likened it to Jonas coming out of the whale.[1] Peter d'Ailly, the Bishop of Cambrai, whose name turns up at every vicissitude in the great drama, had just brought out a work on the religious crisis of the realm that had attracted much attention. This writing is called *De materia concilii generalis*. The writer divides his subject

[1] *Opp. Gersonii,* ii. col. 147.

into three heads. The first deals with the matter and form of the council which was to put an end to the Schism. The second sets forth and clears up the following question: Ought obedience to be given to Benedict before the meeting of this council? Finally, the third had to do with reforms that were necessary in the Church.[1]

According to Peter d'Ailly's ideas, this council concerning obedience to Benedict ought to refrain from dealing with matters of faith or questions of reform. Nor should accusations of perjury, heresy, or schism, brought against the Pope of Avignon, be submitted to the Synod. The assembly should not look for new means of coming to an agreement, as the *three ways* already indicated were enough: but it should only concern itself with guaranteeing liberty of discussion and maintaining peace between the head and the members.

There were to be no fresh rules, but merely the application of common law and old ecclesiastical precedents. There was to be no intervention on the part of civil authority, which was often so ready to encroach.

[1] This treatise was thought by Baluze to be of such importance that he had it copied afresh in 1687, after the MS. 820 Colbert. There are three copies at the Bibl. Nationale (1480, 1571, and 3124). This work is at least as important as Durand de Mende's more general treatise of the same title. It is divided into three chapters: the first part has been ascribed to Gerson and printed by Ellies-Dupin among the chancellor's works (ii. col. 24) under the heading: *De Concilio generali unius obedientiae*. The order of the ideas is not the same, but the substance is almost identical. The second part is wholly unpublished. As for the third, Peter d'Ailly reproduced it thirteen years later with slight modifications, and presented it to the Council of Constance. It is the famous treatise which Protestants have so often misemployed, entitled: *Tractatus super reformatione Ecclesiae in Concilio Constantiensi*. *Cf.* Petrus de Alliaco, Pref. xxxii. and p. 120. It will be referred to again later on in chaps. xv. and xviii.

Then the bishop attacked the question of the most pressing practical importance: should obedience be restored to Benedict before the meeting of the council? He set forth with some prolixity the three opinions then current. The first called for the immediate restitution of obedience pure and simple. Although d'Ailly does not say so, this was the idea of Gerson and the Duke of Orleans. The bishop supports this view with a number of passages of canon law.

The second was absolutely contradictory, and denied the necessity and even the propriety of restitution, and relied on the charges brought against Benedict by the three cardinals sent to Paris by the Sacred College in 1399.[1] The offences with which it was attempted to saddle the Avignon Pope have already been mentioned. The Dukes of Berry and Burgundy, part of the doctors of the University, and the patriarch Simon de Cramaud were for maintaining the *status quo*.

Finally, the third view, which was to triumph in 1406 at the council, occupied the exact mean between the two extremes and laid down certain distinctions. It said: There are rights, a pre-eminence, and honours due by divine right to the Pope, because he is the head of the universal Church. Others are accidental and at times usurped to the prejudice of prelates and inferior Churches: such are collations of bishoprics, reservations for ecclesiastical benefices, and other recent privileges and abuses, called rights of the Apostolic Chamber, which were unknown to St Peter and his venerated successors. Let the former privileges be restored to the Pope, for that is just: but to give him the latter would be unjust and harmful.

Long juridical arguments were used in support of this

[1] See the preceding chapter.

opinion, and what is known of the character and other works of d'Ailly leads one to conclude that the author belonged to this third party.

The dissertation ends with this touching prayer: "In this great diversity of opinions may the Lord Jesus grant us to choose what He knows to be best and most fitting for the honour of His Name and the salvation of Holy Church! Amen."[1]

On account of these differences of opinion, the discussion might have continued long to no purpose, had not the Duke of Orleans hastened matters with the King's consent and put an end to the debates. He ordered the metropolitans to collect the votes of their subordinates secretly and in writing, then he assembled the prelates at Paris on May 28, 1403, in the royal mansion of St Paul's, while the King and his uncles, the dukes, were away. The partisans of the restoration of obedience were in a majority. As soon as Louis of Orleans had ascertained this, he took care to inform the King. Charles was glad and publicly gave his support to this reparatory scheme (May 28, 1403). He took a solemn oath, and had a formal record drawn up, and ordered a *Te Deum* to be sung at Paris and St Denis. In spite of the opposition of the King's uncles, the University fell in with Charles' proposals by a large majority.

The Bishop of Cambrai had been chosen to make a solemn announcement of the restitution of obedience at Notre-Dame in Paris. During the Mass which was said by the Cardinal of Poitiers, Peter d'Ailly spoke before the King, the dukes, the bishops, and a large congregation

[1] MS. 1480 of the Bibl. Nat., f. 108. I have given no analysis of the third part, which has been often printed (*Opp. Gersonii*, ii. p. 903), and which, moreover, has nothing to do with the present subject.

(May 30, 1403). His discourse has not come down to us, but the *Chronicles of Charles VI.*, written by the monk of St Denis, have preserved the articles of the agreement, which he read in conclusion.

These were the conditions of the restitution of obedience: "The Pope undertook to accept the way of *cession*, if his competitor came to abdicate, die, or be deposed. He withdrew all his protests, and undid all proceedings that had taken place during the withdrawal of obedience, and forgave all offences done to his person.

"On the other hand, the nobles of France united with the Duke of Orleans to beg the Pope to reduce the charges on the churches of the kingdom, to approve and uphold the collations and promotions made during the withdrawal of obedience by the ordinary prelates.

"Benedict lastly undertook to convoke, within a year, a council of all the prelates of his obedience to deal with the restoration of union, reform in general, the liberties of the Church, and the subsidies received by the Holy See from France."[1]

No doubt this last article was due to the personal influence and the recent work of the learned Bishop of Cambrai.

After this great demonstration the Cardinal de Thury and several members of the University gave their adhesion to the restitution of obedience. An important embassy went to carry the happy news to the Pope.[2] The Bishop of Cambrai and the Archbishop of Aix appeared before Benedict to demand a speedy and

[1] *Chronic. Karoli VI.*, lib. xxiv. c. 6. *Cf.* Ehrle, vii. p. 280. He publishes a copy of this document in French.

[2] *Ibid.*, c. 8. Martène et Durand, *Thesaurus*, ii. col. 1301. *Appointement final auquel sont d'accord le Conseil du roi et des églises de France sur le fait du Schisme* (May 28, 1403). MS., Vatican Library, according to Montfaucon, *Bibl. bibl.*, i. p. 70.

complete fulfilment of his promises (September 1, 1903).

The restoration of obedience was conditional, and everything depended on the way in which Benedict conformed to the four articles of the agreement. Unfortunately the Pontiff's natural disposition soon gained the upper hand. Daily he invented a subterfuge or started a fresh difficulty. He showed himself more and more cautious in word and tortuous in action. Sometimes he refused to confirm promotions made during the withdrawal, and deprived persons of high character of their benefices ; sometimes he burdened the Churches of France and of the University [1] with taxes and tenths, multiplied reservations and revived all the pretensions that had but lately alienated the French clergy. He refused to listen to his most intelligent and faithful supporters.[2] His temporary successes seemed to have made him only more arrogant and obstinate, and to have bound him still more closely to his dubious dignity.

Nevertheless he thought himself obliged to observe some moderation, to satisfy the French princes, and especially the Duke of Orleans, by giving them vague assurances and by beginning some vain proceedings for the restoration of unity. Thus on January 8, 1404, he put forth, one after the other, five bulls promising on his side that he would make every sacrifice for the restoration

[1] *Chronic. Karoli VI.*, lib. xxiv. 16 and xxvi. 1 and 2. *Cf.* Mollat, *Annales de St Louis des Français*, 1902.

[2] Thus he turned a deaf ear to the vigorous objurgations addressed to him by Gerson in sermons preached before him at Marseilles, and afterwards at Tarascon, Jan. 1, 1404. *Opp. Gersonii*, ii. col. 50, 54. The old chancellor of the University thus laid down his part : "Prosequere pacem Ecclesiae latratu quo potui, ego de genere catulus." *Opp. Gersonii*, ii. col. 74.

of religious unity.[1] Thus it is that, in June of the same year, he gave an assurance that he would send duly appointed ambassadors to Boniface his rival. He did so, as a matter of fact, and the embassy was led by the Bishop of Saint-Pons. It was ordered to renew the following proposal, which we have already seen formulated by Benedict and which France had long before rejected. The two rival pontiffs should have an interview in a place agreed upon to concert together as to the means of restoring peace. The French Pope offered to go to Italy to some neutral territory. He proposed to forbid his cardinals to elect a successor if he died, but asked that Boniface should do the same.[2]

§ 3. *Death of Boniface IX.—Election of Innocent VII.*

The Italian Pontiff was already in failing health when the ambassadors reached Rome, on September 22, and he was unable to receive them. The envoys then had him informed that the way they proposed would be very advantageous for him. The Pope asked them to specify these advantages; but they insisted on the proposal for an interview, and made no further advance.

A few days later, Boniface breathed his last (October 1, 1404). In a letter addressed to the King of France, Benedict relates that this unexpected death was hastened by a warm dispute between the Pope and the French envoys. The latter had behaved very disrespectfully, and replied sharply to the attacks of which the Avignon

[1] Raynald, a. 1404, n. 4-6. Ehrle, v. p. 464. Jarry, *La vie politique de Louis de France*, p. 301. Valois, iii. p. 372.

[2] Niem, *De Scismate*, lib. ii. 23. Martène et Durand, *Veterum Script.*, nova collectio, praef. lxiii. and 686.

Pope had maintained that he was the object.[1] If Benedict's story is true, it is a discreditable one for his ambassadors. But it is contradicted by an official note sent a little later to the University of Paris by Boniface's successor.[2]

This report adds: the Sacred College did not wish to go into conclave until they had sent for the French envoys to know whether they had instructions for such an unforeseen occurrence, and if they had enough authority to put in a resignation on behalf of Benedict. In such circumstances, the cardinals would have made it their duty to postpone the election of the future Pontiff. The ambassadors declared that they had no orders on the point from their master. Then it was proposed that they should depute some of their number to go to the Pope of Avignon to obtain such an order. They refused, saying that Benedict would never consent to the way of *cession*. Just at this time there was a great disturbance in the Eternal City. They requested the envoys to delay their departure, for there was no security for them if they were to leave in the midst of the turmoil. But they would not listen and quitted the city. They had the misfortune to fall at once into the hands of the commander of the castle of St Angelo, who had them flung into prison, and only let them go for a ransom of five thousand ducats. The cardinals made a number of efforts to get them out of their difficulty, but could avail nothing, as they had no authority over the owner of the castle while the conclave lasted.[3]

[1] Martène et Durand, lib. vii. praef. lxiv. and 690. Hefele, x. p. 131. *Chronic. Karoli VI.*, lib. xxv. c. 22.

[2] *Ibid.*, lib. xxvi. c. 2 and 3. The monk of St Denis makes no secret of his preference for the Bishop of Rome's version, though he is on the side of Avignon.

[3] *Chronic. Karoli VI.*, *ibid.* Niem, lib. ii. c. 24. Du Boulay, v. p. 109.

In Paris, as many doubted the truth of this story, the Duke de Berry asked for a corroboration of it from Rome, and obtained an answer in perfect keeping with the official report that had already been forwarded.[1] This report was signed "Innocent VII.," the newly-elected Sovereign Pontiff. This Pope was called Cosmo Meliorati, and came from an obscure family of the Abruzzi. He had been archbishop of Ravenna, then of Bologna, and it was in the latter town that he had been made cardinal. He was of exemplary life, of more than ordinary learning, and the purity of his morals was above reproach. Before his advancement, like all the other cardinals, he had taken an oath to work with all his strength, should he be elected, for the suppression of the Schism, and to resign his office if it were necessary.[2]

Innocent began by keeping the promises he had made as Cosmo Meliorati, and immediately proclaimed a council for his obedience. Unfortunately Rome was disturbed. The Orsinis and Colonnas were taking up arms against each other with the same ardour as of old. Neither the memory of the Ghibellines, the secular enemies of the Popes, nor that of Rienzi, the ardent revolutionary, had faded from the popular mind. The Pontiff was obliged to have recourse to the arms of Ladislas, King of Naples. The latter put down the rebellion, but his protection cost dear. This intervention and sanguinary disturbances threw the Pope into the thick of political passions and reprisals, and alienated the feeling of the Romans from him more and more, for they obliged him to fly to Viterbo. The Vatican and the

[1] *Chronic.*, lib. xxvi. c. 3. A Register bought at Lord Ashburnham's sale, p. 17. The letter is dated the end of April 1405.

[2] *Vita Innocentii VII.*, apud Muratori, iii. p. ii. p. 832. Martène et Durand, *Thesaurus*, ii. col. 1274.

cardinals' palaces were sacked, the Pope's servants killed, and Rome was in anarchy throughout this reign.[1]

In the midst of these troubles he lost sight of the only essential question, that of the suppression of the Schism. On his side, Benedict was not anxious to return to Avignon, which for him had so long been a place of captivity. Salon, Tarascon, Marseilles, and Nice saw him within their walls one after the other. He solemnly declared that he wished to go to Viterbo in order to negotiate with his adversary there. On May 16, 1405, six galleys hung with flags reached Genoa.

Boucicault was there in command in the name of France, and gave a magnificent reception to the Pontiff whom his disreputable brother had but lately besieged at Avignon.

Processions followed banquets, and solemn receptions pompous reviews of the troops brought by the Pope. St Vincent Ferrier came to the town at Benedict's request, and astounded the whole country by his gift of tongues, the number of his miracles, and the fruits of sanctity. St Colette was about to ask the Pope at Nice to receive her into the Order of St Francis. Peter d'Ailly preached before him on the Feast of the Holy Trinity, and got the festival ordained for the whole of his obedience. Benedict's nomadic pontificate was not without a certain brilliancy, and it was kept up until the day when his obstinacy obliged the most saintly and the most devoted to the Church to abandon him to his unhappy fate.[2]

Meanwhile, the more Benedict sees that Innocent is harassed with political difficulties, the more he multiplies his more or less sincere efforts and advances to

[1] Guiraud, *L'État pontifical après le grand Schisme*, p. 14.

[2] *Chronic.*, lib. xxvi. c. 6.

show his desire for unity. Already he had sent a request to the Pope of Rome for safe-conducts that his nuncios might enter Italy, but the latter refused them. Then he gave out his plan of going himself to his rival at Viterbo to come to an understanding with him, and he begged King Charles to send him some princes of his court as a guard of honour. The sovereign agreed and deputed the Duke of Bourbon. In order to defray the expenses of this proceeding, Benedict put new tenths on the property of the French clergy; and the clergy paid without too much protestation, persuaded that union was near.[1]

The Pope of Avignon asked Innocent VII. again for a safe-conduct; and the latter persisted in refusing it, on the ground that his competitor's proposals were not seriously meant.[2]

But Benedict's display of zeal increased in proportion as he saw his rival show indifference. He asked the Republic of Genoa to give him enough galleys to take him to Rome.[3] But time was lost, and the plague broke out in the town and all along the coast. In order to escape it, the Pope was compelled to wander in his ship from Genoa to Savona, from Savona to Monaco, from Monaco to Nice, and lastly from Nice to Marseilles. In this last town he convoked a general council of his obedience for Whitsuntide in the year 1407.

§ 4. *Warm Discussions in Paris.*

Meanwhile the Pope of Avignon, at the beginning of 1406, sent the Cardinal of Chalant to the capital to

[1] *Chronic.*, lib. xxvi. c. 1. Martène et Durand, *Veterum Script.*, vii. col. 686.

[2] Niem, ii. 37.

[3] Jean Jouvenel des Ursins, p. 171.

attach the dukes to his party more and more firmly. They were then the real masters of France, for the King only had the use of his reason at intervals. The legate was coldly received, and he was specially censured when he called the University a " nest of mar-plots."[1] He renewed his attacks upon it when he obtained a solemn audience, and treated those who accused Benedict as gossips unworthy of confidence.[2]

This violence was not without reprisals, nor were these attacks without a reply. There was then at Paris a professor of theology who later on won an unenviable celebrity : this was the doctor, John Petit. A Norman in origin,[3] a poet when in the mood,[4] an eloquent speaker, passionate, sarcastic, and, above all,a perverse politician, he was to distinguish himself later on by his apology for tyrannicide.

In 1406, he posed as the official defender of the University against the attacks of Benedict and his legate. On May 17, Petit boldly took the offensive and proposed to refuse obedience anew to this Pontiff of Avignon, who was crushing the Gallican Church with his exactions.

On June 7, 1406, one of the most enthusiastic professors of theology, Peter Plaoul, attacked the letter of the University of Toulouse in defence of Benedict, and called for the criminal prosecution of its authors. He

[1] *Chronic.*, lib. xxvi. c. 27.

[2] *Ibid.*, lib. xxvii. c. 1.

[3] Simeon Luce and Tschackert make him to be a Dominican : Hefele, Hergenröther and Michelet a Friar minor. He was really one of the secular clergy. He was buried at Hesdin in the Franciscan house in 1411. Denifle, *Chartul.*, iii. p. 462.

[4] The Rouen Society of Bibliophiles has just published *Le Livre du champ d'or*, and other imprinted poems of John Petit, one vol. quarto, li. + 247 pp.

compared the place of the King in his kingdom with that of the Pope in the Church: "The King is lord of his subjects," he said, "but the Pope is not lord of the Church, but her servant. The Church is confirmed in her faith, in which she does not err, but the Pope can err."[1]

Then John Petit resumed speaking and made a host of reproaches against Benedict in a long speech full of warmth and violence. "Obedience was restored to the Pope," he said, "on certain conditions, and these conditions have not been fulfilled. Benedict has shamelessly broken his oaths and promises. You all know how eager he has been in the exaction of procurations, annates, tithes, and services invented by some of his predecessors to the great loss of the clergy."

Next day, Jouvenel des Ursins, the King's advocate, again took up all these arguments, and gave his legal decision. It covered three points:—

1st. The memorial of Toulouse University in favour of Benedict and the restitution of obedience was to be burnt.

2nd. The King is within his rights in opposing the requests for money so frequently repeated by the Pope.

3rd. Benedict had not fulfilled the conditions laid down for the restitution of obedience. The King, then, had the right of refusing it afresh.[2]

The two first conclusions were accepted without any difficulty.[3] The third was graver, and might plunge France again into all the disorders and evils of the withdrawal of obedience. On their side, the Pope's partisans made efforts to secure delay. The Parliament decided not to come to any decision before the French prelates

[1] *Arch. nation.*, x. 1; 4787, f. 359.
[2] *Chronic. Karoli VI.*, lib. xxvii. c. 2. Hefele, x. p. 136.
[3] The first was accepted on July 17, and the second on September 11.

had met, which they were going to do on All Saints' Day of this same year, 1406.

In Italy, the business of union was going badly. Innocent, who was fairly well-disposed towards it at first, was cooling down. He got some of the *curia* and some ambassadors to resolve that he was not bound to keep the oath he had sworn to the conclave, that he would work effectively for the peace of the Church. His friends were highly astonished at this sudden right-about-face. His ear was offended by their proposals, and he imperiously declared to his Great Penitentiary and his Vice-Chancellor that they must quiet these chatterers, because he did not wish to hear any more said about the matter of union.

Such, then, was the respective position of the two obediences at the end of 1406. No way had been successful; no political or military expedient had reached a happy result. Peace seemed further away than ever, and the friends of the Church could only bewail the ruin of their hopes, that had vanished as soon as they had been apprehended.

About this period, a distinguished woman, of Italian birth, but French by adoption, wrote the *Book of the Deeds and Good Conduct of the Wise King Charles V*. "O what a scourge!" she cried, "O what a mournful mischief, that still endures and has already endured for twenty-six years! Nor can this pestilence be cut off or made to cease, if God, in His holy mercy, do not remedy it! For this abominable wound is already festering, and has become chronic. . . . It is indeed much to be feared that there is great danger of the Christian religion as a consequence some day suddenly dying out." [1]

[1] *Livre des fais et bonnes mœurs du sage roi Charles V.* (Collection of memorials relating to the history of France, 1st series, vol. vi.), p. 116.

CHAPTER XI

THE COUNCIL OF PARIS IN 1406

§ 1. *Preliminaries and First Debates.*

THE fourth great ecclesiastical assembly since the accession of Benedict was, then, to be held in Paris.

Its object, which was well laid down by the King's advocate Jouvenel des Ursins, was not to formulate a decision on any point of faith or discipline. Nor was it to indicate a new method of putting an end to the Schism. All had been tried and all had been found unfruitful.

But it was necessary for the clergy to give the King useful counsel on this fine point: should Benedict be adhered to, or was it necessary to abandon him afresh? Is it expedient to resume the extreme measure called withdrawal of obedience?

This was the question that the bishops and doctors of the University were called to resolve.

The problem was a grave one, for this was to create anew a schism within the Schism, and to reopen wounds that they wanted to heal. It was a question that should not have been brought forward, for if the clergy of France considered Benedict legitimate, it belonged neither to the episcopate, nor to the University, nor to royalty to refuse him obedience either in part or altogether. But in revolutionary days, when once legitimate authorities have been set at naught, one is condemned from the very outset not to be able to stop, and to fall lower than one intended to do at the beginning.

The initiative of this schismatic resolution was due to the University, which had long been dissatisfied with the Pope of Avignon. The part played by *Alma Mater*, after having been conciliatory from 1390, had become more and more aggressive and disrespectful towards the French Pope. Clement and Benedict had been spared neither censorious proceedings, nor interested demands, nor bitter words, nor even threats of deposition.

Certain professors of this learned body, puffed up with the importance they had gained from the chance of circumstance, showed no greater docility with regard to the bishops, and assumed a rôle that was presumptuous and extravagant.

From 1391, these professors had not shrunk from coming forward as if they possessed a mission to violate the rights of episcopal authority. They claimed to be the function of *reason* in the body of the Church, prescribing what is good and what is bad, what should be done or avoided. They allowed the prelates the function of the *will*, executive power, the moral obligation of acting according to the light they received from the intelligence represented by themselves.[1] The teaching office appeared to them to be a sacrament. It was unreason in practice finding utterance in the language of pedantry.

In the synod of 1406, *Alma Mater* was only too faithful to this usurped position. She sought to make her views prevail, and also her policy, and even her anti-

[1] A Dissertation by Gilles des Champs or John Gerson. *Cf.* DENIFLE, *Chartularium,* iii. Nos. 552, 596, and 1663. DU BOULAY, iv. p. 806.

pathies, and cried out that she was insulted if anyone dared to oppose her.

Royal authority did not show less sensitiveness, and one may easily imagine amidst what difficulties the bishops gathered at Paris had to speak and act.[1]

Sixty-three prelates and doctors had met at the palace by command of the King on November 18, 1406. In order to enlighten the council as to the points in dispute, it was first decided that each party should select a certain number of theologians and canonists to set forth the pros and cons on behalf of either side. At bottom, it was a struggle between the University and the Pope whom she had imprudently recognised and subsequently obstinately defended.

The defenders of the University were in the first place Master Pierre-aux-Bœufs, Master John Petit, the Patriarch of Alexandria, Simon de Cramaud, and afterwards Peter le Ray, Abbot of Mont-Saint-Michel, and Peter Plaoul of Liège. They divided between them the arguments to be put forward and the replies made to the reasons of their opponents.

The Pope's orators were Master William Philastre, Dean of the Church of Reims, the Archbishop of Tours, Ameilh du Breuil, and the Bishop of Cambrai, Peter d'Ailly. They agreed to reply to Benedict's detractors.

The Advocate-General, who spoke in the name of the King and had to sum up the case, was Jouvenel des Ursins.

On November 18, 1406, after a solemn Mass, celebrated by the Archbishop of Rouen, all the prelates, doctors,

[1] Bourgeois du Chastenet has published the speeches from an MS. of St Victor, pp. 94-234. They are partly summarised in the *Chronic. Karoli VI.*, lib. xxvii. c. 17; in Du Boulay, v. p. 132; and in the *Opp. Gersonii*, i. p. xix. See the French MS. 23,428 of the Bibl. Nationale.

and professors went in procession to the little hall of the palace on the Seine, and appeared at the audience. It was in the presence of the Duke of Guyenne—whom the speakers call a "worthy heir of France, the flower of purity and innocence, the new Josias with the face of an angel"—of the Duke of Berry his uncle, and of Louis, King of Sicily, that this great meeting took place.

The Parisian Cordelier, Pierre-aux-Bœufs, doctor of theology, opened the discussion. He was the representative of the University, which seems to have made a great mistake in choosing him. In his emphatic exhortation he drew a picture of the religious troubles that had ensued upon the election of Clement VII. He likened the Schism to a halo about a star: it was an endless circle; and compared with it, previous theological dissensions were but semi-circles or straight lines. Then he compared the bishops to planets, and their beneficiaries, who had been blinded by their advancement, to night-birds, "who hide their beaks in their feathers at the rising of the sun." The different members of the human body, and flowers and fruits provided him with other similes, and the orator came to the end of his prolix discourse without reaching any conclusion.[1] It was a commonplace, pretentious, and burlesque introduction. In one passage he spoke of "the leafy verdure of fine words, essentially meaningless": it was the best description of his own discourse.

Very different is the speech of Master John Petit against Benedict. He begins by making an apology for his bluntness of nature, and accuses himself of speaking "with haste and warmth as if he were in anger."

The irascible doctor gives a historical summary of all

[1] Bourgeois du Chastenet, p. 95.

that had been done to secure unity during the last twelve years: he violently attacks the Pope of Avignon, his perjuries, and his exactions, his numerous and disloyal subterfuges. Nor does he spare the Roman Pontiff, and sets himself to prove that both are schismatics and strongly to be suspected of heresy.

"The restoration of obedience to Benedict was conditional," he says; "the four conditions have not been fulfilled at all: therefore France should separate again from the Pope who has broken his word."[1]

After John Petit's attacks, the Patriarch of Alexandria ascended the tribune, and made a speech that was full of more worthy and higher reasoning, but tainted with grave theological errors.

He claimed to show "that the request of the University should be granted, and that the King and the people of his realm ought not to obey either one or the other of the two competitors of the papacy."

Starting with the assumption that the rival Pontiffs, *the two foxes*, as he called them, were *schismatics*, he set himself to show that these Popes could no longer promote to bishoprics and cures, that their ordinations were dubious, and that those whom they had made bishops or priests were guilty of mortal sin in administering or receiving the Sacraments; a number of extravagant inferences from a gratuitous hypothesis.[2] "I know not how we put up with such enemies of our faith, such Antichrists and destroyers of Christendom," he exclaimed. Simon de Cramaud even went further: "Whoever pretends to hold the true faith, and despises the traditions of the holy fathers and holy doctors, and

[1] Bourgeois du Chastenet, pp. 105 and 113.

[2] *Ibid.*, p. 120. He quotes passages of law, and sometimes makes a rather macaronic mixture of Latin and French. The theological errors are refuted in our preceding chapter ix., p. 180 ff.

on that account divides the Church, is a heretic. He who damnably keeps the Church in Schism is even a heresiarch, according to the holy doctors."[1]

Simon de Cramaud is indeed himself far more schismatic when he suggests that French prelates can judge all appeals in the last resort. The bishops and archbishops were to appeal finally to the primates of France. "Have we not archbishops of Bourges, Vienne, and Lyons who are primates? It would be more fitting to have French causes judged in France and not in Italy. Nevertheless," he concluded, "I wish to say nothing against the liberties and immunities of the holy Roman Church." Until these troublous times this audacious proposal had never been put forward. Before the days of this orator of 1406, no prelate had ever dared to dispute the right of the Holy See to decide upon important cases in final and supreme appeal. The pragmatic sanction of Bourges, the whole of Gallicanism, and the despotic spirit of Napoleon in 1811 are in embryo in this pretentious and rebellious speech.

On December 3, a few days later, Benedict's defenders replied before the King and the dukes. William Philastre, Dean of Reims, and subsequently a cardinal, was first on the scene. After making some excuses "as to his ignorance and the roughness of his equipment,"[2] after comparing the different faculties to the four animals of the Apocalypse, he wondered at their audacity in attacking and desiring to judge the Pope. "Methinks," said he, "that not all the nations together can condemn the Sovereign Pontiff. How, then, can you judge him with your council, which consists of a

[1] Bourgeois du Chastenet, pp. 122 and 157.

[2] *Ibid.*, p. 125. Elsewhere he says: "I am a poor man brought up in the fields: I am rough by nature, and have not lived among kings and nobles," p. 163.

small minority as compared with the rest of the Church, being barely a fourth or fifth part of it? Kings cannot deprive the Pope of his authority, but the Sovereign Pontiff has sometimes set up a king in France. He has deposed Frederick the Emperor, and he finds a prince for Portugal." These historical reminders were little to the taste of the élite congregation who listened to this speech on behalf of the Pope, and still less to the liking of the Duke of Berry. Later on, Philastre was obliged to offer a humble apology, so quick were princely susceptibilities to take offence.

Then the orator, with more vigour than skill, made a complete apologia for the Pontiff of Avignon: like the latter, he declared in favour of the way of agreement, which included all the rest, and against cession, which he thought useless. He showed up all the inconsistencies of the conduct of France in the matter, and begged that there should be no fresh withdrawal of obedience.

On December 4, the Archbishop of Tours, Ameilh du Breuil, addressed the assembly, and made a prolix lecture of a historical character. He reminded them that the numerous schisms that had occurred before had never been "done away with or extirpated" by the way of cession, but rather by general councils.

He overlooked the fact that, in all the former troubles of the Church, the circumstances were different. Then the question was how to put an end to a usurpation that was clear to everyone, whereas in 1406 it was uncertain on which side the real vicar of Jesus Christ was.

The Dean of Reims had been wanting in style and prudence; the Archbishop of Tours had made use of arguments that were little to the point; the Bishop of Cambrai entered the lists on December 11, and showed his great superiority to the preceding speakers. It was upon his diplomatic skill and well-known eloquence that Benedict relied above all.

Peter d'Ailly remained much more calm than his opponents: his words therefore had all the more weight when they recommended peace and moderation, and when he complained of the bitter words and passionate accusations brought against the Pope by the babblers who had ascended the tribune before him.

From his point of view, the way of *cession* was in reality the best: a general council was also to be desired, particularly for the question of Church reform;[1] the withdrawal for five years had brought about no results: hence those who would not return to that stale and inefficacious method should not be treated as schismatics. Taking up several propositions that he had formerly put forth, d'Ailly regretted that the whole of the University had meddled with the business, and not the faculty of theology alone, which solely was competent. He urged the prelates to give, not definite and peremptory decisions, but rather well-reasoned counsels. He declared that Gerson and more than eighty-six masters of the faculty of theology were of his view, and that they further believed in the great utility of provincial councils to be held annually to prepare for the future council of Benedict's obedience, and subsequently for a general council of the two obediences.

Lastly, he energetically defended the conduct of the Pontiff of Avignon, and declared that the Pope was neither a schismatic nor a heretic in the true sense of the

[1] Bourgeois du Chastenet, p. 153. D'Ailly asked for a *general council* first of all in 1381, and then demanded *cession* in 1395. He never had approved of the too difficult way of *compromise*, nor of the too barbarous way of *action*, nor of that of *agreement*, a dilatory expedient invented by Benedict after his election. In 1406 he extolled and defended the two first means, which ended in prevailing at the Council of Constance.

word, and claimed that he was ready to convoke a general council.

All these arguments ran directly counter to the ideas of the University.

Yet the speaker had taken care that his sentiments towards *Alma Mater* should be neither open to attack nor even to suspicion. Let us quote part of his exordium: "I protest that I wish to give offence to no one, and say this with special reference to my mother the University, whom I always love affectionately, and to whom I am much bound. For in and through her I have received many benefits and honours, whereof I was not worthy." [1]

But these oratorical precautions did not succeed in preserving d'Ailly from attacks and enmities. The University gave him small thanks for his frankness. She refused to regard him any longer as one of her members, for she complained that he had injured her reputation. She asked to be allowed to justify herself before the King through John Petit as her representative. He immediately began his address, and in his protests one finds the usual violence of character and the statements and methods that distinguished this impetuous Norman.[2]

Nevertheless, the rhetorical position of the Bishop of Cambrai had been unexceptionable. Cool, methodical, with his speech under perfect control, he had neither let himself be moved by interruptions nor calls to order, but had carried out his masterly argument to the end.

Like Simon de Cramaud, the Abbot of Mont-Saint-Michel and Peter Plaoul maintained anti-papal opinions and tried to secure the acceptance of all the prejudices of the University.

The abbot did not shrink from saying that obedience

[1] Bourgeois du Chastenet, p. 151. [2] *Ibid.*, pp. 198 and 228.

should be refused to the Pope when he abused his authority : and Benedict was in this position, for he was only working for the destruction of the Church. Peter Plaoul declared that the two Popes were obstinate schismatics, and consequently heretics.[1]

In reading their speeches, one becomes more and more convinced that belief in the divine institution of the Papacy had received serious shocks in these biased minds, and that the rights of the supreme Pontiff were scarcely any longer recognised by all these errant University men.

§ 2. *The Case of the King's Advocate.*

Lastly, Jouvenel des Ursins, the King's advocate, addressed the meeting to state the case. He spoke as a rather Gallican statesman, a forerunner of Achille de Harlay and Denis Talon. Alas ! for four centuries there has been scarcely any change in the language of French political advocates when the Church is in question !

" The King," he said in substance, " had the right to convene the council. In the name of Charles VI. I demand withdrawal of obedience, the suppression of the taxes imposed by Benedict, and the establishment of the jurisdiction of ordinaries, both for collation of benefices and for the hearing of disputes." [2]

After this speech, Jouvenel invited the members of the meeting to give their votes in writing. Simon de Cramaud nominated himself to preside over the ballot, to the great dissatisfaction of the council. The ques-

[1] *Cf.* Schwab, *Johannes Gerson*, p. 178. Tschackert, *Peter von Ailli*, p. 124. Ehrle, *Dietrich von Nieheim*, p. 19 ff.

[2] Bourgeois du Chastenet, pp. 106 and 229.

tion was this: "Is it advantageous to declare for a fresh withdrawal of obedience?" Opinions were very divided.

Some were for making new petitions and filial remonstrances to the Pope. Others were more radical, and declared for entire and unconditional withdrawal. This was the opinion of the University.

There were indeed some who were less bold, and put forward a mixed view, and who would have preferred half-measures. They were for maintaining the obedience in things spiritual, and for repudiating it in things temporal; that is to say, as to collations to benefices, prelacies, and dignities. This middle position received a majority of votes, and on January 4, 1407, the assembly adopted it.

It was, as will be remembered, the opinion which the Bishop of Cambrai had put forward in the work now in manuscript that we have already analysed.[1] The patriarch and several dukes came over to this view, and the King himself approved of this grave decision on February 11 following.

As was only to be expected, this decree provoked lively dissatisfaction. The Duke of Orleans and Guy de Roye, Archbishop of Reims, energetically opposed its execution. They represented the work to the King as an act of hatred, and also that it encroached not only on the personal authority of Benedict, but also on the indefeasible rights of the vicar of Jesus Christ, and on ecclesiastical privileges. Their influence was successful in staying the execution of this royal order. Hence resulted quarrels, insults, and resentments, that did not forward the work of uniting the two Churches.[2]

[1] *De materia concilii generalis*, 2a pars.

[2] Du Boulay, v. p. 141. *Chronic. Karoli VI.*, lib. xxvii. c. 17.

Thus ended the famous meeting of 1406. Its character is remarkable and perhaps unique of its kind, as indeed was the trial through which the Church was passing at this period.

If one considers the composition of a council of this kind, held before the court, it is not like the states general of the three orders that had been inaugurated at the beginning of the preceding century by Philip le Bel. It was rather like the great assemblies of the clergy of France, at which Le Tellier and Colbert, François de Harlay and Bossuet appeared later on.

It might specially be compared with the council of 1811, in which the great papal question and the question of the means to be taken for getting rid of the Pope in the Church were also at stake. Simon de Cramaud, a Gallican before the days of Gallicanism, is like the Cardinals Fesch and Maury. Jouvenel des Ursins, who summed up the debate and laid down the conclusions, appears to have been the model imitated four hundred years afterwards in the same town of Paris by the minister Bigot, when he claimed to intervene in the midst of episcopal commissions and to impose his will.

Let us hasten to add that the comparison, which we would not press unduly, here ceases.

The discussions of this unusual gathering are also curious reading. The style of oratory is familiar and picturesque. D'Ailly complains of "being indisposed with a cold, and of not being as facile as he could wish."[1] He asked for a recorder at the meeting, "that the words uttered in it may not be thrown to the winds."[2] He calls for the speedy conclusion of the discussions: "for," says he, "we are like lawyers who, after having

[1] Bourgeois du Chastenet, *Preuves*, p. 140.
[2] *Ibid.*, p. 162.

spoken very strongly against each other, go off to dine together."[1]

The Dean of Reims quotes at great length commonplace apologies borrowed from the versified stories of the day. In his pleadings we have already noted the fable put into verse by La Fontaine and entitled "The Child and the Schoolmaster."[2] He tells popular tales, well-known proverbs, which set those present laughing. In the same speech he complains that he has not brought his books, and that "he can neither cite chapters nor doctors."[3] An assembly of to-day would doubtless easily forgive the omission.

When a speaker like Peter Plaoul is obviously tiring the Court, the Chancellor rises and remarks: "Our Lordships are getting bored, Master Peter; have you much more to say?" And the object of the interrogatories replies unruffled: "I shall not finish very soon: I have still much matter. If you like, I will finish to-morrow."[4]

Indeed the speeches of those days would often exceed the limits of the hearers' patience of our times. They had three divisions, and sometimes one of these contained eight or twelve subdivisions.[5] The speakers put forth their propositions, not as formal assertions or explicit decisions, but as simple questions for discussion and deliberation, especially when the Church, the Popes and their rights were concerned.[6] Thus they left themselves convenient loopholes and easy excuses.

Although our language lends itself more to discussion, and offers greater facility for impromptu replies, all the

[1] Bourgeois du Chastenet, p. 163.
[2] *Ibid.*, pp. 200, 207, 222.
[3] *Ibid.*, pp. 126 and 200.
[4] *Ibid.*, p. 188.
[5] *Ibid.*, p. 205.
[6] *Ibid.*, pp. 126 and 151. This lack of frankness in argument is to be seen in all the disputants of these days. See p. 11 of this work.

speakers made excuses for speaking French: "These are high matters," said d'Ailly, "and not easy to explain in French."[1] "I would much rather speak Latin," added the Abbot of Mont-Saint-Michel. "I am not accustomed to speaking French, and also I am nervous and not certain of what I am saying. I beg you to bear with my deficiencies and put up with me."[2]

Oratorical eloquence was scarcely born in France: it was still stammering in the rhetorical bouts of the prelates.

Extraordinary amplifications and the forced application of Holy Scripture sometimes hide the underlying thinness of certain speeches. In other speakers the soundness of the reasoning is weakened by flourishes that were certainly useless, and by comparisons in doubtful taste. Moreover, there was a mania for borrowing quotations from ancient writers without imitating their style, and a habit of cramming speeches with tags of Latin. It is, indeed, easy to convince oneself that the humanism of the time was only pedantry. "The knowledge of those who spoke so wretchedly must have been prodigious," remarked La Bruyère.

Yet, such as they are, these harangues are a most curious monument of the language spoken at that period, and are interesting from more than one point of view.

§ 3. *The Election of Gregory XII.—The Hopes to which it gave Rise.*

About the same time, news of the death of Innocent VII. reached Paris. The Pope had been warmly entreated by the Romans to return to the Eternal City,

[1] Bourgeois du Chastenet, pp. 126 and 157.

[2] *Ibid.*, p. 164. *Cf.* Denifle, *Chartul.*, iii., Introd. p. xv.

and at last had consented to leave Viterbo, where he had taken refuge. But exile and grief had undermined his health, and he only returned to Rome to languish. He died on November 6, 1406, after reigning for two years amidst the tumult of political faction and ecclesiastical dissension. Circumstances had reduced him to be the plaything of the unbridled passions with which he was surrounded.

Fourteen cardinals immediately gathered in the chapel of the apostolic palace. They unanimously declared that the way of *cession* was the fairest and most reasonable for securing unity. They swore that, if one of them were elected, he would adopt this as the only practical method and renounce the Papacy, provided that Benedict on his side would do the same.

This declaration was much clearer than those that had gone before it, and it seemed as if nothing were wanting to assure the peace of the Church [1] in the near future. But human ambition has many ways of getting out of all promises, even when the gravest and holiest interests are at stake, as will be clearly seen once more.

Nevertheless the Sacred College seemed to have made a very fortunate choice. The votes had been cast in favour of Angelo Corrario, Cardinal of St Mark's, and he had taken the name of Gregory XII. He was a Venetian, and under Innocent VII. had been entrusted with very delicate missions.

He had always led a very austere life; [2] he was "of holy life and primitive severity," [3] and sixty-three years of age. Seeing him pass with his tall and emaciated form, one might have said, "A soul conducting a body."

[1] Martène et Durand, *Veter. Script.*, col. vii. 722.
[2] Muratori, iii. p. ii. col. 837.
[3] *Ibid.*, xvi. col. 1191, and xix. col. 925.

Hence it might be hoped that purely human considerations would have less hold over a Pontiff so aged and of such a stamp.

After his election on November 30, 1406, Gregory renewed all his oaths and appeared to be sincere in his intention to keep them.[1]

Hence joy and hope reigned in the court of Rome. They were soon shared by the whole of the Catholic world, when Gregory notified Benedict of his election, and of the conditions under which he had accepted it (December 12). "It is not the time to dispute about rights," he wrote: "on the other hand, it is rather the time for making them yield to public interests. The true mother would rather give up her rights than see her child cut in twain. I therefore propose to you to give up the tiara, if you on your side agree to do the same thing."[2] "I will go to see Benedict," he added, "even if I had to make the journey alone with only my stick, or in a little skiff."[3]

The Pope of Avignon at first appeared to enter into his rival's views. He received Gregory's ambassador courteously, and immediately replied that he consented to have a conference with him.

Thenceforward it appeared as if each of the two Popes were no more than a steward, temporarily entrusted with the affairs of his Church, and ready to abdicate on the first sign.

Such a new and unexpected situation was thought to pave the way for negotiations which could not fail to end in tangible results. An important embassy was

[1] *Cf.* Niem, *De Scismate*, lib. iii. 2.

[2] *Chronic.*, lib. xxvii. c. 21. *Cf.* Christophe, *Histoire de la Papauté au XIVe siècle*, iii. p. 234. Finke, *Acta Concilii Constanc.*, i. p. 280.

[3] Raynald, a. 1406, 13. Niem, *op. cit.*, 6. This writer always calls Gregory *Errorius*.

sent from Paris to Marseilles, where Benedict had gone to settle the place of the future interview between the two Popes.

The French legation consisted of very important persons. Among them were the Patriarch of Alexandria, the Archbishop of Tours, Peter d'Ailly, John Gerson, Peter Plaoul, John Petit, William Philastre, and almost all the speakers of the Council of 1406. A young graduate in canon law, then almost unknown, but destined to attain later on an unenviable celebrity, was with the embassy: he was Peter Cauchon, the future Bishop of Beauvais.

Meanwhile envoys left Rome to come to an understanding with the Pope of Avignon about the same matter.

Malatesta of Pesaro, an eloquent and amiable prince, had offered to go as ambassador at his own expense, and he was recommended by the cardinals. Unfortunately Gregory's preference was for his nephew, Antony Corrario, Bishop of Modon, whose stupidity and pretensions more than once nearly wrecked everything. There was much difficulty in coming to an agreement as to the place of the proposed conference; but at last, on April 20, 1407, the town of Savona was selected.[1]

In the meantime the royal ambassadors reached Marseilles (May 9). Benedict gave them a cordial reception, although several of them, and especially the Patriarch, Simon de Cramaud, had shown little respect for his person at the Council of Paris.

At the request of the King's envoys, the Pontiff publicly accepted the way of *cession*; nevertheless, when they begged him to confirm his words by a solemn bull,

[1] *Chronic.*, lib. xxviii. c. 2 and 3.

he blankly refused. He pretended that this act would be a loss of time as well as a sign of mistrust.[1] He was asked to promise that, in case of his death, he would require that no successor should be chosen, and that the cardinals of the two colleges should meet to elect a single Pope. He postponed an answer.

The French ambassadors begged the cardinals to interpose with Benedict. Malesset did so in the name of his colleagues, and got nothing from the obstinate Pontiff. The envoys of the Duke of Orleans, the faithful upholder of the Avignon Pope, met with no better success. The Bishop of Cambrai, and then Gerson, d'Ailly's friend and pupil, joined the Abbot of St Denis in taking a fresh step; but with as little result as those that had gone before it. The inflexible Benedict refused the bull they requested of him: "My acts," he said, "will prove to you better than my words that I have only the honour of God and the interests of the Church in view. You may be sure that I wish for nothing so much as to please the King, France, and all Christian people."[2]

No entreaty could induce him to go any further, and the ambassadors took leave of him without being able to obtain any further concession. At this they were very dissatisfied: all their apprehensions awoke anew, and they began to suspect the good intentions of Benedict. When they reached Aix-en-Provence, several were for an immediate proclamation of the withdrawal of obedience in accordance with the instructions they had received.

D'Ailly and Gerson opposed these arguments energetically, and succeeded in winning a victory for more

[1] *Chronic.*, c. 8 and 9.

[2] *Ibid.*, lib. xxviii. c. 12. Valois, iii. p. 514.

peaceful views, and in deferring a total rupture.[1] While several of their colleagues returned to Paris, the Bishop of Cambrai and the Chancellor set out for Rome with the Patriarch, in order to maintain and stimulate the good dispositions of Gregory.

Then all Catholics looked full of hope towards the little town of Savona, where the noble meeting was to gather which should at last restore peace to the Church, which had been divided for nearly thirty years.

Later on, through similar gatherings, Pisa, Constance, and Trent were destined in turn to attract the general attention of the Catholic world.

Four centuries later, in still more unhappy circumstances for the Church, Savona was to draw to itself the looks, not only of all true Catholics devoted to Pius VII., but of all men who are touched with the sight of crushed weakness struggling against injustice crowned and triumphant.

For the assembly of 1407, the republic of Genoa put three well-armed galleys at the disposal of the Pope; Lucca and Florence offered him their support; John de Boucicault, governor of Genoa in the name of the King of France, was to protect the coming meeting. King Charles had written to the inhabitants of Genoa and Savona to urge them to give a good reception to the two Popes, and these towns willingly opened their gates and palaces for them.[2] France and Italy seemed to be full of the best dispositions, and all Christian hearts were rejoicing beforehand at the happy result of the negotiations that were about to begin.

[1] Martène et Durand, *Thesaurus*, ii. p. 1329. *Chronic.*, xxviii. c. 13.

[2] Bourgeois du Chastenet, *Preuves*, p. 504. Letter of June 11, 1407. On the 13th, Charles sent similar instructions to his ambassadors and officers, p. 516. See Finke, i. p. 280, a detailed report from Simon de Cramaud to Sigismund.

CHAPTER XII

THE CARDINALS FORSAKE THE POPES

§ 1. *Failure of the Proposed Interview.*

As we have seen, the French ambassadors, Simon de Cramaud, Peter d'Ailly, Gerson, and a few others were on their way to the Eternal City. Though they were getting near Rome, the envoys were not without anxiety about the success of their mission, so often already had their strongest hopes come to nothing. At Viterbo, some of them met the Cardinal of Liège, John Gile, and Cardinal Orsini, who added to their uneasiness as to the Pope's disposition. At Rome, where they arrived on July 4, 1407,[1] these apprehensions further increased. Gregory appeared slack and inactive in the midst of this movement towards unity that he had himself set going. His former ardour had given way to marked coolness.

What were the causes of the change? They were of two kinds, the one political, the other personal. Ladislas of Naples had found in Gregory a Pontiff devoted to the interests of his crown, and put every hindrance in the way of his thinking about *cession*. On the other hand, the rigid attitude of the King of France with regard to Benedict made the Pope of Rome fear that he might meet with similar disrespect if he were at Savona under the heavy hand of Boucicault.

But the motives that chiefly influenced the old man's weakness were of a more intimate character. His

[1] P. d'Ailly and others coming by sea arrived on July 16.

nephews, for whom he always showed an extravagant affection, daily urged upon him that, if he gave up the Supreme Pontificate, the fortune of their house would fall and even vanish completely. The mind of the old Pontiff grew more and more liable to these perfidious counsels, and his zeal for unity became ever more and more lukewarm. It was the interest of his family rather than love of supreme authority that played upon his heart, to the confusion of poor human nature. When the French ambassadors appeared in audience, he made use of a number of ways to evade the stipulations of the Marseilles agreement. Being a Venetian, he would rather go to Savona in Venetian galleys, and refused those of Genoa, the old enemy of his country. On the other hand, he would willingly go by land in spite of war, plague, and difficult roads; only his means were insufficient. These were miserable shifts, and childish or rather senile subterfuges, which the Pope nevertheless dared to repeat in the presence of the envoys of Charles VI., and of the legates of Benedict, met in solemn audience on July 28, 1407.[1]

Neither remarks nor proposals made by the ambassadors, nor their conferences with the cardinals, nor their entreaties with the senator, nor their objurgations to the conservators and nobles of Rome, were able to make the Pontiff change his mind, and he showed himself as obstinate as his rival of Avignon.

After several requests on the one side and as many refusals on the other, the French envoys, cruelly deceived, set out on their way home (end of July 1407). On reaching Genoa, on August 21, two of them drew up monitories and sent them to Rome.

[1] *Chronic. Karoli VI.,* lib. xxviii. c. 24. Martène et Durand, *Thesaurus,* ii. col. 1347 ff.

The author of the first was James de Nouvion, who wrote to the Bishop of Todi and his colleagues who had stayed with the Pope. It is a document full of pertinence, elegance, and, at times, of eloquence.[1]

The second letter, addressed to the Pontiff himself, remains unpublished: its author was the learned and able Bishop of Cambrai.[2] At Rome he had succeeded in winning the confidence of the Pope, and he wished to turn it to good account for the greater welfare of the Church. Therefore he begged Gregory to fulfil all the conditions of the Marseilles undertaking, to go to Savona and to trust the King of France. He was frank enough to urge upon him the scandal to which his refusal would give rise and the loss that would result to the Apostolic See.[3]

All these counsels and attempts remained unavailing. When Benedict at Lerins, where he held his court, heard the issue of the steps that had been taken with his competitor, he secretly rejoiced. The less Gregory was for carrying out the Marseilles agreement, the more his rival pretended that he wished to be faithful to it.[4] He left Lerins with six well-armed galleys, and after a short stay at Nice, reached Savona on September 24, 1407. On his side, Gregory set out with extreme slowness, and reached Viterbo on August 15. He stayed there twenty days in spite of all the entreaties of the French cardinals and deputies; and finally consented to go as far as

[1] *Chronic.*, c. 26. *Cf.* Scheuffgen, *Beiträge zur Geschichte des grossen Schismas*, p. 91.

[2] Hefele, *History of the Councils*, x. p. 158. *Bibl. de l'École des Chartes*, 1902, p. 233 ff.

[3] MS. in the Vatican Library, No. 4192, f. 29. *Cf.* Salembier, *Petrus de Alliaco*, p. 71. Gerson collaborated in the letter dated September 15.

[4] "Quia Gregorius fugiebat, ipse Benedictus obviam ire videbatur," Sozomène of Pistoia in Muratori, xvi.

Siena, with the vague notion of getting as far as Lombardy and stopping there.

In giving an account of all these tergiversations, Leonard Aretino said later on, with more mischievousness than respect: "The first, he of Avignon, is a sea-monster that cannot travel by land; the second, Gregory, is a land-animal that cannot endure the sea."[1]

Benedict awaited his rival long at Savona while the latter was purposely delaying at Siena, and staying there from September 4, 1407, till January 1408. Gregory wasted his time in writing letters to the King of France, the Dukes of Burgundy and Berry, the University, and even to Boucicault, whom he both feared and hated. Thus he took care to inform Ladislas how impossible it was for him to go to Savona, and the latter, not at all well-disposed towards unity, was only too glad to be convinced.[2]

The Pope of Rome frequently allowed the time fixed for the meeting to come to an end. He chose different places, one after the other, and lastly he sent three nuncios to Savona to make excuses. He did not think that he was bound by the Marseilles contract, and asked for another to be drawn up on fresh grounds.

After many parleys, Benedict consented to go as far as Porto-Venere, not far from Spezia. Gregory came to Lucca, and refused to come any nearer to his rival. Yet they were scarcely separated by a day's walk. He feared, he said, the armed galleys and the aggressive character of his competitor: he believed, or pretended

[1] Muratori, xix. col. 926. *Cf.* Lenfant, *Histoire du Concile de Pise*, i. p. 193.

[2] Niem, *De Scismate*, iii. 20, 21. *Nemus unionis*, tr. iv. 1. Martène, *Thesaurus*, ii. col. 1339. *Veterum monum. amplissima collectio*, vii. col. 760.

to believe, that Benedict had a hostile intent and a treacherous plan for seizing him by force.[1]

Meanwhile Ladislas was marching upon Rome with a powerful army, and appeared under the walls on April 24, 1408. He reckoned on the perpetual dissensions between the Orsinis and Colonnas, on the latter of whom he relied. Paul Orsini, the governor of the town, made a show of wishing to defend it with vigour; but next night he hastened to give Rome over to Ladislas, who thus triumphed almost without striking a blow (April 25). Instead of being cast down by this violent capture, Gregory appeared to rejoice at it. He called the usurper "very dear son," and seemed only to see in this intervention a way of ridding himself of the cardinals and of the entreaties of those who were urging him in the direction of union.[2]

Doubtless none of these operations prejudiced the rights of the Pope of Rome in any way. The proud despotism of Louis XIV. and the degrading vices of Louis XV. did not prevent their being the legitimate successors of Henry IV. and St Louis. Only these proceedings on the part of the Pontiff, like those of Urban VI. not long before him, made these rights less respected and, so to say, less inviolable in the eyes of the cardinals, even of those who had elected him.

Was Benedict any more sincere? Certainly he kept up appearances better; but all these tergiversations, incessantly renewed, disappointed the expectations of the Christian world, and especially those of France.

[1] Niem, *De Scismate*, lib. iii. c. 23.

[2] Muratori, ii. c. 4, a. 1408. "Ultra modum laetificati fuerant," says Niem, *De Scismate*, iii. 28. "Gregorius fuit valde alacer, nam clam de voluntate ejus rex capiebat terras ecclesiae." Sozomène in Muratori, xvi. p. 1192.

§ 2. *Charles leaves Benedict, and the Cardinals abandon the Popes.*

A terrible assassination came to terrify the Court and the whole country. John the Fearless had his nephew Louis of Orleans killed in the streets of Paris (November 23, 1407). This frivolous but chivalrous prince had always defended Benedict against the ill-will of his uncles, the plans of the cardinals, and the threats and violence of the University. In striking him down, the Duke of Burgundy had dealt a terrible blow to the Avignon party. Thenceforward the King was delivered over irretrievably to the enemies of the Pope. The withdrawal of obedience had been, as we have seen, resolved upon but not carried out. The Pontiff, with his interminable wranglings, seemed to deserve all severity. Charles decided to let drop the sword of Damocles that had been so long suspended over his head. In two edicts, dated January 12, 1408, the King informed the two claimants that if union had not taken place by the Feast of the Ascension, he would declare himself neutral and leave Benedict's party.[1]

On getting this unexpected news, the Pope of Avignon issued bulls in which he complained with unrestrained bitterness and threw all the blame upon his rival. On April 18, 1408, he threatened the King with excommunication and other canonical penalties,[2] and on May 14 he carried out his threat.

The Court and the University were aroused by this attitude, and declared that Benedict and the distributors of these documents, pronounced to be seditious,

[1] Du Boulay, v. p. 131.

[2] *Chronic. Karoli VI.*, lib. xxix. c. 2 and 4. D'Achery, *Spicil.*, i. p. 803.

were guilty of high treason. The masters of the University do not even seem to have had a thought of turning towards Rome, and of recognising and acclaiming Gregory to hold Benedict in check, a step that would have brought the Schism to an abrupt and complete conclusion. On May 21, in full meeting, Master Courtecuisse, in the presence of the University and the people, brought fresh charges of heresy and schism against the Pope of Avignon amidst the applause of the whole of the royal council. "In the future," said he, "we will no longer obey Benedict, or call him Pope or Cardinal. His bulls are false, unjust, null, prejudicial to France and hurtful to the King's majesty." The complete withdrawal of obedience was proclaimed afresh, and was approved by the whole of the assembly. Violence carried on what inconsistency, presumption and a spirit of schism had begun. The Pope's bulls were brought and openly cut up with a penknife by the hand of the Rector himself. The two envoys of the Pontiff were loaded with ill-treatment.

At once Benedict's supporters were seized with fear. The Dean of St Germain of Auxerre, a venerable old man, was taken bodily by the King's men and cast into prison on a charge of high treason.[1] The Bishop of Gap and the Abbot of St Denis were also arrested. Guy de Roye, the Archbishop of Reims, who had openly attacked neutrality, refused to give explanations before the Assembly of Paris, and was forced to seek hiding. Peter d'Ailly, who had just come from a council held at Reims,[2] had a warrant of indictment issued against him, and had much difficulty in escaping an arrest at the hands of Walerand

[1] *Chronic.*, xxix. c. 4 ff. Du Boulay, v. p. 143.
[2] Marlot, *Histoire de la Ville de Reims*, iv. p. 144.

of St Pol.[1] Clémangis, one of his dearest pupils, formerly Benedict's secretary, was obliged to withdraw to the Chartreuse of Valprofonde at Béon, near Sens, and he tried to end his days in oblivion there.[2] It was a *coup d'état*.

The University followed up its work of vengeance and passion. It attacked Benedict and his supporters with the same fury as it had lately shown in defending them.

At Genoa, Boucicault received orders to seize the Pontiff, if he could, and to keep him in prison. Germany and Bohemia, Hungary and Navarre followed one another in making the declaration of neutrality that had been decreed by France.

An assembly met at Paris from August 11 till November 6 to settle the details of the government of the Church in the new state of things.[3] In it a multitude of schismatic usurpations were resolved upon, and the bishops and provincial synods were accorded powers that rightfully belonged to the Apostolic See.

The King informed the two Sacred Colleges of the steps that had been taken, and *Alma Mater* wrote to Gregory's cardinals to beg them to meet with those of Avignon and to work together for the suppression of the Schism.

The ground had been prepared in Italy. Grave events had happened at Lucca, where was Gregory,

[1] See *Revue des Sociétés Savantes*, 1868, 2nd half, viii. p. 139. *Documents relatifs à P. d'Ailly et découverts au couvent de Saint Julien à Cambrai*, by Lefebvre, called Faber. Archives of the Communes of Cambrai, Inventory List A.A., 120.

[2] *Epist. ad Petrum Cameracensem episcopum*, xliv. p. 133 (Ed. Lydii). *Cf.* Du Boulay, v. p. 158. Münz, *Nicholas de Clémanges, sa vie et ses écrits* (Strasbourg, 1846).

[3] *Chronic.*, lib. xxix. 6 ff. Hefele, x. p. 242.

the legitimate Pope of Rome. The differences between him and his cardinals had become accentuated and had assumed an acute form. On May 4, 1408, he had convened the members of the Sacred College and threatened them, and had tried to stifle their protests by intimidation. He had forbidden them to leave the town, or to meet without his expressed permission. The cardinals fled in terror, and nine of them gained Pisa in various disguises. Moreover, they had long been dissatisfied with the Pope. Gregory's obstinacy in refusing all interviews with his rival, and his blind affection for his nephews, whom he had just made cardinals, made the cup overflow, and precipitated a development that had been foreseen, and finished the rupture.

From Pisa, the dissentient cardinals sent memorials of an incriminatory character to Gregory and the Christian princes, and definitely showed their intention of joining the cardinals of the opposite side. The Pope of Rome set himself to refute their allegations and to bring their plans to nothing, but could not succeed in doing so.[1] Four of Benedict's cardinals met at Leghorn, where they had an interview with those of Gregory.

In the meanwhile the Pope at Avignon heard that his authority was more and more set at naught at Paris, and that his supporters had been thrown into prison.

He wanted immediately to escape the attempts of Boucicault, whose high-handed methods and energetic activity he knew well. Yet the obstinate Pontiff by no means gave up: he convoked a general council at

[1] Mansi, xxvii. p. 36. Hardouin, viii. p. 143. Raynald, 1408, 9-19. Niem, *De Scismate*, iii. 33. *Nemus unionis*, vi. 18 ff.

Perpignan for the ensuing Feast of All Saints, and then, with his soul full of bitterness, betook himself thither by sea.[1] On the coast of Italy he left six of his cardinals, who immediately joined those of Gregory.

The two Sacred Colleges had determined to follow up the question of Church unity in spite of everything, and to give their adhesion henceforward to neither one nor the other of the competitors. In case of the death of either of the Popes, they declared that they would appoint no successor, and that they would not recognise any election by the rest of the cardinals if made. On July 28, 1408, the Roman cardinals wrote in this sense to all the faithful of Gregory's obedience, and urged them to follow their example and to break with him.

The Pope of Rome, finally alarmed at this insubordination that threatened to become serious, tried to pacify the dissentients by promises or threats; but his letters, equivocal like the weakness that yields or distrust that holds back in reserve, had no success whatever.

Was the peace of the Church to arise from this new revolt?

Were the cardinals, taking over thus abruptly the guidance of the universal Church, directing her efforts towards unity, and addressing the sovereigns and bishops immediately, going to secure obedience? It was to be dreaded that they would not be followed when they made use of the means they had adopted for putting an end to the Schism. Moreover, what would be the new procedure employed by the two

[1] June 15, 1408. This is a notable date. It is the end of the residence of the Popes at Avignon, which had lasted 103 years. Perpignan then belonged to Spain.

colleges? Would it succeed, when so many others had already proved useless?

§ 3. *The Simultaneous Convocation of Three Councils.*

Such were the questions that the Christian world was asking when the assembled cardinals addressed an encyclical letter to the princes and prelates (July 2 and 5, 1408). They summoned them to a general council of the two parties, which was to be held at a town in Italy not yet specified. The cardinals took care to inform their respective Pontiffs.

No sooner was their proposal put forth (July 6), than Gregory on his side summoned a council to meet in the province of Aquileia or Ravenna. Later on he had created ten new members of his Sacred College and had taken refuge at Rimini under the protection of the faithful Charles Malatesta, the brother of Malatesta of Pesaro. He had received a letter from his cardinals which named the place and date of the future council of the two obediences. This meeting was to gather at Pisa on the feast of the Annunciation, March 25, 1409.

Benedict for his part had not acknowledged the receipt of the very respectful letter sent him by his cardinals. Later on he received from them a second letter summoning him to the Council of Pisa (November 6). This time he answered them, making a long apology on his own account, and wondering at the boldness of their procedure, and then he bade them come to the council he wished to call at once at Perpignan (November 7).[1]

[1] Bibl. Nat., Latin MS. 12,542, f. 143. *Cf.* d'Achery, *Spicil.*, i. col. 820. Mansi, xxvi. col. 1180.

This way of a council, at first recognised as the best, which had been put forward so long before and had been so persistently opposed, thus at last obtained great, and even too great success, since three conciliar assemblies were to meet at the same time, at Aquileia, Pisa, and Perpignan. It was not advantageous, for the only remedy was the meeting of a single assembly which should unite in it prelates from both obediences and from every quarter of Christendom.

Benedict's synod at Perpignan had little success. The number of bishops did not exceed sixty, although the Pope had waited some time for late-comers, and had created for the occasion new patriarchs of Constantinople, Antioch, Jerusalem, and Alexandria.

The Pontiff of Avignon made a circumstantial narrative of the sufferings he had endured, and of the sacrifices he had made for the welfare and peace of the Church. All those who were present applauded; but when they had to determine what should be done, opinions were divided and the council broke up, to a large extent without having decided anything.[1] The eighteen members who remained begged Benedict not to be intractable, but to get ready to abdicate and to send nuncios of acknowledged ability and with full powers to the Council of Pisa. After raising a number of difficulties, Benedict ended by agreeing to depute several prelates belonging to various nations to the future council.[2]

On the other hand, the increasing unpopularity of

[1] Hefele, *History of the Councils*, x. p. 244. Tolra de Bordas, *L'Antipape Benoît XIII. en Roussillon*, *Revue du monde catholique*, xv., April 1866, p. 20. Ehrle, *Archiv.*, vii. p. 576. Martène et Durand, *Coll. ampliss.*, vii. 915. Mansi, xxvii. col. 907, 1079, 1089.

[2] Mansi, xxvi. col. 1097 ff. Hardouin, vii. p. 1955 ff. Niem, *De Scismate*, iii. 37. Valois, iv. 49.

Gregory prevented any hope of success from his Council of Aquileia. There remained the Council of Pisa, upon which all eyes were now turned, as well as all the anxieties and hopes of the Catholic world. Many objections and many obstacles arose as to the plan of the cardinals who had abandoned the Popes. Never had the Catholic world been in an analogous position, and never has such a case of canon law occurred since the fifteenth century.

It was separation from their head; was it a usurpation of powers? Was it appealing to rebellion to re-establish order? Was it not, on the other hand, a natural method of putting an end to a Schism that was in danger of becoming chronic?

The two Pontiffs protested against the proceedings of the cardinals, who, according to them, could not convoke a council without the Pope. They relied upon several texts of canon law, and an anonymous writer summed up their arguments in a pamphlet that created a great sensation at the time.[1]

In general, however, these legal subtleties, literal interpretations, and legal scruples found no echo among the prelates, nor particularly amidst the great schools.

The Universities of Paris, Oxford, and Bologna, that is to say, the three most authoritative voices of Christian learning, had given advice in accordance with the desires of the cardinals, and highly approved their conduct. They took their stand in the main on the difficulty of the times and circumstances, on the natural and divine right of the Church, in virtue of her constitution, to discover in herself the means of maintaining and recovering, if needs be, her essential unity.[2]

[1] Mansi, xxvii. p. 223. [2] *Cf.* Martène et Durand, vii. col. 894 and 898.

Nevertheless Bologna went too far when it claimed that when a Pope has pledged himself to restore peace to the Church when she has been troubled by an intruder, and does not fulfil his promise, a simple provincial council may refuse him obedience.[1]

France, indeed, had ventured to give this example in lately withdrawing her obedience from Benedict; but if the Church ever admitted this principle, she would give her solemn sanction to utter anarchy within her borders. Is it not a point to which a saying of Bossuet's applies: "If there are strong examples for, there are strong reasons against"?

D'Ailly openly declared in favour of the Council in several works publicly approved by theologians and jurists. On the way to Pisa with Cardinal de Bar,[2] he passed through Aix, Tarascon, and Genoa, and in writings dated from each of these towns he asserted the absolute right of the cardinals, as well as the duty of the two rival Popes, to send representatives to the future meeting and to obey its decisions.[3]

Gerson added his voice to that of his illustrious friend, and gave the Council of Pisa the benefit of his popularity.[4]

[1] *Cf.* Martène et Durand, vii. col. 896.

[2] Louis de Bar was connected by birth with the royal family of France. He was Canon of Cambrai in 1403, and then became successively Bishop of Langres, Châlons, and Verdun. He had been created cardinal by Benedict in 1397. He died in July 1430.

[3] Two of these documents, those of Aix and of Genoa, are in the complete works of Gerson, ii. col. 110 and 112. The editor ascribes them to Gerson himself, but d'Ailly claims them as his own in his *Apologia Concilii Pisani*. *Cf.* Tschackert, *Peter von Ailli*, App. xii. p. 31 ff. The third, dated Tarascon, is in Martène et Durand, *Veter. Script.*, vii. col. 916.

[4] *De auferibilitate Papae*, *De unitate ecclesiastica*, *Propositio facta coram Anglicis*, etc., *Opp. Gersonii*, ii. col. 113 ff. Gerson is not the author of *Octo conclusiones quarum dogmatizatio utilis videtur ad exterminationem moderni schismatis*, *Opp. Gers.*, ii. col. 110. Martène et Durand, vii. col. 892. This work is rightly claimed by d'Ailly in the *Apologia Concilii*

Zabarella, as we have seen, claims for the Emperor the right of calling a general council,[1] while Niem, never very friendly to the Popes, recalls the history of Otho I., who convoked a council to depose John XII. He takes advantage of the circumstance to attack the Papacy in terms that recall those of Wicliffe, and for which certain members of the Councils of Paris had unfortunately provided him with a precedent (1398 and 1406). For all of them a scandal-giving Pope is *ipso facto* deprived of all right of command.[2]

In all these tracts, which are sometimes strange in doctrine, one sees a fatal consequence of the disputes of the School and of the deep perplexity that the Schism had caused even in the most highly gifted minds. We repeat [3] that these opinions are barely less than a clear echo of the doctrines of Marsilius of Padua and William Occam, and the troubles of the Church had only accentuated them.

§ 4. *Christendom becomes more and more Divided.*

The grave question of the council not only engrossed the attention of theologians, it also interested the King of the Romans and German politicians.

Robert of Bavaria, elected in place of Wenceslas,[4] was

Pisani in MS. at St Mark's Library, Venice, Latin cod. 120, f. 93. Richer and Ellies-Dupin have attributed to Gerson many documents of the time which were not composed by the famous chancellor, *e.g.* the *De modis uniendi*. A revision of his works is desirable. Bossuet asked for it even in his days, *Defensio declar.*, p. ii. lib. v. c. 12. He only had Richer's edition (Paris, 1606).

[1] See his treatise in Schardius, *De jurisdictione imperiali*, p. 696.

[2] *De Scismate*, iii. 9 to 12. Simon de Cramaud, Peter le Roy, Giles des Champs, Matthew de Krakow, and Gerson all use the same language.

[3] See chapter vi. of this work, p. 110.

[4] *Cf.* chapter ix. of this work, p. 179.

a convinced partisan of the Pope of Rome, whose predecessor Boniface had deposed his rival to the Empire in 1403. He had received an ambassador from the Council of Pisa, the Cardinal Landulph de Bari, but had given him an icy reception. At the diet of Frankfort he had bestowed all his favours on Gregory's nephew, Antony Corrario, whom the Pope had just sent to Germany as legate.

The King had even allowed Antony in full meeting to insult the cardinals gathered at Pisa, and in particular their ambassador Landulph, in spite of the murmurs of the nobles and prelates.[1]

Did Robert desire to profit by the discord between the Pope and Wenceslas to strengthen his position on the imperial throne and to get himself crowned with the crown of the Cæsars at the hands of his protégé Gregory XII.? Did he hope to play once more the part of Astolph, of Henry of Franconia, and of Frederick Barbarossa, and to unite all Italy under one sceptre, that of the Emperor of Germany? Some have thought so. So would Dante have had it, and after him many writers who were more patriotic than catholic.

But, at this time, the King of the Romans feared above all things the influence of France. Gregory showed him the cardinals acting on behalf of Charles VI. and seeking to attack and ruin the Empire. The future council would only be an instrument of French policy.

Robert, tossed to and fro between his ambition and his fears, had little confidence in the result of the efforts of the assembly that was gathering at Pisa. Nevertheless he agreed to send three representatives to the council, and we shall presently see the part they had to play.

[1] Niem, *De Scismate*, lib. iii. 39.

In the South of Italy the council hardly met with more favourable dispositions. The ambitious Ladislas reigned at Naples, and he too has his place amongst the many who have dreamt of Italian unity. In the centre and the North he wanted to crush successively all the little republics that were so proud of their independence, and to establish his supremacy from Bologna to Bari, and from Florence to Reggio. *Aut Caesar aut nihil* was his proud motto. He had already obtained important concessions from Gregory, and forced himself upon him as an imperious protector, and took upon himself to raise taxes in the Papal States.[1]

He rightly feared, too, the warlike spirit of Louis II. of Anjou, who had abandoned none of his father's claims to the throne of Naples, and who was getting ready to make them good by force.

To succeed in his ambition and to triumph over his rival, the King of Naples must have the Pope acknowledged in the whole of Italy, and keep him as an obliging ally, if not as a submissive accomplice. Like Robert, and for the same object, he held to the friendship and alliance of Gregory XII. Thus the Pontiff appeared to be delivered over beforehand as a victim to the covetousness of these two royal personages.

Unfortunately for the ruler of Naples, his plans failed miserably. Found out by the Florentines, who made a formidable league against him, and forced to give up the Papal States, Ladislas had to return to Naples with an army that was still numerous, but disgraced. His attack was as wanting in success as in principle.

Happily for Gregory he had a more substantial ally, one more faithful to the Church and less anxious for his

[1] Mansi, xxvi. pp. 1139, 1219. Hardouin, viii. pp. 8 and 79. Gregorovius, *Geschichte der Stadt Rom*, vi. p. 605.

own political interests, in the person of Charles Malatesta, Lord of Rimini. This prince was an eloquent and chivalrous protector to the Pope of Rome, and he would have saved the position for the Pontiff had it been possible to save it.

He was almost alone in his disinterested fidelity to the old Roman Pope, deserted by his cardinals and surrounded with equivocal, self-interested, or compromising allies. A noble type of prince is Malatesta; a figure that stands out alone amidst all the sovereigns of the period.

From this date onwards, the Great Schism enters upon a new phase. Of all the methods proposed for putting an end to religious division, one only is left: it is that of a general council. All other projects or expedients, whether they were the outcome of an honest heart or of fanciful prepossession, have failed one after the other. Whether these ways be called cession, compromise, the "way of action" under Clement VII., or of a convention under Benedict XIII., they have been given up in turn.

Christendom was now face to face with, on the one hand, two Popes without cardinals, and on the other, confronted with cardinals without a Pope. France, moreover, after many fluctuations, had resolved to leave the Pontiff of Avignon who had refused to enter into her views, and to prosecute and punish Benedict's most intelligent and determined supporters, the true heads of the French Church.

The situation was more extraordinary, more acute, more critical than ever. Kings, prelates, and peoples, too long deceived, ceased to reckon on the goodwill of the rival Popes; they were about to act independently of them, in spite of them, and sometimes against them.

They had resolved to rely upon the Sacred Colleges gathered at Pisa to bring success by way of a general council, which, after years of effort, after new and tragical vicissitudes, was at last to restore unity and peace to the Church.

CHAPTER XIII

THE COUNCIL OF PISA

§ 1. *Opening of the Assembly.*

THE cardinals had had a happy inspiration in selecting Pisa as the seat of the council which was to put an end to the Schism that had lasted far too long.

Divided by the Arno into two unequal parts, this famous town had long seen ships coming in with the treasures of the West and the spoils of the East. For three centuries its hardy sailors had furrowed all the seas, winning victories over the fleets and armies of Genoa, Lucca, and Florence, and conquering kingdoms among the infidels at the time of the crusades.

Later on, intestine divisions amongst the citizens, frequent rebellions of the subjects who inspired in more than one prince a dread of Ugolino's fate in the Tower of Hunger, the ardour that urged the republic in its fealty to the Guelphs against the other Ghibelline cities of Tuscany, a series of deadly epidemics that had ravaged the city, the repeated exactions of *condottieri* who overran and laid waste the country, and the taking of the town by the Florentines (1406) lowered the renown and diminished the forces and lessened the riches of these proud rulers of the sea.[1]

At the time of the meeting of the august assembly,

[1] MURATORI, xv. p. 973; xiv. p. 641. TARTINI, *Chroniche della città de Pisa* del VINCENZIO COLLETTI, i. p. 311.

Pisa had lost some of the rays of its ancient glory: it was only a secondary town of Tuscany, and, so to say, a shadow of its former self. Then, as to-day, it was wrapped in the calm and poetic sadness of fallen cities. Such is Bruges on the North Sea; such, on the Mediterranean, is Aigues-Mortes, where the crusaders of St Louis embarked of yore. Thus Pisa, still filled with memories of its ancient splendour, and henceforward sitting in quiet solitude, seemed to be particularly fitted for appeasement and for the negotiations which were being arranged.[1]

To the right of the Arno, now without ships, to the north of the old city, extends a solitary district which, from an artistic point of view, remains one of the wonders of the world. There was first of all the cathedral that was to receive the fathers of the council, with its fine naves, its hundred yards of length, its flying cupola, and its columns of white marble with their varied incrustation. A thousand victorious trophies reminded Christians of the Pisan expeditions against the Saracens.

Then, by the side of the basilica was the eleventh century baptistery, with its superb pillars and artistic bas-reliefs. It was the *Campo Santo*, an incomparable cemetery where slept in earth brought from Mount Calvary twenty generations of Pisans.

It was on the walls of this building that Bennozzo Gozzoli, Lorenzetti, and other artists were to paint the most wonderful scenes from Scripture and the triumph of Death. But the most unique marvel was the leaning tower, with its colonnades and galleries, its airy peals of bells, and above all, with its startling slant. Doubtless its appearance more than once suggested to the fathers a striking comparison. Was there not here, they might

[1] Niem, *De Scismate,* iii. 26, p. 262.

have asked, an image of the Church that then seemed to totter to its fall, and which, humanly speaking, had never been so near ruin. But she had promises of life eternal, and soon her bells would proclaim her triumph over death.

Such indeed was the result desired by the four patriarchs, the twenty-two cardinals, and the eighty bishops who were to compose this Council of Peace. An imposing procession wended its way on March 25, 1409, through the streets of the city. Starting from St Michael's Church, on the banks of the Arno, it betook itself to the cathedral, which opened to welcome the members of the council. Besides the prelates, one might note amidst the ranks of the clergy the representatives of more than a hundred bishops who were absent, eighty-seven abbots with the proxies of those who had not been able to reach Pisa, and forty-one priors and generals of orders.

Before them marched in splendid military array the armed defenders of Christendom, the Grand-Master of Rhodes with sixteen commanders, the Prior-General of the Order of St Sepulchre, the General-Procurator of the Teutonic Order. The deputies of the University of Paris and of the other Universities of the Christian world might have saluted on their way that other abode of science, which was to be honoured by Galileo, and which was called the University of Pisa. Three hundred doctors of theology and canon law, and the ambassadors of all the kingdoms of Christendom completed the train, which was the finest that had ever been seen in the ancient capital of the Pisans.

Cardinal de Malesset, Bishop of Preneste, was appointed president. We have already made the acquaintance of this prelate, whom his great age marked out for this honour, for alone among his colleagues he owed his dignity to Gregory XI., the last Pope before the Schism.[1]

Next day, Peter Philarghi ascended the pulpit and vigorously assailed the two Popes. It was he who a few months later would be elected to take their place.

Legal proceedings commenced at once. Two cardinal deacons, two archbishops, two bishops, and two notaries solemnly advanced towards the doors of the Church, had them opened, and summoned the two rival Pontiffs in a loud voice in Latin. No one replied. "Is anyone bidden to represent them ?" they added. The silence was unbroken.

The delegates returned to their places and requested that Gregory and Benedict should be pronounced contumacious.

Three days in succession the same solemn ceremony was gone through, with the same absence of result. The formal declaration of contumacy, however, was only pronounced at the fourth session.

Then the Council of Pisa truly began. It passed through three phases, and ended in the election of the new Pope. We shall note at first the exercise of German pressure, and then of Italian influence ; and at last, the episode of Aragon will precipitate the final issue.

§ 2. *The Germans at Pisa.*

At the beginning of 1409, it has been said that Cardinal Landulph of Bari had been sent to Frankfort by his brethren of the two obediences to invite the German prelates and princes to come to the Council of Pisa.

[1] The nephew of this Pope, he was made a cardinal at Avignon on December 20, 1375, and long had the title of Cardinal of Poitiers. At first a partisan of Urban's, he had subsequently come over to the obedience of Clement. He died at Paris in 1412.

The Pope of Rome had, moreover, always upheld Robert, who very fairly gave him his support in return. Furthermore, the fathers of the council, at the instigation of the same Cardinal of Bari, declared openly for his rival Wenceslas of Bohemia, who was represented at the assembly.

This led to the sending of a deputation to Pisa that was unfavourable to the plans of the assembled cardinals, and entrusted with the raising of difficulties. These German ambassadors were John, Archbishop of Riga, Matthew, Bishop of Worms, and Ulrich, Bishop of Verden. On April 15, these prelates appeared at the fourth session of the council, and Archbishop John solemnly addressed the assembly. He put forth, one after the other, twenty-three objections, a great number of which are excellent, but which had the disadvantage of being presented without order or logical connection.

In the first articles, the delegates dispute the lawfulness of the initiative taken by the Sacred College when it refused obedience to Gregory. They denied that the cardinals had any authority to summon a council; for this right belonged only to the Pope, *i.e.* Gregory, who had been fairly elected, recognised, and proclaimed. Moreover, if his election was illegal, how could the cardinals whom he had appointed be sure of the legitimacy of their titles? Next the deputies disputed the legality of the uniting of the two colleges, on the ground that only the nomination of the cardinals of one of the two parties could be considered regular.

So far, nothing could have been better. But the envoys went on to discuss the dates, and reproached the council with having indicated beforehand the object they had in view. This was "to limit the action of the Holy Spirit," they said. But, on the contrary, at the end the deputies appeared to recognise the legitimacy of the Assembly of Pisa, and were perplexed at the final refusal of Benedict, and made out that the interval allowed for coming to the council was too short.

In conclusion, they proposed to the assembled fathers to ask Gregory to select another meeting-place.

A canon of Spires, Conrad of Soest, undertook to give the Synod in writing the long list of these propositions. There is no need to cast any doubt upon the goodwill of Robert's envoys, but the militant disposition of the assembled prelates would not admit of their giving a kindly reception to such criticisms and urgent difficulties. In reality, the effect on the members of the council was grievous for the Germans. They felt this so clearly that they quitted Pisa, as if they were fugitives, on April 21,[1] leaving behind them a new document, in which they aggravated the clumsiness of their criticisms by the violence of their protests. They did not wait for the answer of the fathers. The latter thought it their duty to make one, nevertheless, and entrusted the drawing up of this reply to the learned professor of Bologna, Peter of Ancorano, one of the lights of the council.[2]

We will not enter into these legal discussions in detail. The eminent master sums up the criticisms of the German delegates under four heads, and explains the ideas of the prelates of Pisa as to the withdrawal of obedience, the summoning of the council, the invitation of Gregory to attend the meeting, and as to the union of the two colleges of cardinals. This vigorous reasoning

[1] Mansi, xxvi. p. 1188. Hardouin, viii. p. 49. Hefele, x. p. 255. *Cf.* Pastor, *Histoire des Papes*, i. p. 200. J. Weizsäcker, *Deutsche Reichstagsakten*, vi. p. 496.

[2] *Cf.* Fabricius, *Bibl. medii ovi*, i. p. 235; v. 713; vi. 346. Tiraboschi, *Storia lett. ital.*, ii. p. 370. Schulte, *Geschichte des canonischen Rechts* (Stuttgart, 1877), ii. 278.

almost always gave a sufficient answer to the objections of the envoys of the King of the Romans.[1]

§ 3. *The Italians at Pisa.*

Very different and much more skilful was the line taken by Charles Malatesta, Prince of Rimini. While Robert, as an awkward friend, was compromising the otherwise excellent case for Gregory, Charles defended it as a man of letters, an orator, a politician, and as a chivalrous defender.

First he tried to bring about a reconciliation between the Pope and the fathers, and suggested to four of the cardinals to change the place of the conference, or to put it off.

The Cardinal of Albano replied in the name of his colleagues: "It is the two claimants who themselves mentioned the name of Pisa. It is there that the Popes have been summoned to appear. The cardinals have no right to change the place, for the previous summons would then be null. Moreover, many members are present, others are coming, and a great number of ambassadors are on the way. All change of this kind would be unbecoming."

Malatesta replied: "The conditions upon which Gregory accepted Pisa have changed. Besides, the essential point is the peace of the Church, and the Pope will do everything he can to secure it. Let the cardinals take care: if they continue their present line of action they will have three Popes instead of one."[2]

The cardinals replied in substance: "Let Gregory

[1] Mansi, xxvii. p. 367. Hefele, x. p. 271.

[2] Hefele, x. p. 260. Martène et Durand, *Veter. Script.*, vii. p. 1005. Mansi, xxviii. p. 252.

come to Pisa or decide to abdicate at Rimini. What a joy it would be for your city, Prince! What a glory, too, for it would be there that the election of the future Pope would take place."

"I want neither the honour of my capital nor my own," Malatesta was pleased to observe, "I only want the welfare of the Church."

The negotiations made no progress. The council then named a commission, composed of the Archbishop of Pisa, the Bishop of Cambrai, and two other members, to address fresh entreaties to the protector of the Roman Pope. D'Ailly in particular exerted himself to show that he ought to persuade Gregory to yield or to force him to do so. He tried to prove to him that the proposal to change the place of the council was contrary to law, and could only injure the restoration of peace.

Malatesta was not at all convinced.

In another interview, the Cardinal of Milan, Peter Philarghi, was no more successful. To a promise of abdication made by the prince he replied: "Gregory will not abdicate: he clings to reigning too much." The prince replied with vivacity: "There are people who would not hesitate to overthrow the Church to ascend the see of St Peter. How can you wonder if Gregory requires urging to get him to leave it?" "I have no ambition for the tiara," replied Philarghi. "Perhaps, though, you would have no great repugnance to putting it on some day," replied Malatesta. And herein the Prince of Rimini prophesied true.

Finally, for the good of the Church, the cardinals consented to an interview with Gregory at Pistoia. Malatesta offered to do his best to get the Roman Pontiff to accept this rendezvous and left for Rimini.

But when he gave the Pope an account of his mission and its result, the feeble old man began to weep. "What am I to do?" he cried. "If I accept, I betray my supporters and my family; if I refuse, I raise great scandal in the Church."

Malatesta insisted energetically and eloquently and urged the Pontiff to go to Pistoia. "Never will I go to a town depending upon Florence," said Gregory in reply. "Besides, I could not abandon my neighbours, like King Robert of the Palatinate and King Ladislas of Naples, my devoted supporters." This was all that could be obtained: henceforward his destiny was to be rapidly fulfilled.

§ 4. *The Aragon Incident.*

There remained the intractable and crafty Benedict, who, in retirement at the foot of the Pyrenees, had not yet given up all hope of seeing the triumph of his cause. His deputies were awaited at Pisa from moment to moment, and they were deliberating as to how they should be received by the council. In spite of a few members of the Sacred College who were still attached to the Pope of Avignon, it was declared that his ambassadors should be treated with no sort of honours. After many deliberations the synod also proclaimed that the union of the cardinals of the two obediences was in accordance with law, and that the assembly had been lawfully convened. It affirmed, moreover, that the Council of Pisa was a true œcumenical council, enjoying the authority of the highest tribunal in the world, and having a sovereign right to decide between the two claimants.

The members of the council arrived in larger and

larger numbers from every part of Christian Europe. It was then that, in order to establish greater order amongst the different special congregations, it was thought advisable to have each country represented by a certain number of delegates, and to give out opinions nation by nation. There were four, those of France, Italy, England, and Germany. Later on we shall see the Council of Constance use the same method of procedure, unknown to former synods.

The assembly, after drawing up a memorial of all the incidents of the Schism, asked each of its members to abandon the obedience of Benedict and Gregory, declared to be obstinate.

Nearly the whole of the month of May was devoted to taking the evidence of witnesses against the two claimants. Then, on May 23, the assembly outlined the sentence that was to be pronounced. Numerous masters of the University took part in the debates, and were not among the least ardent in their condemnation of the Pope of Rome and even of Avignon.

On this date the cardinals received Benedict's bulls. "I have taken knowledge of your summons to the council," he declared, "but I shall not come, and I forbid you to elect another Pope in my place."

They took no notice, and on June 5, 1409, met for the fifteenth solemn session. The cardinals fulfilled for the last time the formality of citing the claimants at the gates of the Church, then the procurators of the council demanded that a definite condemnation should be pronounced against Peter de Luna and Angelo Corrario.

The fathers of Pisa were about to return a sentence until then unexampled in the history of the Church. All were stirred when the Patriarch of Alexandria,

Simon de Cramaud, addressed the august meeting: "Benedict XIII. and Gregory XII.," said he, "are recognised as schismatics, the approvers and makers of schism, notorious heretics, guilty of perjury and violation of solemn promises, and openly scandalising the universal Church. In consequence, they are declared unworthy of the Sovereign Pontificate, and are *ipso facto* deposed from their functions and dignities, and even driven out of the Church. It is forbidden to them henceforward to consider themselves to be Sovereign Pontiffs, and all proceedings and promotions made by them are annulled. The holy See is declared vacant and the faithful are set free from their promise of obedience.[1]

Scarcely had the patriarch done reading this grave sentence, when joyful applause broke out in the vast enclosure. The *Te Deum* was sung, and a solemn procession was ordered next day, the feast of Corpus Christi.

All the members of the august assembly appended their signatures to the grave deed of condemnation that had just been pronounced.

Thereupon there entered the council the ambassadors of the King of Aragon, who had to announce that the nuncios of Benedict had finally reached Pisa. These envoys were abbots and religious, among whom was Boniface Ferrier, the brother of St Vincent.[2] They

[1] Hardouin, *Concil.*, viii. p. 85 ff. Von der Hardt, *Rerum Conc. œcum. Constant.*, ii. col. 136.

[2] Like his brother, Boniface was a violent partisan of Benedict's. He wrote a vehement letter against the French who were present at the council, and especially against the Bishop of Cambrai. Here is the title of his pamphlet—*Specula contra vasa irae super haeretica pravitate pisana*, Martène et Durand, *Thesaurus*, ii. col. 1447. Peter d'Ailly replied with his *Apologia Concilii Pisani*, recently printed in the *Peter von Ailli*, by Tschackert, *Appendix*, p. 31.

had not come to bring Benedict's adhesion to the conciliar meeting; they had only been ordered to publish Benedict's renunciation, if Gregory did the same, a conditional clause that savoured of mockery in the circumstances.

They made their entry into the council on June 14, but their pretension soon aroused the protests, and then the ironical laughter, of those who were present. The people of Pisa gave them a still more unfavourable reception, and at times heaped threats and insults upon them. The chancellor of Aragon was heard somewhat impatiently, and the Archbishop of Tarragona raised a terrible uproar when he began his speech thus: "We are the nuncios of the only true Pope, Benedict XIII." It was a declaration of war that showed more audacity than capacity.

Moreover, the ambassadors soon saw that all their proceedings at the council would be fruitless, and that everything was being got ready for the election of a new Pope. It was necessary to inform them that their lives would be in danger if they persisted in upholding the so-called rights of the Pontiff of Avignon. In much fear the envoys left the town secretly and tried to reach Gregory. For this purpose they asked Balthazar Cossa, then the governor of Bologna, for a safe-conduct. "Whether they come with or without a safe-conduct," he replied with brutality, "let them know this, that if I take them, I will have them burnt alive."[1] More and more alarmed, the nuncios of Benedict returned to their master.

The latter did not allow himself to be cast down by

[1] Martène et Durand, *Veter. Script.*, vii. p. 1112. *Thesaurus*, iii. p. 1476. Hardouin, viii. 17, 89. Lenfant, *Histoire du Concile de Pise*, p. 284.

these repeated blows, but appointed twelve new cardinals to carry on the Schism which he had done so much to bring into being and to prolong.[1] It was a vexatious expedient to add to so many others, and it aggravates the responsibility of its author in the eyes of the Church and of posterity.

§ 5. *The Election of Alexander V.*

All was ready for the conclave which, according to the hopes of the Sacred College, would bring about the unity of the Church. On June 15, the cardinals met in the archiepiscopal palace of Pisa to proceed with the election. The conclave lasted eleven days. Few obstacles intervened from outside to delay the election of the new Pope. Within, it is said, there were a few intrigues concocted for the election of a French Pope. But at last, through the influence of the energetic and ingenious Cossa, the votes were unanimously cast in favour of Peter Philarghi, a cardinal who took his title from the twelve apostles. He was elected on June 26, 1409, and took the name of Alexander V.

Like Silvester II., Saint Gregory VII., Adrian IV., and several other Pontiffs, Alexander was of the humblest extraction.[2] It is hardly known whether he was of Greek or Italian origin. He had been forsaken by his parents from his earliest years, and spent his childhood at Candia, where he begged his bread. A Friar Minor, who took an interest in him, educated him, made him

[1] Niem, *De Scismate,* lib. iii. 14, p. 310. Ciaconius, *Historia Pontif. Roman. et Cardin.*, ii. p. 741.

[2] In 1881 appeared a Greek biography of Alexander, entitled: Μάρκου Ῥενιέρη Ἱστορικαὶ Μελέται. ὁ Ἕλλην Πάπας Ἀλέξανδρος έ! Τὸ *βυζάντιον καὶ ἡ ἐν* Βασιλείᾳ Σύνοδος. *Cf.* Pastor, i. p. 200.

join the order, and then took him to Italy. A student of Oxford, a doctor and then a professor of Paris, he was distinguished alike as master and preacher, and showed himself a determined supporter of Urban VI. Recalled to Italy, he became the tutor of the son of John Visconti, Duke of Milan; and subsequently was Bishop of Placenza (1386), Vicenza (1387), and then of Novara (1389). In 1402[1] he was advanced to be Archbishop of Milan, and Innocent VII. invested him with the purple. Under Gregory XII. he actively took the side of the dissentients; he discharged certain important negotiations with undoubted success, and largely contributed to the meeting of the Council of Pisa.

His election was expected and hoped for; and as soon as the sound of bells made it known, everyone hastened to testify his respectful joy to him. Perhaps many of the greetings were interested, for they knew that the new Pontiff could not resolve to refuse a favour. Munificent kindliness was the salient feature of his character. Niem himself, who shows little friendliness as a rule when the Roman Pontiff is in question, is forced to praise his generosity of disposition.[2] Alexander was solemnly crowned, on July 7, by the Cardinal of Saluzzo, in the midst of general rejoicings, for everyone thought that the Schism was ended for ever.

The new Pope hastened to send legates to all the sovereigns of Christendom to announce his election, and he received from every quarter of the world marks of lively sympathy for himself and for the position of the Church. Charles VI. wrote to him, through his secretary

[1] *Cf.* Gams, *Series episcoporum*, p. 796 (Ratisbon, 1873).

[2] Niem, p. 321. *Cf. De difficultate reformationis in Concilio universali* (August 1410). This work was long ascribed to d'Ailly, but it is probably by Thierry de Niem: this is Lenz's opinion, and also Schwab's and Hergenroether's. *Opp. Gersonii*, ii. col. 872.

John de Montreuil,[1] and France honoured the humble Friar Minor, now Pope, as if he were descended from royal blood. He presided over the four last sessions of the council, confirmed all the ordinances made by the cardinals after their refusal of obedience, and united into one the two Sacred Colleges. He subsequently declared that he would work energetically for reform in concert with the élite of the prelates of every nation. Nevertheless,[2] Alexander immediately distributed favours and privileges with both hands, particularly to the Minors and Augustinians, and gave his friends bishoprics and abbeys with too much generosity. It was a bad way of beginning reform by acting thus inconsistently with it.

The assembly, before breaking up, took several fresh legal measures, and settled certain circumstances to the greatest advantage of the prelates, abbots, and nobles; another fatal example given by the expiring council. Nevertheless, it was resolved that in three years' time, that is to say, in 1412, another general council should meet, and that in the meantime metropolitans should convene provincial councils and look into the question of reform with them. These decisions were undoubtedly sincere, but it gives one a painful impression to see the bishops and abbots thinking of increasing their personal powers, and diminishing the charges they had to pay before thinking of their own amendment. "*Et haec fuit ipsa reformatio ultro promissa!*" cries a contemporary in sorrow, "Such is their long-promised

[1] *Cf.* Martène et Durand, *Veter. Script.*, ii. col. 1374. Mgr. Hautcœur, *Histoire de Saint Pierre de Lille*, ii. p. 161.

[2] Later on the French deputies protested at the Council of Rome against these exaggerated favours, at which the University of Paris was very dissatisfied. *Cf.* Finke, *Acta Concilii Constant.*, i. p. 162.

reform!"[1] It might be feared that deeds would not correspond with words, and that the reform, so perseveringly hoped for, so openly proclaimed, would yet remain long a dead letter.

In the meantime, Gregory XII. endeavoured to assemble a council at Cividale in Frioul. Hardly anyone attended, and sentences were pronounced that the precarious position of the Pope made necessarily ineffective. The results were such that the Pontiff deposed at Pisa had to fly disguised as a merchant (September 6, 1409).

As for Benedict, he saw his soldiers obliged to leave Avignon before the French troops, and he prudently made haste to cross the Pyrenees and to place himself more and more under the protection of his royal friend, Martin of Aragon.[2] He was leaning on an already bruised reed. On May 31, 1410, King Martin breathed his last, and the obstinate Benedict was deprived by Providence of one of his best supporters.

§ 6. *Judgment on the Council of Pisa.*

Despite the checks received by the condemned claimants, what was the position of the Church in law and in fact at the end of 1409?

The right of the cardinals to convene a general council to put an end to the Schism seemed to themselves indisputable. It was a consequence of the natural principle, as has been already observed, that demands for a large corporation the capacity of discovering within

[1] MANSI, xxvi. p. 1090 ff. RAYNALD, a. 1409. L. SCHMITZ, *Römische Quartalschrift*, 1894, p. 245 ff.

[2] TOLRA DE BORDAS, *L'Antipape Benoît XIII. en Roussillon*, *Revue du Monde catholique*, xv. p. 24 (1866).

itself a means of safety: *Salus populi suprema lex esto.* Everything must be subject to the safety of the Church, and to the preservation of her indispensable unity. Moreover, the tergiversations and at times the perjuries of the two pretenders seemed to justify the united Sacred Colleges. "Never," said they, "shall we succeed in ending the Schism while these two obstinate persons are at the head of the opposing parties. There is no undisputed Pope who can summon a general council. As the Pope is doubtful, the Holy See must be considered vacant. We have therefore a lawful mandate to elect a Pope who will be undisputed, and to convoke the universal Church that her adhesion may strengthen our decision." Famous Universities urged and upheld the cardinals in this way.[1]

And yet, from the theological and juridical point of view, their reasoning might seem false, dangerous, and revolutionary. For if Gregory and Benedict were doubtful, so were the cardinals whom they had created. If the fountain of their authority was uncertain, so was their competence to convoke the universal Church and to elect a Pope. Plainly this is arguing in a circle. How, then, could Alexander V., elected by them, have indisputable rights to the recognition of the whole of Christendom? Further, it was to be feared that certain spirits would make use of this temporary expedient to transform it into a general rule and to proclaim the superiority of the Sacred College and of the Council to the Pope.

This is, indeed, what happened. Zabarella, appointed

[1] This is the principle extolled in the treatise that has so long been attributed to Gerson, *De modis uniendi Ecclesiam . . . Opp. Gersonii*, ii. col. 163. *Cf.* Pastor, i. 203. Lenz, *Drei Traktate aus dem Schriftencyklus des Constanzer Concils Untersucht* (Marburg, 1876), p. 29.

cardinal later on, had already laid it down as a principle that the Sacred College should be like a permanent commission set over the government of the Church, to the detriment of the Holy See.[1] For him the Pontiff is only the first minister of the Church, the *caput ministeriale*. Later on, Richer and his school spoke in much the same strain. The same Zabarella dares also to affirm that, when the College of Cardinals cannot or will not convoke the council, this right belongs to the Emperor: a theory of which the application will be seen at Constance. The spirit of Cæsar succeeds to that of revolution: this is part of the constitution and logic of facts.

The means used by the cardinals could not succeed even temporarily. The position of the Church became still more precarious: instead of two heads, there were three: three wandering Popes, persecuted and exiled from their capitals. The two first obediences did not disappear, and they only succeeded in making a fresh one. Yet, from certain points of view, the position of Alexander is better than that of Clement VII. and Benedict XIII. He was not elected in opposition to a generally recognised Pontiff, nor by schismatic methods. An almost general opinion asserts that both he and his successor John XXIII. were true Popes.[2] If the Pontiffs of Avignon had a colourable title in their own obedience, such a title can be made out still more clearly for Alexander V. in the eyes of the universal Church.

[1] This famous treatise entitled *De schismatibus auctoritate imperatoris tollendis* is published in Schardius, *De jurisdictione imperiali*, pp. 688, 741. *Cf.* M. Lenz, *loc. cit.*, p. 71. Plaoul had already maintained this principle at the Council of Paris in 1406. *Cf.* Bourgeois du Chastenet, *Preuves*, p. 191.

[2] Bellarmine, *De Concil.*, lib. i. c. 8. Muzzarelli, *De auctor. Rom. pontificis*, ii. p. 414. Tosti, *Storia del Concilio di Costanza*, i. p. 55.

In fact, the Pope of Pisa was acknowledged by the majority of the Church, *i.e.* by France, England, Portugal, Bohemia, Prussia, a few countries of Germany and Italy, and then by the Comtat-Venaissin,[1] whilst Naples, Poland, Bavaria, and part of Germany continued to obey Gregory, and Spain and Scotland persisted in remaining subject to Benedict.

Thus the election of Alexander did not immediately bring about the peace that many of the faithful had hoped for. Peter d'Ailly, one of the most far-seeing men of his time, had foreseen this result, and had not at all hidden his apprehensions. "If the council makes a new election," he wrote, "it will not do to go on with it before making sure of the adhesion of the whole of Christendom, or at any rate of the greater part of it. . . . Otherwise it would be grafting a new schism on the old one, and the second mistake would be worse than the first."[2]

He was not heeded by the fathers of Pisa, who, confident of their omnipotence, were desirous of hastening on the solution and refused to take the precautions that were desirable for bringing it about. At the time of the convening of the council they did not trouble to prepare public opinion and to withdraw it gradually from the Popes who had to be overthrown. They sent no legate to Hungary and the regions of the North, and they left Spain and its various kingdoms on one side. If, as will be seen later on, the Council of Constance succeeded in restoring unity, it is because it took care to follow an absolutely opposite plan. It overthrew the successor of

[1] *Cf.* SIMON DE CRAMAUD's letter in *Acta Concilii Constanc.*, i. p. 285.

[2] Advice given at Tarascon, January 10, 1409, by the Bishop of Cambrai. MARTÈNE et DURAND, *Veter. Script.*, vii. col. 917 and 1464. *Cf.* N. DE CLÉMANGIS, d'Ailly's disciple, *Opera*, p. 71. GERSON, *Propos. coram Anglicis*, *Opp. Gersonii*, ii. col. 128. TSCHACKERT, *Peter von Ailli*, p. 152.

the Pope elected at Pisa, but, in this important and delicate affair, it proceeded with a wise deliberation, and surrounded itself from the start with all the conditions likely to achieve success.

Why did the Council of Pisa declare that it was œcumenical, why did it put forth the claim of speaking for the universal Church, when it knew that several nations were unrepresented? It ought not to have wondered at all if its decisions were not unanimously approved. Again, why were the two claimants accused, not only of schism, but of real heresy? Such are the charges that passion invents, but such as neither theology nor justice can maintain.

Moreover, the same Peter d'Ailly was able to add later on: "Although the celebration of the Council of Pisa and the election of Alexander V. were held to be legitimate and canonical by the obedience of John XXIII., yet the two opposing obediences maintain the contrary, not without probability, and the difficulties in law and in fact are no less than they were previously."[1] And Gerson thought so too: "The present Schism offers so many doubtful points," he wrote, "that it would be rash, hurtful, and scandalous to pronounce the upholders of such and such a party outside the way of salvation."[2] So, then, even according to the supporters of the council, the canonicity of its acts and the value of its decisions are open to question. How, then, can it be reckoned œcumenical, especially if one knows beforehand that the legitimate Pope, whoever he might be, neither convened it nor presided over it, and that the council did not at all represent the universal Church?

[1] *Cf.* Bouix, *De Papa*, i. p. 497.

[2] Bess, *John Gerson u. d. Kirchenpolitik Parteien Frankreichs von der Konzil zu Pisa* (Marburg, 1890).

Further, theologians and canonists have been hard upon the synod of Pisa.

On the one hand, to the extreme left of the doctors, we hear a violent partisan of Benedict's, Boniface Ferrier, call it a "conventicle of demons."[1] Theodore Urie, one of Gregory's mainstays, seems to doubt whether they gather at Pisa with the sentiments of Dathan and Abiron, or those of Moses.[2] St Antoninus,[3] and Cajetan after him, as well as Turrecremata and Raynald, openly call it a conventicle, or at any rate cast doubts on its authority.

On the other hand, the Gallican school either approves of it or pleads extenuating circumstances. Noël Alexander, at the end of a long dissertation, asserts that the council destroyed the Schism *as far as it could.*[4] Bossuet says, in his turn: "If the Schism that devastated the Church of God was not exterminated at Pisa, at any rate it received a mortal blow there, and the Council of Constance consummated it."[5]

Protestants, who follow out all the consequences of their principles, applaud this council unreservedly, for they see in it "the first step to the deliverance of the world," and greet it as the dawn of the Reformation.[6] Perhaps it is wise to say with Bellarmine that this assembly is a general council which is neither approved nor disapproved.[7] On account of its illegalities and

[1] *Thesaurus anecdot,* ii. col. 1461.

[2] Von der Hardt, i. 147.

[3] *Summa historialis,* p. iii. tit. xxii. c. 5, par. 2. "*Per Pisanum concilium vel conciliabulum non erat ablatum schisma, sed augmentatum.*"

[4] T. viii. (Ed. in fol.), p. 360.

[5] *Defensio declarationis cleri gallicani,* pars. ii. lib. v. c. 12.

[6] Gregorovius, *Geschichte der Stadt Rom in Mittelalter,* vi., 3rd Ed., p. 577.

[7] Bellarmine, *De Conciliis et Ecclesia,* ii. c. 8, p. 13 (Ed. 1608, Paris). *Cf.* Bliemetzrieder, *Die general Konzil im grossen abendlandischen Schisma,* Paderborn, Schöningh, 1904.

inconsistencies it cannot be quoted as an œcumenical council. And yet it would be unfair to brand it as a conventicle, to compare it with the robber-council of Ephesus, with the pseudo-council of Basle, or with the Jansenist council of Pistoia. This synod is not a pretentious, rebellious, and sacrilegious coterie. The number of the fathers, their quality, authority, intelligence, and their zealous and generous intentions, the almost unanimous accord with which they came to their decisions, the royal support they met with, remove every suspicion of intrigue or cabal.[1] Nevertheless it is not a council that resembles any other, and it has a place by itself in the history of the Church. Unlawful in the manner in which it was convoked, unpractical in its choice of means, not indisputable in its results, and having no claim to represent the universal Church, such was the character of the Council of Pisa. The original source of all the historical events that took place from 1409 to 1414, it must be considered as the preliminary of the Council of Constance.

[1] The Popes of Pisa have their place in the monumental gallery of medallions which adorns the frieze of St Paul's outside the Walls. Those of Fondi and Avignon are not among them.

CHAPTER XIV

THE COUNCIL OF ROME AND THE PRELIMINARIES OF THE COUNCIL OF CONSTANCE

§ 1. *Alexander V. and John XXIII.*

Pope Alexander had been elected owing to the zeal of Balthazar Cossa. He did not forget it, and either through gratitude or timidity he remained dependent upon him who was his legate and as it were his prime-minister. His opinions and decisions never did aught but reflect the counsels, if not the commands, of Cossa.

On November 1, 1409, the Pontiff issued a fresh bull against the ambitious Ladislas of Naples, who had possession of a large part of the States of the Church, and upheld the cause of Gregory XII. Here he obtained more success, for the usurper was soon forced to quit Rome. Instead of immediately betaking himself to the Eternal City which was expecting him, Alexander yielded to the entreaties of Balthazar and settled at Bologna in order to end his days there. They were not of long duration. From the beginning of 1410, the Pope renewed all the condemnations pronounced against his two rivals. Struck with a mortal illness at the beginning of May 1410, he gathered all the cardinals about his death-bed, confirmed anew the decrees of Pisa, urged them to concord, and then breathed his last. He was seventy-one years of age, and had held the pontifical throne for ten months and eight days.[1]

His successor was plainly marked out: his confidant and supporter, Cardinal Cossa. He was elected by seventeen cardinals, after a conclave of three days, on May 17, and took the name of John XXIII. He was ordained priest immediately afterwards, then was consecrated bishop, and solemnly crowned on May 25.

Here we take in hand the history of a man whom calumny has not spared and who may have often given occasion for it. His enemies made him out to be a sort of crowned monster, but one only has to run through the long list of misdeeds for which he is blamed by them to be struck with the evident exaggeration of the charges brought against him.

Balthazar Cossa was a Neapolitan, born of a noble family and gifted with a rare intelligence. That he had been a pirate in his youth, and had long scoured the seas of Sicily, is an allegation of the atrabilious and vindictive Niem,[2] but it appears very difficult to prove it. We prefer to follow the opinion of Platina,[3] Valori,[4] and the monk of St Denis,[5] who were all contemporaries, and who show him to us as a student at Bologna, obtaining a double degree as doctor of law.

Boniface IX. appointed him his chamberlain, and Thierry de Niem accuses him of having dealt in the traffic of indulgences.[6] Appointed Cardinal of St

[1] Ciaconius, *Vitae et resgestae Pontif. rom.*, ii. p. 776. Wadding, *Ann. Minorum*, ix. p. 273. Platina, *De vitis Pontif. rom.*, 1645, p. 248. Niem, *De Scismate*, iii. 53.

[2] *De vita et factis Johannis XXIII.*, Von der Hardt, *Rerum concil. oecum. Const.*, ii. 338.

[3] *Loc. cit.*

[4] *Archivio storico italiano*, iv. 1843, p. 261.

[5] *Chronic. Karoli VI.*, lib. xxxiii. c. 28.

[6] Von der Hardt, ii. p. 340.

Eustache and Legate of Bologna, it is certain that, in this difficult position, he exhibited very remarkable political skill. He was both administrator and general, and soon succeeded in getting back all the land to the obedience of the Church.

According to Thierry's own avowal,[1] the legate very heavily fined debauchees, usurers, and gamblers. Can it be thought that he would have fallen himself into all these vices, and that he united to the skill of Cardinal Albornoz, the sometimes brutal behaviour of Cardinal Robert of Geneva, and the shamelessness that has occasionally been laid at the door of Cardinal Dubois, though without sufficient proof?

Let it, however, be frankly owned that John XXIII. appears to have been inspired with ideas that were rather political than religious. One looks to find the Spirit of God in him and only discovers the spirit of the world, combined with a love of money, and an unscrupulous ambition which sticks at nothing. St Antoninus judged very well of him when he wrote: "*Vir in temporalibus magnus, in spiritualibus nullus.*"[2]

Was he the Pope who was wanted for the president of the future council that was to set forward the great reform? Was his election at such a time a grace from God or a providential punishment? Certainly Balthazar can always be accused of having coveted the supreme pontificate, of having bought the conscience and the vote of certain cardinals, and even of having accelerated the death of his predecessor, without arousing too much astonishment and protest on the part of those who knew him.[3] Here must one not repeat what our readers must have thought more than once in going through the

[1] Von der Hardt, p. 350. [2] *Summa historialis*, p. iii. tit. 22, c. 6.
[3] *Cf.* Hefele, x. p. 428.

ecclesiastical annals of this sad period? God must have well guaranteed the immortality of His Church when He allowed His representative to be sometimes so unworthy of her. In the like circumstances, any other purely human institution must have disappeared amidst public contempt. But, as St Leo remarks, "the Papal dignity loses nothing even when he who inherits it is unworthy of it." There are to be seen evils, scandals, but not mortal wounds. One cannot but pity as well as condemn those who are guiltily responsible for them; and a certain brotherly sympathy must be extended to those who undertook to be the recorders of these troubled times, and who, in order to be faithful to historical truth, are obliged to relate what is not for edification. So many glorious deeds are inscribed on the credit side of the account of the Sovereign Pontiffs in the course of nineteen centuries, that certain temporary lapses can be forgiven them. Supposing we wished to hide some things, our lies are no good to them. We have already quoted the saying of De Maistre: "The Popes want nothing but the truth."

Monstrelet relates that, at the ceremony of the coronation, the cardinals, following time-honoured custom, lighted a tow fire before the new Pope, and said to him three times: "Holy father, thus passes the glory of the world." [1]

John XXIII. was soon to learn this by experience. Until then his cleverness had never left to chance what good counsel or foresight could provide, and he had been happy in all his undertakings; and his ambitions, even when most daring, had been crowned with success. From the time of his promotion to the pontifical throne, Balthazar no longer appeared the same person.

[1] *Chroniques,* livre i. ch. 68.

He seemed to have lost some of the fine penetrating insight, the energy of will, and rapidity of execution that had marked out his youth. No one showed himself weaker, more clumsy in policy, more unlucky in war, and more destined to be the plaything of fortune, which was to spare him no humiliation.

No sooner was he elected, than John tried, by an embassy of Cardinal Landulph of Bari in Spain, to detach the Kings of Aragon, Navarre, and Castile from the obstinate Benedict. The legate did not succeed, despite his efforts and his undoubted skill.[1]

On the other hand, the Pontiff tried to open negotiations with Malatesta to get him to make Gregory decide to resign ; but the prince either could not, or would not work efficaciously in that direction and prepared to declare war upon the new Pope.

At the same time the fleet of Louis of Anjou, the supporter of John XXIII., was beaten and routed by that of Ladislas, Cossa's old enemy. Several towns of the Romagna had to open their gates to the victor. It was the first of a series of unexpected disappointments.

Happily, events that were more favourable to the Pontiff were taking place in Germany. Robert of Bavaria, King of the Romans, the constant protector of Gregory XII., had just died. Sigismund, King of Hungary, brother of the dethroned King Wenceslas, presented himself as a candidate for the Empire, and endeavoured to secure a triumph by relying upon John XXIII. But this prince's cousin, Jodocus of Moravia, also claimed the dignity of King of the Romans. On his part the drunken Wenceslas did not cease to try to make good his rights to the throne, of which he had been declared unworthy. Thus there were three competitors for

[1] Finke, *Acta concilii Constanciensis,* i. pp. 2, 20 ff. [2] *Ibid.*, p. 4 ff.

the imperial crown, as there were three claimants for the tiara. But Jodocus died almost immediately; Sigismund was elected at Frankfort on July 21, 1411, and was afterwards confirmed by Gregory XII. He hastened to be reconciled with his brother Wenceslas. The new sovereign, as fair as he was courageous, played henceforward a great part in the history of the time. To him all looks were to turn: on the King of the Romans, the born protector of the Papacy, everyone was to depend for convoking the council which would put an end to so many spiritual and temporal evils.

Among the first, the indefatigable Malatesta became the champion of this idea, and directly addressed the new emperor. In a detailed report, he made warm complaints of John XXIII., adjured the German monarch in fine to come to the rescue of the Church, and begged him above everything not to assemble the future council in a town where the Pontiff would have a twofold power, both spiritual and temporal. He was not listened to. In the meantime the Prince of Rimini went on with the war he had declared against John XXIII., and united his efforts with those of Ladislas.

The King of Naples was conquered by his rival Louis of Anjou at Roccasecca, on May 19, 1411; but the French prince could not turn his victory to good account, and returned to Provence as rapidly as if he had suffered a defeat. It was the fate of the Dukes of Anjou never to succeed in Italy, which has sometimes been called the Frenchmen's grave. Louis II. was no more fortunate than Charles of Anjou had been in 1282, Louis I. of Anjou in 1383, or than René of Anjou was in 1438. Each of them was enticed with the hope of carving out for himself a powerful kingdom at Naples with the edge of the sword, and all died in disappointment.

The triumph gained by Louis II. had no morrow, and its only result was to inflate the magnificent expectations of John XXIII. one day, and then to let them fall as quickly into ruin. On his side, Malatesta occupied Emilia, and kept it in the obedience of Gregory XII., whilst Bologna drove out the new Pope's legate.

§ 2. *The Council of Rome.*

At the end of its sessions, the assembly of Pisa had decided that a new council should take place in three years, *i.e.* in 1412.

John XXIII. convened it for April 1.[1] In order to make some partisans for himself, he nominated fourteen cardinals, and his selection was generally approved.

They were Peter d'Ailly, Bishop of Cambrai; Gilles des Champs, Bishop of Coutances; his friend William Philastre, Dean of Reims, less skilful and less eloquent; Zabarella, Bishop of Florence, whose ideas about the Church were open to question, but whose cleverness and initiative were very noted; Robert of Hallum, Bishop of Salisbury, who was to bind England to the new Pope, and several others who were less well known (June 6, 1411).

Two years later he also promoted Simon de Cramaud, Archbishop of Reims, to this dignity.

Among the thus elected are to be noted the principal doctors of the University of Paris. John made a point of conciliating this powerful and illustrious corporation for good and all; but his intentions were soon doomed to cruel disappointment.

He was less happily inspired when he decreed a crusade

[1] The bull which convoked the council given in Raynald is faulty. See the true text in Finke, i. p. 127. It is dated April 29, 1411.

against Ladislas. This self-interested appeal met with no success. The Pontiff was soon forced to conclude a disadvantageous peace with the King of Naples, and to grant him a number of privileges, in some cases of a very onerous character.

Circumstances were growing favourable to the holding of a council at Rome. Only a few French prelates were there under the guidance of the Bishop of Amiens, Peter d'Ailly, and Simon de Cramaud. King Charles had charged them with the defence of his interests and those of the Church of France.[1] From 1411, the University had drawn up *avisata* concerning the reform of the Church,[2] and Peter d'Ailly for his part had written a summary of the points upon which the attention of the future council should be brought to bear.[3] The two programmes are so like each other that it may be suspected that they came from the same source.

Many delegates arrived in turn from Italy, Bohemia, Hungary, and England, but slowly and in small numbers.[4] The Pope was obliged to prorogue the council several times, and it hardly began with the year 1413. The only important enactment was one condemning the books of the heresiarch Wycliffe, and forbidding anyone to comment on them in the pulpit before the people.[5] It was a disapprobation of the doctrines and practices which John Huss was beginning to introduce into Bohemia.

The Cardinal of Cambrai, who arrived on December 1, 1412, could not get his remarkable project for reforming

[1] *Chronic. Karoli VI.*, lib. xxxii. c. 41.

[2] Finke, i. p. 132.

[3] The *capita agendorum* are in Von der Hardt, i. col. 506. He ascribes them to Cardinal Zabarella, but Lenz, Steinhausen, and Tschackert prove that they are d'Ailly's (1417). *Cf.* Clémangis, *Vota emandationis*, in Von der Hardt, i. p. ii. col. 45. Valois, iv. p. 203.

[4] *Cf.* Mansi, xxvii. col. 505.

[5] Finke, p. 163.

the calendar discussed and accepted, and its final acceptance was deferred until the end of the troubles of the Church.[1] The French ambassadors had scarcely reason to be satisfied at the result of their mission. Like all the fathers of the council, they soon perceived that John did not wish seriously to take in hand the questions of reform which were of such keen interest to the University as well as to the whole Church. As soon as the discussions reached these burning questions, the skilful Zabarella immediately addressed the meeting and put the proposals on one side.[2]

The French delegates, not wishing to be dupes, demanded that the meeting should be prorogued and transferred elsewhere. The Sovereign Pontiff consented willingly, and put it off till the month of December without mentioning any definite meeting-place. Afterwards he acknowledged, in his bull convening the Council of Constance, that the Universal Church was not adequately represented in this Roman assembly.[3]

The Pope, moreover, must have been far from ready to convoke the bishops again, for before as well as after the council he had heard from the lips of the Cardinal of Bari, and certain others, stern truths and severe reproaches, which his conduct too often deserved. Cardinal Orsini and the Cardinal of Cambrai were witnesses of it. These remarks were unhappily of no avail, as the future was to show.[4]

[1] *Cf.* Von der Hardt, iii. col. 70. It is analysed and discussed in my *Petrus de Alliaco*, p. 192. In this treatise d'Ailly just touches on the errors of the Julian calendar. Unfortunately his plan was only adopted in 1582 by Gregory XIII. Thus the Cardinal of Cambrai is one of the authors of the Gregorian calendar.

[2] Muratori, *Rerum italic. Script.*, iii. p. ii. p. 846. Duschesne, *Liber. pontif.*, ii. p. 536.

[3] Raynald, a. 1412, No. 5; a. 1413, Nos. 1-4.

[4] Finke, i. pp. 125, 163. Hefele, x. p. 429. Bibl. Nat., Latin MS. 9513.

No sooner had the fathers left Rome than the King of Naples declared war,[1] and entered into the Eternal City through a breach (June 8, 1413). He devastated it, and perpetrated such horrors as had not been seen since the time of the Vandals. The Pope was put to flight and vigorously pursued.[2] Florence refused to open its gates to the fugitive, and help came from nowhere in spite of his embassies and entreaties. Cardinal d'Ailly, sent as a legate to Germany, could not get the permission of Venice for the passage of the imperial troops through its territory on their way to help the Pope.[3] But, on the other hand, the senate promised that it would not oppose the meeting of a council at Bologna, where John XXIII. had long wielded absolute authority.[4]

Fortunately he was soon delivered by a death, which was both disgraceful and tragic, from the sacrilegious and voluptuous Ladislas, who had just sacked Rome a second time, and who had ridden on horseback into the Church of St John Lateran. Ill as a consequence of his debaucheries, and perhaps poisoned, he had himself carried to Naples, where he succumbed (August 6, 1414). This made one less obstacle to the peace of the Church. It may be observed, by the way, that the taking of Rome has always proved fatal to conquering adventurers, either through its fascinating seduction, or else because of the inevitable disappointments that it prepares for them. Genseric and Odoacer were in this respect the precursors of Otho, Barbarossa, Ladislas, and many others known to history.

[1] Finke, p. 105.

[2] Niem, in Von der Hardt, ii. p. 380. Thierry, who was then recorder of Curia, was present at this rout (p. 381).

[3] Letters lately discovered in the State Archives of Venice. *Cf.* Finke, pp. 106 and 167.

[4] Guiraud, *L'État pontifical après le grand Schisme*, p. 23.

§ 3. *Preliminaries of the General Council.*

On his part, Sigismund obstinately pursued the object that several prelates, distinguished writers, and particularly the public voice,[1] had assigned to his efforts: the convening of a General Council that should definitely restore the peace of the Church.

Coming down into the North of Italy, he omitted nothing that might secure the success of his plan. The state of Christendom was much more in his thoughts than the particular interests of John XXIII.

The latter, forced by circumstances to take up the idea of a council again, wished to hold it in a town that would be under his rule, or, at any rate, neutral, and above all independent of the Empire. In this sense he had definitely instructed his legates, Cardinals de Chalant and Zabarella.

But at the last moment, seized with an unaccountable fit of bewilderment and blundering, he said to them: "I had meant to specify to you certain towns and to prevent your choosing others. To-day I have changed my mind, and I leave it to your discretion, giving you full powers."[2]

The two legates left for Como, where they found Sigismund. He had already fixed his choice on the imperial town of Constance, the advantages of which had been pointed out to him by his friends. He easily succeeded in getting the Pope's delegates to share his views.

[1] Thierry de Niem, or Andrew Escobar, have mainly re-echoed it in a book entitled *De modis uniendi*, written in 1410. Von der Hardt, i. p. v. p. 68. *Opp. Gersonii*, ii. p. 161.

[2] These letters have been recently printed by Palacky, *Documenta Mag. J. Hies*, p. 512. *Cf.* Muratori, *Rer. italic. Script.*, xix. p. 928.

Moreover, these prelates, like most of those about John XXIII., had but a very moderate amount of esteem for him. They were more attached to his fortunes than to his person, and endured rather than loved him. They sometimes corresponded with his rivals, and were ready for any possible desertion. Peter d'Ailly himself did not believe in John's good faith, for he had tried to get himself carried off by the troops of Ladislas in order not to be present at the council that was being got ready.[1]

At bottom, the cardinals in general were anxious, no matter how, to get rid of this compromised and compromising Pontiff.[2] When John XXIII. learnt of the choice made by Sigismund, and when he saw his own plans so openly thwarted, he bitterly deplored his blindness. It was too late: the head of the Empire was urging events on, and hastening negotiations with Catholic kings, and was arranging secret understandings with Gregory XII.[3]

On October 30, 1413, he announced to Christendom that, in consequence of an understanding with the Pope, a General Council would commence at Constance on November 1 of the following year. He would attend in person, and he invited the three claimants and princes to be present.

The King of France, sincerely attached to John XXIII., gave a very cool reply to Sigismund. In a vague way he doubtless understood that the King of the Romans was taking up a rôle which he himself had formerly fulfilled. Charles VI. at first limited himself to a statement that he would hinder no one from going to Con-

[1] Finke, pp. 182 and 344.

[2] *Ibid.*, p. 345.

[3] *Ibid.*, p. 239 ff. Leonard Aretinus, in Murator, xix. i. 928. Mandonnet, *Hist. Jahrbuch*, 1900, p. 388.

stance: but later on he changed his mind, and yielded so far as to send a representative.

The new King of Aragon, Ferdinand, on the contrary, gave an energetic reply, and warmly disputed the superiority that the King of the Romans took upon himself.

The Pope would have vainly offered some resistance, but he finally resigned himself to issuing from Lodi a bull convoking the council (December 9, 1413).

This resolution was made with little spontaneity and not without regret. When the republic was proclaimed at Rome, after the shameful death of Ladislas, the Pontiff wanted to return to his capital in order to restore his authority there, as he said. Perhaps he was hoping in this way to escape the council which he feared, and the cession that he anticipated.

The cardinals opposed the journey: they succeeded in making him believe that the meeting at Constance would not last long, that it would confirm him in his rights, and that he could afterwards enter the Eternal City with greater authority than ever.[1]

Always distrustful, because he knew that he was legitimately regarded with suspicion, John exacted numerous and substantial guarantees for the protection of his person from the citizens of Constance. Since the citizens of the town put a certain amount of difficulties in his way, the Pope sent John de Brogny, Cardinal of Ostia, to smooth them down and to prepare a solemn entry for him.

At last, on October 1, 1414, John left Bologna for Constance. He passed through the Tyrol, and there met Frederick V., Duke of Austria. He immediately bound

[1] Gregorovius, *Geschichte der Stadt Rom im Mittelalter*, vi. p. 596 ff. S. Antoninus, *Summa historialis*, p. iii. tit. xxii. c. 6. Finke, i. p. 237 ff.

himself to him with the bonds of an interested friendship: and he did not conceal his fears from him, and they concluded a sort of defensive alliance together. The Pope felt that he was not above reproach, nor was he without fear, and he thought that he could afford to neglect no precaution that would ensure his liberty in the council. These apprehensions, it is said, were shared by those around him. His jester, making an allusion to a certain game of chance and the town of Trent, near which he happened to be, said to him one day, "Holy Father, he who goes higher than Trent (thirty), loses."[1]

We have seen at Constance the ancient manuscript of Canon Ulrich of Richenthal about the council that was going to begin. This volume is decorated with naïve and rather coarse designs. In one of them the old chronicler represents John XXIII. falling out of his carriage in the Tyrolese mountains and exclaiming: *Jaceo hic in nomine diaboli.*[2] Another page shows him arriving on the banks of Lake Constance, discovering the town and saying: "Here is the fox-trap!"[3]

His former boldness had given way to a strange fatalism that paralysed every thought and all power of resistance in him. One day Bartholomew Valori told him to be on his guard against the dangers he might run in attending a synod held in a strange town. "I know that the Council of Constance will not be in my favour,"

[1] Lenfant, *Histoire du Concile de Constance*, i. lib. i. p. 19.

[2] A similar engraving is in the curious book that bears the name of Heinrich Stegner, and which was printed at Augsburg in 1536. The original copy of Ulrich is in the Rosgarten Museum at Constance, as well as a copy of Stegner. As to Richenthal, *cf.* Marmor, *Das Konzil zu Konstanz* (Constance, 1898).

[3] *Cf.* Richenthal, p. 24. Trithemius, *Chronicum Hirsangiense*, ii. p. 336.

answered the Pope, "but what can I do about it if my fate carries me thither?"[1]

While all these events were taking place in upper Italy and lower Germany, the legitimate Pope Gregory carries almost everywhere his wandering authority with him, and is the sport of political and religious strife. Never, perhaps, was good right more misunderstood, spiritual power more questioned, the temporal power more despised.

Pursued by numerous enemies, the Pontiff passed from Gaeta into Dalmatia, from Dalmatia to Cesena, and from Cesena to Rimini, where reigned the faithful Malatesta. He had just refused a pension of 50,000 florins offered him by John XXIII. if he would give up. He declined the invitations to the future council given him by the King of the Romans, but agreed to send a representative. Surrounded with a few trusty and prudent cardinals, like Condulmaro[2] and Dominici,[3] and convinced that the council would only become œcumenical if he took part in it, he resigned himself to waiting upon events, and to coming forward at the most favourable moment for the peace of the Church.

[1] *Vita di B. Valori,* in *l'Arch. stor. ital.,* iv. part i. p. 262. *Cf.* Pastor, *Histoire des Papes,* i. p. 205.

[2] The cardinal was a Venetian by birth, and commendatory abbot of St George Major. In 1431 he became Pope Eugenius IV.

[3] John Dominici was born of humble parents at Florence. He became a Dominican quite young. He was nominated by Gregory to the archbishopric of Ragusa, and soon afterwards cardinal (May 9, 1408). As eloquent as he was pious, and as learned as he was zealous, he played a large part in the events that followed, and carried on negotiations with Sigismund for two years on behalf of Gregory. See his Life by Rosler (Freiburg, 1893).

CHAPTER XV

THE COUNCIL OF CONSTANCE—FIRST SESSIONS

§ 1. *Opening of the Council.*

In history the city of Constance had already had a glorious past. Its annals recorded its foundation by Constantine, and that the Emperor had given it his name, as he had done to Constantinople. He had fixed its site at the meeting-point of three lakes connected with one another, the largest of which is a regular sea, washing Suabia on the north, and reflecting in its southern waters the heights of the Appenzell and the Vorarlberg.

In the earliest Christian ages Constance had sent missionaries to Gaul. In the course of the seventh century, which was called the golden age of sanctity, the North had taken from it St Omer, St Momelin, St Ebertraume, and St Bertin.

Later on, it had seen founded, almost under its walls, the Abbey of Reichenau, which, in its literary and apostolic influence, soon rivalled Bobbio, St Gall, and Luxeuil, the fertile foundations of St Columba and his disciples.

Charles the Fat, conquered and plundered, found a grave in these cloisters, where legions of monks lived, studied, and prayed. The churches of the Isle of Reichenau, their old paintings, and their relics, are the only genuine memories of the illustrious past, now almost perished.

Still later in the tenth century, the bishops Conrad and Gebhardt II., whose monumental statues adorn the bridge over the Rhine, had been celebrated for their sanctity and for their services.[1] In the eleventh, Henry III. had held a great council (1043) at Constance, and had induced the clergy and the people to restore peace. In another synod, in 1094, Bishop Gebhardt III. had encouraged the reforms of Gregory VII. and had abolished a host of abuses. It was this twofold pacificatory and reforming object that was to occupy the great council of which we are about to speak.[2] In 1183, Frederick had here granted the famous *pax Constantiae*.[3] In the Middle Ages, the diocese of Constance, owing to its great abbeys, had enjoyed a certain liturgical and more specially an intellectual leadership over the ecclesiastical province of Mayence and over all the dioceses of the Empire.[4]

It is in the libraries of the surrounding monasteries of Reichenau, Weingarten, or even of St Gall, that Poggio and other humanists conducted their researches so ardently and successfully between the sessions of the council. It is there that they discovered and copied the manuscripts of the masterpieces of Cicero, Quintilian, or Statius, lovingly preserved by the monks;[5] it is there that they prepared the literary movement of the renaissance.

At the beginning of the fifteenth century the imperial town of Constance was in full possession of every

[1] Pertz, *Monumenta, Scriptores,* iv. and x.

[2] Hefele, vi. p. 285 and vii. p. 26.

[3] Pertz, *Monumenta,* Leges, ii. p. 175.

[4] *Cf.* E. Misset, *Le premier livre imprimé connu,* in the *Bibliographe moderne,* September 1899.

[5] *Cf.* Voigt, *Pétrarque, Bocace, et les débuts de l'humanisme* (French translation by Le Monnier, 1894), p. 237.

municipal franchise, and made free use of them behind its seven gates and thirteen towers. When the city agreed to receive the council, it was not without taking most elaborate precautions for the maintenance of its rights and ancient liberties.

After having been a centre of missionary and scientific work, Constance was about to become the headquarters of Catholic unity, and for a time the heart of Christendom. In anticipation the Christian world hailed it in the words of Peter d'Ailly: "O happy town of Constance," he cried, "I share thy joy, for it is among the German towns that have been laid under my charge as legate that thou hast been selected!" [1]

From another point of view, Thierry de Niem boasted the wealth of its vines and fields, *ager cui benedixit Dominus*, the beauty of its lakes and of its river, the purity of its air, and the justice of its laws for the protection of strangers.[2]

In 1414, Constance was to write the fairest page in its history, for the council was the most brilliant that had been ever held in Germany. Like Pisa, which had been also the seat of a similar assembly, since then it has only decreased in importance and renown. To-day, almost all the curiosities that Constance has to show the traveller date from the council and from the events that distinguished it.

It was a magnificent sight when Pope John XXIII., on October 28, 1414, made his solemn entry into the city by the fine Kreutzlingen gate, which may be seen still to-day.

[1] *Sermo de adventu Domini. Cf. Tractatus et Serm.* (Strasburg, 1490). *Opp. Gersonii,* ii. col. 918.

[2] Von der Hardt, ii. col. 398. On the part of Niem at the Council of Constance, *cf.* H. Finke, *Forschungen und Quellen zur Geschichte des Konstanzer Konzils*, p. 132.

Nine cardinals accompanied him, and a great number of prelates and nobles. The Count de Montfort and a Prince Orsini of Rome led his ambling nag by the bridle, while Henry of Ulm, Burgomaster of Constance, and three other notables bore the baldachin which was over his head. The Pope was received alike as an angel of the Lord [1] and also as a conqueror in this old cathedral that was to witness such important events. Then he went to take possession of his apartments in the palace of the bishop, Otho of Hochberg.

Every day the town saw the arrival of eminent prelates, of princes with numerous trains of cavaliers, and of delegates of the Universities.

Cardinal Zabarella proclaimed that the first session of the council would begin on November 16.[2] The delay was used to hold preliminary meetings, to make arrangements for good order, and all sorts of preparations.

The auditors of the Roman Rota took their places in the Church of St Stephen's, which still exists, in order to administer justice three times a week. Thus it was that the maximum tariff for the board and lodging of strangers, their servants and horses, was settled by common agreement.[3]

Further, full liberty of speech was claimed for members of the council, and promoters, procurators, and councillors were appointed to control the proceedings. On November 17, Cardinal Peter d'Ailly arrived, who was to be the soul of the great assembly, and he was received with the greatest respect. He had a retinue of forty-four persons. It was rather smaller than that of Angelo,

[1] *Chronic Karoli VI.*, lib. xxxv. c. 35.

[2] On this prince of the Church, see Kneer, *Kardinal Zabarella* (Münster, 1901).

[3] *Cf.* Rossmann, *De externo Concilii Constant. apparatu* (Jena, 1856).

Cardinal of Praeneste, who had forty-eight, and of Peter de Foix, Cardinal-priest titular of St Stephen's of the Caelius, who had fifty-two, according to Richenthal.[1] Louis Fieschi, Cardinal of St Adrian's, was accompanied by sixty-two servants, while John de Brogny, Cardinal of Ostia, had eighty-eight. But nothing came up to the splendour of the Archbishop of Mayence, John of Nassau, who arrived with an escort five hundred strong,[2] excepting perhaps the luxury of Louis, Count Palatine of the Rhine, elected protector of the council, who entered the town at the head of more than five hundred horsemen.

Soon five patriarchs, twenty-nine cardinals, thirty-three archbishops, more than five hundred bishops, a hundred abbots, three hundred doctors, and about eighteen thousand ecclesiastics filled the town. A hundred thousand men and thirty thousand horses had to be fed daily, according to the chroniclers of those times.[3] All this crowd of persons, mostly made up of knights, soon gave themselves up to tourneys, and to other amusements even less worthy of the majesty of the council and of the gravity of the subjects that it had to deal with.

Until then, however, they had not been joined by the most important personage of all, the King of the Romans.

He had just had himself crowned at Aix-la-Chapelle (November 8), and this grand ceremony had kept about him the greater part of the German nobility.

At the repeated entreaties of the Pope, he was on his way towards the seat of the council. On Christmas Eve,

[1] Ulrich von Richenthal, *Kronik des Constanzer Concils,* 1414-1418. He often makes mistakes, both about the names and titles of the prelates.

[2] Jungmann, *Dissert. selectae in hist. eccles.,* vi. p. 295.

[3] Theod. Urie in Von der Hardt, i. col. 155. Lenfant, *Histoire du Concile de Constance,* ii. p. 365-386. Hefele, x. pp. 392.

the 24th December, his arrival on the lake of Überlingen, connected with that of Constance, was notified.

The same evening, an immense crowd pressed towards the gates of the town, to be present at the reception of the head of the Empire. The cold was severe and the night was far advanced when the vessel carrying the King and his suite at length came to under the walls of the town, amidst popular applause. Queen Barbara of Celje accompanied him, as well as several princes and princesses, and a large number of knights. Perhaps the shores of the lake had never seen a royal entry of such an extraordinary and solemn character.

After a short rest, Sigismund went to the Cathedral, which was brilliantly illuminated. The Pope was waiting for him in order to celebrate the Christmas High Mass. The King put on a deacon's dalmatic, placed the crown upon his head, mounted the ambo, and solemnly chanted the Gospel of the Nativity.[1]

Then he took his seat on a magnificent throne, surrounded with all the princes of the Empire, bearing the insignia of his sovereignty. His Holiness then gave him a sword that had been blessed, and charged him to wield it always for the protection of the Church. The prince took an oath to do so, and as a matter of fact, he set himself to keep it during the events that subsequently took place.

§ 2. *Departure of John XXIII.*

The representatives of the two authorities had met: and the bishop without protected the bishops within with his sword: serious discussion was about to begin.

[1] Marmor, *Das Concilium zu Konstanz* (1898), p. 42. Theod. Urie in Von der Hardt, i. col. 15.

Some already wanted to declare that the present council ought to be satisfied with confirming that of Pisa, suspended in 1409 by Alexander V.[1] His successor, John XXIII., and the Italians in general attached much importance to this formality, for thereby the canonical lawfulness of the latter would be decreed, and at the same time the indisputable validity of the pontifical election with which it had closed. Thenceforward, the measures finally taken against the claimants would have had nothing to do with John XXIII., but only with his rivals Gregory and Benedict.

The fathers refused to share these interested views.

Peter d'Ailly, supported by Cardinal Philastre, laid down a counter-proposal on December 7. "The Council of Constance," he said, "is only the logical continuation of the Council of Pisa. In the same way as the Rhine is always the same river as it was a hundred years ago, although between its banks not a single drop of the same water remains. It is therefore useless to ask this assembly to confirm the one that went before it. This step might be dangerous in vexing those who deny the legitimacy of the Council of 1409. According to the decisions of Pisa, in virtue of their oath, the Pope and the cardinals are obliged to work for the unity of the Church, and for reform *in capite et in membris*."[2]

In a second document, presented to the council on December 14, the Cardinal of Cambrai added: "With regard to the claimants, first every possible means of persuasion must be tried to secure voluntary *cession*. Gregory and Benedict, if they consent to annul their functions, must be offered important compensation and

[1] Von der Hardt, iv. p. 23. Mansi, xxvii. p. 581.

[2] Von der Hardt, ii. col. 192, 201. Mansi, xxvii. col. 542. *Cf.* H. Finke, *Forschungen und Quellen*, pp. 120 and 249.

a suitable position. If they resist, no new election will be made on their death." [1]

In this document, as in several others reproduced by Von der Hardt, Peter d'Ailly desires to exhaust all the means of conciliation before coming to methods of severity. He does not even shrink from repeating his doubts as to the validity and efficacity of the Council of Pisa. He is right, but unfortunately he makes the mistake of here reiterating his view of the fallibility of general councils. "They have sometimes been mistaken," he says, "in fact and in law, and even in the faith. The Universal Church alone has the privilege of infallibility." [2]

In this false and grave assertion, we have the prelude of the heterodox decisions taken at the first sessions of the council.

Two other serious discussions took place in January 1415.

In the School, the importance of the theological decisions uttered by the Sorbonne had already been exaggerated, and the doctors had had an authority ascribed to them which the Church until then had never recognised and will never grant them.

D'Ailly, Gerson,[3] and the first Gallicans often exalted this sort of magisterial omnipotence, both immoderately and unreasonably. No doubt, doctors may be consulted by the highest ecclesiastical authorities. Their advice, when asked for, often has great weight, but it is merely a theological consultation. It is worth just what the proofs it contains are worth. The doctor, in this case, is like the lawyer, who, in the interpretation of the

[1] Von der Hardt, col. 196. Finke, p. 125.

[2] Von der Hardt, *Ibid.*, col. 201. *Cf.* chapter vi. p. 111 ff.

[3] *Opp. Gersonii,* i. col. 10. *Cf.* Puyol, *Edmond Richer,* i. p. 211. See also farther back in this book, p. 206.

law, puts forth an opinion which is always open to dispute by a jurist, and never the irrevocable decision of a supreme judge, for he has no legal jurisdiction.

This was not understood by a large number of the members of the council. Also, when this question was raised at the council, many members of the University of Paris, *brought up amidst* the cries of the School, showed their eagerness in favour of this democratic and multitudinist tendency, which Marsilius of Padua, John of Jandun, and Occam had already proclaimed a hundred years before, which Gerson and Courtecuisse maintained about the time we are speaking of, and which Richer and Vigor were to bring out again in the seventeenth century.

D'Ailly, true to false principles, threw himself headlong into this movement. He asked that at Constance the bishops and abbots wielding jurisdiction should not be the only persons to have a definite vote, but that doctors in theology, canon law and civil law (there were more than three hundred) should also be granted to exercise the suffrage.[1]

"They," said the Cardinal of Cambrai, "have a greater doctrinal authority than an ignorant bishop, or an abbot who is only titular and without any effective jurisdiction. It cannot be admitted that these inferior prelates should have as much influence as the Archbishop of Mayence, for example, or any other bishop with an immense diocese. . . . I ask the same favour for kings and princes, and also for their ambassadors and the proxies of absent bishops and of chapters. Since the most important thing is to get rid of the Schism, it

[1] He had already expressed exaggerated opinions on the point in his speech before the Avignon Pope against John de Montson, *Jacobita perfidissimus*, as he calls him (1387), *Opp. Gersonii*, i. col. 710. D'ARGENTRÉ, *Coll. Judic.*, i. p. ii. p. 76.

would be neither reasonable nor right to try to exclude kings and princes and their delegates.[1]

This dangerous doctrine, as unfounded in canon law as in tradition, had already been put into practice at the Councils of Pisa and Rome. It was approved of afresh at Constance. At bottom, it was merely an expedient for neutralising the influence of the prelates of the second rank, Italians for the most part, who had flocked to the council in large numbers to sustain the cause of John XXIII. Later on, the Council of Basle renewed the experiment; and it was the source of its impotence and the cause of its rebelliousness.

Another expedient, quite as dangerous and as contrary to ecclesiastical tradition, was likewise used against the Pope whom they wished to overthrow.

It was voting by nations and not by heads. This measure was intended to bring to nought the numerical superiority of the Italians. It was resolved, as at Pisa, that the assembly should be divided into four nations: Italy, France, Germany and England. Later on, a fifth was added, Spain.

Each nation was to nominate a certain number of delegates, either ecclesiastics or laymen. Over the deputies of each nation there was a president who was changed every month. Moreover, each nation was to meet separately to examine questions and to report its decisions to the others.

When an understanding on a given point had been reached, a general gathering of the four nations was to be convened *nationaliter*. When this gathering had agreed on one point, they were to submit it to the general

[1] Von der Hardt, ii. col. 224. Mansi, xxvii. p. 560. Hardouin, viii. p. 223. *Cf. Petrus de Alliaco*, p. 274. Next year d'Ailly set forth the same principles in his treatise *De potestate eccl.*, Von der Hardt, iv. p. 18. *Opp. Gersonii*, ii. col. 941.

council *conciliariter.*[1] The Sacred College was unable to get any recognition from the nations, as a definite body having an autonomy and authority of its own. Each cardinal had to vote with his nation.

All these decisions, adroit as they may have been in a political sense, deprived John XXIII. of any advantage he might have obtained from numbers, but they had the disadvantage of being derogatory to the most respected traditions. They introduced national and particularist divisions into the council, such as should find no place in a catholic assembly, which is universal in character. Like the former one, this procedure was revolutionary with regard to supreme authority: it injured the rights of cardinals and bishops, and was merely a contrivance intended to strike at the Sovereign Pontiff.

This blow, which was already very evident, was not the only one then aimed at John XXIII. An anonymous person, probably an Italian, brought out a pamphlet against the Pope, full of the most odious charges.[2] This defamatory publication was put into the hands of the four nations at the same time as a request for legal inquiry. Thus the enemies of the Pope wished to dishonour him, as they had tried to do in the case of Boniface VIII. a century earlier (1303). Informed by

[1] Von der Hardt, t. i. col. 157. *Cardinalium, nationumque consult.*, *Ibid.*, t. ii. col. 230, and t. v. p. 53. Peter d'Ailly, *Opp. Gersonii*, ii. col. 940. The Cardinal of Cambrai, learning from experience, later on criticised this system, the manifold disadvantages of which he had quickly perceived. He preferred voting by ecclesiastical provinces. See his dissertation read at Constance on November 1st, 1416, *De Reformatione Ecclesiae.* The text found in the works of Gerson, ii. col. 915, is not the same as that of 1403, the date of the first edition. The original text, in the Bibl. Nationale (Latin MSS. 3124, 14579) and copied by Baluze (No. 1571) has a lacuna of thirty-eight lines. D'Ailly added these *desiderata* on presenting his treatise to the council.

[2] Von der Hardt, ii. col. 391. Hunger, *Zur Gesch. Papstes Johanns*, xxiii. (Bonn, 1876).

one of his servants, John was first of all thrown into consternation. He consulted some cardinals who had remained true to him.

The latter advised him not to enter into discussion with his adversaries, but they were of opinion that he had better abdicate to avoid a still greater scandal.

The Pope accepted their counsels : and thus out of evil came a certain amount of good. The calumnies or slanders which were heaped upon the Pontiff led to the *cession* so earnestly desired, and prepared the way for a definite solution of difficulties.

On February 16, John XXIII., more and more alarmed, got Cardinal Zabarella to read a document wherein he said : "Determined to restore the peace of the Church, I agree to resign my powers, provided that Peter de Luna and Angelo Corrario, who have been pronounced to be heretics, also renounce all their claims to the tiara."[1]

The form of this document was reviewed by the fathers, and found too violent for the rival Popes : but already the council put the three Pontiffs on the same footing : the work of Pisa was thus a failure in their view. A second document was considered no more satisfactory. Sigismund proposed a third, which met with no better fate. Finally, after many negotiations, John read in public an express and formal renunciation, which contained only one condition, that Benedict and Gregory should abdicate in turn. On March 2, 1415, in the second solemn session, he repeated this important declaration.[2]

This act was received with delight by the council.

[1] Von der Hardt, ii. col. 223 and 292. Mansi, xxvii. p. 564.
[2] Hefele, x. p. 387.

The *Te Deum* was sung and all Constance rejoiced. On March 7, the Pope issued a bull confirming and solemnly promulgating his promised *cession*.[1]

What is the use of relating events that now followed with rapidity? The innumerable vexations suffered by John XXIII., the plans of Sigismund who wanted to go to Nice to confer with Benedict, the refusal of the Pope to accept the King of the Romans as a proxy entrusted with abdicating on his behalf, the burning and virulent discussions between different nations, and the threats addressed to the French people?

Troubles were increasing, relations between John and Sigismund were becoming more and more strained: a report ran, that the Pope desired to leave Constance with the help and protection of Frederick, Duke of Austria. The Pontiff hoped that his withdrawal would break up the council and put an end to the persecution of which he complained.

On March 20, a great tourney took place at Constance. The head of the Empire was present with his princes, knights, and a great concourse of people. For the moment, there was a truce to the grave debates of the council. The Duke of Austria and the Count of Celje, the brother-in-law of the King of the Romans, were to meet in a contest of strength and skill. While the magnificent spectacle engrossed all minds and eyes, an old man in a worn-out grey dress and mounted on an old horse, and with a cross-bow on the saddle, appeared at the gate of Kreutzlingen with his face concealed. In this disguise, who could recognise one who had passed through the same gate four months previously in all the

[1] Hefele, x. p. 390. Christophe, *Histoire de la Papauté pendant le XIVe siècle*, iii. p. 385. H. Finke, *Forschungen und Quellen*, p. 265. Valois, iv. p. 281.

pomp of the sovereign pontificate? John XXIII. was only accompanied by a child. No one took any notice of travellers of such a pitiful appearance.

The Pope gained Ermatingen in Thurgau, embarked on a boat which had been got ready by Frederick, and reached Schaffhausen next morning.

Scarcely had he left Constance when he sent a trusty messenger to inform the Duke of Austria, who nevertheless took part in the tournament. But the same evening the Duke took horse and flung himself on the road to Schaffhausen, where he rejoined the papal fugitive.

Next morning, the news of the Pope's flight spread in Constance and at first created astonishment, and then consternation and confusion.

Most of the fathers thought the council was over, and got ready to leave: others, and even some cardinals, thought of setting out to rejoin him whom they still looked upon as their legitimate head.

On the other hand, invectives broke out against John XXIII., whose palace was at once abandoned to the pillage of the populace. Disorder kept increasing, and fear with it, when Sigismund mounted on horseback, and went through the streets of the city. His presence raised their drooping courage, restored peace, and prevented hasty departures.

The King immediately convened an assembly of the four nations and declared his fixed determination of defending and upholding the council, even at the risk of his life. The cardinals gathered about him, but told him, that before taking steps against the Pope, an embassy should be deputed to go to him. Three members of the Sacred College were invited to leave for Schaffhausen with the Archbishop of Rheims, while

Sigismund accused Frederick of treason, and summoned him to appear before the council and himself.

In the assembly, the French delegates were remarkable for the violence of their writings [1] and words, as well as for the schismatical errors of their teaching about the Church.

Gerson and others put forward theories subversive of papal authority, and exalted the omnipotence of a general council beyond all measure.[2] All these audacious opinons were about to force a certain number of fathers to most lamentable deviations in doctrine and conduct. Already they clearly upset certain heads, and led on to utterances exaggerated to the point of injustice and so mistaken as to be heretical.

Ecclesiastics of the second order, who had been wrongly called to take part in the assembly, showed themselves more carried away and more intractable than the rest. They seemed ready to accept the most far-fetched conclusions.

This state of mind explains without excusing all that remains to be told, and all that took place at subsequent sessions of the council.

§ 3. *The Third, Fourth, and Fifth Sessions.*

The next meeting had been fixed for March 26th, for the assembly made a point of showing as quickly as possible that it did not look upon itself as dissolved through the Pope's departure. On the other hand, John sent to all the Sacred College a command to come and

[1] *Cf.* the violent placard attributed to Benedict Gentian, representing the University of Paris. Martène et Durand, *Thesaurus*, ii. col. 1620.

[2] Von der Hardt, ii. col. 265. J. B. Schwab, *Johannes Gerson*, p. 507. Martène et Durand, col. 1623. Valois, iv. p. 290.

join him at Schaffhausen within six days under pain of excommunication. Thus, his intention of making the council impossible was evident. At the same time he complained to the King of France and his uncles, as well as to the University of Paris, of the bad treatment which he had experienced at the hands of the council, of the distrust that had been shown towards him, and of the plots that had been made by Sigismund against the liberty of the fathers and of himself. The new procedure followed at Constance and the so-called wrongs inflicted on the French people also evoked his interested remonstrances.[1]

Two days later, on March 25, John XXIII. sent the Archbishop of Rheims to the town and bade him make a verbal declaration to the assembly. "It is not fear, but the unhealthiness of the air," he said, "that obliged me to leave Constance. I am even ready to help Sigismund and to pacify the Church." In a letter addressed to the cardinals, he appointed them all as his representatives in the work of *cession,* and ordered three of them to make his abdication publicly known, as soon as Benedict and Gregory had given in their resignation.[2] In fine, the Pontiff capitulated!

Without awaiting the return of the members of the Sacred College who had been sent to Schaffhausen, it was decided to hold the third session immediately, and, in fact, it took place on March 26. The business was to promulgate *conciliariter* what the four nations had decided upon *nationaliter.* Most of the cardinals, uneasy

[1] Von der Hardt, ii. col. 253 (not 153, a printer's error in the book). Mansi, xxviii. p. 14. In the Vatican Library, Nos. 4173-4179 refer to the Council of Constance. The reports of the Congregations were not drawn up at Constance at all: hence much uncertainty in the actual text.

[2] Von der Hardt, iv. col. 68. Mansi, xxvii. p. 576.

as to the provisions enacted by the council, and vexed by its proceedings, refrained from putting in an appearance at the meeting. There were only seventy prelates present, but, on the other hand, there was an abundance of ecclesiastics of the second order. Cardinal d'Ailly took the chair after having solemnly sung Mass. Cardinal Zabarella read the following resolutions, which had already been approved by the nations: that the council had been legitimately convened, opened, and held at Constance; that the withdrawal of the Pope had not dissolved it; that it could not be dissolved before the Schism was exterminated and the Church reformed; that the assembly could not be transferred elsewhere, and that all its members ought to remain at Constance till the work was over.

These fine points were adopted *conciliariter* by the cardinals and all the members who were present. Nevertheless d'Ailly and Zabarella thought it their duty to make a public protestation of their fidelity to the authority of John XXIII., as long as he persisted in his intention of resigning his prerogatives. If they consented to attend this session, it was because they hoped to see the Pope ratify their decisions later on.[1] One cannot but feel that the two cardinals were themselves growing alarmed at the violent and revolutionary turn things were taking.

Meanwhile, the three members of the Sacred College sent to Schaffhausen returned to Constance. On March 28, Maundy Thursday, the Cardinal of Pisa, Alemanno Adimari, made a report of his mission. The Pope upheld his original declarations, but persisted in wishing to reside outside the town for some weeks,

[1] Von der Hardt, iv. p. 70-74. Mansi, xxvii. p. 579. Hardouin, vii. p. 246.

keeping an adequate court about him. Moreover, he asked that his protector, Frederick, should not be prosecuted, at any rate within a certain time.

These propositions were unfavourably received and gave rise to violent discussions. The King of the Romans and his partisans would admit none of the Pope's reservations. In his requests they saw mere subterfuges for preventing the progress of the council, for suspending its deliberations, and for bringing about its dissolution. All resolved to hold a new session without delay, and it was fixed for March 30, Holy Saturday.[1]

But in the interim, on Good Friday, the nations of France, Germany, and England, gathered at the Franciscan convent, drew up *nationaliter* four articles, which have become as historically famous as the notable declaration of 1682.

1st. The Council of Constance, lawfully meeting in the Holy Spirit, making an *œcumenical council* and *representing the Church militant*, holds its authority directly from God. All the faithful, *the Pope included*, are bound to obey it in the matter of things of faith, and of the extinction of the Schism, as well as of the reform of the Church alike in her head and members.

2nd. Whoever, *even if he were the Pope himself*, obstinately refuses to conform to the decrees, statutes, and ordinances of the holy council, or any other general council canonically convened, on the points already mentioned, or others like them, will receive the penalty he deserves, and other lawful means shall be employed if necessary.

3rd. The flight of the Pope is a reprehensible action and scandalous: it throws him open to the suspicion

[1] Several dates in HARDOUIN and MANSI, *loc cit.*, are faulty.

of desiring to favour the Schism, and even of having fallen into heresy.

4th. John XXIII., and all other persons invited to the council, have always enjoyed and still enjoy the fullest liberty.[1]

Every reader can see how these propositions, adopted by three nations out of four, are far from being satisfactory from a theological point of view. The two first contain the whole of the essence of Gallicanism: they are full of its schismatical venom.

It is to be noted that the cardinals and the very numerous Italian nation took no part in drawing up these articles. On the contrary, they showed that they were very discontented with them. They went to Sigismund, reminded him of the Pope's promises with regard to *cession*, and begged him not to allow these four articles to be published next day in the general sitting *conciliariter*. Indeed, they drew his attention to the fact that several of the decrees proposed by the three nations were inadmissible. They tried to modify them and to replace them by others. The King of the Romans fully understood that a rupture between the Sacred College and the council was to be avoided at all costs. He sought to get the nations to listen to reason, but he had great difficulty in securing a delay of a few hours before the opening of the fourth session.

Sigismund succeeded in turning this brief respite to good account. He operated with such firmness and shrewdness that when the sitting opened, the cardinals and the national deputies were agreed in suppressing everything that could wound the Sovereign Pontiff. No

[1] Von der Hardt, iv. p. 81. Hefele, x. p. 401. The translation of the second article in this author appears defective. Schelstraete, *Tractatus de decretis Constantiensibus* (Rome, 1686), p. 3.

doubt the majority of the members of the council were not in the secret, but it was intended to snatch a surprise vote.

The fourth session then opened on Holy Saturday, March 30, 1415, under the presidency of Cardinal Orsini, the Cardinals of Viviers and Cambrai being, or pretending to be, ill. Great was the astonishment of the majority when they heard Cardinal Zabarella read three articles which were entirely different from the four that they had approved *nationaliter* the day before. Only the first point was approximately the same; and here again the words "*reform of the head and of the members*" had been suppressed.

The second article was conceived thus: John XXIII. shall not be able, without the consent of the fathers, to withdraw from Constance the members and servants of the Roman Court, whose absence would threaten to dissolve the council.

The third article: All penalties decreed by the Pope since his departure from Constance against the supporters and members of the assembly shall be null.[1]

These three articles were much milder than the four proposed by the nations. The skill and influence of the cardinals had succeeded in avoiding the reefs. But the dissatisfaction of the bitter enemies of the Pope was extreme, especially among the delegates of the University of Paris.

An unexpected occurrence came to drive into fury those who were hostile to John XXIII. On Good

[1] Animated discussion has arisen as to the text of the decrees of the fourth session, and particularly as to the words: "*reform in the head and the members.*" They are not to be found in sixteen MSS., but appear in some others, as well as in the printed deeds of the council. Probably Zabarella omitted them in reading them: and this was doubtless the cause of the lively reproaches afterwards directed against him.

Friday, the Pontiff had left Schaffhausen and had taken refuge in the castle of Laufenburg, fourteen leagues to the west of that town. He feared, he said, that Sigismund threatened an immediate attack on the Duke of Austria, and he was increasing the distance between himself and Constance. The nations saw a fresh hostile act and a perfidious manœuvre in this second flight.

What was far more important, the Pope was said to have declared before a notary that all the concessions he had made at Constance had been extorted from him by force, and that they were therefore null.[1]

Thenceforward, abusive and threatening protests were redoubled and it was resolved not to mince matters, to strike blow for blow and to make John XXIII. feel how far the council was superior to him. There seemed to be nothing more opportune than to resume the four violent articles that had been passed on Good Friday by the nations of France, Germany, and England.

The fathers were hastily assembled in a general meeting: and the session was held on the Saturday in Easter week, on April 6. It was the fifth. Cardinal Orsini presided again. D'Ailly, the Cardinal of Viviers, and several others did not appear. Nevertheless, seven cardinals were present, but they took care to declare beforehand that they only did so in order to avoid giving scandal, and not to approve the extreme decisions which they expected to see formulated. No doubt they dreaded a phenomenon, which is peculiar to deliberative assemblies, and which has been lately named general insanity. The Bishop of Posen immediately read five articles demanded by the nations, and embracing all the points agreed to on Good Friday and Easter Eve. The first was the one we have already noted with the adden-

[1] Niem, *Vita Johannis XXIII.*, apud Von der Hardt, ii. col. 399.

dum demanding *reform in the head and members of the Church.*

The second, which was quite as deplorable and offensive, called for rigorous measures against the Sovereign Pontiff, if he refused to obey the decrees of the Council of Constance or of any other general council.

The third and fourth were nothing more than the second and third of the fourth session. They forbade the Pontiff to summon the curia to himself, and annulled all the condemnations issued against the council.

The fifth was in accord with the fourth of the gathering of March 29. It affirmed that Pope John and the members of the council had always enjoyed the fullest liberty.[1]

What a sad page is this in the Church's history! It shows how true was the reflection of Pellisson when the four articles of 1682 were accepted: "Ecclesiastical jurisdiction is a matter which is hardly ever dealt with without carrying people further than they intend to go."

§ 4. *Estimate of the Decrees of Constance.*

Such in their schismatical essence are the famous articles of Constance, taken up and further exaggerated by the conventicle of Basle, and extolled in 1682 once more. In germ they contain the whole of Gallican doctrine, which has done such harm to the Church of France, and which has perhaps been "the most formidable and deeply rooted of our errors."[2]

These four articles are merely an act of war and ill-feeling, the outcome of a hasty vote at a time of trouble

[1] *Histoire de Louis XIV.*, i. p. 227.

[2] MONTALEMBERT, *Des intérêts catholiques*, Œuvres, v. p. 35.

by an incompetent assembly, which perhaps only intended them as a temporary expedient, but which in any case declared that it was œcumenical without any right to do so, and which on this point has never received the approval of the Sovereign Pontiff.[1]

That this thesis of the superiority of the Council over the Pope was until then unknown in the Church cannot be disputed by any theologian, unless he pushes his foregone conclusions to the point of choosing as the speaking-trumpet of the true doctrine such and such a heterodox doctor, this or that Gallican bishop, or some one or other professor of the Faculty of Paris at the end of the fourteenth century. That this opinion, which was until then considered heretical, was put forward at this period merely as a means of bringing the Schism to an end, is clearly acknowledged by all the corypheuses of Gallicanism. That it was passed *ab irato* in a vindictive spirit, and to wreak vengeance on the proceedings of John XXIII., all who have followed our narrative will agree.

There is every reason to believe that the human spirit in its weakest inspirations had a greater share in all these deliberations than the Spirit of God.

Moreover, these articles, which were so contrary to the most honoured traditions, and of such an extraordinary cast, were prepared, drawn up, and promulgated in passionate haste.[2] Three sessions of the council were held one after the other within twelve days (from March 26 till April 6), and each of them altered for the worse the measures and decisions previously adopted. It was an *opus tumultuarium*, thus well described by de Maistre :

[1] *Cf.* Gerson, *De Potestate Ecclesiae,* Consid. x. and xi., ii. col. 240 ff. Bossuet, *Defensio,* vi. c. 19.

[2] This is the opinion of Bellarmine and the doctors of Louvain. *De Concil. auctoritate,* xix.

"Let us put ourselves," he says, "in the place of the bishops of Constance, torn by all the passions of Europe, divided into nations, opposed to one another in interest, weary of delays, irritated by contradiction, separated from the cardinals, and to crown all other evils, under the influence of jarring memories. Is it, then, any wonder that since they were also urged on by intense desire to have done with the most lamentable Schism that had ever afflicted the Church, these bishops should have said to themselves: "There is only one way of restoring peace to the Church and of reforming her in head and members. We must command this head himself. We must declare that he is obliged to obey us." Men of splendid intelligence, in subsequent centuries, have argued no better."[1]

And it is these decrees of passion and conflict, drawn up in such scandalous haste, without precision, and without reserve, that some would compare in value with the articles of faith of the ancient councils, which were so long expected, so thoroughly weighed, so learnedly deliberated on, and so plainly approved!

What, then, is the true scope of these resolutions of Constance? Were they intended to have the force of law in the future, at all times and in all places, or had they merely in view the precarious position of the Church at the beginning of the fifteenth century. Have we to do with an absolute thesis or a transitory expedient? Is it a question of a dogma, proclaiming the superiority of the Council over the Pope, or of a means invented for a time of Schism in order to escape from an embarrassing and perilous position? Many grave theologians have declared that these decrees are exceptional and that they are inapplicable to ordinary times in which the

[1] De Maistre, *Du Pape*, lib. i. ch. xi.

Church obeys a single and undisputed Pope.[1] They find a support in the very text of the articles, which set forth the sole and exclusive end of the gathering assembled at Constance, *pro extirpatione praesentis schismatis, ad consequendum facilius, securius, et liberius unionem et reformationem Ecclesiae.* They remark, moreover, that certain other terms of the decrees are intended to fix limits: they only have to do with the present council and the extraordinary circumstances in which the Church then was. What matters it, they add, if the conventicle of Basle claimed to give these articles an absolute value and to establish the claims of the Council as against the Pope in a permanent manner? Is it not right to deny altogether the authority of this meeting of schismatic prelates, which can only be likened to the robber-council of Ephesus of 449? [2]

Thus do these authors speak, and their arguments are not at all wanting in force, although the whole Gallican school has ever desired to give these conciliar declarations a general application.[3]

Others more reasonably, as it appears to me, dispute the value of these decrees, not so much with regard to their bearing, as with reference to the source whence they proceed.[4] No doubt, they say, the council

[1] MUZZARELLI, *De auctor. Summi Pontificis,* ii. c. xvii. §§ 2-7. PALMA, *Praelect. hist.,* iv. p. 1ª, c. iv. p. 63. CHRISTOPHE, *Histoire de la Papauté pendant le XIVe siècle,* iii. p. 485. JAGER, *Histoire de l'Église,* xiii. lib. 39, p. 107. TURRECREMATA, *Apol. in Conc. Floren., Summa de Eccl.,* vol. ii. c. xcix.

[2] *Cf.* ch. vi. above, p. 117.

[3] *Cf.* BOSSUET, pars ii. lib. v. c. 13-21.

[4] BALLERINI, *De Potestate Ecclesiae,* c. vii., in MIGNE, *Theol. cursus completus,* iii. col. 1350-1359. BOUIX, *De Papa,* i. c. vi. p. 460. PASTOR, *Histoire des Papes,* i. p. 208. HEFELE, *Histoire des Conciles,* x. p. 406. JUNGMANN, *Dissert. select. in hist. eccl.,* vi. p. 308. HERGENROETHER, *Histoire de l'Église,* iv. p. 558. Other authors rely upon both reasons, RONCAGLIA, MANSI, LITTA, ROHRBACHER.

of 1415 declared itself to be œcumenical. This could not be helped, if the inference was to be drawn *that all persons, of any and every position or dignity whatsoever, even if it be papal, are obliged to obey it*, but was it really œcumenical ?

It is not enough to make a claim to establish it. Two obediences were not at all represented at Constance, and never approved the famous decrees. The cardinals protested in a body. Moreover, the Pope John XXIII. was absent, nor had he sent any legates to represent him, so that the flight of the Pontiff, which gave rise to the schismatical decrees, is at the same time one of the reasons that deprives them of any value whatever.

But what is a council without a Pope, except a number of members without a head ?

In the present case, whatever opinion one may hold about the legitimacy of the Pope, it is certain that there was discussion and separation between the council and the true Pontiff. Without a Pope there can no more be an œcumenical council than without a head there can be a living body.

So, then, the assembly of Constance was from the start merely a particular council, or a meeting of four nations, convoked by the head of the Empire to deliberate about the particular case of the Schism, and not about the general question of the prerogatives of the council and of its superiority to the Roman Pontiff. It only became œcumenical after its thirty-fifth session, when Gregory XII. had resigned, and when Sicily and the county of Poix, together with the Spanish peninsula, had repudiated Benedict's obedience. Only in its nine last sessions could it claim to represent the universal Church.

But, answer the Gallicans, the decrees of the council

were approved by Martin V., a Pope universally recognised.[1] What, then, is wanting to give them legal force?

Where are the authentic documents that prove this approbation? one may reply.

It is inaccurate to say that the Sovereign Pontiff ever accepted these irregular articles and sanctioned them with his supreme and sovereign authority. On the contrary, when, in 1418, the ambassadors of the King of Poland wanted to get the Pope to utter a solemn condemnation of the Dominican, John of Falkenberg, who was already found guilty by the nations *nationaliter*, Pope Martin V. opposed them and replied: "All that has been decreed by the present council in *matters of faith and conciliariter* must be believed and held inviolably. I approve and ratify it, but not what has been done in any other way, *non aliter nec alio modo*."[2] But at Constance *conciliariter* is always opposed to *nationaliter*.

This restrictive decision was reiterated by Augustine of Pisa, the fiscal procurator, who in the Pope's name asked the protonotaries and notaries to publish all the documents that had to do with the assembly in full, and who relied upon this important distinction.

But what had the council determined in matters of faith besides the articles condemning Wicliffe and Huss? It is these articles that the Pope approves, and the same affirmation is to be found in the series of

[1] *A Sede apostolica comprobata*, says the second article of the declaration of 1682. FUNK understands this word of the Pope's in a restricted sense: according to him, it only applies to the Falkenberg affair. HUBLER appears to be of the same opinion, *Die Konstanzer Reformation* (Leipzig, 1867), pp. 263-280.

[2] BOUIX, *De Papa*, i. p. 524. HEFELE, i. pp. 50 and 59. JUNGMANN, *Dissert. select.*, vi. p. 310. LABBE et COSSART, xiii. p. 258. VON DER HARDT, iv. p. 1558. *Cf.* FUNK, *Kirchengeschichtliche Abhandlungen und Untersuchungen* (Paderborn, 1897), p. 491. VALOIS, iv. p. 506.

questions ordered by Martin V. to be put to all who were suspected of Wicliffite or Hussite heresy [1]

The five propositions already cited are not of this nature, for they are not invested with the solemn formulæ which ordinarily guard decrees of faith that are binding on the belief of all the faithful. The fathers themselves considered them for the most part as simple synodal declarations having an application to a given case. They never condemned as heretics, drove out of the Church, or excommunicated those who might think otherwise.[2]

Furthermore, did the assembly act *conciliariter* in its fourth and fifth sessions? No, and this has been proved. At this date, during the months of March and April, the council was not yet œcumenical. Whatever it decreed was decided by the nations, who formed so many little particular synods, deliberating independently, and of very unequal numbers and value.

These articles were acknowledged without any participation on the part of the cardinals and against the will of part of the assembly, but with the votes of more than three hundred simple priests or married laymen, voting without any right to do so.

Lastly, in his bull of February 22, 1418, Martin V. makes the œcumenical character of the council binding on the belief of the faithful, but he makes an important reservation when he adds: "Hold for certain whatever it has determined in favour of the faith and for the good of souls." Thereby he seems to exclude certain decrees, without wishing to express himself more formally on the point, so as not to disturb the peace. It would have

[1] Hefele, xi. p. 58. *Cf.* Ballerini, in Migne, *Theol. cursus completus*, iii. col. 1353.

[2] Ballerini, col. 1359.

been so dangerous, at this date, to enter into a conflict with the expiring council.

So it was with Eugenius, Martin V.'s successor. In 446 he was quite willing to approve of all the decisions of Constance, "that were not in any way prejudicial to the rights, the dignity, and the pre-eminence of the Apostolic See."

Judge whether the decrees accepted at the first sessions are in favour of the faith and of souls, and whether they could be acknowledged without doing grievous wrong to the superior authority of the Sovereign Pontiffs.[1] These reservations are significant and must be taken into consideration.

Martin V. and Eugenius IV., therefore, did not approve of these decrees, but implicitly repudiated them as not belonging to matters of faith, as approved merely *nationaliter*, and not by the whole assembly *conciliariter*. Moreover, the Popes who came after always permitted the opposite to be taught to what had been decreed by the Council of Constance.

This was also the opinion expressed by Cardinal d'Ailly in general terms, and he was intimately connected with the whole of the events and is considered as one of the fathers of Gallicanism. "This deliberation carried on by the nations outside the assembly, without votes cast at a common sitting, appears to many persons not to be ranked as a deliberation made by the general council, *conciliariter facta*. . . . However this may be, I submit the definition of this matter to the will of the holy council."[2]

Therefore, a year after the famous sessions, d'Ailly

[1] *Cf.* Hefele, xi. p. 110. Valois, iv. p. 507.

[2] *De Ecclesiae concilii generalis et Summi Pontificis auctoritate, Opp. Gersonii*, ii col. 940 and 960. *Cf.* Ballerini, col. 1351.

and many others thought that these decisions, which were so novel in the Church, had not been taken *conciliariter*, and awaited a definite determination of the point.

He who, according to Bossuet,[1] was the light of this assembly, he who gave the best explanation of its decisions, thus appears to give up the work of the three sessions, although in the eyes of Gallicanism this work has always seemed the decisive argument and the capital proof.

A day came when he, who after d'Ailly was the greatest of the defenders of Gallican privileges, Bossuet, was tired of incessantly turning back to a number of sophisms and inconsistencies where his downright mind and strong good sense were ill at ease. The concession that he thought himself forced to make to the civil power and national prejudice rightly appeared to him exaggerated. Perhaps, too, he bethought him of the account he would have to give to God of the part he played in the assembly of 1682, and of the *Defence* of the too notorious declaration which was the sin and the torment of his life.

Hear de Maistre: "One cannot consider this great man without interest, nailed, so to speak, to an ungrateful task, which he could never give up or bring to an end. After having made, re-made, changed, corrected, abandoned, resumed, mutilated, supplemented, erased, interlined, and annotated his work, he concluded by turning it completely upside down. He changes the title, and binds himself to make no further mention of the four articles."[2] He would have modified the book

[1] "Sancti conventus lumen et in dogmatibus explicandis facile princeps." *Def. declar. cleri gallicani*, c. 30.

[2] *De l'Église Gallicane*, lib. ii. ch. ix. *Cf.* Gérin, *Recherches historiques sur l'Assemblée de* 1682, p. 345.

from beginning to end, had his infirmities and death not cut his time short.

The attitude of Peter d'Ailly is like that of Bossuet, and the Cardinal of Cambrai holds the articles of Constance cheap, like the Bishop of Meaux holds the decrees of Paris. Both are hampered with their own work and with the consequences that may be drawn from their principles. Are not these two judgments, separated as they are by more than two centuries, the best theological criterion and the soundest commentary on the declarations of 1415 and 1682?

Nevertheless, several centuries had to pass before the Vatican Council would strike a mortal blow at the doctrine which was too long taken advantage of by the enemies of the Church. The great act of 1870 has put an end to all the fluctuations of thought and to all the hesitations of obedience, of which this beginning of Schism was the cause. It has shed light in a definite fashion on this point of dogma, and has closed the important debate that the fourteenth century saw arise, and which had lasted down to our own times.

CHAPTER XVI

HERETICS AT CONSTANCE

§ 1. *Heresies and the Schism. John Huss.*

At first blush one would suppose that this chapter has only an indirect connection with the great division in the Church of which we have undertaken to record the history. And yet heresies naturally and logically grow out of Schism. When the infallible *magisterium* is repudiated, disputes quickly arise, and then dogma gets denied. If schism breaks up social communion, heresy immediately comes after it to break down doctrinal communion. England, at first schismatical and then heretical, will soon afford us a sad example: so will it be with Russia and Greece. "When schisms continue, new heresies arise." Such is the historical and theological law laid down by Henry of Langenstein in the fourteenth century.[1]

The Great Schism, though essentially and originally differing from that of England and Russia, leads to the same results and gives rise to similar troubles. A dubious Papacy has no authority, a disputed Sacred College has no prestige; councils, when belittled and despised, are powerless to attain their peaceful ends; certain bishops at times put forward strange propositions from a dogmatical point of view; a few doctors, members

[1] *Invectiva contra monstrum Babylonis,* partly printed by A. Kneer, Rome, 1893, after a Breslau MS., cod. 320, v. 253 and 797. *Entstehung der konziliaren Theorie,* pp. 127-129.

of famous universities, approve and maintain heretical opinions to the very last.

John Huss is the most celebrated of the revolters. His errors prepared the way for deeper revolutions that were to shake the world to its foundations and drench the future with blood.

In the first book of his *History of the French Revolution*, Louis Blanc relates, with his usual burning and gloomy eloquence, which is often impassioned to the point of injustice, the drama of John Huss appearing before the fathers of Constance. In this historical fact he sees the first act of the great struggle between the Church and the Revolution, between divine authority and human individualism. The heretic at the bar of the council is for him the intrepid champion of fraternity, which has been changed by the Church, and of equality between all men, priests and laymen. It is John Huss who is the first defender of this new spirit, the apostle of the most radical social reforms. "Until then," says the revolutionist historian, "revolts of conscience and the cry of the people, the movement of the human mind and the tremblings of the travailing earth had only issued in theological revolutions. . . . Insolence (that is to say, authority) branded as heresy what in our days it condemns as rebellion. The Revolution, which was prepared for by philosophy and carried on by politics, and will only be achieved by socialism, had to begin with theology." And the radical writer adds in conclusion: "Clearly it is a great question that is in debate between the council and John Huss."[1]

Perhaps it was even still more grave than was suspected by those who were to be the judges of the bold innovator. The fathers of Constance had just pro-

[1] L. Blanc, *Histoire de la Révolution Française*, i. ch. i.

claimed the superiority of the Council over the Pope. In doing so, they had inflicted a blow on the monarchical form of the Church, opening up the way to the stormy government of assemblies, and leading on to the superiority of the latter over kings. "Why should a temporal monarchy be more absolute than a spiritual one? Was a crown more sacred than a tiara?"[1] The Council of Constance had yielded on the question of the supreme power of the Roman Pontiff: was it to abdicate before the heresy of Huss? Was it to open with its own hands the era of religious and social revolutions that John Huss was preparing, and to leave a free field to all innovations? The attitude of the fathers in the suit of this heretic will show that here the council knew how to uphold and defend all the rights of truth.

There are two well-marked divisions in the agitated life of the professor of the Bohemian University: the first, in which he appears as a more or less demagogical innovator; the second, in which he is a determined and obstinate heresiarch. Whoever studies his history will find in him first a Lammenais and then a Luther.

Born in 1369, in a Bohemian village, John Huss soon made his way into one of the Universities, which in those days were open to the least of fortune's favourites. He rapidly became a professor, and then Dean of the Faculty of Arts, and finally, in 1412, rector of the University. He was a tall man, with a lean, ascetic face, skilful in dialectics, of a rough eloquence, full of vigour, energy, and subtlety. He swept people along with him rather than persuaded them, was more of a tribune than of an orator or professor, and bitter invective was his favourite weapon. Juvenal and Dion Chrysostom were his masters rather than St John or St Irenæus.

[1] *Ibid.*, chs. i. and vi.

He was ruthless against whatever he took to be erroneous, and never spared even the highest personalities. Especially did he fall upon the clergy, seduced one section of them and attacked the rest, with the animosity of an obstinate and ill-balanced mind. He called for reform, even if it were to bring revolution in its train.

The first errors of John Huss reached him from abroad. Wicliffe had preached subversive doctrines in England: he had stirred up the people by attacking both ecclesiastical and civil power. From 1385 his philosophic theories had made their way into Bohemia, and about 1402 his theological works were circulated there most extensively. John Huss had the same feelings and hatreds as the English heresiarch. Soon he embraced all his errors.[1]

As a professor of the University, he was received with applause by youthful enthusiasts. Preaching in the Czech language in a Prague church, he carried away an ardent and ignorant people by his sectarian violence and fanatical ardour. As confessor of Queen Sophia, he had acquired powerful friends and protectors at the court of the weak and voluptuous Wenceslas.

From 1407 the master more and more inclined towards Wicliffe. He wrote to his partisans in England, and openly defended his errors, notwithstanding the opposition of the archbishop and of the majority of the clergy.

Patriotism soon came to confuse the situation by firing people's minds still further. Then, as to-day, two parties divided the University of Prague. On the one

[1] *Cf.* J. Loserth, *Hus und Wiclif* (Prague, Leipzig, 1884). J. B. Schwab, *Johannes Gerson*, p. 527 ff. Budensieg, *J. Wiclif und seine Zeit* (Gotha, 1885). Stevenson, *The Truth about J. Wiclif.* Krummel, *Leben des J. Huss, eines bekannten Reformatoren* (Kempten, 1873), and other works on the question by the same author. Like Palacky, Krummel is an admirer of J. Huss, but he sometimes makes reserves.

side were the Germans, attached to Gregory XII. and hostile to the new teaching; on the other were the Bohemians, upholders of the Council of Pisa, and mostly addicted to Wicliffism. The Germans had three votes to one in the Bohemian *Alma Mater*; but Wenceslas took sides against them, and decided that henceforth the Czech nation should have three votes, and the three German-speaking nations (Germany, properly so-called, Saxony, and Poland) only one (January 18, 1409). By way of reply the Germans withdrew in a body. The Czechs, who had long been under their yoke, greatly rejoiced. In order to accentuate the meaning of this step still further, John Huss was nominated rector of the University thus reduced. No doubt it emerged from the struggle less numerous, but more united and emboldened by an unexpected victory.

The cause of the Bohemian Wicliffites was taken before Pope Alexander V., who summoned the King to take proceedings against them. A synod, under the presidency of the archbishop, condemned the works of the heresiarch, whom Huss and his party took as their leader, to be burnt.

The University protested in the name of the reputation of Bohemia for orthodoxy. The Czechs took all the theological novelties as a symbol and instrument of their national awakening.[1] It was to avenge the insult suffered by the Bohemian nation that John Huss appealed to the new Pope John XXIII., and his whole party heaped insults on the Archbishop of Prague and the priests who had held true.[2]

[1] Goyau, *Le Vatican* (Paris, 1895), p. 119.

[2] "In his language one recognises rather the frenzy of a sectary than the wisdom of an Apostle." Such is the admission of a Protestant, Émile de Bonnechose, otherwise a great upholder of the reformer. *Les Réformateurs avant la Réforme, Jean Hus*, lib. i. ch. iii. p. 128.

A knight named Jerome of Prague, a former student of the University of Paris, had become one of the heads of the party. He openly upheld the innovators, and outstripped the violence of the master whose punishment he was afterwards to share.

Henceforward the demagogue, smitten with a desire for unwholesome popularity, was to become a heresiarch; and he flung Bohemia into a long and bloody religious revolution and became one of the forerunners of the apostate of Wittemberg.

" After John Huss, the world in its bitterness brought forth Luther," says Bossuet. Both of obscure origin, they were naturally endowed with an eloquence that carries away the crowd. Both proclaim at the outset a deep contempt for the Roman Pontiff and for the bishop, and let loose religious passion with a light heart. The one, like the other, relies subsequently on the laity, gives up to them the government of the Church, and places it without either repugnance or reserve in the hands of Cæsar, Pope and King.

Like Luther, John Huss was summoned before the court of Rome, and condemned by it. Like him, too, the Bohemian heresiarch appealed to a general council, and continued to preach his doctrines with ardour despite all prohibitions. At Prague, as a century afterwards in certain German diets, civil authority, troubled and irresolute, allowed itself to be checked by a few hypocritical protests, and the sword of justice to become blunted in its hands. John Huss relied on the Czech nobility and on the lord of Austia, as Luther did on the Elector of Saxony and Ulrich von Hutten. The first found an asylum in the castles of Kozihradek and Krakovec, as the last did in the dungeon of the Wartberg.

Even the doctrines of Huss are closely related to those a century afterwards taught by Luther. The Bohemian heresiarch, too, began by an assault on the Catholic teaching as to the crusades and the publication of indulgences (1411).[1]

But this first dispute was only to give rise to a more extended rupture. For him the Church was merely a society of the predestinated (*praedestinati*). Those who are not among them, those whose damnation God foresees (*praesciti*), can never become a part of the mystical body of Jesus Christ.[2]

There is no acquisition or preservation of merit. Faith only and not keeping the law is the means of salvation.[3] Wicliffe had already maintained these ruinous and distressing doctrines.[4] The Church was founded on Christ and not upon Peter ; the first of the Apostles had never been its true head. For John Huss the true Pontiff was Jesus Christ alone. The Church could be governed without any vicar of Christ. The Pope was sometimes Antichrist, sometimes the servant of Antichrist. Sometimes he had taught heresy ; and he ought to have no material possessions. This heretic was not afraid of attacking papal bulls in the most disgraceful manner, and to all who were willing to listen he related the story, as apocryphal as it was shameful, of Pope Joan.[5] Bishops, priests, and monks, especially

[1] Palacky, *Documenta*. Hefele, *Histoire des Conciles*, x. p. 350.

[2] Cappenberg, *Utrum Hussii doctrina fuerit haeretica* (Munster, 1834). Friedrich, *Die Lehre des Joh. Huss* (Ratisbon, 1862), p. 13. Hefele, pp. 356, 462-504.

[3] Arminius Jepp, *Gerson, Wiclef, Hussus inter se cum reformatoribus comparati*, p. 61 (Göttingen, 1857). *Cf.* Winkelmann (Joa. Cav. Aug.). Same title and same date.

[4] Jepp, pp. 33 and 38. Wiclef, *Dialogus*, ii. 73 ; iv. 22.

[5] Hus, *de Ecclesia*. *Ibid.*, 2nd letter to Christian de Prachatic, in Höfler, *Jean Hus*, p. 222. *Ibid.*, 5th letter.

those of the mendicant orders, were loaded in succession with insult and contempt.

After having thus villified and cast aside the living rule of faith, the reformer ascribed all doctrinal authority to one among dead rules, I mean Holy Scripture and the law of Christ. He held that the Pope's decrees were only so far obligatory as they were in accord with this law ; but everyone was to be a judge of this concordance or not. Here we have the right of private judgment, the infallible authority of the reason of the individual, as proclaimed by Luther.[1] Huss, moreover, claims for everyone permission to read, and the right to interpret, the Bible.

In expounding the doctrine of the Sacraments, this innovator claims communion in both kinds for all the faithful, *i.e.* the chalice for the laity. This was long the chief point in dispute between the Bohemians and the Roman Church.[2] With less daring than Wicliffe and Luther, he used ambiguous language as to the permanence of the substance of bread in the Host after the consecration.[3] Auricular confession was unnecessary, contrition being enough for salvation.[4]

As for veneration of relics, ecclesiastical censures, and the foundation of civil authority, the opinions of Huss hardly differ from those of Luther.[5] Moreover, the latter more than once acknowledged the influence of the doctrines of the Bohemian apostate on his mind and

[1] Palacky, *Documenta,* p. 448. Hefele, x. pp. 350, 520. A. H. Wratislaw, *The Commencement of Resistance to Papal Authority on the Inferior Clergy* (London, 1882).

[2] Jepp, p. 56. Hefele, *Op. cit.*, pp. 372, 448, 477.

[3] Hefele, pp. 360, 455, 502.

[4] Jepp, p. 64.

[5] See the thirty propositions condemned at Constance, and the thirty-nine articles on which suspected heretics were cross-examined. Denzinger, *Euchiridion,* No. 522 ff.

conduct, and he honoured him as a great Christian martyr, while blaming him for timidity. On the first page of a Hussite hymn-book kept at Prague is an engraving which represents Wicliffe striking a light, Huss supplying the coal, and Luther waving a burning torch.[1] It is a true symbol of the relations which morally bound the three men together, though they never met in this life. The heresiarch of Wittemberg wrote thus insultingly to the Pope : " Everything you condemn in Huss I approve, and everything you approve I condemn. Here is the retractation you have bidden me to make. Do you want anything more in that line ? " " The most violent fevers do not produce such outbursts as these," says Bossuet, in relating the matter.[2]

§ 2. *Judgment and Sentence.*

At the time we have just reached, the Council of Constance was about to open. Sigismund bade several Czech nobles invite the innovator to appear. The latter had several times appealed from the Pope to a general council, and therefore could not refuse this invitation. Was it arrogance and infatuation ? Was it mental aberration ? Huss had a naïve and presumptuous confidence in the goodness of his cause, and he never belied it. Therefore he decided to expound his doctrines to the reforming council and to attempt to justify himself. He replied to Sigismund : " I have always taught openly and never in secret, and I demand the right of speaking in public assembly and of debating with my opponents. I have nothing to fear in confessing Christ, even if, in

[1] *Cf.* Janssen, *Allemagne et la Réforme*, i. 580 ; ii. pp. 83, 155, 413.
[2] *Histoire des Variations*, i. ch. 25.

order to defend His faith, it were necessary to risk the last penalty."[1]

He had already often said in public debate: "I am ready to undergo the penalty of being burnt, provided that my accusers suffer the same punishment if defeated."[2]

He had, indeed, obstinate adversaries, who were prepared to attack his dogmatic novelties before the Council, and who had already collected together the proofs of their main charges in Bohemia. The reformer left Prague on October 11, 1414, accompanied by numerous friends. Almost everywhere he met with a favourable reception, though he had not yet received the safe-conduct promised him by Sigismund.[3]

On arriving at Constance, on November 3, he obtained an assurance from Pope John that he had nothing to fear for the moment, that the excommunication he had incurred had been suspended, and that his trial would not begin before the arrival of the King of the Romans.

The Pontiff had forbidden him to say Mass and to

[1] Palacky, *Documenta*, p. 60. Höfler, *Magister J. Hus*, Part ii. p. 260. *Jean Hus et le concile de Constance*, Analecta juris pontificii, 1872.

[2] *Documenta*, p. 18. Höfler, Part i. p. 164. Hefele, pp. 348, 353, 518.

[3] The safe-conduct, which has been made the ground of so many charges, was brought to Constance on November 5 by Wenceslas from Duba. It was meant to guarantee Huss from illegal violence *en route*, and not from legal proceedings before the Council. It was only to facilitate his journey *in his quae celeritatem et securitatem itineris concernunt, tam per terram tam per aquam*. In a similar document addressed to Jerome of Prague, we read that it is intended to keep him *a violentia, justitia semper salva*. A safe-conduct is only a passport, which cannot be used to free its bearer from a penalty which he has incurred, or to guarantee him against the sentence of a court to which the accused has often himself appealed. *Cf.* Hefele, pp. 336, 459, 521 ff. Höfler, *Histor. polit. Blätter*, iv. p. 421. It should be added that several German writers admit a certain amount of duplicity in the Emperor. *Cf. Literarische Centralblatt*, Aug. 12, 1901.

preach: nevertheless Huss celebrated every day and spoke on every occasion without the least reserve. This disobedience, as contemptuous as it was imprudent, displeased the Pope and the cardinals. They invited the reformer to give an account of his conduct and opinions. As his answers seemed to them unsatisfactory, they put him under ward in the Dominican convent, near the lake, on December 6, 1414. Several months he remained in this modified captivity, receiving visitors, and keeping up a constant correspondence with his Bohemian friends, to whom he related his hopes as a false prophet, and later on his dreams as a visionary.

On April 6, at the fifth session, the Council entrusted the examination of the Hussite doctrines to Cardinals d'Ailly and Philastre, assisted by the Bishop of Dol, Stephen Cœuvret, the Abbot of Citeaux, and several doctors. The Cardinal of Cambrai agreed to make a report to the Council as to the questions of faith; but he demanded and obtained an order that lawyers should argue and conduct the case. He was less happy in begging the fathers to give sentence against Wicliffe and Huss in the name of the Council alone, without mentioning the Pope, because the Council was superior to him. The commission appointed to investigate the question reported against him by a large majority.[1] This took

[1] Hefele, p. 414. Von der Hardt, iv. p. 136. Palacky, *Documenta*. Schwab, *Johannes Gerson*, pp. 549-609. Ballerini, *Op. cit.*, iii. col. 1362. Only twelve out of forty theologians agreed with Peter d'Ailly. Hence the majority did not wish the decision of April 6 to be binding on general belief, so that the superiority of the Council to the Pope should be an article of faith. It is also remarkable that the Cardinal of Cambrai does not quote the decrees of the fifth session in favour of his opinion. Nor does he mention it in the treatise he published seventeen months later, entitled: *De Ecclesiae, Concilii generalis, Romani Pontificis et Cardinalium auctoritate.* He rather appeals, as we have seen, p. 308, to a future decision of the council. But this doctrinal decision was never reached.

place on April 17, 1415, eleven days after the famous fifth session of April 6. It was like the first contradiction by the council of the anti-papal decrees it had carried in a moment of passion.

While awaiting the appearance of John Huss, the Czech nobles, his partisans, several times attempted in vain to obtain his liberation. They had to be satisfied with bringing him out of the Dominican convent and getting him transferred to Gottlieben, a castle of the Bishop of Constance, on the banks of the Rhine and not far from the town.

I have seen the old ivy-covered tower in which the heresiarch was locked up. Crowns with laudatory inscriptions in the Czech language have been deposited in it: and, on the large wooden cage where he is said to have spent some weeks, an unknown hand had just placarded the famous safe-conduct, violated by his imprisonment, according to some historians, as a retrospective and permanent accusation.

At the beginning of June 1415, Huss was transferred to the Franciscan convent at Constance and underwent several cross-examinations.

We will not enter in detail into this theological controversy, or rather tragic duel, prolonged for five weeks, and ending in the death of one of the combatants.

Suffice it to say that the sessions were conscientiously presided over and directed, that the innovator was examined about matters involving the faith, and that two hundred witnesses were heard. The Cardinal of Cambrai was chairman of the commission of inquiry. Huss replied sometimes with lying denials, sometimes with sophistical reasoning that convinced nobody. When witnesses were brought against him, he merely appealed against them to his conscience or to Christ and treated his opponents as calumniators. He refused to subscribe freely to the condemnation of the forty-two articles taken from Wicliffe,[1] and would not always admit as his the thirty-nine articles taken from his own books.[2]

D'Ailly, however, who presided with more firmness than indulgence, observed to Sigismund, in the presence of the accused, that the exact and original terminology of his subversive theories had been softened down more than once in the formal allegations. Then, at the end of the third examination, the cardinal repeated to him what he had already said in the presence of, and with the approval of, the King of the Romans: "John, two ways are open to you: the first is to throw yourself simply and unreservedly on the clemency of the council, which, out of regard for the princes and yourself, will not fail to treat you with humanity and indulgence. The other is to persist in the defence of some of your articles. In the latter case you will have further hearings; but I warn

[1] *Cf.* HEFELE, pp. 455 and 468.

[2] It is, however, to be regretted that the cross-examiners mixed up the opinions of the School more than once with the theological discussions. In these grave circumstances, what had philosophical quarrels between nominalists and realists to do with opinions ascribed to Huss as to impanation? What could d'Ailly have answered, if the accused had made this objection: "But you yourself formerly acknowledged that my opinion was possible, as being repugnant neither to reason nor to Biblical authority, and as being easier and more reasonable than any other theory"? (*Quaest. super.*, i. iii. iv.; *Sententiarum*, Q. vi. a. i. f. cclxiv.) Also if John Huss had remarked with regard to his explanation of *Tu es Petrus*: "My opinion is the same as yours, and you have defended it in public theses. You said before me, and like me, that the rock is Christ and not Peter, *non in petra Petrus, sed in petra Christus est intelligendus*; have you forgotten this?" *Recommendatio sacrae Scripturae.* D'Ailly had composed this treatise at the end of his course in 1380. It is found in the works of Gerson, i. col. 604. *Cf.* SALEMBIER, *Petrus de Alliaco*, pp. 232 and 235. This is another proof of the danger of the novelties of the School, and of the paradoxical theses wherein the young doctors doubtless only saw an encounter of wits and matters for free discussion. See ch. vi. above, p. 109.

you that men of distinction and learning will oppose you, and I fear you will be on the losing side."

"I ask to be allowed another hearing," replied the accused; "I want to give explanations of the incriminated articles."

D'Ailly was urgent, and Sigismund united in his entreaties without obtaining anything. The writings of the reformer were condemned to be burnt, but immediately afterwards (June 24) Huss wrote to his Bohemian friends letters recommending that they should read them. His fixed idea is always to rely entirely on Scripture and to wish to discuss its text with the fathers,[1] as if the council were a parliament and not a tribunal. He lived tossed between hope and fear, but obstinately refused to sign a form of retractation, in spite of the requests of d'Ailly and Zabarella.

At last, on Saturday, July 6, all the fathers were convoked for the fifteenth general session and met in the Cathedral of Constance. The Cardinal of Viviers presided, and the King of the Romans was present, arrayed in all his majesty. The great trial, which had held all minds in suspense, had to be finally decided. John Huss was brought in and placed on a bench. On a table lay the sacerdotal vestments, which were to be used for the purpose of public degradation, if the innovator continued to prove obstinate.

After a short homily by the Bishop of Lodi, the articles against Wicliffe were read, and then the thirty charges specially brought against the Bohemian heresiarch. After each allegation, Huss spoke and tried to defend himself with more or less adroitness.

Several charges brought against him in the preceding

[1] *Documenta Johannis Hus*, p. 137 ff. Ep. lxxxv. HEFELE, pp. 493 and 496.

sessions had not been maintained, but the thirty articles which had been retained seem directly opposed, not only to the doctrinal authority of the Church, but to secular authority also. From the session of June 8, Sigismund understood this, and declared himself openly against the innovator.[1] "In all Christendom there is no more dangerous heretic than Huss," he exclaimed.

The reading of the minutes of the preceding cross-examinations continued on July 6, amidst the interruptions and protests of the accused. The tribunal had prepared two forms of sentence, the first to be read in the event of his repentance, and the second if he persisted in his rebellion. But, in spite of all entreaties, not a word of retractation passed the lips of John Huss. Thus the Bishop of Concordia was obliged to read the second sentence: "The holy Council has proofs that John remains obstinate and incorrigible," he said, "and that he refuses to return to the bosom of the Church, and to abjure his errors. The assembly therefore decrees that the guilty one shall be deposed and degraded, and that, after having been cut off from the Church, he shall be given over to the secular arm."[2]

§ 3. *The Execution.*

The fate of the heresiarch was to be fulfilled. Two bishops approached the condemned man and degraded him with the customary forms and imprecations. The chalice was taken from his hands, and the sacred ornaments one after the other were removed from his body, and his tonsure was deformed as a sign that he had lost all his ecclesiastical privileges. Then his head

[1] Hefele, p. 466. [2] Mansi, xxvii. p. 733. Hardouin, viii. p. 410.

was covered with a paper mitre bearing the words: *hic est heresiarcha.* Thus Huss was delivered over to the secular arm. Sigismund immediately summoned the Count Palatine of the Rhine: "Here is the guilty man," said he. "Treat him as a heretic." The Count in turn said to the Provost of Constance: "Seize Master John Huss, and burn him as a convicted heretic."

Immediately the sergeants and the executioner laid hold of the condemned man and made a path for him through the three thousand soldiers and the countless crowd that thronged the square. The cortège left the town dragging John Huss through a mob inspired with various feelings. He was asked if he wished to make his confession, and he accepted the invitation. The chaplain, Ulrich Schorand, approached him provided with full powers. "Master," said he, "I cannot give you absolution unless you retract your errors." Huss then refused, and wanted to begin a sermon in German. The Count Palatine opposed this, and had the execution hastened on. When bound to the fatal stake, and surrounded with wood and straw, he again refused to save his life by a withdrawal. At last the pyre was set on fire. The victim cried out thrice:[1] "Christ, Son of the living God, have mercy on us!" Then he died, and his body was soon consumed. The cinders, with the smoking remains of the pyre, were thrown into the Rhine.

This tragic death, the dark and mystic words uttered by the innovator, and the words that were put in his mouth at the last moment, all helped to stir popular opinion at the time very deeply, and called forth posthu-

[1] There is no contemporary account by a Catholic. Our only narrative is by Mladenowitz, a strong supporter of John Huss. The story attributed to Poggio, and printed at Reutlingen, in 1846, is a pure invention. *Cf.* Orthuinus Gratius, *op. cit.*, p. 152.

mous sympathy which may still be traced to-day. Constance has kept the cart in which he reached the town, and also the gate of his dungeon; and it has decorated with sculpture and painting the houses where he dwelt and the prisons where he was locked up. Three great pictures, all in honour of the heresiarch, decorate the immense hall which is wrongly called the council-chamber; and they give Huss the noble, grave, and ascetic face of Munkacsy's Christ, and to his judges and guards angry and mean features.[1]

A granite memorial has been raised at Brühl on the place of the heretic's execution, and despite the Hussite doctrine about relics, certain bones found on the spot where he was punished are kept with religious care.[2]

But the memory of the reformer was specially glorified in Bohemia. There the sectarian spirit united with an ill-informed patriotism to crown him with an aureole of sanctity, and to prepare a vengeance that was worthy of him. Do you see "kingdoms in revolt, Germany in flames, armies a hundred thousand strong urged on to a war of extermination: numerous populations flying from their homes armed with a gospel and a sword, changing their manner of life, and living only under the open sky, always shuddering, clothed in iron, living in nomadic cities made of waggons, a terrible series of massacres, fabulous combats, and embraces; and to preserve the memory of all this fury, the country, like it was after the defeat of Varus, whitened with bleaching bones? Such in principle and in practice was to be the war of which the trial of John Huss was the bloody germ."[3]

[1] These paintings are by Pecht and Schwarer (1875). The Council, as has been said, always met at the Cathedral, and never in this hall. The conclave of 1417 was held in the *Concilium Saal*.

[2] Rosgarten Museum at Constance.

[3] L. Blanc, *Histoire de la Revolution Française*, i. ch. i.

The letters sent by way of notification and explanation by the Council to the Bohemians did not succeed in calming people's minds. The torture of Jerome of Prague, on the contrary, renewed all their anger and resentment.[1]

This knight in the service of John Huss, a scholar who was as much of a sectary as his master, this Hütten of another Luther had been arrested in the Palatinate for insulting the Council. First of all his captivity had made him wiser, and he had yielded to the entreaties that had been pressed upon him. He had accepted the condemnation of his master's errors at a general session, and publicly anathematised his perverse doctrines (September 23, 1415).[2] In a letter written to a friend he had affirmed that the heresiarch had been justly condemned.[3]

The cardinals had demanded his immediate release, but Jerome's compatriots who were at Prague, and who had remained orthodox, were opposed to it, for they had doubts about his sincerity. Like his master, he wished to appear before the Council in person, to reply to the numerous charges brought against him, and to develop to the utmost his own defence. As a matter of fact he appeared in the midst of the general assembly on May 23, 1416, defended himself to the best of his ability, made an extravagant eulogy of John Huss, and violently attacked the Pope and the cardinals.

Next Saturday, May 25, the Council met in general session (its twenty-first) to pronounce the final sentence.

[1] Palacky, *Documenta*, iii. p. 369. Von der Hardt, i. col. 425, and liv. pp. 495 and 559. Denis, *Hus et la guerre des Hussites* (Paris, 1878).

[2] Theodor. Urie, *Historia Concil. Constant.*, in Von der Hardt, i. col. 181. *Ibid.*, iv. p. 490. Mansi, xxvii. p. 791.

[3] *Documenta*, p. 598. A letter to Lord Lacek of Krawar, Seneschal of Moravia.

Before the fathers, Jerome ventured afresh on a long diatribe against the clergy and retracted his retractation. Like his master he was given over to the secular arm, and died equally courageously at the stake in the square of Brühl.[1]

A few years ago a Protestant theologian, Dr Arminius Jepp, in a grave thesis delivered before the Faculty of Göttingen, claimed to show the similarity of the doctrines of Wicliffe, Huss, and Gerson. As for the Bohemian heretic, he wrote: "Huss's stake is where the roads of the Roman and Evangelical Churches part, never to meet again. The blood of the Czech doctor still burdens the conscience of Rome; and the memory of this martyr is still dear to our communion."[2]

This Göttingen professor is only the echo of many other reformers. We have related the facts. It will be easy to establish the right if we put ourselves in the social surroundings of the fifteenth century.

John Huss, the originator of the gravest error of his times, was responsible both to religious and civil society. He had to answer to the former, which he had sinned against in attacking dogma, and to the latter, which he had disturbed by his revolutionary and anti-social teachings. The religious tribunal, the Council, judges and condemns the heretic; temporal authority, the secular arm, receives the guilty man, strikes him

[1] *Cf.* Von der Hardt, iv. p. 770. Palacky, *Documenta*, p. 624. Poggio's letter to Leonard Aretinus is also given by Von der Hardt, iii. p. v. col. 64. The author was an eye-witness, and speaks thus: *Vidi hunc exitum, singulos actus inspexi. Sine perfidia, sine pertinacia hoc egerit, certe ex philosophiae schola verum interemptum esse descripsisses.* He then compares Jerome to Scaevola and Socrates. The sceptical character and licentious tone of the writings of the humanist Poggio are well known. *Cf.* Hefele, x. p. 584.

[2] Jepp, Gerson, Wiclef, *Hussus inter se cum Reformatoribus comparati*, p. 68.

down and executes him, since he persists in propagating rebellion as well as heresy.

According to canon law, the accused is not summoned before his judges to discuss dogma, to raise questions, and to suggest doubts. He is examined to give an account of his beliefs, and to be judged according to the higher law constituted by the doctrine of the Church. It is a public examination of conscience undergone by the guilty one, not a discussion which he undertakes and maintains. To-day, after such an ecclesiastical cross-examination, the penalty is purely spiritual. It is excommunication, suspension, or inhibition. Formerly, in the society of the Middle Ages, the condemned cleric came under common law, and the temporal sanction followed on the sentence pronounced by the tribunal of the Church. "He who broke off from religion was cut off from human society: and the infidel was judged by the faith of the general public. Society had the right of defending its necessary beliefs, and of hindering a blind Samson from bringing down the pillars of the temple."[1]

Thus the two *fora* agreed together, and mutually supported each other for the legitimate defence of Christian society. The first passed sentence, and the second carried out the decree, whatever it might be.

But what was the civil and criminal penalty in the Middle Ages? Note first, that it never touched secret heretics who did not propagate their errors, or who only erred in ignorance or repented openly and sincerely.

Moreover, we know that the sword never faltered in the hand of the State. Mediæval legislation was incomparably more severe and sanguinary than it is to-day. Blasphemy, moral misdemeanours, false coining were punished with fire; thieving and housebreaking met

[1] Étienne Lamy, *Revue des deux Mondes*, 15th Aug. 1897, p. 722.

with hanging. In Saxony and Suabia, on which Constance depended, the penal code ordered the heretic, who was condemned by an ecclesiastical court, to be burnt.[1] John Huss was not unaware of this, and he faced this terrible alternative, this crowning consequence of his obstinacy.

The conciliar tribunal could only pronounce according to the laws in force in the fifteenth century. Provisions that seem severe to-day appeared neither extraordinary nor unjust in the days of John Huss. Protestants who blame us need only search through their own history till they read of the principles of Bucer, Calvin, and even of the gentle Melanchthon, on the same question. They know how the first reformers practised toleration, and they should show some reluctance in finding fault with the judges of Constance, and in taxing them with cruelty. Whatever the supporters of Huss may think, we believe it would have been better for Bohemia and for the Church if this false doctor and rebellious priest had never been born.

§ 4. *Condemnation of some other Innovators.*

The condemnation of John Huss was of interest alike to civil and to ecclesiastical society. The affair of John Petit and tyrannicide also concerned both the power of the State and the authority of the Church.

Let us briefly recall the facts. On November 23, 1407, the Duke of Orleans fell in a Paris street, killed by assassins hired by his cousin, the Duke of Burgundy. John the fearless, " an offender against God as well as

[1] *Der Sachsenspiegel*, ii. a. 14 (Heidelberg, 1848). HUILLARD-BRÉHOLLES, *Histoire diplom. de Frédéric II.*, iv. 1a pars, p. 198. *Cf.* PERTZ, *Leges*, ii. p. 287. J. HAVET, *Bibl. de l'École des Chartes*, xli., 1880, p. 488.

against his own blood and honour,"[1] boldly accepted responsibility for the *fait accompli*.[2] He ventured to plead his cause before King Charles VI., the brother of his victim, and he committed his defence[3] to his councillor, John Petit, the Norman (March 8, 1407). The orator was bold enough to plead the following proposition amongst several others: "Any subject or vassal who makes any attempt on the King's health, through cupidity, fraud, or witchcraft, may be killed as a tyrant by any other subject, without any command or order. It is proved by laws natural, moral, and divine."[4]

In his pedantic elaboration of the subject, the author sets himself to prove his assertion, alleging twelve reasons in honour of the twelve apostles. The first three are drawn from the holy doctors; the three next from Aristotle, Cicero, and Boccaccio; three others from civil law; and the three last from Holy Scripture. He concludes that, "according to his rough and rude understanding, our lord the King ought to love more than he did before my said lord the Duke of Burgundy."

All this defensive display, which was at once immoral and burlesque, caused more astonishment than conviction.

This subversive teaching was referred by Gerson to the judgment of the Bishop of Paris and certain masters

[1] GEORGES CHASTELLAIN, recorder of the Duke of Burgundy, Philip the Good, *Œuvres* (1863), published by Kervyn de Lettenhove, i. p. 16.

[2] *Chronic. Karoli VI.*, xxviii. c. 31. Bibl. Nat., col. of Burgundy, lvii. p. 66. NICOLAS DE BAYE, *Journal*, i. 206; ii. 294. CABARET D'ORRONVILLE, *Œuvres*, published by the French Historical Society, p. 206.

[3] *Cf.* KERVYN DE LETTENHOVE, *Bulletin de l'Académie royale de Belgique*, p. 558, *Jean sans Peur et l'apologie du tyrannicide*.

[4] MONSTRELLET, *Chroniques*, i. ch. 39. *Cf. Opp. Gersonii*, v. col. 27. Nearly all the 5th vol. of the Ellies-Dupin Ed. is filled with details of this affair. J. B. SCHWAB, *Joh. Gerson*, pp. 449, 609. BESS, *Frankreichs Kirchenpolitik . . . und der Process des J. Petit.*

of theology. The doctors at first condemned seven, and afterwards nine of John Petit's assertions, and ordered them to be burnt (February 23, 1414). The King gave his approval, but the Duke of Burgundy appealed to Pope John XXIII. On his side, Gerson denounced the nine articles condemned at the Council of Constance, (7 June, 1415). Martin Porrée, Bishop of Arras, and the too notorious Peter Cauchon,[1] vidame of Rheims, were ordered by the Duke of Burgundy to ask the assembly for decisions on all these points. The fathers appointed Zabarella and several other cardinals, with whom they associated the bishops and doctors of each nation. They decided not to condemn John Petit by name, and consequently, not the Duke of Burgundy, but they repudiated a proposition cast in general terms, without naming the author[2] (July 6).

The Cardinal of Cambrai and Gerson later on, wanted to get from the council a more formal and open condemnation of tyrannicide and its apologist.

The Chancellor spoke in the name of the King of France on May 5, 1416, and showed much eloquence in his peroration : " I address myself to you, Bishop of Arras," he exclaimed, " answer me, or rather I will myself answer for you. Are you concerned for the temporal and spiritual salvation of the illustrious Duke of Burgundy ? Yes, I know you are. Are you anxious for the safety of his descendants in his hereditary

[1] He had shown himself a Cabochian in 1413. He was then counsellor of the Duke of Burgundy and the University of Paris protected him. Later on he became the Pope's referendary. His deplorable behaviour in the affair of Joan of Arc is well known. "He was a one-sided and dangerous man," said a barrister in the parliament of Paris in 1444. Impartial history might be even more severe without injustice.

[2] Von der Hardt, iv. p. 489. Hefele, p. 485. *Cf.* Wicliffe's xviith proposition condemned at Constance.

domains ? Yes, I do not doubt it. And therefore, truth, reason and piety are triumphant with you. I beg you, for your soul's sake, to let them triumph. Shun the punishment of those who willingly are self-deceived, a punishment that must fill you with dread and which you must avoid at all costs." [1]

Gerson was everwhelmed with insults and persecutions because of this speech, and yet he was a good prophet at the time. Three years afterwards, John of Burgundy was to fall assassinated on the bridge of Montereau, by the order and before the eyes of the Dauphin. He who had smitten with the sword perished with the sword. It was a case of the law of retaliation : sometimes through the injustice of men the justice of God is worked out. Thus events themselves undertook to oppose and to condemn the propositions of John Petit, which certain political anxieties had hindered from being anathematised at Constance. Next year, the Dominican, John of Falkenburg, who had made analogous declarations with regard to the King of Poland, was also smitten, but in congregation and not in general session. His book was committed to the flames.[2]

More than once, in the course of time, this question was to come up for fresh discussion. In the middle of the fifteenth century, the first humanists, imbued with the examples of classical antiquity, wished to make pagan civilisation spring to life again, and to cause what they called the era of liberty to flourish once more, getting rid of all whom they called tyrants. What they preached in theory, they tried to get put into practice. New Harmodii, and fierce Bruti arose, and took up the

[1] *Propositio facta coram Concilio Constantiensi, Opp. Gers.*, ii. col. 328. Schwab, p. 626.

[2] Van der Hardt, iv. pp. 1091, 1513. Hefele, xi. p. 68.

poniard against the Medici, and the Sforzas, and though it was a still deeper error, against the saintly and learned Nicholas V.[1]

The first Protestants welcomed this doctrine, and after the murder of Charles I. of England, Milton defended it in several writings against the learned Saumaise. In Spain, the Jesuit Mariana, breaking away from the general teaching of the Company, allowed anyone to kill a tyrant after the formal manifestation of the will of the people. It is well known, how French parliaments, infected with Gallicanism, took advantage of this to attack the Jesuits and Rome itself, whom they made jointly answerable for such opinions. Later on, appeared the immortal calumnies of Pascal, and finally the Constitution of 1793 made the same doctrine a dogma of the revolution.[2]

Amidst all these quarrels, the defenders of sound doctrines made it their duty to recall the reasonable, energetic, and eloquent protests of d'Ailly and Gerson at the Council of Constance.

We shall only speak by way of reminder of the doctrines of the Dominican, Matthew Grabon. He was author of a pamphlet against the new religious orders, and claimed that the vow of poverty could only be well observed in the ancient institutions approved by the Holy See. The Brethren of the Common Life, particularly the worthy precursors of our Brothers of Christian Doctrine, excited his animadversions and inflamed the ardours of a zeal which was more sincere than enlightened. "They are excommunicated," he said, "and those who favour them are guilty of sin."[3]

[1] De l'Epinois, *Nicholas V and the conspiracy of Stephen Porcari* in the *Revue des Questions histor.*, 1882, 61st no. Pastor, *Histoire des Papes*, ii. p. 199.

[2] Article xxvii. of the Constitution.

[3] Hefele, xi. p. 103.

Condemned by d'Ailly and Gerson, this William de St Amour of the fifteenth century, retracted and abjured his doctrines, which were more eccentric than really harmful.[1]

The Council of Constance also declared against the Flagellants. These penitents had lost the profoundly religious spirit that had inspired them at the outset. They had fallen into all the errors of a false mysticism, and had laid themselves open to the suspicion of many true believers, who protested in several countries against their doctrines and practices.

Soon this sect disappeared entirely from the Catholic world.[2]

To complete our narrative, a few words must be added as to the part of the Council in the case of the Bishop of Strasburg.

William of Diest was a not very commendable prelate who was in dispute with his chapter and with the magistrates of the town, and the latter had cast him into prison at Molsheim (December 3, 1415).[3] A commission of sixteen was appointed to judge the case, which had been extremely complicated by certain circumstances, and an embassy was sent to Strasburg. It did not succeed in getting the Bishop immediately set at liberty. This was

[1] *Opp. Gersonii*, i. col. 467.

[2] J. Boileau, *Historia Flagellantium*, Paris, 1700. Thiers, *Critique de l'Histoire des Flagellants*, Paris, 1703. Von de Hardt, iii. col. 92. *Opp. Gersonii*, iii. col. 660. Frédéricq, *Bulletin de l'Académie royale de Belgique*, 1903, p. 688.

[3] Hefele, x. p. 545. ff. ; xi. p. 2 ff. Von der Hardt, ii. p. 426 ; iv. p. 551. Dr H. Finke has dealt exhaustively with the subject in his *Forschungen der deutschen Geschichte* (Göttingen, 1883), p. 501. He remarks on the untrustworthiness of Von der Hardt. Sometimes the subject announced by the author is not dealt with ; sometimes facts are badly reported, official documents are not given at their proper dates, and the narrative becomes unintelligible. All the statements of this annalist must be verified by comparison with contemporary documents.

not done till after June 3, when the chapter and the town had been excommunicated and the town laid under an interdict. Finally, the Bishop appeared before the Council, and the dispute was ended, November 6, 1417, by a condemnation of the chapter.

It is thus that, in spite of genuine griefs and very irregular proceedings, the Council gathered at Constance yet could undertake to defend the rights of the Church and the interests of the State, striking disturbers of the peace and the insubordinate, passing sentences that were just and that history can recognise with respect. Its part, so far as this is concerned, is unassailable, in spite of the use of forms of justice which have fallen into desuetude.

CHAPTER XVII

END OF THE SCHISM

DURING all these grave disputes, the principal work of the Council went on with varying fortunes. The heresies were wounded unto death. Schism itself was about to disappear, thanks to the persevering efforts of everyone.

When the assembly held its first sessions, it was all over with the precarious solution, which had been invented at Pisa, and matters had fallen into the deplorable state from which that synod had sought to extricate them by illegal acts. It seemed as if there were no Pope because there were three, and the sovereign pontificate was humbled as it had never been before in the persons of each of the three.

John XXIII., the butt of the proceedings of the Council and of the King of the Romans, continued his wretched wanderings through the Germanic countries, expecting to be thrown into prison by the Fathers, and then was judged and deposed by them. Never perhaps had the venerable title of Pontiff been more exposed to opprobrium and gibes, nor subjected to more indignity of speech and action. How happy would it have been for him had he less deserved these manifold disgraces! Pius VI. and Pius VII., who suffered as cruelly, present another appearance in the eyes of posterity.

In Italy, with his courtier in misfortune, Charles of Malatesta, old Gregory XII. preserved his pontifical functions. He may have given rise to charges of nepotism, and have committed political errors, and at one time have seemed to hold too tenaciously to his supreme position, to which, however, he had been lawfully appointed. But he could neither be reproached with disorderly conduct, nor with scandalous obstinacy, and later on, he knew how to give up the pontifical throne with a dignity and resignation that rallied everybody's sympathy to him.

At the foot of the Pyrenees, Benedict maintained the part which he had been given to play for more than twenty years. He had always the same stubbornness and tenacity in following out his aim, as well as the same suppleness and skill in the choice of means. We get a vivid insight into his character when we see him struggling single-handed against the Council, the King of the Romans, the Kings of Aragon, Castile and Navarre, and further against the peoples of Christian Europe who had remained under his obedience and who were not yet represented at Constance. *Etiamsi omnes, non ego*, seems to have been his device, in which there may be some pride, but still more of obstinacy. Thus it is that he shut himself up henceforth in the futility of his interested and systematic opposition, and in the scandal of his schismatic retreat at Peniscola.

§ 1. *Deposition of John XXIII.*

The fathers of Constance did not hide from themselves that, so far as John XXIII. was concerned, they had committed at least an irregular act in promulgating the decrees of the fourth and fifth sessions.

They at once felt the need of justifying themselves, which they did by sending to all Christian princes as well as to the Universities a detailed memorial on the progress of events at the council, on the Pope's flight, and also about the negotiations they had entered into with him. These letters were sent off at the sixth session (April 17). But the Pontiff had already quitted Laufenburg for Freiburg in Breisgau, then for Brisach, a stronghold belonging to Frederic his protector. Outlawed from the Empire by Sigismund, the Duke of Austria had seen all his neighbours rise against him. And because John was not safe at Schaffhausen, Laufenburg and elsewhere, he had determined to take flight in his wretchedness anew.

In the same session, which, like all that followed it, was presided over by the Cardinal of Viviers, the form of abdication which was to be suggested to the Pope was adopted.[1] Under the influence of momentary passion, it was drawn up in terms too hard for John's acceptance. And in fact, when the deputation entrusted with these proposals, reached Brisach, the Pontiff feigned illness and refused them an audience. Finally, he consented to receive them, but on April 25, without giving the delegates notice and without leaving any answer behind him, he left early for Neuenburg, meaning to go to Avignon by Burgundy. But his protector, the Duke of Austria, would not allow him to stay there, and had him brought back to Brisach, and thence, on the 27th, to Freiburg.

Meanwhile, a skilful negotiator, Duke Louis of Bavaria, succeeded in obtaining Frederic of Austria's submission to Sigismund and the Council. Frederic in turn got John to have an interview with the deputies

[1] Hefele, x. p. 410.

from Constance. The Pope then allowed himself rather easily to be convinced of the need of resigning unconditionally. As he was without resources, support or friends, his will appeared to be annihilated. He promised to resign with no other stipulation this time than that his competitors should do the same. He would resign all his powers as soon as the council had assured him of a suitable indemnification.[1]

Without taking account of these concessions, the fathers decided in their seventh session (May 2), that John XXIII. should be summoned before the Council with every legal formality, but also with the most liberal guarantees. The summons was publicly fastened up over the same Kreutzlingen gate, by which the Pope had fled on the preceding March 20. The Duke of Austria, who was the Pope's accomplice in this flight, might have seen this official document when he returned to Constance to undergo a public and cruel humiliation in the presence of the King of the Romans and a crowd of princes and nobles. He had to beg for pardon, and to place himself entirely, with his subjects and possessions, at the discretion of Sigismund, who hardly showed himself generous. On May 9, 1415, the council sent a deputation to the Pope to notify him of the summons. John XXIII. complained bitterly of the Fathers, and put off his departure for Constance from day to day. On May 13, when the ninth session opened, he had not yet arrived. D'Ailly, Zabarella and Philaster, whom the Pope had chosen to defend him, refused to take up this too compromising office, and a commission of thirteen was appointed to hear the witnesses for the prosecution.

May 14 was the date of the judgment. The council

[1] Von der Hardt, ii. col. 402; iv. p. 135. Mansi, xxvii. p. 621.

in its tenth general session solemnly pronounced a decree of suspension against John XXIII., and forbade the faithful to obey him henceforward.[1]

This grave step was only preparatory to another still more terrible, the sentence of deposition. Indeed, the heads of allegations against the unfortunate Pontiff amounted to not less than seventy-four,[2] and their exaggeration showed the spirit of hatred and vengeance which inspired the accusers.

The deputies who were bidden to take John XXIII. his summons to appear, had also received orders to give him an assurance of his personal safety, and to bring him back to Constance. They had led him to Radolfzell, five leagues from the town, and locked him up in a dungeon, no longer existing, under the guard of three hundred Hungarian soldiers. There it was that he was joined by the five cardinals and among them by d'Ailly, delegated to notify the Pontiff of the decree of suspension. The accused submitted to everything and offered his resignation. "If they depose me," he added, "I shall offer no resistance. I only ask to be allowed to safeguard my honour, my person, and my rank." Then, he signed the report with his Christian name "Balthazar."[3]

At last, on May 29, at the twelfth general session, in the presence of the King of the Romans and of fifteen cardinals, John was solemnly deposed. The decree was very hard on the accused, and condemend him "as guilty of simony, a dissipator of the goods of the Church, and an unfaithful administrator of the Church, both in things spiritual and temporal." It also roughly criti-

[1] Hardouin, viii. p. 324. Mansi, xxvii. p. 655.

[2] Von der Hardt, only gives 70 (iv. p. 196). They were afterwards reduced to 54. *Cf.* Hefele, pp. 427 and 438. Bibl. Nat., MS. lat. 9513.

[3] Mansi, xxvii. p. 681. Von der Hardt, p. 210 ff.

cised his conduct, which it qualified as a scandal to Christendom. Therefore the holy Council released all the faitful from their oath of obedience to John XXIII., and forbade them to call him Pope any more. It further ordered that he was to be placed in safe confinement under the supervision of Sigismund. Finally, the fathers decided that neither Balthazar Cossa, Angelo Corrario, nor Peter de Luna, should be capable of being raised to the pontifical seat in the future.[1]

The Bishop of Arras read this weighty act in the presence of the council, and each father answered: *placet*. The pontifical seal was broken with a jeweller's hammer and the arms of John XXIII. were destroyed. It was the counterpart, perhaps the penalty, of the severe judgment passed upon Gregory XII. and Benedict XIII. by the Council of Pisa, on June 5, 1409, under the influence of Balthazar Cossa. Does not Providence sometimes smite with the law of retaliation?

A deputation went to notify the Pope of his final condemnation on May 31. It came to Radolfzell. John gave it a suitable reception, and ratified the sentence without making any opposition. He submitted in advance to all the further decisions of the fathers and threw himself upon their clemency.

On June 3, he was transferred to the other side of the Rhine to the very castle of Gottlieben, which John Huss had just left. The Count Palatine, Louis of Bavaria, a personal friend of Gregory XII., undertook to watch over him. Soon he found that this prison was not safe enough, and had the Pontiff taken to his Heidelberg residence, and then to Mannheim, where he made his captivity still more strict.

[1] Von der Hardt, iv. p. 281. Mansi, xxvii. p. 715. Hardouin, viii. 376. *Journal de Philastre*, p. 177.

The unfortunate prisoner passed his time in making Latin verse on the instability of human affairs. Louis kept him thus a prisoner, until in 1418; but at that date, he got entangled in a dispute with Sigismund, and set the Pontiff free in return for a ransom of 30,000 golden florins.

The work of Pisa, was thus brought to nought by the humiliating fall of John XXIII. He lived yet long enough to recognise Martin V. as the true Pope at Florence, and to protest that he intended to live and die in his allegiance. The new Pontiff was so touched at this, that he gave him the first place in the Sacred College with the title of Cardinal-bishop of Tusculum.[1] Cossa died in December 1419, after profiting by the rude lessons of adversity. His tomb is in the celebrated baptistry of Florence. It bears this brief and strikingly simple inscription: Here lies the body of Balthazar Cossa, who was Pope. "This tomb," says Gregorovius, "is a memorial monument of the great Schism: it is the last raised to a Roman Pontiff outside Rome."[2]

§ 2. *Abdication of Gregory XII.*

While these events were taking place at Constance, and in its neighbourhood, Pope Gregory continued to reign in the town of Rimini, under the protection of the chivalrous Malatesta, lord of the town and governor of the Romagna for the Holy See. He was then aged 89, and, in spite of the baneful influence of his nephews, Antony and Paul Corrario, he secretly yearned for the

[1] Von der Hardt, iv. p. 1497. Mansi, xxvii. p. 1172. Hardouin, viii. cols. 834, 871.

[2] Gregorovius, *Grabmäler*, p. 84.

peace of the Church. Nevertheless, with regard to the future council, his first idea was a mixture of distrust and aversion. He had not wished to go to Constance, in spite of the entreaties and promises of Sigismund. Balthazar Cossa had always been an object of horror to him. He looked upon him as the principal cause of the defection of his cardinals, and called him "a worker of iniquity, and son of perdition."[1]

In the letters he wrote to Louis of Bavaria, he spoke of this freely. Louis indignantly repudiated the Council of Pisa, and added: "May it please God not to let the Council of Constance bring down upon us still graver evils. We should expect more from the King of the Romans."[2]

Two months later, Gregory complains of the "sacrilegious conciliabule," writing to the same correspondent. He recommends him to oppose this detestable assembly, and to avoid it like the pest.[3]

About the same time, Cardinal John Dominici, who had been negotiating secretly for two years with the King of the Romans,[4] sent Sigismund some theological remarks about papal power and the indisputable rights of Gregory. He notified him at the same time of the Pontiff's feelings, who was ready to lay down the tiara, if his two rivals would do the same.[5]

Later on, Gregory was glad to be represented at the Council of Constance by the same venerable Cardinal, who was also Archbishop of Ragusa. The latter betook himself to the conciliar city. Over the doorway of the

[1] Hefele, x. p. 311.

[2] Letter of Feb. 21, 1414. *Cf.* Finke, *Acta Concilii Constant.*, p. 268. Von der Hardt, ii. col. 467.

[3] Finke, letter of April 7; *Ibid.*, p. 270.

[4] *Cf.* Nandonnet, *Histor. Jahrbuch*, 1903, p. 392.

[5] Finke, p. 272.

Augustinian convent, an abode which had been assigned to him by the magistrates of the town, he had the arms of Gregory XII., whose plenipotentiary he was, set up. They were taken away on a November night.[1] John protested energetically, and this incident formed the subject of all conversations in Constance during several days. The arms were not allowed to be restored before the arrival of Gregory, who was always expected to appear in person.

The Pope, however, was not slow in changing his mind. He had always a deep love of the Church, and the time had come to show it otherwise than by word only. On March 15, 1415, he sent Sigismund a bull, wherein he named his dear son Charles de Malatesta his procurator to the prince, and bade him renounce really and actually in his name all right, title and possession of the papacy.[2]

When this bull reached Constance, on May 13, they also received a letter from Malatesta, dated from Brixen and addressed to the nations, wherein the governor of the Romagnas made excuses for being delayed and said that he would soon arrive.[3]

Two days later, a bull from Gregory intended for the Cardinal of St Sixtus was read at the Council. Therein the Pontiff declared his intention of renouncing the tiara and agreed to acknowledge the Council in so far as its summons had been made in Sigismund's name. He would not listen to any mention of Balthazar Cossa, as he called him ; and laid it down as essential that the latter should not preside over the Council or even be present at it.[4]

[1] Mansi, xxvii. p. 540. Lenfant, *Histoire du Concile de Constance*, i. p. 35.

[2] The text of this remarkable bull is to be found in Finke, p. 270.

[3] Von der Hardt, iv. p. 177.

[4] *Ibid.*, p 192.

It must be acknowledged that Gregory carried through the business of his resignation with a logic, a spirit of continuity and a dignity, which contrasted strangely with the procedure of John XXIII. On June 15, Charles of Malatesta, furnished with full powers, made his solemn entry into the city of Constance, where he was magnificently received by the King of the Romans and the prelates.[1]

He first of all declared to Sigismund that he had been sent to him, and not to a Council that the Pope had neither summoned nor acknowledged.

After several preliminary negotiations came the great day of the fourteenth general session, July 4, 1415.[2] All the Fathers were present as well as the King and his court to attend the almost unheard of spectacle of the resignation of a Pope. The bulls that had been read, showed all Gregory's greatness of soul, which, combined with his correctness of attitude, called forth general and respectful admiration. In everything he acted as a legitimate Pontiff, and had his conditions accepted.

First of all, the bull was published which appointed Charles of Malatesta and Cardinal Dominici of Ragusa,[3] as his proxies. Then the Cardinal himself read the summons of the Council, a document, the skill and importance of which are obvious to everyone. Gregory held to the logic of his position. He was faithful to

[1] Von der Hardt, p. 341.

[2] *Ibid.*, p. 346.

[3] Abbé Christophe seems very hard upon this saintly and worthy archbishop, (*Histoire de la Papauté au XIVe siècle*, iii. p. 275). He accuses him of flattery and obsequiousness: "He is," he adds, "one of those feeble beings who cannot be faithful to a conviction, who are carried away by circumstances and seduced by preferments." This summary judgment seems full of injustice. John was the friend of St Antoninus and proclaimed "Blessed" by Gregory XVI. Nothing he did gives any foundation to the criticisms of this writer who is usually more happily inspired.

what he owed to himself, and to what he owed to his supporters.

"I convoke this holy council," solemnly said the papal mandatory, "and I authorise and confirm all that it may do henceforward, *omnia per ipsum agenda*." [1]

This manner of procedure and of speech gave rise to no objection, and yet did not this acceptance seem to prove an implicit recognition of the lawfulness of the Pontiff and of his predecessors, Innocent, Boniface and Urban? Gregory XII., gave no approval to anything that had been done at the preceding sessions of the Synod of Constance. He declared that he recognised this assembly as henceforth legitimate and ecumenical, in order to make union possible, reform effective and heresy vanish.

Immediately the Council declared that the supporters of Gregory XII., were fully reconciled with those of John XXIII., and only formed one body, and that all the censures pronounced at the time of the Schism against one side or the other were revoked.

The venerable Cardinal of Ragusa then wished to become a simple bishop, but the Sacred College would not allow it. In order to affirm the fusion of the two obediences still more, John received the brotherly embraces of the cardinals who were his equals and immediately took his seat in their midst.

The Synod was thus regularly constituted in the eyes of all. Malatesta proclaimed the full powers he had received from Gregory XII., to renounce the papacy in his name. "Does the assembly," he asked, "think it more opportune to receive the Pope's abdication before the departure of the King of the Romans for

[1] Von der Hardt, *loc. cit.* Mansi, xxvii. p. 730 ff. Hardouin, viii. p. 384.

Nice? Or would it rather defer the ceremony until it has taken cognisance of Benedict's intentions?" Sigismund had been induced to go to Nice to confer with the King of Aragon and the Pope of Avignon. The council decided for immediate renunciation.

The Prince of Rimini pronounced the formal resignation in a few words then and there, and gave a written copy of the act to the assembly. They chanted the *Te Deum*, and Malatesta, whose pious efforts had contributed so much to such a happy result, received the solemn thanks of the whole meeting.[1]

The fathers hastened to announce the voluntary resignation of Gregory to the towns of his obedience, and at the same time informed them of the deposition of John XXIII. The venerable Gregory was appointed Bishop of Porto and perpetual legate at Ancona. He took care to renew the testimony of his perfect submission to the Council, and to express his gratitude for the respectful regard which had been shown towards him.

He died at Recanati, not far from Ancona, on October 18, 1417, without being able to pay his respects to his legitimate successor, Martin V.[2]

His last words were these: "I knew nothing of the world, and the world knew nothing of me." He still lies at rest in Recanati Cathedral, amidst the land of the Marches and the Romagnas, which was always faithful to him. Thus this line of pontiffs came to an end. Its rights ran back to Urban VI., and for thirty-two years it had occupied the pontifical throne.

[1] Von der Hardt, iv. p. 341-380. Mansi and Hardouin, *loc. cit.* Hefele, x. p. 486.

[2] Von der Hardt, ii. col. 470.

§ 3. *Decadence of Benedict XIII.*

While Gregory XII. was thus giving way honourably with the most praiseworthy resignation, Benedict was isolating himself more and more in his scandalous obstinacy, and, forsaken by all, seemed to boast of the unpopularity attaching to his name.

We have said that the King of the Romans was preparing to leave for Nice in order to meet the obstinate old man and to obtain his abdication. Peter de Luna and his supporters, whom the memoirs of the time called *Lunatici*, were henceforth the sole obstacles to the peace of the Church. Sigismund left Constance on July 18, 1415, accompanied by sixteen delegates chosen by the fathers,[1] and by four thousand horsemen, and provided with all the authentic documents proving the renunciation of Gregory XII.

He had taken every precaution to ensure that the deliberations of the Council should be undisturbed during his absence.

While he is on his way to the South of France by Basle, Lausanne, Chambéry, Lyons, Vienne, and Valence (August 5), let us see what Benedict is doing now that French troops have compelled his soldiers to leave Avignon. The activity of this old man of eighty continued as great as his stubbornness. From Morella, which he had chosen as a retreat in the kingdom of Aragon, he maintained the best of relations with King Ferdinand, and through him with the Queen of Castile.

[1] Von der Hardt, iv. p. 264. De Dynter, *Chronica ducum Brabantiae* (Ed. Ram.), iii. p. 279. *Cf. Bulletin d'histoire eccl. et. d'archéol. de Valence,* v. p. 127, 1884. Aschbach, *Regesten u. Itinerar des römischen Königs Sigmund von* 1. *Juli* 1414 *bis Schluss des Jahres* 1419. Fromme, *Die spanische Nation und das konstanzer Konzil,* p. 8. Ant. Morosini, *Chronique,* French Historical Society, 1889, ii. pp. 36, 56, and 86.

Both of them were guided solely by his advice in Church affairs.[1] He intrigued in Italy with Jane of Naples and her brother Ladislas, then Cossa's enemy.[2] He even tried to maintain correspondents in Rome, and to draw over Soriano, the city prefect, to his side, and to weaken the fidelity of the Cardinal of St Eustache, John XXIII.'s vicar. His agents were commissioned to explain to the Romans, who were ruined by the Pope's absence, Benedict's keen desire to bring the curia back to the Eternal City, and the efforts he had made and the expenses he had incurred for that end [3] (October 1414).

In all remaining documents of this date the Pope of Avignon displays all his animosity against what he calls the conventicle of Pisa, against its promoters, "hated of God," and against "the idol they have made." He hopes for the revision of this great suit and for the final admission of his rights. At the same time he protests his zeal for unity, setting forth the means he intends to use to secure it. Benedict agrees in accepting the town of Nice as a meeting-place with the King of the Romans in the month of June, and takes every possible precaution against surprise.[4] But he refuses to go to Constance, and does not believe that this new conventicle "will have the good fortune to do anything pleasing to God."[5] On his side, Ferdinand appoints his proxies for the Constance assembly, which, however, he will not recognise as a general council. He protests beforehand against any decisions it may take to Benedict's disadvantage, since

[1] Finke, i. p. 310 ff.

[2] *Ibid.*, p. 312. Valois, p. 334.

[3] *Ibid.*, p. 316. These hitherto unpublished documents are taken either from the Archives of the Crown at Barcelona, or from the Archives of the Vatican. *Cf.* Hefele, x. p. 542.

[4] Finke, p. 330 ff.

[5] *Ibid.*, p. 333.

he is "a Pope certainly and without doubt," he says (October 1, 1414).

The representatives of the Pontiff and of the King of Aragon arrived at Constance, and on March 4 they begged Sigismund to go to Nice as quickly as possible to be present at the proposed conference.[1]

Benedict XIII. flattered himself that his rights would be recognised there, though he was almost alone in thinking them unassailable. Moreover, everything continued to maintain the Pope in his incorrigible delusions. He was told that the greatest nobles of France would entreat King Charles to declare in his favour afresh.[2] He heard from Paris that, despite certain indications to the contrary, John XXIII. would have nothing to do with the Council of Constance, of which he dreaded the results for himself, and that his cardinals and friends were ready to abandon it. His correspondent, John Humbert, a clerk of the island of Majorca, and a student of the University, also gave him information as to the state of mind of the French Court, the masters and pupils of the *Alma Mater*, and strengthened in the Pope's heart hopes which a near future would show to be vain.[3]

Some time before the meeting-place had been changed and it was decided to meet at Perpignan, then belonging to the kingdom of Aragon. Benedict had come there in the month of June in accordance with previous arrangements. When he saw that Sigismund did not come, he left Perpignan precisely at midnight on the last day of June, and declared that the King of the Romans was as contumacious as a criminal who does not answer to his summons. Here is but one more proof of the intractable character of the Pope of Avignon, whose

[1] Lenfant, *Histoire du Concile de Constance*, p. 62.

[2] Finke, p. 311. Valois, p. 338.

[3] *Ibid.*, p. 343.

pretensions increase inversely in proportion to his power.

Sigismund, however, arrived at Narbonne on August 15, and on the 19th was at Perpignan, where he met the King of Aragon, whose travelling had been hindered by illness. What is the use of relating what took place at these conferences? The old man showed that he was like himself, and as we have already seen him on several occasions. He made complaints as to points of etiquette and form of summons, made exaggerated and unacceptable proposals to the King, demanded the cancelling of the sentences pronounced at Pisa, proposed to appoint arbitration commissions for the election of the new Pope, etc.[1] . . . Subterfuges, delays, complaining susceptibilities, shifts worthy of an artful attorney, but where no generosity can be discerned, no greatness of spirit, and no pity for the Church in her distress.

The King of the Romans asked for resignation pure and simple, a step which had been so often and so vainly demanded.[2] Benedict persisted in his dilatory expedients. Sigismund and the envoys from Constance acted hastily and left Perpignan.[3] At the beginning of November all seemed to be broken off. Ferdinand, already ill, was despairing; and other sovereigns, till then attached to Benedict, made no secret of their annoyance. They wrote to the King of the Romans to beg him to delay his departure. "We are determined to leave Benedict," they said to him, "if he persists with his insensate resistance."[4]

[1] Mansi, xxviii. p. 1111. Martène et Durand, *Thesaurus*, ii. p. 1684.

[2] *Cf.* Chapter vii. of this volume.

[3] Tolra de Bordas, *L'Antipape Benoît XIII. en Roussillon*, p. 29.

[4] Döllinger has published two letters of the King of Aragon and King of the Romans on this question. *Cf. Materialien zur Gesch. des* 15. *und* 16. *Jahr.*, ii. p. 378.

Sigismund agreed to send envoys to Perpignan afresh, but he maintained his proposals: he must resign at all costs. Benedict saw that the King would not yield, and fled on November 13 to Collioure. He only stayed there three days, and then betook himself to the castle of Pensicola, situated on the sea to the north of Valencia. A few cardinals followed him to this solitary dungeon belonging to his family, and formerly illustrious with the exploits of the Cid. On entering this refuge, the fugitive fired a threat of anathema and deposition like a Parthian arrow against the kings who wished to withdraw from his obedience. All the princes who had been thus defied met at Narbonne, and, in accord with Sigismund, concluded a celebrated concordat (December 13, 1415).

According to the tenor of this document, the cardinals and prelates met at Constance were to invite their colleagues, who had hitherto remained faithful to Benedict, to join them within three months, in order to make a truly general council. They undertook to do nothing prejudicial to the interests of the princes, bishops, and officers who had been attached to the Pope of Avignon. They would proceed to depose this Pontiff, and then to the election of a new Pope, with the concurrence of the cardinals of Benedict. The Council would annul all sentences which had been pronounced during the Schism, and ratify all favours accorded by the deposed Pope.[1]

The assembly took several other resolutions as to details, and then Sigismund, the envoys of the Spanish kings, and the Archbishop of Rheims representing

[1] Mansi, xxvii. p. 811, and xxviii. p. 224. Von der Hardt, ii. col. 487. Hardouin, viii. p. 473. Labbe, xii. c. 177. Valois, p. 347.

France, solemnly swore to observe all the articles. The delegates of the council took the same oath.

From December 14, the King of the Romans informed the Council of the concordat that he had just signed, then he came to spend the feast of Christmas at Avignon, and betook himself to Paris, where he made his solemn entry on March 1, 1416. Thence he went to England, and afterwards returned by Zealand, Holland, Germany, and Cologne. He returned to Constance in great state on Wednesday, January 27, 1417, after winning over to the work of the Council, to religious peace and a future crusade, all the sympathy of all sovereigns and peoples.[1]

Nearly a year before, on January 30, 1416, a detailed report of the Narbonne concordat had reached Constance and caused general joy there. The treaty was immediately ratified in general assembly.

Thanks to the energetic efforts of Vincent Ferrier and to his renown for sanctity, Aragon (January 6, 1416), Castile (January 15), Navarre (July 16), and the county of Foix (August 3) threw over their obedience to Benedict. The wonder-worker, so long and so genuinely attached to the Pontiff, himself declared at Perpignan, though much against the grain, the withdrawal of obedience, and read the skilful and firm declaration of the King of Aragon from the pulpit.[2]

Several times the Council declared the Pope of Avignon rebellious and contumacious, and then, in the thirty-seventh session, it proclaimed his irretrievable fall as an incorrigible and notorious heretic and schismatic (July 26, 1417).[3]

[1] Morosini's *Chronicle*, ii. p. 122.

[2] P. Fages, *Histoire de St Vincent Ferrier*, ii. pp. 118, 141. Fromme, pp. 12, 13.

[3] Von der Hardt, iv. pp. 1128, 1314, 1134, 1374. Hefele, xi. p. 32.

The stubborn Peter de Luna dwelt seven years more near the sea on the bare and impregnable rock of Pensicola. This new sort of stylite only had under his obedience a few servants and soldiers, but his misfortunes had in no way abated his pride. When almost a centenarian, he still replied, in striking his throne, to the ambassadors from Constance: "All mankind was in the ark with Noah: all the Church is with me on the rock of Pensicola."[1] He cherished an implacable hatred against the Council and Ferdinand. Every day he had a sentence of excommunication pronounced against the then dying King. Benedict died on November 24, 1422,[2] but he made the three cardinals around him swear to give him a successor. This phantom succeeding a phantom was a canon named Gil Mûnoz. He took the name of Clement VIII. (June 10, 1423). This very doubtful election was even disputed by a fourth cardinal, named John Carrier, then besieged in the castle of Tourène in Rouergue, another Pensicola. This cardinal, who considered that the whole Sacred College consisted in himself, secretly elected one named Bernard Garnier, sacristan of Rodez, who took the name of Benedict XIV.[3]

This new Benedict was excommunicated by Martin V., as well as his protector, Count d'Armagnac. The latter once applied to Joan of Arc to ask her who was the true Pope, but she only gave him an evasive answer.[4]

Meanwhile, the Pope of Pensicola, Clement VIII., was reconciled to Martin V. in 1429. Bernard Garnier,

[1] Hefele, p. 21. Mansi, xxviii. col. 263. Hardouin, viii. col. 827. Bossuet, *Defensio declarationis*, ii. lib. v. c. 24.

[2] *Cf.* Valois, iv. p. 450.

[3] Valois, pp. 458, 475. Martène et Durand, *Thesaurus*, ii. col. 1738 ff. Pastor, i. p. 282.

[4] J. Quicherat, *Procès de Jeanne d'Arc*, i. p. 243 ff.

the false Benedict XIV., died after winning some supporters in the south. John Carrier then took his place and his name, refused to retract, and ended his days in prison in 1433, at the castle of Foix. These pontiffs of Pensicola and elsewhere did not even get what Balthasar Cossa obtained, a dole of pity. Thus, in open rebellion, in impotence, in ridicule and shame vanished the great Schism of the West.

Providence has fixed a strange gradation between the three Pontiffs who were then disputing for the tiara.

Gregory XII., a true Pope in spite of his deposition proclaimed at Pisa, leaves the pontifical throne with calm majesty and resigns his functions into the hand of the Council with dignity.

John XXIII., the successor of Alexander V., the elect of Pisa, is condemned and deplored by the assembly of Constance, and is at any rate to be honoured for his resignation and repentance.

Benedict XIII., sprung out of Schism, and knowingly perpetuating the fatal division, remains obstinate till death, and is stigmatised in history as an Antipope. After having held his own against five Pontiffs, all more legitimate than himself, against two councils, two emperors, and ten others sovereigns, he dies excommunicated and excommunicating.[1]

These events, guided by the hand of God, have made a clean sweep. All rivals have disappeared, and now a new election, which shall give peace to the Christian world, can be proceeded with without any hindrance.

[1] "Observas in Joanne XXIII. miserabile spectaculum, in Gregorio XII., mirabile factum, in Benedicto XIII. lacrymabile exemplum, et in electo Papa Martino admirabile negotium." VON DER HARDT, iv. 1586.

CHAPTER XVIII

THE END OF THE COUNCIL

§ 1. *The Question of Reform.*

BOSSUET begins his *Histoire des Variations* with these words: "For several centuries the reformation of ecclesiastical discipline had been wished for. . . . St Bernard had incessantly warned nations, clergy, bishops, and even Popes of the need of it. He did not shrink from also warning the religious, who like him were distressed about it in their solitude. . . . Since then abuses had increased. The Roman Church, the mother of Churches, was not free from evil, and from the time of the Council of Vienne, a great bishop laid it down as the foundation of the work of this holy assembly, that the Church needed reform in both head and members. The Great Schism put this word more than ever in the mouth, not only of certain doctors like Gerson and Peter d'Ailly, but also of councils, and the Councils of Pisa and Constance are full of it!"[1]

But the great doctor of the Church of France is speaking of the true reformation, and not of that which is brought about by schismatical rebellion and outbursts of passionate invective. He speaks of that which is worked in the Church by the Church and by the authorities lawfully established by Jesus Christ. Lastly, Bossuet

[1] *Histoire des Variations*, i. ch. i.

shows by terrible examples what "reform in a crooked sense can do with obstinate minds." [1]

This pacific revolution, so generally desired, was about to be inaugurated in an effective way. But there were difficult obstacles to be overcome within the Council itself: these were the manifold divisions which reigned in it. The vexatious dogmatic discussions of 1415 about the pre-eminence of the Council over the Pope had left more than one mark on the assembly. The pontifical seat was vacant, and several asked whether it was not the time to give definite shape to this superiority, in order to make general councils more frequent, and to increase and regularise their power. They claimed to organise them as a permanent and essential institution, to set up a sort of spiritual parliament which should meet at fixed times, and to which sovereigns should send their ambassadors, substituting a constitutional oligarchy for a monarchy that was certainly elective, but absolute. They aimed at nothing less than changing the form of the Church, giving it up to the play of parties, and risking all the useful advance that had been made by the Papacy for three centuries.

In another direction the Sacred College had aroused bitter hostility against itself. Its conduct in the preceding pontifical elections and throughout the agitation of the Schism had given rise to much fault-finding and to reproaches, some of which were well founded.

The Christian people, the monks, and the lower clergy rightly attributed to the intrigues and antipathies of the cardinals the long division which had inflicted so much harm on ecclesiastical discipline and on the Church herself. But, at the close of the Council, dissension reigned in the Sacred College, and several bishops,

[1] *Cinquième avertissement aux Protestants*, xxxv.

struck with these scandals, loudly demanded the exclusion of the cardinals from the conclave that was about to open. They dared to go even further, and to call for the abolition of this ecclesiastical institution. D'Ailly had declared long before that the body of cardinals also urgently needed reform.[1] In fact, they only escaped from all these exaggerated demands by suppleness and diplomatic skill.

Furthermore, some French prelates were eager to deprive the Pope of the privilege which gave him almost exclusive patronage of benefices. On the other hand, the University men preferred that this right should be retained by the Pontiff, because they placed their more special interests before everything else. They wished to see their names still filling the *Rotuli* presented to the Pope. From then it was difficult for the members of the University to call for a reduction of pontifical privileges, to which they were often glad to have recourse. The bishops also energetically pressed for a diminution or for the extinction of annates, reservations, expectations, and all the contributions that the Roman Pontiff had the right of levying on the whole Church.

Certain German deputies were still more radical in their demands, and more violent in their reproaches. They attacked not only pontifical privileges, but even the Pope himself. "For about a hundred and fifty years," they write, "certain Popes have not sufficiently respected the rights of other Churches and benefices of the clergy. They have granted commendams, multiplied expectations, and stripped the dead. . . . Councils have not been summoned, and hence ambition, avarice,

[1] P. d'Ailly, *De reformatione Ecclesiae*, *Opp. Gersonii*, ii. col. 906. The Cardinal of Cambrai had come to the Council full of anti-papal prejudices and plans of reform. He was obliged to give up a large number of these ideas, and to recognise their impracticability.

heresy, simony, and schisms have raged in the Church. So let us take advantage of the vacancy in the Holy See to purify it of all its stains. Otherwise the newly elect, however virtuous he may be, will necessarily get some taint."[1]

The Germans then pressed for priority to be given to the consideration of reform. Some cardinals were of the same opinion, and the King of the Romans was especially strong on their side.[2] A general commission had been appointed in 1415, and already many projects of reform had come before it for discussion. On the other hand, the Italians, the French, and the Spaniards demanded a new Pope before everything else, and energetically protested against all the delays put in the way of his election. "The most urgent reform," said they, "and the one that is immediately pressing, is to get rid of the anomaly of a Church without a head. Let us then make haste to elect a Pope!"

If, to all these causes of discord, questions of precedence and patriotic quarrels be added, the incessant conflicts between Castilians and the people of Aragon, between English and French,[3] between the Amagnacs, and the Bourguignons, even between Sigismund and the cardinals, it will be seen how deeply disturbed the Council was on the eve of the important decisions that remained to be taken.

"It is verily a tower of Babel," says a historian. "At Constance, as many different tongues are spoken, as

[1] Von der Hardt, iv. p. 1419. Hardouin, viii. col. 862.

[2] At Trent, Charles V. and the secular princes put forth the same pretensions later on. In a conciliatory spirit the fathers decided to take in hand dogmatic definitions and reform simultaneously. *Cf.* Baguenault de Puchesse, *Histoire du Concile de Trente*, Paris, 1870, p. 49.

[3] Fromme, *Die spanische Nation und das Konstanzer Konzil*, chaps. ii. and iii.

many contradictory opinions are shown, as there are representatives of various nations to be met with."[1]

In the meantime an English bishop, Henry of Winchester, uncle of King Henry V., arrived at Constance. He intervened in all these quarrels, succeeded in pacifying Sigismund, in calming the minds of the fathers, and had an agreement drawn up as to the following three points: I. A conciliar decree was to be carried that, immediately after the election of the Pope, the question of Church Reform should be seriously taken in hand. II. Before the election the reforming decrees, as to which all nations were agreed, should be promulgated. III. The mode of election should be settled by special commissaries.[2]

Of these three resolutions, the second was immediately carried out, and the five following decrees were promulgated at the thirty-ninth general session (October 9, 1417):—

I. General councils shall meet every ten years. Before the close of the first, the Pope, with the consent of the fathers, shall name the place of the next meeting. Such is a summary and the exact meaning of the decree *Frequens*, so often quoted since at schismatic conventicles like that of Basle, and in suspicious Pragmatical Sanctions like that of Bourges (July 7, 1438).[3]

[1] CARO, *Das Bundniss von Canterbury*, Gotha, 1880, p. 5.

[2] VON DER HARDT, iv. p. 1447.

[3] As to the Council of Basle, *cf.* HEFELE, xi. p. 188 ff. As to the Pragmatic Sanction of Bourges, *Ibid.*, p. 486. Modern writers have also demanded the periodical holding of general councils, and have wished to make them a permanent instrument of the life and authority of the Church. See MGR. MARET, *Du Concile général et de la paix religieuse*, ii. p. 414, and the article of the *Correspondant* published on the eve of the Vatican Council by M. COCHIN (October 10, 1869). *Cf.* EM. OLLIVIER, *L'Église et l'État au Concile du Vatican*, ii. p. 73. See too BOSSUET, *Defensio declar. cleri gallicani*, p. i. lib. v. c. 16.

II. In order henceforward to forestall all danger of Schism, in the event of two or more pretenders to the Papacy, a council should assemble *ex-officio* within a year to settle the difference. All prelates shall be bound to be present without further summons.

III. Each Pope, before election is published, shall be obliged to place a profession of the Catholic faith in the hands of his electors. The Council gives the form.

IV. Translations of prelates from one see to another shall not take place without the consent of those concerned. The Pope must give up his right to successions and procurations. Alexander V. had already consented to this.

V. Certain reservations of procurations that came to the visitor-bishops, and the right of spoils shall be justly done away with.[1]

Without entering into detail as to these regulations, it is clear that most of them spring from questionable law, and are animated with a spirit of mistrust of the supreme Pontiff. The prelates are taking precautions against future Popes. Another decree shows the same anxieties and requires the new Pope, in concert with the members of the Council and of the nations, to settle on reforms which are to apply, not only to the Roman curia, but also to the future head of the Church.

§ 2. *Election of Martin V.*

Finally, the fathers resolved to settle the question that took precedence of all others, the election of a new Pope. How should this conclave be proceeded with,

[1] *Cf.* Hubler, *Die konstanzer Reformation*, p. 23. Hefele, xi. p. 41. Bossuet, *Ibid.*, c. 17.

which was to meet in such extraordinary circumstances? Who would be the electors? Who would be the elect?

In consequence of the distrust shown towards the cardinals, the Council did not wish them to be allowed to take part in the election of the Pope by themselves. To the twenty-three members of the Sacred College were added for this time only thirty other prelates, six from each nation.[1] This decision, which was new to canon law, was taken on October 30, 1417, at the fortieth solemn assembly.[2] D'Ailly had already counselled this in his sermon at Whitsuntide (May 30). The King of the Romans had had the vast warehouse, which can still be visited on the banks of Lake Constance, prepared for the conclave. He had chosen the guards among the most illustrious princes of all nations; he had made them take an oath in his presence, and had forbidden the people to pillage the house of the elect. Finally, on November 8, the fifty-three electors went into conclave, and before Sigismund took an oath to choose a virtuous prelate who should be capable of reforming the Church. The doors were then shut and soldiers guarded all the exits.

Next day work began amidst prayers and exhortations. Daily a solemn procession left Constance Cathedral, and filed through the hall of the conclave, reciting the *Veni sancte spiritus*. Six candidates were at first to the front, and then there remained only four. At last, after long discussions, just when the King of the Romans, the princes, and the clergy were passing

[1] The two chief deputies for France were William de Boisratier, Archbishop of Bourges, and James Gélu, Archbishop of Tours.

[2] *Modus eligendi summum Pontificem.* *Cf.* *Tractatus et Sermones*, Strasburg, 1490. Von der Hardt, ii. p. 586; iv. p. 1452. *Cf.* Fromme, *Die Wahl Martins V.*, in the *Römische Quartalschrift*, x. pp. 133-161 (1896).

beneath the conclave windows in procession, all votes fell unanimously to Odo Colonna, cardinal deacon of Saint George, who took the name of Martin V. (November 11).

The new Pontiff was forty-two years of age. He belonged to the noble Roman family of Colonnas, whose connections were Ghibeline, and who had been so long hostile to the Orsinis. It had already provided the Church with twenty-seven cardinals, but Martin V. was the first of his race to ascend the see of St Peter.[1] The learned had a high appreciation of his deep knowledge of canon law; and the simple folk revered him as a kindly, peaceful, and modest prelate, who was independent of partisan intrigue and compromise. At the first news of his election, crowds rushed headlong to the place of the conclave, and displayed a joy that was soon shared by the whole Church. Sigismund also came up himself and congratulated the electors, and kissed the foot of the newly elect. Pope Martin embraced the King and thanked him for having so powerfully contributed to the maintenance of unity and peace.

In the evening, at the solemn procession, Sigismund and the Elector Palatine led the Pontiff's charger by the bridle as far as the cathedral, and then Martin V. went to the bishop's palace to take possession of the rooms left by John XXIII. Next day he was ordained deacon, Saturday priest, and Sunday bishop. Then he received everyone's oath of fealty. Next Sunday his solemn coronation took place in the great court of the episcopal palace.

The new Pope, without being pledged to any party,

[1] Ughelli, *Elogia Columniensis familiae*, Roma, 1650. Guiraud, *LÉtat pontifical après le grand Schisme*, p. 50.

sincerely desired such reforms as were necessary. He was skilful and popular, and was believed to dispose of all the means of success. But the task was an arduous one, and soon it was seen that he could not bring it so quickly to a good issue. The time had not yet come, and reforms did not seem to be ripe. The Council, although it had become œcumenical since its thirty-sixth session, and though it had henceforth a legitimate head, had nevertheless to acknowledge that several of its members were not sufficiently keen for reform. Indeed the Roman Pontiff received scarcely any assistance from them. Each wanted to begin by reforming his neighbour, and divisions had not been abolished by the election of the new Pope. "It is enough for one nation to desire a reform for another to reject it"; thus spoke the delegate of the University of Vienna before the Council. This simple remark shows the disintegrating effect of national divisions, and also explains the sterility of the fathers' efforts. Sigismund took steps with Martin V. to hasten the conclusion of business. A new commission was appointed,[1] and the burning question of benefices was put down for discussion. The Italians, English, and Spaniards wanted all collations to be reserved to the Pope; whereas the French and the Germans claimed to restrict the privileges of the Holy See within the limits of ancient law. They were agreed as to the reduction of the revenues of the Sovereign Pontiff, without taking into account the fact that the regular revenues were far below the requirements that had to be met. On the other hand, apart from the nations, the cardinals tried to maintain and to multiply still further the reservations to be given to the Roman Pontiff.

[1] Von der Hardt, iv. p. 1492.

Martin V. began by declaring that he meant to grant all the points as to which the nations were unanimous; but they were not agreed on a single one.

Weary of strife, everyone recognised the impossibility of reforming the Church by universal decrees. There were too many differences of view, too many opposing interests at stake. So it was decided to make a division in the legislation; one part was to be for the general needs of the Church, the other for the particular needs of each country. The first should include all points on which the nations were agreed; the second should be settled by special concordats.

Among the manifold reforming projects which were then put before the Council, let it suffice to mention Peter D'Ailly's treatise, *De Reformatione Ecclesiae.*[1]

The requests of the German nation were presented to the Pope, and then came French and Spanish demands. Martin V.'s suggested plan of reform corresponded roughly with the eighteen points of the memorial worked out by the Germans. But the nations could only agree upon seven of the proposed articles: these were the decrees of general reform read at the forty-third session, presided over by the Sovereign Pontiff in person.

The first decree abolished all exemptions granted by Popes since Gregory XI.; and replaced all churches

[1] *Opp. Gersonii,* ii. col. 903. As already remarked, this little work, which is full of novel and often good ideas, is only the third part of the treatise *De materia concilii generalis,* composed in 1403. See chap. x. of this book, p. 192. The Cardinal of Cambrai first deals with the whole body of the Church and with the councils, then with the Sovereign Pontiff and the Roman curia, the bishops, monks, and nuns, and lastly with the clergy and laity, specially kings and princes. Many of these reforms were also proposed at the Council of Trent by Cardinal Bartholomew of the Martyrs. *Cf. Analecta juris pontificii,* xci. and xciii. a. 1869 and 1872.

and monasteries, that were exempt, under the sway of ordinary jurisdiction.

The second revoked from the same date associations and incorporations, which had not been granted for right and sound reasons.

By the third, the Pope gave up first fruits and revenues of churches and monasteries during vacancies, and placed them at the disposal of those who were legally entitled to them.

The fourth decree pronounced all those who had been ordained simoniacally to be suspended. All elections and confirmations tainted with this radical vice were annulled.

Benefices are given on account of the offices they presuppose, said the fifth decree. It is absurd of the beneficiaries to refuse or neglect to fulfil their professional duties. Bishops and abbots in this position must be consecrated or blessed without delay, otherwise they will be deprived of their offices and benefices.

In the sixth article the Pope forbade all his subordinates to impose tithes. He himself undertook not to demand any from the whole body of the clergy, unless some grave cause concerned with the universal Church were in question.

The seventh decree regulated the important question of the life and morals of the clergy. He reminded ecclesiastics of the most useful and wise laws, which neglect had sometimes led to be disobeyed, but for which pontifical authority had always demanded respect.

Subsequent Councils renewed these regulations concerning behaviour and discretion in the form in which they are generally observed to-day.[1]

These articles were sanctioned on March 21, at the

[1] Von der Hardt, iv. p. 1533. Hefele, xi. p. 84.

forty-third session, at the same time as the special concordats with each nation. The latter were then nearly finished. They regulated the number and quality of the cardinals, who were henceforth to be chosen in each Catholic nation,[1] and in this respect they were in complete accord with the proposals made by Martin V. in response to the requests of the Germans. The other articles contain decisions, differing according to countries, concerning reservations, collations to benefices, expectations, and confirmations of elections. They also deal with annates, major causes which should be carried before the Roman curia, commendams, indulgences, and dispensations.

These concordats deal with very grave matters, and make the princes concessions which would never have been granted by Pontiffs of the early mediæval period. They inaugurate a new era. Relations between Church and State take a form hitherto unknown, and on which faith and discipline could not always be congratulated.

§ 3. *Martin V. and the various Nations.*

Amidst these cold measures of canon law, the Holy Father contrived to introduce an affectionate expression of compassion for the disasters from which France had been suffering so long, especially since the fatal day of Agincourt (October 26, 1415). " On account of the wars and misfortunes that afflict this country," said Martin V., " the Pope, moved by a feeling of pious sympathy,

[1] HEFELE, xi. pp. 59, 88, and 99. D'Ailly had already put forth this proposal in his treatise (*Cf. Petrus de Alliaco*, p. 121). Unfortunately he neglects to point out that the initiative for such a reform should come from the Pope. The same question came up at the Council of Basle. *Cf.* HEFELE, xi. p. 348.

desires to alleviate all the ecclesiastical dues that weigh upon the kingdom, and specially is anxious to relieve institutions of public charity."[1] Were these measures, which were so affectionate and full of consolation for the eldest daughter of the Church, a reply to the brutality and threats with which the English, in the Council itself, had loaded the French ambassadors, and Peter D'Ailly himself? Perhaps, too, the Pontiff wished to show that he did not share Sigismund's sympathy for the King of England and the Duke of Burgundy.

Unfortunately, owing to crises of ill-health, Charles VI. reigned no longer: he was now only the saddened witness, impotent, and sometimes unconscious, of his own reign and of the decadence of his kingdom.

Being only a sovereign in name, he could make no reply to these very touching marks of pity. On the other hand, meetings of prelates, doctors of the University, and members of the chief council had just taken place from February 28 to March 16. An answer had to be made to the knight, Luke Fieschi, who had been sent by the Pope to notify his recent election to the King. These meetings had been made distrustful of Martin V., owing to the part which Sigismund, recently won over to English policy, had played in the last events of the Council and the conclave. They replied to the cardinal ambassador that, before declaring himself, the King wanted to wait to obtain certainty as to the freedom and legality of the pontifical election.

An explanation of these unjustifiable suspicions is necessary. From the beginning of the fifteenth century, the bishops and doctors had placed themselves at the head of a movement in favour of certain pretensions of a

[1] Hefele, p. 98. Von der Hardt, iv. p. 1566. This concordat was registered on April 15 and published on May 2.

particularist and quasi-schismatical character, which they pompously termed "the ancient rights and privileges of the Churches of France." An order of February 18, 1407, had settled, independently of the Pope and against the Pope, questions which could only be determined by mutual agreement. The Gallicans counted on the Pontiff or on the council to settle the points in dispute. But the Pope of Avignon would give no decision, and the Council of Constance would do no more, in spite of the urgency of the French ambassadors.[1]

Then they wished to act with authority, and decided that the order of 1407 [2] should be put into practice without the intervention of the Pope. But this measure, as unlawful as it was hurtful, could not be carried out without opposition and without delay. This explains why the gathering at Paris put difficulties in the way of recognising Martin V.; it wished to take precautions before the Pontiff would be able to exercise his authority in France.

More than anything else, the money question was a source of anxiety to the court and to the court prelates. It was quite perceptible when the two royal orders of March and April 1418 were read. The first protested against abuses and simoniacal practices, and against a large quantity of gold and silver going out of France. The second formally forbade gold, silver, or jewels to be taken to Rome when benefices were vacant, and forbade asking the Pope for the favour of expectations. The University had already protested energetically, and had hastened to send to Constance its lists of benefices

[1] *Cf.* De Beaucourt, *Histoire de Charles VII.*, i. pp. 279, 361.

[2] *Les libertés de l'Église gallicane prouvées et commentées*, Durand de Maillane, iii. p. 621. *Registres du Parlement*, i., in the same work. P. Dupuy, *Traité des droits*, xxii. No. 16.

(*rotuli*). It preferred to depend on the Roman Pontiff rather than on the bishops.[1] Martin V. on his side showed a proper displeasure at seeing the ungrateful way in which his paternal advances were acknowledged. He had promulgated the concordat for France, and he protested forcibly against the two orders that annulled it. Meanwhile the Duke of Burgundy came into power. Already he had had the concordat published in his states; and, wishing to conciliate to himself the good graces of the Pope, he had a decree made that repealed the two orders (September 9).

It is much to be regretted that Germany and England followed in this matter the footsteps of France, and the concordat made by them with Martin V. met with no better fate.[2]

The Roman Pontiff was no happier in his negotiations with the Greeks. An embassy from the Emperor and Patriarch of Constantinople arrived at Constance on February 19, 1418. This step resulted in the same way as a number of others had done, after being tried by the schismatics of the Lower Empire. There was a want of straightforwardness at Byzantium, and just misgivings caused them to fail at the Papal Court.

But we must not omit an important document that was destined to stifle the heresy of John Huss in Bohemia and Moravia.[3] The twenty-four articles were added to the famous bull *Inter cunctas*, put forth by Martin V., on the same question. This document contained a summary of the errors of the Bohemian heresiarch in forty-five points. All persons under suspicion of heresy on arrest were to be cross-examined in a long series of

[1] See p. 360 above.

[2] Hubler, *Die Konstanzer Reformation und die Concordate von* 1418, Leipzig, 1867.

[3] Von der Hardt, iv. p. 1514.

propositions shown in the pontifical bull. Unhappily, Bohemia was still too violently agitated to listen to the voice of the Pope. Soon afterwards it became necessary to preach a crusade against the Hussites, who were forcing their doctrines upon people at the sword's point, and who seemed to have borrowed from Mahomet his famous device, "Believe or die." One need only mention the names of Ziska, Procopius, and the fierce Taborites to revive the memory of a multitude of excesses in doctrine and behaviour, of innumerable scenes of devastation, sacrilege, and horror.

Let us only note, among the decrees carried against Wicliffe, the condemnation of the thirty-seventh proposition: "The Pope is not the immediate Vicar of Jesus Christ." Gallicans have affirmed, as we have seen,[1] that Martin V. had admitted and approved of the famous propositions brought forward at the fourth and fifth sessions. If the superiority of the Council over the Pope is a true doctrine, then the Council and not the Pope is the immediate Vicar of Jesus Christ. Martin V., in condemning Wicliffe, thus indirectly struck at the doctrine of Constance.[2]

There is another and equally cogent proof of this. Among questions to be put to persons suspected of Hussite heresy is the following: "*Do you believe that the canonically elected Pope is the successor of blessed Peter, having supreme authority in the Church of God?*" If the Constance proposition is true, the accused should reply: "No, the Council has this supreme authority." The suspected heretic then could not have been reconciled,

[1] See above, chap. xv. p. 305 ff.

[2] Hefele, p. 75. *Cf.* Cajetan, *De auctoritate Papae et Concilii,* tr. i. and ii. Gonzalez, *De Infallib.,* disp. xiii. sub. v. § 5, No. 2. Bossuet thinks these arguments are scholastic subtleties, p. ii. lib. v. c. 15, of the *Defensio declarationis cleri gallicani.*

had he upheld the doctrine of the earlier sessions of Constance.

What conclusion can be drawn from this twofold argument, but that Martin V., far from confirming the propositions afterwards called Gallican, on the contrary formally condemned them?[1]

§ 4. *Departure of the Pope and the King of the Romans.*

The Council had settled nearly all the questions that had been submitted to it. For nearly four years the fathers had been gathered together, not without real disadvantage to the many dioceses so long deprived of their legitimate pastors.

Perhaps no council had been so numerous or lasted so long since the beginning of the Church, as no crisis had been so terrible as that of the Great Schism.

At last, on April 22, 1418, the forty-fifth and final session was held. The Pope presided and Sigismund was present at it. The customary ceremonies and prayers were performed in the most solemn manner. A general emotion seized the fathers when they heard the Cardinal-deacon Raynald, titular of St Vit, exclaim in the name of the Pope and of the members of the Council: *Domini, ite in pace.* "My lords, you may go in peace." *Amen*, answered the assembly with one voice.

After a final incident, brought about by the Falkenberg affair, of which we have spoken,[2] a sermon was preached by the Bishop of Catania. When it was

[1] Hefele, p. 80. [2] See above, chap. xv. p. 306.

over, the Cardinal of Chalant solemnly arose and read the decree dissolving the Council of Constance. *Placet*, replied the Cardinal of Ostia in the name of all the bishops. A consistorial lawyer then acted as interpreter to the King of the Romans. He thanked the cardinals and the fathers, as well as the envoys of the Universities and Christian princes ; and finally protested the invincible attachment of Sigismund to the Holy Church as well as to the new Pontiff whom she had just elected.

The Pope and the King of the Romans remained a few weeks more at Constance to settle a few matters of minor importance there, but the hour of the true dissolution of the Council was at hand. During four years the town had been stirred and sometimes disturbed by all the echoes of an assembly that was more stormy than the waves of its lake in the most tempestuous weather. It had often resounded to the clang of arms, the flourish of trumpets, and the cries of triumph, when magnificent tourneys were given by Sigismund to the warlike nobility of Switzerland and Germany. A final passage of arms of greater brilliancy than all the rest was to assemble the princes and knights once more in the presence of Sigismund and to bring these great days to a splendid close. This mingling of sacred and profane, of theological discussions and jousts of chivalry, was according to the manners of the times.

Every day brought news of the departure of a cardinal, a famous bishop, or a prince with his numerous and brilliant train.[1]

[1] Simon de Cramaud had left Constance in the month of January ; G. Philastre left on April 2. P. D'Ailly, who had been the soul of the council, started on March 30 for Avignon, where he had his palace, and where he died on August 9, 1420. More than fifty authors are mistaken as to the date of his death, and most of them put it in 1425.

Every day saw the enormous and mingled crowd, brought together by the Council, grow less. The announcement of the departure of the Pope and King of the Romans hastened on all other departures, and was to deprive the city of a glory and distinction that it has never recovered.

Martin V. officiated pontifically for the last time at Constance on Whit Sunday, May 15, 1418.[1] Next day, at seven in the morning, he left the town in state. Sigismund and the other princes held the reins of his horse in turn, counts of the Empire bore the daïs above his head, and forty thousand horsemen accompanied him on his way. At Gottlieben, boats waited for him at the foot of the historic castle, which had held John Huss and John XXIII. successively as prisoners. The Pope gave his benediction to the King of the Romans, whom he was never to see again, and then embarked on the Rhine, while his suite lined the banks of the river. He turned his course towards Bern and Geneva (June 11), and was everywhere greeted with glad cheers by the Catholic populations. Finally, he reached Milan, where he consecrated the high altar of the cathedral. He made a long stay at Mantua (November 9) and Florence (from February 26, 1419, till September 14, 1420) before returning to the Eternal City, which he entered in state on September 28, 1420.

Sigismund too left Constance on May 21, 1418, to visit his fair towns of Alsace, and then finally returned to his own states. The King of the Romans had just done eminent services to the Church. During the whole of this stormy period his prudence and almost

[1] F. Contelorius, *Martini V. vita ex legitimis documentis collecta* (Roma, 1611), p. 12 ff. Reumont, *Beiträge zur italienischen Geschichte*, iv. p. 304 ff.

incessant moderation were all the more meritorious from his being naturally of an ardent and active disposition. We will not compare him to Constantine, present at the Council of Nice, and giving its decrees the force of law; nevertheless, apart from a few errors, his part was honourable. His respect for ecclesiastical authority was undiminished, in spite of the regrettable scenes he sometimes witnessed at Constance, and in spite of the too natural temptation to increase his imperial power in proportion as he saw ecclesiastical authority becoming lessened. He would have wished plans of reform to take precedence in the assembly; for he rightly thought that, when once the Pope's election was over, everyone would be glad to have done with it and to get away.

He would have also liked to modify the constitution of the Empire at the same time,[1] but he passed the whole of his life in struggling with pressing difficulties, in elaborating a host of projects, in entering into innumerable negotiations which could hardly ever come to anything. Brave, active, and chivalrous, he had all the qualities that later on distinguished Francis I. of France. We may add that he also resembled the latter in his taste for pleasure, in his love of dangerous enterprises, in his want of continuity, and in his prodigality, which made him a needy sovereign. For a time, however, Sigismund allowed himself to be carried away by the conventicle of Basle, which went beyond the bad doctrines of Constance, but he soon acknowledged his error as well as the good right of the

[1] *Cf.* Carl Koehne, *Die sogenannte Reformation Kaisers Sigismunds*, *Neues Archiv*, 1898, p. 690. F. Miltenberger, *Das Itinerarium Martins V. von Constanz bis Rom*, in *Mittheilungen des Instituts für östreichische Geschichtsforschung*, xv. (1894), p. 662.

Pope. He became once more what he had often been in the Council, the external bishop, and one of the firmest upholders of the faith.

Such was the part of the last Emperor of the family of Luxemburg, before, during, and after Constance.

CHAPTER XIX

THE END

In his letter on *Historical Studies*, Leo XIII. laid down this great law: "The perpetuity of the Church cannot fail: God himself stands surety for this and history bears witness to it: *Sponsor Deus, historia testis.* Providence, sometimes in spite of men, makes use of events for the progressive development of the society He has founded." [1]

The history of the Great Schism is perhaps the most striking proof of this axiom; this acute and extremely dangerous crisis would have dealt a mortal blow to the Papacy, had not the promise of Christ made it immortal.

The centuries as they pass do not all help to throw as much light on this distinctive mark of the true Church. There are some which hardly contribute to enhance her splendour and to increase her influence: they may be called the iron ages. Of these were the tenth and eleventh, and, after the glorious revival of the twelfth, and particularly of the thirteenth centuries, the end of the fourteenth and the beginning of the fifteenth brought a fresh intermission in the development of dogma, in the realisation of projects of reform, and in the progress of pontifical authority.

When Martin V., henceforth the only Pope, closed

[1] *De studiis historicis* ad Cardinales Pitra, de Luca et Hergenroether, 1883.

this era of discord and restored peace and unity to the Church, under these three heads there took place an awakening to which history must testify, while regretting that the results were not such as one might have expected.

§ 1. *Doctrinal Progress.*

In several passages of his writings, St Augustine sets himself to show that the appearance of heresies was one of the causes of this development: "Errors teem at certain periods," he says, "but they are the occasion of a closer study of doctrine, and truths get better understood and proclaimed with more energy. Thus it is that an indiscreet question raised by an innovator becomes an occasion for a fresh manifestation of doctrinal progress." [1]

This happy result does not always immediately follow. Sometimes a man's life is too brief for him to witness the birth and growth of evil, and to testify to the salutary effect of the remedy. We have seen how heresies developed during the forty years of schism. The University of Paris with its theological audacity, Wicliffe with his violence of mind and pen, John Huss with his revolutionary enterprises, compromised everything and risked the loss of everything.

The tares were sown in the fourteenth and fifteenth centuries, and it is not till the sixteenth that the Master tears them up to make room for the growing of the good grain. Luther must appear for the Church to hold solemn assizes at Trent and give the Christian universe the decrees that govern us still. The particular evil called forth general good: *Oportet et haereses esse.* On

[1] *De Civ. Dei,* xvi. 2. *In Psalmis,* liv. 22. *Confess.,* vii. 19.

another point, which was not less fundamental, the result kept the world longer waiting; and, to say the truth, it is only the end of the nineteenth century that reaps the benefit.

We know the tenor and the disastrous sense of the famous decrees of the fourth and fifth sessions of Constance: we know how they aimed at nothing less than modifying the fundamental constitution of the Church.[1] Martin V. had not acknowledged them, but his resistance had been rather passive: he had not been able to fight openly against a movement which at the bottom of his heart he believed to be fatal. In spite of himself he summoned a council at Pavia in 1423 to obey the decree *Frequens*, which was animated with the same distrust as that which ordered a general synod every ten years.[2] When the assembly had to be transferred to Siena, the Pope was able to convince himself that his most pessimistic apprehensions were well founded.[3]

As for the conventicle that gathered at Basle in 1431, it was too often a mere mob: and what a singular and too often scandalous spectacle it presented to the world is well known. It dared to set the Lord of Ripaille, the Anti-pope Felix V., against the true Pope Eugenius IV. Eugenius in turn summoned the synod of Ferrara to cope with that of Basle. There were not only two Popes, but two councils; and one might have imagined that things had reverted to the worst days of the Schism.[4]

These excesses, which were as ridiculous as they were scandalous, did not, however, fail to have one result. They discredited the decree *Frequens*, which ceased to

[1] See chap. xv. above, p. 294.

[2] See chap. xviii. above, p. 362.

[3] *Cf.* JOHN OF RAGUSA, in *Monumenta Conc. Gener. Saec.*, xv. t. i. pp. 12 ff.

[4] HALLER, *Concilium Basiliense, Studien und Quellen zur Geschichte des Concils von Basel.* Bâle, 1896-1897.

be applied, and they put at the same time an obstacle in the way of the periodical reunion of general councils, which could never be one of the ordinary means of government.

On the other hand, these deviations did not hinder future rebels from appealing to a later council against the Roman Pontiff. When a prince like Louis XI. or Louis XIV. desires to usurp the rights of the Church, when bishops like those of 1682, such as Febronius and Grégoire, mean to shake off the Papal yoke, when rebellious innovators put forward daring and incendiary propositions, when a doctor such as Döllinger refuses to believe in Papal infallibility, all, despite the repeated vetoes of the Supreme Pontiffs, appeal to a future council as to a jurisdiction superior to that of the Pope.[1]

In their turn, at the instigation of men like Dumoulin, Pithou, and Dupuy, parliaments will apply such legislation as that of the *placet*, the *exequatur*, and the *appeal against abuses*. The maxims of Constance and of Basle will give rise to tendencies and procedures of that suspicious Gallicanism which was to keep France in a spirit of chicanery and peevish independence with regard to the Pope, and in a semi-schismatical condition. In the hands of the lawyers of Charles VII. and his successors, these decrees will become, to use the words of Guizot, a *terrible and fatal instrument of tyranny*. Fénelon was well situated for forming a judgment, and his definition of the so-called "Liberties" of the Church of France is well known: "Liberty so far as concerns

[1] This appealing to a future council, which was already rebuked by Cœlestine I. in the fifth century, was again censured by Martin V., Pius II., and Julius II. *Cf.* de Marca, *de Concord. sacerd. et imperii*, iv. c. 17. It forms the 78th privilege of the Gallican Church, demanded by Pithou and the French legists. *Cf.* Durand de Maillane, *Les libertés de l'Église gallicane prouvées et commentées*, ii. p. 729. Lyon, 1771.

the Pope, slavery so far as concerns the King. The King's authority in the Church has passed into the hands of secular judges. Laymen rule bishops."[1]

Voltaire in his turn has passed judgment on these fatal privileges: "The 1682 assembly thought the time had come for setting up a *Catholic Apostolic* Church in France, which would not be *Roman*."[2] It was neither more nor less than an advance towards the idea of a national Church with a common faith, but without one head. It was the preparation of a civil constitution for the clergy.

Jansenists and Josephites, liberals who were more or less revolutionary, and despots who were more or less absolute, all considered these principles as a sacred ark. "I require people to profess the four articles and Gallican liberties," said the Emperor to Abbé d'Astros. "Moreover, I have the sword at my side, so take care."[3]

All these distressing discussions scarcely favour dogmatic advance. The University of Paris, which had been up to this period one of the great exponents of doctrinal tradition, was within an ace of being ruined when the victorious Bourguignons persecuted it in 1418.[4] Later on, when too much under England, it played its too well-known part in the condemnation of Joan of Arc, and in the pragmatic sanction,[5] it rejected the very idea of a crusade on behalf of the Greeks.[6] Its influence,

[1] Fénelon, *Plans de Gouvernement*, iii. p. 433, Ed. Didot, 1870.

[2] *Siècle de Louis XIV.*, ch. xxxv.

[3] D'Haussonville, *l'Église romaine et le premier Empire*, iii. ad finem.

[4] *Ordonnances des rois de France*, x. p. 485. Du Boulay, v. p. 352. Gerson, *Opp.*, iv. col. 527 ff.

[5] Avroles, *L'Université de Paris au temps de J. d'Arc*, 1902. Du Boulay, v. pp. 632, 636, 642.

[6] *Ibid.*, pp. 609, 617.

disastrous from a patriotic point of view, became absolutely null as to theology. It only had enough signs of life left to send its *rotuli* and *libri supplicationum* to Rome, and to defend to the very last the benefices it had once obtained. Its professors, removed far from Paris by the troubles of the times, founded rival institutions in foreign lands.[1] The number of students diminished in proportion as the glory of the masters became dimmed. The time when thousands of pupils were seen around the professorial chairs of *Alma Mater* passed away, never to return. The days of Albert the Great, Thomas and Bonaventura came to a close. No more *Theological* "*Summae*" issued from the University. Compared with such works of genius, Augustine of Rome's doctrinally unsafe books,[2] those of the ardent Thomist, Henry of Gorcum, and even of the learned and many-sided Nicholas of Cusa might be called works of decadence.

Without being too severe on the Scotist, Gabriel Biel, what can be said of John Major and James Almain his disciple, the rabid defenders of all Gallican theories ?[3]

Some of these theologians, like William of Varillong, fall into all the eccentricities of style and explanation that mark false scholasticism. Others, like Paul Cortesine, were elegant humanists, without precision, solidity, or depth.

It is especially on the subject of the constitution of the Church that theological errors crop up. Some authors

[1] Cologne, Erfurt, Wurzburg, Leipzig, Cracoria, St Andrews in Scotland, Valentia in Spain, Palermo, Turin, and Cremona in Italy, Orange Aix, Perpignan.

[2] Condemned at the 22nd session of the Council of Basle. See John Turrecremata's report in Mansi, xxx. p. 979 ff.

[3] Some of their works are in Gerson, ii. col. 961 ff.

think that they are obliged to maintain *à outrance* the decrees of Constance, and to defend aristocratic and conciliar theories against the monarchical authority of the Pope. These theologians and legists rely upon kings and parliaments as in the days of Occam and Dubois. The Cæsarian and individualistic spirit makes headway even before Luther's time.

But, on the other hand, true science protested, and the Council of Florence, in the presence of Latins and Greeks united, proclaimed the Roman Pontiff the first authority in the Catholic world, the true vicar of Christ, the head of the Church, the father and teacher of all Christians. A century later, the Council of Trent, rather by actual facts than by formal definitions, proclaimed the same truth. The theologians of the sixteenth century gave up the fatal theories that had prevailed during the whole of the fifteenth, and revived a great doctrinal era.

Nevertheless the disastrous current continued, specially in France. Gallicanism, whether theological or parliamentary, too often held sway in the assemblies of the clergy, in books infected with Jansenism or Josephism, and in royal courts and parliaments. It survived revolutions and changes of dynasties, modifications of régimes, and the appearance of new codes. Governments imbued with liberal principles went to fetch from the arsenal of absolute laws rusty arms for use against the Church. The Vatican Council had to silence the doctors and parliamentarians who invoked the maxims of Constance and Basle, and boasted of being disciples of Gerson and Bossuet in religious policy. And thus it was that the stream of sound doctrine finally made its way through the errors which had arisen from the great Western Schism.

§ 2. *The Question of Reform.*

The Schism, both from the prejudices which it aroused and from the disorder which it fomented, was not calculated to favour the ideas of reform which so long had filled the loftiest minds. The grave complications that ensued after the Council of Constance, and the obstacles incessantly interposed by human passion in the way of such restorative ideas, hindered the latter from coming to anything. Here again opposing currents were plainly evident.

On the one hand, the reforms decreed at Constance and repeated in the concordats that followed were received with favour and applied with success. Thenceforward the question of reform was part of the order of the day. The example was given from above. Excellent Popes, generous friends of science, enlightened protectors of the arts, almost always displayed an energy and zeal which rose to the full height of the most difficult circumstances. Doubtless Martin V., Calixtus III., and Sixtus IV. were not free from all accusations of nepotism, but this defect may have had extenuating circumstances.[1] All endeavoured to reform the Roman curia, in spite of a certain amount of interested opposition,[2] and found prelates who were ready to second their efforts.

The cardinals, henceforth gathered into a single college, ceased to make the Christian world groan with their intemperate extravagance. The honours of purple were granted to many men in every way worthy of their august functions. Suffice it to mention John

[1] PASTOR, i. p. 236. GOYAU, *Le Vatican*, p. 134. HEFELE, xi. p. 148.

[2] PASTOR, ii. p. 40 ff.

Dominici, the peace-bringing legate at Constance, blessed Nicholas Albergati, the skilful negotiator of the treaty of Arras, the humanist Julian Cesarini, who commanded armies, the learned Capranica, who made some celebrated foundations and who was twice offered the tiara.[1] At Constantinople, Cardinals Isidore and Bessarion, so different in character and life, shed a last ray of glory on the clergy of the East. Later on, Pius II. placed Saint Antoninus on the commission which he had entrusted with reforming the curia.[2]

Members of the Sacred College were sent as legates to all the places in which reform was to be undertaken, but none of them surpassed the wise and good Cardinal Nicholas of Cusa in zeal and influence. "To purify and renew, not to destroy or to crush," such was his motto. "Man has not to reform religion," he added, "but religion has to reform man."

It was his work to get rid of the bad influence of the Conventicle of Basle in all directions, to bring back priests and people to Roman unity, to reform religious houses, sometimes in spite of the opposition of public authority. In Denys the Carthusian he found an indefatigable ally.[3] In Austria, Styria, and Bavaria, he extolled the rule of Bursfeld,[4] and transformed more than fifty Benedictine monasteries as well as a large number of chapters regular of the Augustinians. Everywhere he appointed visitors and convoked

[1] Pastor, ii. p. 453.

[2] Moro, *Di San Antonio in relazione alla riforma cattolica nel sec. XV.* (Florence, 1899).

[3] D. A. Mougel, *Denys le Chartreux, sa vie, son rôle* (Montreuil, 1896).

[4] *Cf.* Dom V. Berliere, *Revue Bénédictine*, eleventh year, Nos. 9, 11, 12; xix. No. 1, Maredsous, 1899, 1900, 1902

synods; at Bamberg, Münster, Mayence, and Cologne he abated scandalous quarrels and smoothed away hosts of difficulties.

At the same period, the famous Augustinian congregation of Windesheim continued its works of edification and salvation, particularly in the low countries.[1]

In the order of St Dominic, the movement began at Bologna, the burial-place of the venerated founder. Its originator was Blessed Raymond of Capua, the confessor and historian of St Catherine of Siena.[2] A few young religious from Flanders and Holland had come to study at the University of Bologna, and they communicated to their native land this generous ardour, and the blessed Rosary soon became a means of reviving primitive fervour. The reformed religious were distributed into several congregations, which vied with one another in renewing themselves in the spirit of their founder. This spirit reinvigorated the whole order and made it blossom anew with saints both male and female.[3]

Among the sons of St Francis, Bernardine of Siena and John of Capistrano set up fervent houses of Friars Minor in all directions, and renewed the wonders formerly wrought by their blessed founder all the world over. Both preached devotion to the holy name

[1] J. Acquoy, *Het Kloster te Windesheim en zign invloed* (Utrecht, 1876). Watrigant, *La Genèse des Exercices de St Ignace* (Amiens, 1889). Bonet-Maury, *De opera scholastica, Fratrum vitae communis* (Paris, 1897), p. 61.

[2] *Cf.* pp. 23, 51, 61, above.

[3] R. P. Chapotin's note, historian of the order of St Dominic. *Cf.* Echard, *Scriptores ordinis Praedicatorum*, Paris, 1719. *Bullaire de l'ordre des Frères prêcheurs*, vols. iii. and iv. Masselli, *Monumenta et antiquitates veteris disciplinae ordinis Praedicatorum* (Rome, 1864). Reichert, *Monumenta O. FR. Pr. historica*, viii.

of Jesus,[1] the first to the enthusiastic crowds who listened to him in Italy, and the second to the Hussites of Bohemia and to the crusaders at the siege of Belgrade.[2]

The example thus coming down from the higher levels of ecclesiastical and religious life immediately had a fruitful influence on the Christian laity. To become convinced of this, one only has to read contemporary accounts of the magnificent manifestations of the Jubilee of 1450. One cannot but wonder at the spectacle of immense crowds filling all the roads of Italy and turning towards the city of pontifical benedictions. Thousands of prelates, princes, and distinguished persons mingled with the enormous influx of pilgrims intent on gaining the Jubilee indulgences. Emperor Frederic III. had himself crowned in the Eternal City in 1452, and people expected a revival of the most glorious days of the Germanic Roman Empire. Everywhere at that time a reawakening of the religious life was witnessed, and it looked as if the most Christian period of mediæval times were to be renewed.

Along with the spirit of faith arose also the spirit of charity. Hospitals and lepers' houses were built or else were restored. Monts-de-piété, those banks of charity, grew up, thanks to Blessed Bernardine of Feltro;[3] hostelries received travellers and poor

[1] *Cf.* Pastor, i. p. 243; ii. p. 366.

[2] *Cf.* De Kerval, *Saint Jean de Capistran* (Paris, 1887). Thureau-Dangin, *Saint Bernardin de Sienne* (Paris, 1896). Alessio, *Storia di S. Bernardino di Siena e del suo tempo*, 1899. Ludovic de Besse, *Bernardin de Feltre*, 2 vols. (1902).

[3] *Cf.* Moirachi, *Vita del B. Bernardino Tomitano da Feltre* (Baira, 1894). Flornoy, *Le bienheureux Bernardin de Feltre*, p. 156 (Paris, 1897).

pilgrims;[1] orphanages were opened for foundlings; popular schools multiplied;[2] more numerous and simple catechisms were put into the hands of all the faithful.[3] The *Imitatio* spread more and more among the masses, and God raised up extraordinary envoys of his love in all directions. Preaching was rarely more general throughout the Church, and it exercised considerable influence.[4]

And still, by the side of these proofs of resurrection and life, many symptoms of disease and grave wounds were shown in the midst of this still Christian society, which was a prey to continual attacks of the spirit of immorality and scepticism.

Certain Popes who came on the scene subsequently, and more than one cardinal, did not always give edifying examples, and the clergy in many of its members ceased to be a model for the people. The humanists, whose presence and aspirations have already been in evidence at Constance, tried to withdraw their uneasy curiosity more and more from the supervision of the Roman Church. They not only stood out as the champions of classical antiquity, but as the imitators and defenders of pagan morality and law. One need only mention the names of Poggio, Valla, Filelfo, and Beccadelli, to immediately revive memories of flighty morals and indifference or hatred for religion.

In their books matter is glorified above spirit, and their work has been rightly and graphically described as the resurrection of the flesh.

It was amidst the nobility first of all that this spirit of disorganisation seethed. Knighthood and

[1] JANSSEN, *L'Allemagne et la Réforme,* French translation, i. p. 572.
[2] *Ibid.*, p. 49.
[3] *Ibid.*, p. 32.
[4] PASTOR, i. p. 42.

chivalry, which had so long been the armed servants of God and the weak, became wanting in grit, changed character, lost their legitimate independence of spirit, and fell under the domination of princes. Remnants of feudalism, too faithfully retained, handed over certain ecclesiastical benefices to nobles who were often ignorant and worldly,[1] and sometimes too young, and sovereigns tried to transform prelacies into fiefs and bishops into vassals. On the other hand, the introduction of Roman regal law into Christian mediæval legislation gave rise to social disturbances, undermined the old political constitutions, destroyed ancient popular privileges, increased the arbitrary powers of princes, and favoured indirectly all enterprises directed against the Church and the Papacy.[2]

The germs of opposition sown at Constance and Basle increased and turned kings and peoples aside from accepting reforms favourably, when their initiative was found in Roman authority.

Later on, Protestantism was to find its strongest support in degenerate courts, and its principal lever for effecting the so-called movement for reforming the morals of the clergy was to be the immorality of princes. Add to this the cupidity of the nobles and the unconscious ardour of popular passion, and we have the three chief causes of the success of the Reformation made in the heart of the Church in spite of the Church and against the Church. Soon the Council of Trent was to

[1] Janssen, p. 575. See Pius II.'s eloquent complaints about France; *Pii II. Comment.* (Francfurti, 1614).

[2] *Cf.* Janssen, *op. cit.*, i. pp. 403, 456, 570. It was particularly the University of Bologna that introduced the exclusive study of Roman law, and Muratori rightly complains of the fatal influence of this pagan legislation in Italy, in spite of the perfection of its legal forms. *Cf. Dissertazioni sopra la antichità italiane*, i. p. 349.

study the decrees *De Reformatione* at the same time as the dogmatic canons, and was to impose them as a whole, as a code of wise and unchangeable laws on all the Catholic universe.

§ 3. *The Temporal Power, and Political and Religious Authority of the Popes.*

Martin V. had a very sincere desire to promote dogmatic progress and to protect all attempts at reform. But he soon saw that he could not attain this double aim without having recovered first of all his complete independence in the sphere of his pontifical domain. He wanted to return to Rome immediately to restore his power there. Through this energetic and intelligent resolution, he shook himself free from the urgency of Sigismund, who wanted to keep him in Germany and who offered him Basle, Mayence, and Strasburg as a place of residence one after the other.[1] At the same time the Pontiff declined the entreaties of the French prelates, who begged him to return to Avignon in order to preside over the coming council there. "My duty is to return to Rome," invariably replied Martin V. "The city is suffering from the absence of its sovereign; the Roman Church is the mother of all the rest; there and there alone the Pope is at his post, like a pilot at the helm."[2] For the twenty-fifth time the Papacy, momentarily in exile, was about to take fresh possession of its secular possessions, and was to be once more at

[1] Von der Hardt, iv. p. 1580.

[2] Platina, *Vita Martini V.*, p. 623. *Cf.* Pastor, *Histoire des Papes*, i. p. 222. Denifle, *Chartul.*, iv. p. 347. Valois, iv. p. 434.

home. With reference to another return of a Pope to Rome, de Maistre alludes to the fable of Antæus regaining fresh strength after having touched earth, his mother. The Pontiff also wished to resume the struggle against error and vice with renewed vigour in putting foot on the blessed ground which his predecessors had won by their sweat and blood.

In what state did Martin find Italy and the Eternal City, which the Papacy had made so glorious? Anarchy reigned everywhere, and the Pope only governed a small part of his temporal dominions. The nobles and the communes had been quarrelling over its remnants, while *condottieri*, foreigners for the most part, overran the peninsula in all directions, scattering slaughter everywhere, and leaving behind them nothing but ruins and death. The Pope's own family, the powerful dynasty of the Colonnas, firmly established in Campania, sought to subdue the Orsini and the Conti, and hoped that the new Pontiff would increase its power with his domains.[1]

The communes had gained strength and become powerfully organised during the troublous times of the Schism. Their jealousy, their pretensions, and even their cruelty, which were in no way behind that of the nobles, were the cause of incessant fights. Rome enters into a struggle with Viterbo, Perugia sets itself to subdue Foligno, Ancona fights with Recanati, and one wonders, in the midst of all these battles, what has become of the legitimate authority of the Pontiffs, who have been kept far from their capital by the misfortunes of the times. With regard to another epoch, no less troubled, Dom Pitra wrote: "The strangest thing is

[1] J. Guiraud, *La politique italienne du Pape Martin V.*, *Revue historique*, 1901.

that the Church could remain where she was. Not without reason do we find the image of the three children in the furnace constantly surrounding the graves of the Popes. They had to live on hot embers, and to rise from the cinders like the phœnix. Old Latium had become a volcano, and the catacombs were hollowed out of burning puzzolana. The most solid edifice under the sun was built on a soil that trembled and burned. Thus will it always be, even after peace has come, even after our own days." [1]

Martin, in recrossing the Alps, knew that he was going to find Rome occupied by the Neapolitan troops of Joan II. They only evacuated the town in 1419, and it was only in 1410 that the Pope was able to return home and to be received there as a saviour, and soon to win the title of *Father of his country*. He restored the Eternal City, assuaged the wretchedness of its inhabitants, took severe measures against the defacing of monuments which had become habitual, and by degrees re-established his authority in the Papal States, and fought with energy to put down the scourge of brigandage, which was endemic in the Roman Campagna. A large number of towns, tired of endless dissensions, got rid of their petty tyrants and united together under the immediate sway of the Pontiff. At his death, peace and order reigned in the Papal States.[2] There were, however, more troubles under Eugenius IV. and Nicholas V.; but the Popes soon got the better of them, either through the warlike energy of the Vitelleschi and the Scarampo, or else by pacific means more in harmony with the mind of the Church.

During the eight years of Nicholas V.'s pontificate,

[1] Pitra, *Analecta novissima* (Tuscul., 1885), p. 16.

[2] *Cf.* Guiraud, *La politique italienne du Pape Martin V.*, *Rev. hist.*, 1901

Rome arose from her ruins with renewed youth, covered herself with an adornment of churches and palaces, and surrounded herself with a strong circle of ramparts. This son of the people, raised to the honour of the tiara, "was the first of the Medicis in spirit, if not in rank."[1] Julius II. would have "Pontiffs to be masters and lords in the game of this world. But at that time in Italy it was necessary for a Pope to be feared to secure respect; it was not a bad thing for him to wear a cuirass: the tastes of Julius II. were appropriate. For several centuries to come he fortified the Papal States and strengthened the old pontifical establishment. From Piacenza to Terracina he made St Peter a strong landowner."[2]

Let us hear the statement of Machiavelli: "But lately, no baron was too small to despise Papal power. To-day it is respected by the King of France."

With the restoration of the temporal power grew the influence of the Popes over Italy and the Catholic nations. The reunion of schismatic Greece with the Church and missionary successes were convincing proofs of it. Already the Council of Basle had worked hard to conclude a treaty of religious alliance between the Church of the Lower Empire and the Roman Church.[3] The minority of the fathers came to an understanding with Eugenius IV., and chose the town of Florence as the place of the future council for union (May 7 and 29, 1437). The Greek envoys arrived in Europe, held discussions at Ferrara, and met the Latins at Florence,

[1] Voigt, *Die Wiederbelebung des classischen Alterthums oder das erste Jahrhundert des Humanismus*, i. p. 413 (Berlin, 1880).

[2] Goyau, *Le Vatican*, p. 135.

[3] Mansi, xxix. p. 1235 ff.; xxx. p. 670. Hardouin, viii. pp. 1185, 1190, 1498 ff. Cecconi, *Studi storici sul Concilio di Firenze*, i. 1869. Haller, *Concilium Basiliense*, i. 4th part.

thanks to the learning of Bessarion[1] and the energy of Isidore of Kieff.

Being badly received in their country because of this alliance treaty, some of these Greek ambassadors betrayed the cause of unity, and fell away again with all their people into schism. In giving up Rome, this unhappy Church gave up herself. The Turks of Mahomet II. soon came to show that the degenerate soldiers of the Lower Empire could only be saved by union with the Latins and a crusade.

This redeeming crusade would have been undertaken later on by Sigismund and Maximilian. Joan of Arc had counselled the Duke of Burgundy, Philip the Good, to undertake it; Savonarola urged Florence and Italy to do the same; Denys the Carthusian in the depths of his cloister, and Christopher Columbus in his adventurous ships, dreamed of arousing the West to fight the Mussulmans. This Eastern Question filled the thoughts of all the greater spirits of this century: it was also a capital affair for the Popes, who alone had influence enough to bring such an undertaking to a successful issue. The question was, indeed, how to unite the petty Italian republics, to urge peace upon the principal powers of the West, to allay the secular jealousies which divided the Poles and Hungarians, to send reinforcements to the Knights of Rhodes, to Matthias Corvin, to Hunyadi, and to Scanderberg, in a word, to arouse Europe, and to hurl it upon Asia before Mahomet II. had time to mass a hundred and sixty thousand men for a march upon Byzantium.

Nicholas V. ceased his artistic and literary occupations to arm vessels and to send help to the besieged Greek capital. The ardent Spaniard, Calixtus III., is above

[1] Vast, *Le Cardinal Bessarion* (Paris, 1878), p. 53 ff.

all the crusader Pope. A new Urban II., he makes a great effort to retake Constantinople. Pius II. addresses fiery harangues to the nations and Christian princes, and multiplies the urgent steps he is taking. Unworthily abandoned by Venice, he dies at Ancona without being able to convey to the East the troops whom his eloquence had assembled. He was the soul of the crusade, and it died with him. In vain Sixtus IV. sent Bessarion to France and England, Borgia to Spain, Capranica to Italy.[1] The spirit of Europe had changed, and unselfish gallantry had fallen away along with faith. The fall of the Eastern Empire, the arrival of Greek exiles in the West, did not get Christendom to shake off its torpor and unsheath the sword; it was all over with the crusades. The East, after having been subject to the depressing leadership of Byzantium, fell under the shameful and sometimes bloody yoke of the Turks for centuries, perhaps for ever.

The Pontiffs of this period also resumed the missionary efforts which Clement V., John XXII., and Clement VI. had inaugurated, and which the Great Schism had miserably interrupted.

In the north of Europe, after sweeping away the remains of the worship of Thor and Odin, they extended the boundaries of the faith and received the sovereign of Denmark and of Norway at Rome.[2] In the East, they set themselves to reconcile the Russian Church with the Roman Church, and to urge the Grand Duke Iwan against the Turks. On the Danube, the Papacy tried to do away with schism among the Walachians, Bulgarians, and Moldavians.[3] In Lebanon, it begs the

[1] Raynald, 1456, Nos. 1 and 8; 1457, Nos. 7, 12, 50; 1458, No. 35.

[2] Pastor, iv. p. 236.

[3] Raynald, a. 1434, 18-20; 1436, 27.

Maronites to bring their rite more and more into conformity with that of the Roman Church.[1]

The merchants of Germany were in touch with all the world, and made the faith known in the most remote regions, before it followed Vasco da Gama on the new road to India which he had discovered.[2] Full of daring in the Far East, the Church kept up her position in North Africa. Soon she was to arrive in America, simultaneously with the boldest of the *conquistadores*. She fought against slavery and immorality; keeping in check alike the passion of the oppressors and the vengeance of the oppressed.

While a part of old Europe was being torn from the hold of the papacy, the latter was making unexpected conquests beyond the sea; and unbounded hopes formed some consolation for inexcusable desertion.

A supernatural Providence guards the Church, disposing of human events in such wise that she never loses the distinctive note of Catholicity, which is the most palpable and evident proof of her divinity.

In writing this page of ecclesiastical annals, we have sometimes cruelly felt the truth of Lacordaire's saying: "History is the long narrative of human dishonour." It indeed appears as if certain years at the close of the fourteenth and fifteenth centuries were accursed.

Thus it is that one reads in Scripture of towns struck by fire from heaven, or of certain countries condemned for a time to desolation and the barrenness of the desert.

In this fatal period, a theological science which has gone astray deceives men's minds and scandalises the faith; virtues supernatural and even natural are under

[1] Raynald, a. 1469, 28 ff.

[2] Janssen, *L'Allemagne à la fin du moyen âge*, i. p. 357.

eclipse; they no longer adorn the crown, the mitre, nor even always the tiara; the Church is the victim of human passion; Popes become the creatures and sometimes the playthings of the Kings whose judges they formerly were; such, in short, is the picture we have had to put before our readers.

On the other hand, at the close of the Great Schism, arts flourished, the exiled muses of Greece found refuge in Italy, learning brought to light the most perfect masterpieces of the past, and the Church began to favour this movement. "She takes a grace from time to adorn her for eternity," as Lacordaire again says.

But why was it that certain humanists preferred Plato to Jesus Christ, and that their mental guides were at Alexandria or Athens, and not at Jerusalem or Rome? Why did the whole of Olympus seem to descend into the palaces of Florence and Genoa, and sometimes even of the Vatican?

An epoch of decadence, say some. A century of renaissance, say others. A mixed period, we will say, like all the ages of history, but in which the world-stream carried on in its troubled waters less gold than sand and slime.

Those who expect to find in every period of history an ever brilliant proof of the divinity and sanctity of the Church, are sometimes liable to cruel disappointments. At certain eras the fact is clearer to the eye of faith than to that of reason.

In a given age, even in a Christian age, we do not always find the Church showing herself in all her glory without spot or wrinkle as the bride of Jesus Christ. Still less do we find her as the Church universally venerated and obeyed.

Rather must she be compared to the cloud, sometimes

dark and sometimes light, which led the Hebrews in their journey towards the land of promise.

The history of the Church, like that of her Divine Master, has a divine and a human side. At certain eras it is the former that shines forth ; in the age we have studied the second is more in evidence. The earthly existence of the Society founded by Jesus Christ sometimes affords matter for criticism and furnishes a pretext for unbelief or strife, but belief in her divine authority surely stores up merit in the sphere of faith, and ever keeps a crown in reserve for the moment of victory.

LIST OF AUTHORITIES

(A) BOOKS

ACHERY (d').—*Spicilegium, sive collectio veterum aliquot scriptorum.* Paris, 1723.

ALMAINUS (Jacobus).—*De dominio naturali, civili et ecclesiastico, in Opp. Gersonii,* t. ii. col. 961 ; *De Auctoritate Ecclesiae et conciliorum generalium, Ibid.,* t. ii. col. 976.

ANTONIN (Saint).—*Summa historialis.* Florence, 1741.

ARETINUS, Leonardus (Brunus).—*Rerum suo tempore in Italia gestarum commentarius ab anno* 1378 *usque ad annum* 1440, dans MURATORI, *Rer. Ital. Scrip.,* t. xix. pp. 909-942. Mediolani, 1731.

ARGENTRÉ (d').—*Collectio judiciorum.* Paris, 1736.

ARNAULD (Antoine).—*Éclaircissements sur l'autorité des conciles généraux et des papes.* An explanation of the real meaning of the three decrees of the fourth and fifth sessions of the Council of Constance against Schelstrate's dissertation, 1701. Place and publisher unknown.

ASCHBACH (J.).—*Geschichte Kaiser Sigmunds.* Hamburg, 1838-1845.

BAETEN (J.).—*Verzameling van Naamrollen Betrekkelijk de Kerkelijke Geschiedenis van het Aartsbisdom van Mechelen.* Malines. Date and publisher unknown.

BALLERINI.—*De potestate ecclesiastica,* in MIGNE, *Theolog. cursus completus,* t. iii. p. 899 et suiv.

BALUZIUS (Steph).—*Vitae Paparum Avenionensium, hoc est historia pontificum Romanorum qui in Gallia sederunt ab anno Christi MCCCV. usque ad annum MCCCXCIV.* Paris, 1693.

BAUDRILLART, *Dictionnaire de théologie catholique,* fasc. xxi. col. 1200. 1907.

BAYE (Nicolas de).—*Journal* of the Société de l'Histoire de France, par ALEXANDRE TUETEY, 1885.

BEAUCOURT (Du Fresne de).—*Histoire de Charles VII.* Paris, 1882.

BENOIST (Charles).—*La politique du roi Charles V., la nation et la royauté.* Paris, 1886.

BERGER.—*Joh. Huss. und König Sigismund.* Augsbourg, 1871.

BERNHARDT (W.).—*Zur Geschichte der Konstanzer Konzils.* Marbourg, 1891.

BESS.—*Joh. Gerson und die Kirchenpolitik Parteien Frankreichs vor dem Konzil zu Pisa.* Marbourg, 1890.—*Frankreich und sein Papst von 1378 bis 1394.* 1904.

BLIEMETZRIEDER.—*Die general Konzil im grossen abendlandischen Schisma.* Paderborn, 1904.—*Die Konzilsidee unter Innocens VII. und König Ruprecht von der Pfalz.* 1906.

BLUMENTHAL (H.).—*Die Vorgeschichte des Konstanzer Konzils.* Halle, 1897.

BONET-MAURY.—*Gérard de Groote, un précurseur de la Réforme.* Paris, 1878.—*Les précurseurs de la Réforme.* Paris, 1904.

BONNECHOSE (Émile de).—*Jean Hus et le Concile de Constance.* Paris, 1847.—*Lettres de Jean Hus,* avec une préface de Martin Luther. Paris, 1850.

BOSSUET.—*Defensio declarationis Cleri Gallicani,* l. x. c. 12 (alias xiv. c. 12).—*Appendix ad defensionem,* l. i. c. 5.

BOUIX (D.).—*Tractatus de Papa ubi et de concilio œcumenico.* Paris, 1869.

BOURGEOIS DU CHASTENET.—*Nouvelle histoire du Concile de Constance.* Paris, 1718.

BRANN (Henry).—*The Schism of the West and the Freedom of Papal Elections.* New York, 1895.

BREVISCOXA (Joannes).—*Tractatus de fide et Ecclesia, Romano Pontifice et Concilio Generali, in Opp. Gersonii,* t. i. col. 805.

BROWN (E.).—*Fasciculus rerum expetendarum et fugiendarum.* Londini, 1690.

CAPPENBERG.—*Utrum Hussi doctrina fuerit haeretica?* Munster, 1834.

CHÉNON.—Dans l'*Histoire générale du IV*^e^ *siècle à nos jours,* publiée sous la direction de LAVISSE et RAMBAUD, t. iii. Colin, 1894.

CHEVALIER (Ulysse).—*Répertoire des sources historiques du moyen âge.* Paris, 1877-1883.—*Le Mystère des Trois Doms.* Lyon, 1887.

CHRISTOPHE (J.-B.).—*Histoire de la Papauté pendant le XIV*^e^ *siècle, avec des pièces justificatives.* Lyon-Paris, 1863.

LIST OF AUTHORITIES

CHRONIC. KAROLI VI. (The Monk of Saint-Denis).—*Collection de documents inédits sur l'Histoire de France* (édit. Bellaguet). Paris, 1839-52.

CHRONIQUES DE FRANCE (édit. Paulin, Paris). Paris, 1836-40.

CIACONIUS (Alph.).—*Vitae et res gestae Pontificum Romanorum et S. R. E. Cardinalium . . . ab August. Oldoino, S. J. recognitae*, t. ii. Romae, 1677.

CLÉMANGIS (Nicolaus de).—*Opera omnia.* Lugduni Batavorum, 1613.

CONTELORIUS (F.).—*Martini V. vita ex legitimis documentis collecta.* Romae, 1641.

CREIGHTON.—*A History of Papacy during the Period of the Reformation*: vol. i. *The great Schism, The Council of Constance.* London, 1882.

DEGERT.—*La fin du schisme d'Occident en Gascogne.* Privat, 1902.

DELALONDE.—*Étude historique et critique sur le grand Schisme.* Rouen, 1875.

DELAVILLE LE ROULX.—*La France en Orient au XIVe siècle.* Paris, 1886.

DENIFLE.—*Die Universitäten des Mittelalters.* Berlin, 1885.

—— *La désolation des églises, des monastères et des hôpitaux durant la guerre de Cent ans.* Paris, 1899.

—— et CHATELAIN.—*Chartularium Universitatis Parisiensis.* 4 vols. Now ready. Paris, 1890 and following.

DENIS.—*Huss et la guerre des Hussites.* Paris, 1878.

DINAUX (Arthur).—*Notice historique et littéraire sur le Cardinal Pierre d'Ailly.* Cambrai, 1821. *Mémoires de la Société d'émulation de Cambrai*, 1825, p. 207.

DÖLLINGER (J.).—*Lehrbuch der Kirchengeschichte*, t. ii. 1re partie, 2e édit. Ratisbonne, 1843.

DOUET D'ARCQ.—*Choix de pièces inédites du temps de Charles VI.* Société de l'histoire de France, 1863.

DROSTE (von).—*Die Dioceze Luttich zu Beginn des grossen Schismas.* Munster, 1904.

DU BOULAY.—*Historia Universitatis Parisiensis*, t. iv. 1300-1400; t. v. 1400-1500. Paris, 1668 et suiv.

DUPUY.—*Histoire du schisme*, 1378-1420. Paris, 1654.

EHRLE.—*Martin de Alpartils, Chronica actitatorum temporibus Domini Benedicti XIII.* Paderborn, 1906.

Epinois (Henri de l').—*Le gouvernement des Papes et les révolutions dans les États de l'Église*, 2e édit. Paris, 1867.

Erler (G.).—*Zur Geschichte des pisanischen Concils* (Programm des Nicolai-Gymnasiums in Leipzig). Leipzig, 1884.

—— *Dietrich von Nieheim, sein Leben und seine Schriften.* Leipzig, 1887.

Eubel.—*Die provisiones praelatorum. Römische Quartalschrift.* Rom, 1894.

—— *Die Avignonesische Obedienz der Mendikantenorden . . . zur Zeit des grossen Schismas.* Paderborn, 1900.

—— *Hierarchia catholica medii aevi.* Munster, 1898 et 1901.

Fages (R. P.).—*Histoire de saint Vincent Ferrier.* Paris, 1893.—2e édit., Louvain, Uystpruyst, 1901.

Finke.—*Acta Concilii Constanciensis*, t. i. Munster, 1896.

—— *Forschungen und Quellen zur Geschichte des konstanzer Concils.* Munster, 1889.

Fraikin, *Les comptes du diocèse de Bordeaux, from* 1316 *to* 1453. Rome, 1903.

Friedrich.—*Die Lehre des Joh. Hus und ihre Bedeutung für die Gegenwart.* Ratisbonne, 1862.

—— *Joh. Huss, ein Lebensbild.* Francfort, 1864.

Froissart (Jehan).—*Chroniques*, édit. Kervyn de Lettenhove. Bruxelles, 1867-1877 ; édit. Raynaud.

Fromme.—*Die spanische Nation und das konstanzer Concil.* Munster, 1896.

—— *Die Wahl Martins V.*, dans *Römische Quartalschrift*, t. x. 1896.

Gams (B.).—*Series episcoporum Ecclesiae catholicae quotquot innotuerunt a beato Petro apostolo.* Ratisbonne, 1873.

Gayet (Louis).—*Le grand Schisme d'Occident.* Paris, 1889.

Gerson (Johannes de).—*Opera*, édit. Richer. Paris, 1606.—Édit. Ellies-Dupin. Antwerpiae, 1706.

Gieseler (J.-C.-L.)—*Lehrbuch der Kirchengeschichte*, t. ii. 3rd and 4th parts. Bonn, 1829-1835.

Goldast.—*Monarchia Sancti Romani Imperii.* Francofordiæ, 1614.

Goller.—*Papst Johann XXIII. und König Sigismund im Sommer* 1410. Rome, 1903.

Gratius (Orthuinus).—*Fasciculus rerum expetendarum et fugiendarum.* Colon. 1535 ; ond. 1590.

LIST OF AUTHORITIES

GREGOROVIUS (F.).—*Geschichte der Stadt Rom im Mittelalter vom fünften bis zum sechszehnten Jahrhundert*, 3e édit., t. vi. et vii. Gotha, 1879-1880.

GRUBE (Karl).—*Gerhard Groot und seine Stiftungen.* Köln, 1883.

GUIRAUD (Jean).—*L'État Pontifical après le grand Schisme.* Paris, 1897.

HALLER, *Papstum und Kirchenreform.* Weidmann, 1903.

HARDT (H. von der).—*Rerum Concilii Œcumenici Constantiensis. . . .* Francofurti et Lipsiae, 1697-1700.—Index by BOHNSTEDT, 1742.

—— *Herman von der Hardt und sein sechs.* Paderborn, Schöningen, 1889.

HARTWIG (O.). —*Leben und Schriften H. von Langensteins.* Marbourg, 1857-1858.

HAUTCŒUR (Mgr Ed.).—*Histoire de Saint Pierre de Lille.* Paris, 1899.

HEFELE.—*Histoire des Conciles*, t. x. et xi., traduits par MM. GOSCHLER et DELARC. Paris, 1869.

—— *Beiträge zur Kirchengeschichte.* 1864.

HENKE.—*Joh. Hus und der Synode von Konstanz.* Berlin, 1869.

HERGENRÖTHER (J.).—*Handbuch der allgemeinen Kirchengeschichte*, t. ii. et iii. Fribourg, 1876-1880. Trad. fr., Paris, 1880-94.

HINSCHIUS (P.).—*System des katholischen Kirchenrechts mit besonderer Rücksicht auf Deutschland.* Berlin, 1869-1883.

HIRSCH.—*Die Ausbildung der Konziliarentheorie.* Vienne, 1903.

HISTOIRE LITTÉRAIRE DE LA FRANCE, t. xxiv. Paris, 1862.

HÖFLER (C.).—*Ruprecht von der Pfalz, genannt Clem, römischer König.* Fribourg-en-Brisgau, 1861.

—— *Anna von Luxemburg, Kaiser Karls IV. Tochter, König Richards II. Gemahlin, Königin von England*, 1382-1394. (*Denkschriften der kaiserlichen Akademie der Wissenschaften, philosoph.-hist. Klasse*, t. xx. pp. 89-240.) Vienne, 1871.

—— *Aus Avignon.* Prague, 1868.

—— *Die avignonesischen Päpste, ihre Machtfülle und ihr Untergang.* (*Almanach der kaiserl. Akademie der Wissenschaften*, 21e année, pp. 231-285.) Vienne, 1871.

—— *Magister Johannes Hus.* Prague, 1864.

HÜBLER.—*Die konstanzer Reformation, und die Concordate von* 1418. Leipzig, 1867.

ILLYRICUS (Flacius).—*Catalogus testium veritatis.* Lugduni, 1597.

ISSET (E.).—*Die Reformation in Konstanz.* Freiburg, 1898.

JAHR.—*Die Wahl Urbans VI.* Halle, 1892.

JANSSEN (Joh.).—*Geschichte des deutschen Volkes seit dem Ausgang des Mittelalters*, t. i. 9e édit. Fribourg-en-Brisgau, 1883. Trad. fr. par E. PARIS, Plon, 1889.

—— *Frankfurts Reichscorrespondenz nebst anderen verwandten Actenstücken von* 1376 *bis* 1519. Fribourg-en-Brisgau, 1866.

JARRY.—*La vie politique de Louis de France, Duc d'Orléans.* Paris, 1889.

JEEP (Arminius).—*Gerson, Wicleff et Huss.* Gœttingue, 1857.

JOUVENEL DES URSINS.—*Histoire de Charles VI.*, Panthéon littéraire.—*Choix de chroniques*, Nouvelle collection de Mémoires (Michaud et Poujoulat), t. ii. 1836.

KAISER (Hans).—*König Karl V. von Frankreich und die grosse Kirchenspaltung.* München, 1904.

KAUFMANN (Josef).—*Ein Tractat über die Frage der Absendung eines Legaten nach Deutschland*, 1394.

KEPPLER.—*Die Politik des Kardinals-Kollegium in Konstanz.* Munster, Doctor-Dissertation, Heiligenstadt, 1899.

KEHRMANN.—*Frankreichs innere Kirchenpolitik von der Wahl Clemens VII. bis zum Pisaner Concil.* Iena, 1896.

—— *Die capite agendorum.* München, 1903.

KERVYN DE LETTENHOVE.—*La Belgique sous la domination des ducs de Bourgogne*, text. lat., t. i. *Chronique de* JEAN BRANDON, moine des Dunes. Bruxelles, 1870.

—— *Jean sans Peur et l'apologie du tyrannicide.* Bruxelles, 1861.

KNEER.—*Die Entstehung der conciliarien Theorie zur Geschichte des Schismas und der Kirchenpolitiken.* Rome, 1895.

—— *Kardinal Zabarella.* Munster, 1901.

KRUMMEL.—*Leben des J. Huss.* Kempten, 1873.

LARGENT (Aug.).—*Leçons données à la Faculté de théologie de Paris*, 1899-90.

L'ÉCUY.—*Essai sur la vie de Jean Gerson.* Paris, 1832.

LENFANT.—*Histoire du Concile de Pise.* Amsterdam, 1724.

—— *Histoire du Concile de Constance.* Amsterdam, 1714.

LENZ (M.).—*König Sigismund und Heinrich der Fünfte von England. Ein Beitrag zur Geschichte der Zeit des Constanzer Concils.* Berlin, 1874.

LIST OF AUTHORITIES

LENZ (M.).—*Drei Tractate aus dem Schriftencyklus des constanzer Concilsuntersucht.* Marbourg, 1876.

LESQUEN et MOLLAT—*Mesures fiscales exercées en Bretagne par les Papes d'Avignon.* Paris, 1903.

LINDNER—*Beiträge zu dem Leben und den Schriften Dietrichs von Niem.*

LOCKE (Clinton).—*The Age of the Great Western Schism.* Edinburgh, 1897.

LORENZ (O.).—*Papstwahl und Kaiserthum. Eine historische Studie aus dem Staats- und Kirchenrecht.* Berlin, 1874.

LOSERTH (J.).—*Beiträge zur Geschichte der husitischen Bewegung.* III. *Der Tractatus de longevo schismate des Abtes Eudolf von Sagan.* (*Archiv für österreich. Gesch.*, t. lx. pp. 343-561.) Vienne, 1880.

—— *J. Huss und Wiclif.* Prague, 1884.

—— *Die Streitschriften.* Vienne, 1893.—*Das Vermeintl.-Schreiben Wiclifs an Urban VI.* Munich, 1895.

MAIMBOURG.—*Histoire du grand schisme d'Occident.* Paris, 1722.

MANDONNET (R. P.).—*Beiträge zur Geschichte des Kardinals Giovanni Dominici, Zusammenberufung des Konzils zu Konstanz. Historische Jahrbuch*, 1900.

MANSI.—*Sacror. Conciliorum nova et amplissima collectio.* Florentiae, 1759.

MARMOR.—*Das Concilium in Konstanz.* Konstanz, 1898.

MARTÈNE (Edmond) et DURAND (Ursin).—*Veterum scriptorum et monumentorum historicorum, dogmaticorum, moralium amplissima collectio.* Paris, 1724-1733.—*Thesaurus novus anecdotorum.* Paris, 1717.

MASSON.—*Jean Gerson, sa vie, son temps, ses œuvres.* Lyon, 1894.

MEYER (Jac.).—*Annales rerum Flandricarum.* Anvers, 1569.

MONSTRELET.—*Chroniques*, édit. Buchon, 1836.

MOROSINI.—*Chronique*, Soc. de l'Hist. de France, 1899.

MULLER (F.). — *Der Kampf um d. Auctorität auf d. Concils zu Constanz.* Berlin, 1860.

MUNTZ (Adolphe).—*Nicolas de Clamenges.* Strasbourg, 1846.

—— (Eug.).—*Les arts à la cour des Papes pendant le XV*[e] *et le XVI*[e] *siècle.* Paris, 1878.

MURATORI (L.-A.).—*Rerum Italicarum scriptores praecipui ab anno aerae Christianae D ad MD, quorum potissima pars nunc primum in lucem prodit ex codicibus, etc. Muratorius collegit et ordinavit, etc.* Mediolani, 1723-1751.

NIEM (Theod. de).—*De scismate*, libri iii. édit. Erler. Lipsiæ, 1890.

—— *Nemus unionis.* Bâle, Guarini, 1566.

PALACKY (F.).—*Geschichte von Böhmen, grösstentheils nach Urkunden und Handschriften*, t. iii. Prague, 1836-68.—*Documenta Joannis Huss.* Prague, 1869.

PASTOR.—*Histoire des Papes depuis la fin du moyen âge*, traduite par FURCY RAYNAUD. Paris, 1888.

PHILASTRE (Guillaume), *Journal de.*—MS. bibl. Vatic., 4173 and 4175, partly edited by FINKE, *Forschungen und Quellen. . . .* Paderborn, 1889.

PISAN (Christine de).—*Livre des faits et bonnes mœurs du sage roi Charles V.*—Dans *Mémoires sur l'Histoire de France*, 1re série, t. v. et vi.—*Nouvelle collection des Mémoires* (Michaud et Poujoulat), t. ii.

PLATINA.—*Opus de vitis ac gestis Summorum Pontificum ad Sixtum IV., pontificem maximum, deductum.* Venise, 1479.

POGGIUS (Joh.-Franc.). — *Epistolae. Editas collegit et emendavit, plerasque ex codd. msc. eruit, ordine chronologico disposuit notisque illustravit* THOMAS DE TONELLIS, vols. i.-ii. Florentiae, 1832-1861.

PUYOL.—*Edmond Richer, étude historique et critique sur la rénovation du Gallicanisme.* Paris, 1876.

RASTOUL.—*L'unité religieuse pendant le grand Schisme d'Occident.* Bloud, 1904.

REINKE.—*Frankreich und Papst Johann* XXIII. Munster, Diss., 1900.

RICHENTAL (Ulrich von).—*Chronik des Constanzer Concils, herausgegeben von* M. R. BUCK (*Bibl. literar. Vereins in Stuttgart*, 158). Tübingen, 1882. Édition de MARMOR, Freiburg, 1873.

RICHERIUS (Edmundus).—*Libellus de ecclesiastica et politica potestate.* Coloniae, 1701.—*Vindiciae doctrinae majorum scholae Parisiensis.* Coloniae, 1683.

ROCQUAIN (Félix).—*La Cour de Rome et l'esprit de Réforme avant Luther*, t. iii. Paris, 1897.

ROSLER (Aug.). — *Cardinal Johannes Dominici, O. Pr.* Fribourg, 1893.

ROSSMANN.—*De externo Concilii Constant. apparatu.* Iena, 1856.

ROTH. — *Zur Bibliographie des Henricus Hembuche de Hassia.* Leipzig, 1888.

SALEMBIER (Louis).—*Petrus de Alliaco.* Lille, 1886.

—— *Deux conciles inconnus de Cambrai et de Lille au temps du grand Schisme.* Lille, 1902.

SALUTATUS LINUS COLUCIUS PIERIUS.—*Epistolae ex cod. MSS. nunc primum in lucem editae a Jos.* RIGACCIO. P. i., ii. Florentiae, 1741-1742.

SAUERLAND (H.-V.).—*Das Leben des Dietrichs von Nieheim nebst einer Uebersicht über dessen Schriften.* Göttingen, 1875.

SCHARDIUS (Sim.). — *De jurisdictione, auctoritate et præeminentia imperiali, ac potestate ecclesiastica variorum auctorum scripta.* Bâle, 1566; Strasbourg, 1618.

SCHELSTRATE.—*Tractatus de sensu et auctoritate decretorum Concilii Constantiensis, sessione quarta et quinta.* Romae, 1686.

SCHEUFFGEN.—*Beiträge zu der Geschichte des grossen Schismas.* Fribourg-en-Brisgau, 1889.

SCHMITZ (J.).—*Die französ. Politik und die Unionsverhandlungen des Concils von Constanz.* Duren, 1879.

SCHOLZ.—*Die Rückkehr Gregors XI. von Avignon nach Rom im Jahr 1377.* Hirschberg, 1884.

SCHULTE (Joh.-Fried. von).—*Die Geschichte der Quellen und Literatur des canonischen Rechts von Papst Gregor IX. bis zum Concil von Trient.* (*Geschichte der Quellen, usw. von Gratian bis auf die Gegenwart,* t. ii.) Stuttgart, 1877.

SCHWAB (Joh.-Bapt.).—*Johannes Gerson, Professor der Theologie und Kanzler der Universität Paris.* Würzbourg, 1858.

SIEBEKING (H.).—*Beiträge zur Geschichte der grossen Kirchenspaltung. Programm der Annen-Realschule zu Dresden.* Dresden, 1881.

—— *Die Organisation und Geschäftsordnung des Constanzer Concils.* Leipzig, 1875.

SORBELLI.—*De moderno Ecclesiae schismate.* Trattato di Vincenzo Perrer, Roma, 1900.

SOUCHON (Martin).—*Die Papstwahlen in der Zeit des grossen Schismas.* Braunschweig, 1899.

STEINHAUSEN (F.).—*Analecta ad historiam Concilii Constantiensis.* Berolini, 1862.

STEINHERZ.—*Das Schisma von 1378 und die Haltung Karls IV.* Mayence.

STEVENSON.—*The Truth about J. Wiclef.* 1883.

STUHR.—*Die Organisation und Geschäftsordnung des Pisaner und Konstanzer Concils.* Schwerin, 1891.

THOMASSY.—*Jean Gerson et le grand Schisme d'Occident,* 2e édit. Paris, 1852.

TOSTI (Luigi).—*Storia del Concilio di Costanza.* Napoli, 1853.

TRUTMANN (A.).—*Das Konklave auf dem Concil von Constanz.* Strassburgische Dissertation, Freiburg in Br., 1899.

TSCHACKERT (P.).—*Peter von Ailli (Petrus de Alliaco). Zur Geschichte des grossen abendländischen Schismas und der Reformconcilien von Pisa und Konstanz.* Gotha, 1877.

URIE (Theod.).—*Historia Concilii Constant.* dans VON DER HARDT, t. i. et t. iv.

VALOIS (Noël).—*La France et le grand Schisme d'Occident.* Paris, 1896 et 1902.

VAN DER HAEGEN.—*Jean Huss, exposé de sa doctrine sur l'Église.* Alençon, 1888.

VOIGT (G.).—*Die Wiederbelebung des classischen Alterthums oder das erste Jahrhundert des Humanismus.* Berlin, 1880-1881.

—— (J.).—*Stimmen aus Rom über den päpstlichen Hof im fünfzehnten Jahrhundert (Raumers Histor. Taschenbuch,* 4e année). Leipzig, 1833.

VON WESSEMBERG.—*Die grossen Kirchenversammlungen des XV. und XVI. Jahrhunderts.* Constance, 1840.

WYLIE (J. H.).—*The Council of Constance to the Death of John Hus.* London, 1900.

ZURITA (Geronimo).—*Los cinco libros primeros de la segunda parte de los anales de la corona de Aragon.* Caragoça, 1669.

(B) PERIODICALS

Almanach der kaiserlichen Akademie der Wissenschaften. Wien, 1851 and following.

Analecta juris pontificii. Geneva, 1872.

Archiv der Gesellschaft für ältere deutsche Geschichtskunde zur Beförderung einer Gesammtausgabe der Quellenschriften deutscher Geschichten des Mittelalters. Herausg. von J.-L. BUECHLER, C.-G. DUMGE und G.-H. PERTZ, Frankfort a. M. und Hannover, 1820-1874.—*Neues Archiv der Gesellschaft für ältere deutsche Geschichtskunde,* t. i. et suiv. Hannover, 1876.

LIST OF AUTHORITIES

Archiv für Literatur und Kirchengeschichte des Mittelalters. Herausg. von P.-H. Denifle und P.-F. Ehrle. Freiburg, 1885-1893.

Archiv für österreichische Geschichte. Wien, 1880.

Bibliothèque de l'École des Chartes. Paris, 1872.

Briegers Zeitschrift für Kirchengeschichte. Gotha, 1877.

Bulletin critique. Paris, 1896.

Bulletin d'histoire ecclésiastique de Valence. 1884-85.

Denkschriften der kaiserlichen Akademie der Wissenschaften philosophisch-historische Classe. Wien, 1871.

Der Katholik. Mainz, 1900.

Études publiées par les Pères de la Compagnie de Jésus. Paris, 1897 et 1903.

Forschungen zur deutschen Geschichte. Göttingen, 1883.

Historische polit. Blätter für das katholische Deutschland. München, t. iv.

Historische Jahrbücher. Munster, 1893, 1894, 1900.

Historische Zeitschrift. München, t. xxviii.

Revue catholique de Louvain. Louvain, 1876.

Revue d'histoire ecclésiastique. Louvain, 1901 et 1904.

Revue du clergé français. Paris, 1904.

Revue des Études historiques. Paris, 1904.

Revue d'histoire et de littérature religieuse. Paris, 1896.

Revue historique. Paris, 1886 et 1901.

Revue de Lille. Lille, 1899.

Revue des Questions historiques. Paris, 1887, 1896.

Revue des Sciences ecclésiastiques, publiée par des professeurs de l'Université catholique de Lille, 1886, 1887, 1889, 1890, 1896. Amiens-Lille.

Römische Quartalschrift für christliche Alterthumskunde und für Kirchengeschichte. Rom, 1887 et 1896.

INDEX

ACHERY, D', 45
Agnani, 54 ff.
Ailly, d', *see* Peter
Alexander V. (Peter Philarghi), 250-255
Alexander, Natalis, 263
Alvarez Pelagius, 12
Amédée of Savoy, 6
America, 3
Antoninus, St, 15, 52, 60, 263
Aquileia, *see* Ravenna
Arcq, Douet d', 135
Arnold of Brescia, 30
Augustinus Triumphus, 12
Avignon, 7, 17, 72, 166 ff., 233

BACON, ROGER, 84, 88
Baeten, 71
Bâle, *see* Basle
Baluze, 23
Bartholomew Saliceto, 84
Bartholomew Valori, 278
Basle, Council of, 115 f., 381 ff.
Beghards, 122
Benedict XII., 18
Benedict XIII., *see* note p. 139 (Peter de Luna), 35, 45, 66, 78 f., 135, 142 ff., 186, 291, 350 ff.
Benedict XIV. (pseudo-pope), 356 f.
Benoist, 63
Berlière, 17
Bernard, St, 8, 17
Bess, 262
Bliemetzrieder, 55
Boniface VIII., 23
Boniface IX. (Peter Thomacelli), 106, 197 ff.
Bordas, Tolra de, 258
Bossuet, 113, 263, 309
Boucicault, Godfrey, 161 f., 167 ff.
Boucicault, John, 6, 200, 223, 231 f.
Boulay, du, 25
Bressolano, 8
Bridget of Sweden, 23, 77

CAJETAN, 10, 263
Casimir, 4
Catherine of Siena, 14, 23 f., 51, 76
Catherine of Sweden, 76
Cauchon, *see* Peter
Charles of Bohemia, 8
Charles IV., Emperor, 67
Charles V. (of France), 49, 58, 66, 140
Charles VI. (of France), 101 f., 125
Charles Malatesta, 241, 249, 269, 270, 279, 339, 346 f.
Chastenet, Bourgeois du, 105
Chenon, 48
Christophe, 25
Clemangis, 132, 135, 188, 231
Clement V., 5, 18, 20
Clement VI., 5
Clement VII., *see* note p. 139 (Robert of Geneva), 25, 34, 44 f., 59, 135 ff.
Clement VIII. (Gil Muñoz, a pseudo-pope), 356
Collette, St, 80, 200
Collucio Salutato, 56
Comneni, 7
Conrad of Gelnhausen, 86, 129
Constance, Council of, 79, 115 f., 280 ff.
Corvin, *see* John de M. Corvino
Cramaud, *see* Simon

DANTE, 15
Delalonde, 66
Denifle, 18, 50, 86
Döllinger, 106
Dominici, *see* John
Durrieu, 60

ECUY, l', 86
Elizabeth of Schönau, 14

England, 66, 68, 121 f., 370
Epinois, de l', 24
Eubel, Conrad, 4, 47, 72
Eugenius III., 8
Eugenius IV. (Condulmaro), 279, 308

Fages, 79
Falkenburg, *see* John
Felix IV., 47
Felix V. (pseudo-Pope), 381
Ferrer, Boniface, 253, 263
Ferrer, Vincent, 31, 78, 125, 130, 200
Finke, 112
Flanders, 68 f., 102
Fleury, 34
Fondi, 49, 57
Froissart, 2

Gams, 4
Gardar, 4
Gatarus, Andrew, 107
Gayet, 25
Geiger, 15
Gerard Groot, 77, 92
Gerson, 112, 114, 116, 120, 191, 196, 206, 262, 287, 294, 332 f.
Gilbert of Ravenna, 2
Goldast, 8
Grabmann, 10
Grabon, *see* Matthew
Greenland, 4
Gregorovius, 3
Gregory XI., 16, 23, 28
Gregory XII. (Angelo Corrario), 219, 344 ff.
Groot, *see* Gerard
Grube, Karl, 78
Guiraud, 108
Guy de Malesset, 34, 46, 65, 68, 95, 191, 222, 245

Hardt, von der, 86
Hartwig, 86
Hase, 24
Hauréau, 100
Hautcœur, Mgr., 70
Hefele, 44
Henry of Langenstein, 61, 85 f., 311
Hubler, 86
Hunyadi, 4, 396
Huss, John, 4, 12, 19, 111, 122, 272, 306, 312 ff., 272

Innocent VII. (Cosmo Meliorati), 199
Ireland, 68

Jahr, 35
Jandun, *see* John
Jane, *see* Joanna
Jarry, 91, 102
Jean de Nevers, 6
Jerome of Prague, 328 f.
Joan of Arc, 126, 333, 356
Joanna of Naples, 57, 71, 76, 102, 184
John XII., 47
John XXII., 5, 11, 20
John XXIII. (Balthazar Cossa), 254, 265 ff.
John Boucicault, *see* Boucicault
John de Brogny, 277
John de Cros, 34, 64
John Dominici, 279, 345
John of Falkenburg, 334
John of Jandun, 11, 288
John of Lignano, 56
John of Monte Corvino, 5
John of Paris, 11
John Petit, 151, 202, 207 f., 332 f.
Jorga, 90
Jouvenal des Ursins, 15,1 203, 214

Kneer, 85
Knopfler, 32

Ladislaus of Naples, 199, 240, 274
Ladislaus of Poland, 4
Langenstein, *see* Henry, 61
Le Clerc, 13
Lenfant, 278
Lenz, 87
Lindner, 27
Livonia, 4
Lodi, 277
Louis of Bavaria, 8, 11, 21
Louis of Bourbon, 6

Maimbourg, 26
Maizieres, Philip de, 9, 90
Malan, Chavin de, 62
Malatesta, *see* Charles

INDEX

Marmor, 278
Marsilius of Padua, 11, 238
Martene, 17, 154
Martin V. (Odo Colonna), 306 f., 365 f.
Matthew Grabon, 335
Mézeray, 26
Mignatz, 23
Miræus, 71
Muratori, 40

Neefs, 71
Nicholas of Cusa, 112, 123
Niem, Theodoric of, 51, 106, 125, 266, 282
Norway, 4

Occam, *see* William
Orsini, 30, 36 f., 299 f.
Oxford, 152
Ozanam, 15

Paleologi, 7
Paris, University of, 9 ff., 57, 64, 74, 94, 104, 113, 131, 383
Paris, Paulin, 90
Pastor, 14, 19
Perpignan, Council of, 235
Peter d'Ailly, 20, 30, 65, 87 f., 104, 111 ff., 124, 135, 138, 192, 200, 207, 216, 261, 273, 282 ff., 296, 375
Peter of Ancorano, 248
Peter of Aragon, 23
Peter Cauchon, 221, 333
Peter de Corbière, 2, 21
Peter Corsini, 33
Peter de Cros, 53 f.
Peter Dubois, 11
Peter Flandrin, 33
Peter Flotte, 11
Peter de Luna, *see* Benedict XIII.
Peter of Luxemburg, 80
Peter Plaoul, 158, 202, 207, 217
Petit, *see* John
Petrarch, 8, 15, 23, 168
Philip the Fair, 13, 110
Pileo de Prata, 69, 83, 96, 107
Pisa, Council of, 235 f., 243
Pisan, Christine de, 50
Pistoja, Synod of, 117
Pius II. (Æneas Sylvius), 116
Poggio, 281, 329, 390
Poland, 4
Polo, Marco, 5
Prussia, 4

Ravenna, Council of, 265 f.
Raynald, 25
Reclus Élisée, 4
Richard II., 68, 152, 184
Richer, 117
Rienzi, 8
Robert of Bavaria (King of the Romans), 179, 238 f., 247
Robert of Hallum, 271
Rocquain, 12, 14
Romanus (Pope), 2
Rome, Council of, 271
Rossmann, 283
Roth, 14, 86
Roulx, J. Delaville de, 6, 73

Samaran, 17
Savona, 221 ff.
Scheuffgen, 55
Scotland, 66
Sigismund (King of the Romans), 270, 275, 285 f., 291 ff.
Silverius (Pope), 47
Simon Borsano, 33
Simon Cramaud, 142, 157, 207, 209, 253, 271
Simon Freron, 65
Souchon, 98
Spain, 93
Stegner, Heinrich, 278

Tamerlane, 5
Tebaldeschi, 33, 39 f., 58
Telesphorus, 123 f.
Thomassin, 18
Tosti, 13
Toulouse, University of, 188
Tschackert, 87

Ulrich of Richtenthal, 278
Urban V., 23
Urban VI. (Bartholomew Prignano), 25, 34, 106
Ursula of Parma, 77

Valois, Noël, 27, 92, 159
Valori, *see* Bartholomew
Vigilius (Pope), 47
Vincent Ferrer, *see* Ferrer

Viterbo, 199 f.

WALDENSES, 122
Wenceslaus (King of the Romans), 67, 84, 152, 154, 178
Wicliffe, John, 12, 19, 121, 272, 306, 314 ff.
William d'Aigrefeuille, 34, 65
William of Bavaria, 11
William of Occam, 11 f., 88, 118
William Philastre, 207, 221, 271, 321, 341

ZABARELLA, 238, 259, 271 ff., 275, 283, 296 ff.

TURNBULL AND SPEARS, PRINTERS, EDINBURGH.